CW00376836

Books are to be returned c
the last date

Contents

1 1

2 8

3 13

4 16

5 16

6 16

7 16

8 16

9 16

10 16

11 16

12 16

13 16

14 16

15 16

16 16

17 16

18 16

19 16

20 16

21 16

22 16

23 16

24 16

25 16

26 16

27 16

28 16

29 16

30 16

31 16

32 16

33 16

34 16

35 16

About the Author 16

Acknowledgements

A huge thank you to my family, friends and supporters.

Dear World,

You don't know me, and as of yet I barely know you. I mean, I am sixteen, I know nothing, or so most adults seem keen to tell me. I am writing to you now because my wall is nearly full of words, and still they keep on coming. They fill my head when I am trying to concentrate, like everything they say, everything they want me to hear is so vitally important. More important than anything else. That's how it feels anyway. I don't know if that's how it is for everyone. Plus, the reason I am writing to you, is there are some things I have become concerned about lately, and most of these are private. I can't write them on my wall or my mum might see. Like most mothers she is incredibly nosy and suspicious. She worries about everything and if she knew only half the stuff I am concerned about, she would freak out completely. She's a very anxious person and anxiety is catching. I am trying to avoid it where I can.

Do you know, when I wake up in the morning, I do the same thing every day? I run my hands down to my belly while I am still half asleep, flattening my palms and pushing them against the softness of my flesh. I try to judge whether it is flatter, or fatter than the day before. Then I move my palms sideways, pushing out towards my hipbones. When I was fatter, I could never really feel my hipbones that well. Now I can feel them, and it is my favourite feeling in the world. I love touching them. I love smoothing my hands over them. I want them to get sharper so I can grab onto them. Bone handles, not love handles! Even if my belly still feels too soft and squishy, I like the way my fingers roll down from the hipbone into a little dip, before they roll back up and onto my stomach. I suppose if I ever smoothed my fingers down from the hipbone and onto a flat, hard plain, with no hill on the other side, then I would be happy. But I am not sure.

I haven't really written a diary since I got one for Christmas when I was ten. It had a little dog on the front wearing a hat. It was the best present I got that year, and I wrote in it faithfully every day. But, like all things in life, the novelty wore off. To be honest, there is not much to write about when you are ten, because life is really pretty simplistic at that age. You go to school, you play out, you eat your tea, you go to bed. You don't worry at that age. You don't think that much. Well I didn't anyway. I'm going to try and stick to it this time. First of all it will help me with my diet. Like I told you before, there are a few things I am concerned about that I can't really discuss with other people, and my diet is one of them. I got the idea from one of my mum's women's magazines; '20 tips to lose weight fast', that sort of thing. They had loads of tips and advice. No wonder my mum buys those things religiously! They really do have some good ideas to keep you on track. One was keeping a food diary, the idea being that once you wrote down and realised how much you actually ate, you would be horrified into action. It works, I can tell you. It gets embarrassing when you write it all down. It makes you want to eat less, so you can write less. Secondly, writing a diary is probably better than writing on my wall, which is what I have been doing for a long time now. It's not like I write personal thoughts and feelings on there or anything; just song lyrics, random musings that I have, the odd stream of expletives, that sort of thing. But like I said already; there are things I nearly write on there, things in my head, and then I stop and remember that anyone can read my wall.

***

It's Saturday today. A Saturday in my house begins the same way as it has always done. I lie in my bed for as long as I possibly can. I drift in and out of sleep, opening and closing my eyes each time I hear footsteps on the landing passing my door. I do not look at the digital alarm clock on my bedside table, because I hate knowing what time it is. Who seriously wants to know what time it is? Whatever it is it will probably depress you. I roll away from the time and face the same wall I have turned towards for sixteen years. I lift a finger and trace it gently over the writing that is scrawled there. It used to be pink wallpaper when my sister and I were little. Pink with fairies all over it. I remember being so excited about that. Which is sort of ironic now, as these days I can think of nothing more vile than the colour pink, and nothing more pathetic than fairies. But there you go. I am a teenager, and my mum reminds me of this daily. She does this in a dopey, bless her fashion, like it's all so predictable or something, how cynical I have become.

Yesterday was my sixteenth birthday, and me and my best friend Joe found something we shouldn't have in his brother's wardrobe. This comes to me now in the foggy ruins of sleep, as I squint and peer, and blink at the writing on my wall. After my sister and me outgrew the fairies, my dad papered it again. It was blue and white stripes on the bottom half, with a frieze going around, and then just blue on the top. I remember it took my dad ages to do it. I still don't understand why he bothered. I scraped it all off when I was thirteen years old. I was into heavy metal and wanted to paint it all black, but neither of my parents would let me. I was only given the choice of magnolia or lilac. I ask you. They were taking the piss with that one, I know.

Now the lilac is faded, nearly white in some places. My dad used to go mental every time he saw I had stuck a new poster up. He was like that about small things. "Blu-tack is better than cello tape," I remember defending myself sulkily. He had responded by storming into my space and pointing viciously to a white mark on the wall. "When you pull the poster off, the blu-tack pulls the bloody paint off!" he had yelled at me. Bloody is still his favourite word. I think he should open a thesaurus one day. He uses it in almost every sentence he speaks. My dad is the opposite to my mum. He is not anxious, just angry. Anger is catching too, in case you didn't know. You probably don't even realise it most of the time, but other peoples personalities can really rub off you. You have to watch out for that, if you are just trying to be yourself, like me. I don't want to be like any of them. Problem is, I don't really want to be like me either.

I didn't start scribbling on the walls until after he left. It was because I felt free then. Mum didn't care about small things the way he did. Mum had other things on her mind. Now, I run my fingers along the blue lines that twist and twirl and dance across my wall. My pen is always under my pillow. I pull it out, not lifting my head at all, tug off the lid and write *'life is fucked up in broken wellies'*. I smile at myself and stick the end of the pen between my teeth. A memory from last winter dances before my eyes. Me walking the dog in the dark, wearing old wellies that had split down the back. They were bent and broken, and the split rubber kept poking me in the heel, rubbing a blister into life. It had pissed me off beyond belief. Not having to walk the dog, because I actually liked that. But walking the dog in broken wellies. Never having anything nice, or new.

***

There is a long rattling knocking at my door. My mum. That is how she knocks. It is a repetitive tapping that runs up and down the door, as if she is superstitious about knocking in the same place twice. It is quite a pathetic knock, in truth. She could take it up a level. "Are you awake in there Lou?" she is asking me. "I need you up."

I need you up. I groan at this remark. That means she wants me to do something for her. My top lip curls slightly. I don't like being needed.

"Nearly," I tell her. "Give me a few minutes."

I hear her walk back downstairs without saying another word, but I can just see her rolling her eyes and shaking her head at me. It won't be long before she is back again. I know that will annoy me immensely, so I decide to get up before she can make it back. That way I won't have to endure that miserable crawling knock she does again. I fling back my covers and swing my feet down to the floor. On the opposite side of the room is my sister's bed. Sara is going to start University in London after the summer. I can't wait to have the room all to myself, but in other ways I am dreading her leaving. When she is gone, mum will have to direct all her pointless shit onto me. I am sixteen, I remember, and I seem to have less and less patience with everything. Probably that is normal, but I don't know. I have also recently started to really enjoy swearing. I mean, *really* get off on it. Me and my best friend Joe have mouths like gutters when we are together. My mum would go nuts if she ever heard us. I don't know why swearing is so funny, but it just is. It's like if your friend trips up over something and looks stupid, you'll make yourself laugh a hell of a lot more if you call them a fucking twat or something. I don't trust people who don't swear. Everyone needs to swear sometimes. You just need to. There are times when a *damn,* or a *bloody*, or even a *Christ* just won't do. It just won't be enough. Believe me.

When I stand up, my head swims; reminding me of the cheap lager Joe and me drank yesterday at his house. I feel a bit icky, and that is as good an excuse as any not to eat breakfast. (One less thing to write in my food diary, you see!) I'll just get out of the house and go and do whatever it is my mum wants me to do, and then I'll go to Joe's. We need to talk about what we found yesterday. I can imagine Joe lying awake on his bunk bed all night, sweating about it. I wanted to stay over with him, but our parents are not keen on us having sleepovers anymore. For some reason, when we got to about the age of thirteen, they all suddenly expected us to start fancying each other. They still can't really accept that we are just friends. They are always lifting their eyebrows at us, and swapping looks with each other which range between amused and horrified. Well, they are all idiots. You'll soon see. Just wait till you see.

There is a chest of drawers in our room. I have the bottom two drawers, and Sara has the top three. We also share the wardrobe, which is slightly better, because it is huge and endless, just like the one in Narnia. You could actually climb inside and get lost if you were a little kid. There are no clean pants in my drawer. I realise this is because they are all screwed up in little colourful knots across the bedroom carpet. My mum flatly refuses to pick washing up from the floor. She will only wash it if it has made its way to the linen bin in the bathroom. I sigh and growl, and scoop them all up and throw them on the bed. I shrug at the thought of wearing the same pants again. I think, fuck it. Who will know? I wonder vaguely what influence wearing yesterday's crusty pants will have on my day. You have to think about these things.

Okay, so here begins the other thing I do every day now. Pull off the t-shirt I wear to bed and stand in front of the full-length mirror that is next to the chest of drawers. Front view. Stomach in, then stomach out. Side view. Stomach in. Stomach let out. Finally back view, head twisted over shoulder to see bum. I only ate half of my dinner last night, and wonder if my stomach does look just a tiny bit flatter because of it. I think it does, which satisfies me for now. I pull on the denim cut offs which are dangling from the end of my bed, shove my phone into one pocket, and throw on a black vest top. I grab a hoodie from the wardrobe, snatch up my manky pants and go to the bathroom. I see my mum half way up the stairs, and she does that face. The mouth drops into an 'o' shape, then snaps shut quickly, and her eyebrows frown over her eyes and she says, "Oh," just like that. Like I have surprised her or something. She does not smile though. She is not really a smiley person. I go into the bathroom and lock the door behind me. I stuff my pants into the overflowing linen bin and wonder how long it will take her to get around to washing them. I wonder if I have any money anywhere to buy some new pants. "Are you off out Lou?" She is outside the door asking me. "I only ask because I need milk and bread, and some letters posted. If you were going out anyway?"

I wash my face and brush my teeth, rolling my eyes at my own reflection. "Okay," I call back to her. Unbelievable. I need you to be up, she had said. I need you to be up in case you were going out anyway? No, that doesn't really make sense mum.

"Okay thanks," she says and goes back down the stairs. I absolutely know what is coming next. I know it so much that I can even mouth the words at the mirror as she calls them up the stairs to me. "Perhaps you could take the dog with you too then?" I do not answer, because it is not really a question. I brush my hair and tie it back and make a face at myself. The thing that pleases me is that I definitely look better with a thinner face. I nod at this. Loads better. Chubby cheeks only look good on babies and toddlers. Fact.

Downstairs my mum pushes money into one of my hands, and the dog lead into the other. I am yawning, and my temples are thudding. "How does it feel to be sixteen?" she asks me for what feels like the hundredth time. I fake a smile and shrug.

"It feels amazing."

"Is that the jumper Nana got you?"

"No, this is an old one,"

"Well where's the one Nana got you? Doesn't it fit?"

I look around, shaking my head. "I think it's down here somewhere."

"Well I hope you haven't lost it young lady!" She fixes me with a warning glare, and shakes her head twice and I feel like shrinking down to the floor away from that look. My Nana died two months ago, but she was one of those extremely well organised people. Even on her deathbed she'd had the forward thinking to get someone to go out, buy me a jumper and wrap it up for her. It warmed my heart to think of her doing that for me, to imagine that I was one of the things on her mind during her last weeks in this world, but the awkward thing is, I really hate that jumper. Her taste in jumpers was a running joke between me and my sister over the years. I mean, when we were little, knitted pink cardigans with teddy bear buttons were okay for a while, although I can never recall *liking* them, but when your Nan buys you a jumper for your sixteenth birthday that looks like it is something she would wear herself? Hmm. What do you say to that? What do you say to that when the poor woman is dead? She would have flipped if she'd known. She was like that. She was feisty and fiery, the kind of old woman people are scared of. I think my mum was always scared of her, but me and Sara adored her. My mum likes to joke that Nan's feisty nature skipped a generation, missing her entirely and landing squarely on Sara's shoulders. There is some truth in this I will admit, but it is one of those pointless comments that my family make endlessly, which never fails to piss me off. Am I not feisty then, I wonder? What am I? No one ever says stuff like that about me. It didn't use to bother me, but for some reason lately I find myself dissecting everything that anyone says to me, you know, turning it over and examining it, reading too much into it most of the time. So I am not only cynical, but slightly paranoid. I don't know if anyone else my age feels like this yet. Most of the time lately, to be honest with you, I just feel sort of stuck and wound up. I can't listen to people if they are boring me and I just drift away.

My mum is not feisty, although she does attempt to be sometimes. Mostly with me, because she can't get away with it with Sara. My mum just wants people to be nice and not argue. My Nan hated my dad, when they were together; she was always snarling and griping about what an idiot he was. My mum would sigh and say 'can't we just all get along?', 'no we can't.' my dad would say, and then he left. It's not her fault she married a bastard.

"I'll find it."

"Hope you and Joe enjoyed your little party?" Mum walks back into the kitchen as she says this. She thinks I don't know, but this is her way of ending a conversation, walking away from it, moving out of earshot, so that if I do answer her, I am pretty much talking to myself.

"It was quiet," I shrug again. Mum frowns back at me.

"Quiet? Didn't sound quiet from here young lady. I nearly went over! But I had Les on the phone."

"Okay, I'll see you later," I say, and that's it, I go. I am hoping eventually she will notice that whenever she mentions her new boyfriends name, I cut her off and stop listening. But somehow I doubt it. Like a lot of adults my mother has a rather thick skin.

I leave the house and look at the dog on the end of its lead, and I sigh and think why does it feel like it is always just the dog and me? I don't often complain about walking the dog, because if I do mum will spend a good five minutes reminding me that it was me who wanted a dog, me who pestered her for years to get a dog, and her that is always stuck with looking after the dog. She let us get the dog when I was thirteen, because that was when my dad walked out. It was almost the first response she had to that door closing, with him on one side, and us on the other. 'We'll get a dog,' she had told my sister and me. 'I know someone who has puppies.'

No one knows what type of dog Gremlin is. We called him Gremlin because he looked like one. Squashed up face, small nose, and big fuck off ears like a bat. He is only about the size of a spaniel, with a long tail and scruffy, wiry fur. It is mostly white, but he has one black ear, and one black patch near his tail. Joe calls him an experiment.

As I walk towards the shop, I keep yawning, and my head keeps thudding, and my throat feels dry, and I think why the hell didn't I make myself a coffee first? I have only recently discovered that coffee reduces your appetite. Well, sort of. If I am feeling hungry, I might have a big sugary coffee instead of food, and it seems to work. I hope Lorraine is not in the shop. Lorraine is Joe's mum and my mum's best friend, and she scares the shit out of me.

There is a little parade of shops just down the end of our road. There is the shop, well it's a Londis at the moment, but it's been loads of things, so everyone just calls it the shop. Then there is the ladies hairdressers, the off licence, and the fish and chip shop. That's it. If you want anything else you have to catch a bus into town. I tie Gremlin up outside the shop and go in. Straight away I see Lorraine is on the till, and straight away she gives me one of her hellish looks. I avoid her for a while, browsing the magazines I have no money for, before I wander around to the chiller cabinet and grab the milk. The bread is near the till. I pick up a loaf of white and put it on the counter with the milk. Lorraine is chewing gum; she is always chewing gum to stop her from smoking. I can still smell nicotine on her though. She fixes me with an icy stare as she scans my shopping. "I hope, young lady," she begins. "That you are on your way round to my house to help tidy up after last night!"

I am slightly stunned by this, but try not to let it show. Joe and me barely had a party at all, so I don't know what either of our mothers are going on about. We stayed in his room, drank cheap lager, and the only other people that came over were Marianne, Josh and Ryan, and they all left by eleven. You can hardly call five teenagers in a bedroom a party, can you?

"What mess?" I ask this as politely and innocently as I can, because the last thing I want Lorraine to think is that I am being sarcastic with her. Apparently, according to her and to my mum, I have been getting very sarcastic lately. They told me this last week in my own kitchen. They were both tapping their feet and giving me their screwed up lipstick face look. Lorraine had even said something about sarcasm being the lowest form of wit. I had wanted to both laugh and scream at her. I had wanted to say, sarcasm is all you deserve when you repeatedly ask such banal and dumb questions! You can't talk to Lorraine. I mean, really you can't. You can open your mouth and let words come out, but she won't hear them unless she wants to, and most of the time she will talk right over them anyway. She lacks even the basic skills in conversation. Like listening.

"What mess, she says?" Lorraine practically throws back her head at this comment and starts to shove the milk and bread into a carrier bag. "No doubt you buggered off home before you saw the state of the kitchen!"

"We didn't go in the kitchen," I tell her, again, trying ever so hard to keep my tone non-confrontational. This is almost impossible with someone like Lorraine, who does not feel human unless she has torn strips off of someone. As I stare at her, I can't help imagining what it would feel like to punch her out. Don't get me wrong, I have never punched anyone in my entire life and I don't intend on ever starting. But sometimes when I am speaking to people who make me uncomfortable, I start to picture slapping them suddenly, or poking them in the eye. What would they say, I wonder? If I just lashed out without warning, like that? What would they do? "Leon and Travis were in the kitchen." I pay her the money and take the bag.

"I don't care which of you people were in the kitchen," Lorraine informs me, her voice getting higher now, as she blatantly ignores the old man who is waiting patiently behind me to pay for his newspaper. "It was your party, and so you can help tidy up the mess! Otherwise I will be having words with your mother."

"Okay," I tell her, shrugging my shoulders and biting down on the strong urge to say *whatever* to her. I know that would drive her wild, so I don't do it. "I'll take this home then go round and help."

This seems to pacify her, and she even pushes a red smile across her face. She screws her lips up so much that when she smiles, you can see all the little creases around her mouth, all filled with shiny red lipstick. She buys the same shade of lipstick from the Avon lady about every six weeks, I once heard her tell my mum. I imagine the shade is called something violent like 'death spray' or 'blood lust'. She is five foot nothing and as vicious as a pit bull. Her hair is a deep brassy blonde, piled high on her head, probably to make her look taller. Joe calls it her Marge Simpson hair and he is right. If it was a foot taller and blue, it would be Marge Simpson's hair. She smiles a sick smile at the old man, and the smile screws up her whole face, I notice, especially her eyes. "Off you go then," she says to me, so I go.

I wander back home with the dog lead in one hand, and the carrier bag swinging from the other. I open the door and call mum to come and get the shopping. She hurries to meet me, waving two brown envelopes at me accusingly. "You forgot the letters!" she practically screams in terror, as if all the letterboxes in the area have probably vanished into thin air in the ten minutes that I have been gone.

"You didn't give them to me," I tell her. She pushes them into my hand, and runs back into the kitchen.

"Got Les on the phone!" she calls back. I slam the door behind me.

Right, I think, as I shove the letters into the post box near the shop, and walk around the back of the parade. That's enough of pleasing the parents for today. There is a car park behind the parade, and I cross it and head down the narrow alley that will lead me to Joe's back gate.

We were drunk last night, and when the others had gone home, we crept into his brothers' room to look for a lighter. We only smoke when we are drunk, otherwise it tastes like shit. Leon and Travis had been in the kitchen all night smoking and drinking. Then Leon had answered a call on his mobile. He and Travis had left the house minutes after. We had watched them go from Joe's window.

We dove into the older boys bedroom, which was pitch black and reeked of sweat and dirt and God knows what else. It really was a vile dungeon. It was me who had opened the wardrobe door, while Joe looked on the bedside table for a lighter. It was me, being nosy. I'll tell you now, before we go much further, that lately I have had a tiny, tiny, *really* tiny crush on Travis. I know, I know, pathetic and predictable, which is why I keep it to myself. Well, between you and me World. It's a sick, sick thing, and you'll see why soon enough. Anyway, I'd felt a little light headed from the lager and the smell of the older boys bedroom. Maybe my hormones had a surge, it being my sixteenth birthday and everything. I had opened the door a crack, running my eyes up and down the shirts and sweatshirts that hung there. I had opened the door another crack. There was an Adidas rucksack, bulging at the sides. I was drunk and giddy and nosy, and had no idea what boys Travis and Leon's age would keep stuffed into a bag like that. Sports kit maybe? Did they play any sports? I had no idea if they did anymore. I had no idea what their lives consisted of. A sinister side of my brain had urged me to unzip it, imagining porno magazines, or stolen goods. What I had not expected to find was several large plastic bags filled with white powder. Joe had peered over my shoulder, his hazel eyes growing larger and larger as he took in what I had found.

"Zip it back up, for fucks sake!" he had hissed at me, his hand suddenly seizing the top of my arm so hard it hurt.

"Okay, okay, sorry," I had mumbled at him, struggling with the zip and panic now breaking through my drunken stupor. Joe had slammed the wardrobe door so hard and so fast he had nearly trapped my fingers. We had run back to the room he shares with his little brother Will.

I find Joe in the kitchen now. He looks hung over and scared. We don't speak to each other for a minute or two. I know it is harder for him, because this is his family, and to be honest, they were already fucked up enough to deal with. But I cannot deny the frizz of excitement that courses through my veins when I see him there, and the silent knowledge passes between us. I remember my Nana once saying everyone should have at least one good summer in their lives, one summer that they never forget. I think, this is not a bad way to start my sixteenth year. This is not a bad way to start our summer. And I give Joe a slow smile.

2

Dear World?

Are you still there? Are you still listening? I've still got so much to tell you.

Like how it still amazes me, how easy it is to not eat. All those years of being fat, and I had thought food was my salvation, my friend, and my crutch to help me limp through a life that bewildered and bored me. I can still remember the day I snapped. I can still remember the jam doughnut that I crushed inside my fist, instead of inside my mouth. I guess it made me feel stronger somehow, more in control, more savage. Less of a fat loser. See, if you want to know the truth I have finally figured out, it's that my worst enemy has always been myself. My biggest problem has always been looking in the mirror and seeing me, still standing there, staring back, when I really want to see someone else. I just don't *want* to, I mean I *expect to.* I am thinking about all this as I enter Joe's house through the back door.

Joe stands in his kitchen, which is cramped and cluttered, with too many chairs around the small square table, and towers of cardboard boxes around the edges of the room. I look around and find myself agreeing with Lorraine; the kitchen is a total mess. The table is normally covered in an old checked tablecloth, with Lorraine's china fruit bowl in the centre. Today someone has used the tablecloth to mop up a spillage on the floor, and the fruit bowl is on the draining board. The table is covered in crushed beer cans and ashtrays. It's Leon and Travis's mess, and we are being blamed for it.

Joe is dressed in tracksuit trousers and a t-shirt. His dark brown hair is all stuck up and messy, as if he has not even had a chance to look in the mirror yet. Like me, he can't stop yawning, and every now and again he touches two fingers to his forehead, as if the same pain rages in his as it does in mine. He has filled the sink with water and washing-up liquid, and starts to dunk cups and glasses into the water while I look on. I think about offering to make us both a coffee. Just then, Joe's step-dad's dog Rozzer comes trotting into the kitchen. He is a German Shepherd cross, and lifts his fluffy tail in a greeting to Gremlin. Gremlin responds by cocking his leg on one of the cardboard box towers. I yank him away by his lead. "Fuck me!" Joe exclaims, lifting his hands from the soapy water. "Isn't that freak show house trained yet?"

"Sorry," I tut, looking around for a cloth. Joe drags a dishcloth out of the water and throws it at me. "He's threatened by Rozzer, that's why," I try to explain. "He's older than Rozzer, but smaller. So it confuses him."

"Looking like a smashed in cat confuses him," Joe responds, and I laugh.

"You love him really."

"He gives me nightmares."

I laugh again, louder this time, and bend down to wipe up the mess. This particular tower of boxes contains crisps. One of the others contains peanuts. Joe's stepfather Mick works at the cash and carry.

"Just seen your mum," I say from the floor. Joe lets out his breath.

"Oh yeah?"

"You better be on your way round to mine to clean up that mess or I'll be having words with your mother!" I relay this in a near perfect imitation of Lorraine's voice, the way she speaks as if her teeth are permanently clenched together. Joe laughs as he washes up. "We didn't even make this mess," I point out uselessly. "We didn't even come in here."

"Well I got that in my fucking ear when I still in bed this morning," Joe sighs.

"Why can't they clean up their own mess?"

"They didn't come back last night." I make a face, my eyebrows rising and my mouth screwed up in thought. Joe looks back at the sink, but jerks his head towards the kettle. "Do you want to make me a coffee? And some toast? I'm fading fast."

"You drank more than me," I point out, heading for the kettle. I get two clean mugs down from the cupboard, and some bread out from the bread bin. I want to ask Joe about the bags of powder in the rucksack. Who does the rucksack belong to? Travis or Leon? What did he think the powder was? I had no idea, but I was pretty sure it wasn't biological washing powder or anything. I put on the grill, and while the kettle is boiling, I poke my head around the kitchen door. I see right away that Mick is sprawled out on the sofa, fag in one hand, cup of tea in the other. He is watching Soccer AM or some such crap. I go back to the oven to check the toast, knowing that this is why we cannot say anything. "Where are the little ones?" I ask, referring to Joe's other brothers, Will and Tommy.

"Will went next door to play," Joe answers. "Don't know where Tommy is."

I suddenly think of the powder in the rucksack and a sick fear grips me and makes all my hairs stand on end. "What about…?" I say quietly to Joe. He turns and looks at me, and I can see the same thought has spread like a germ through his mind too. He shakes the water from his hands and stalks from the room.

"Wait here," he says to me. I turn the toast over and make the coffees. When Joe finally comes back, he is holding his three-year-old half-brother by the arm and the little boy is whining and struggling. I go to the door to watch.

"What's going on?" Mick demands from the sofa. Joe lets Tommy go and he runs for his daddy's lap and climbs all over him, still whining.

"Can you tell him to stay out of my room?" Joe complains. "He's got his sticky fingers all over my stuff!"

I look at Mick as he comforts Tommy, knowing as well as Joe that he is wasting his breath trying to complain. "Just think yourself lucky that you have a room, eh?" comes the haughty, confrontational tone that Mick uses whenever he speaks to one of his stepsons. His tone goes up a notch, his voice is gruffer, quicker, more accusing. Even if he is saying 'pass the potatoes'; it is more like *pass the potatoes!* I can do an excellent take on his voice too, well, his two voices. Because when he speaks to Will or Tommy, his eyes go all dopey, and his tone softens and the speed of his words slows down. "He doesn't even have a bedroom, remember?" Mick directs this statement towards Joe's tired face, accompanied by a puff of grey smoke from his fag. I watch Joe's shoulders drop, and I don't know how he puts up with it.

Joe comes back into the kitchen and gives me a look that I know means; God give me fucking strength. I pass him his coffee toast and he cocks his head at me. "You not having any toast?"

"No thanks."

"You're not still on a stupid diet?"

"It's not stupid, and yes I am."

"You look fine the way you are."

"Well thanks very much."

Joe chews his toast and nods at me. "You girls are all the same."

"We are, aren't we? Me and Marianne. Exactly the same."

Joe rolls his eyes at the mention of our pale-faced friend. "Well not *her* obviously. She doesn't give a shit what she looks like."

"Come on," I say, getting bored. "Let's hurry up and get out of here."

Joe feels the same, I know. His house is suffocating. There is too much stuff. Every room is packed full of furniture; three sofas instead of two, three coffee tables, two units filled with glass ornaments and other nasty shit. Every room has these towers of boxes of stuff Mick brings back from work in case it is needed one day, and people. Too many fucking people. You feel like you are permanently enveloped within a crowd. The house is never empty, ever. I cannot remember us ever being alone there. You are always bumping shoulders with someone, squashing past someone on the landing, or on the stairs. The place reminds me of a rabbit warren.

I can vaguely remember it before Mick came along. We would have been about eight, I suppose. My mum and Lorraine have been friends for years. I have therefore known Joe since before we were even born. We were in our mother's stomachs, face to face almost, forced to sit in uterine liquid and listen to their spiteful gossip endlessly. I am convinced this experience has shaped us into the cynical pair we now are.

Joe's dad Tony left when he was five. He's a long distance lorry driver, and Joe sees him about twice a year if he is lucky. Despite this, we both like Tony a lot. We are not supposed to obviously, him being another one of the men who have left, another useless father who walked out and closed the door behind him. But I don't blame him one bit for walking out on Lorraine. Jesus Christ, how did he last as long as he did? We have to keep our admiration for Tony well hid. God forbid Lorraine or my mum hear us say something positive about him. He is tall and broad, and always wears checked shirts and jeans, and smokes rolls ups. He is quiet and still. He is a softly breaking sunset, while Lorraine is a fucking thunderstorm.

Mick met Joe's mum when he fixed her car. He used to be a mobile mechanic. He still tinkers with cars a lot. I mean, their back garden has three cars in it, and their front garden has two. He never really gets around to fixing them though. He works at the cash and carry now. More money apparently. He moved in when Lorraine got pregnant with Will. I remember feeling sorry for Joe and his older brothers when this happened. Leon and Travis never stopped complaining about this intrusion in their lives, this fake father figure who thought he could tell them what to do, or the two younger half-brothers that soon arrived to drive the house to the brink of its capacity. Joe never said much about anything. He is like his dad that way. He takes it all on the chin. He just takes it all.

We get the kitchen back to its usual clean but cluttered standard, and then we leave. We don't know where to go, or what to do. I can see it all tumbling around inside Joe's head, because his eyes are dark and frowning, and his lips are tight and straight. He looks just like his dad that way. "I'm a bit worried about leaving Tommy there," I say eventually, because as much as I despise the sticky little monkey-faced bugger, this is the thing that is keeping me scared. This is the thing that keeps spinning back into my mind every time I try to shrug it all off and convince myself copious amounts of drugs in my best friends brothers' wardrobe is nothing to get my knickers in a twist about. Joe looks sideways at me.

"I know. Me too."

"There's no lock on their door."

"I know."

"Tommy or Will could easily find that stuff. Whatever it is."

"I know what it is," Joe says then, and I stop walking. We have wandered to the fields behind the estate, so I lean down and unclip Gremlin's lead. I wait for Joe to speak, and I can see a hundred secrets behind his troubled eyes. He releases a heavy sigh that smooth's its way down his body. He is taller than me now, I notice. Only by a bit. "It's cocaine," he whispers, even though there is no one to be seen for miles around. My eyes shoot wide open. "At least I think that's what it is." He lifts and drops his shoulders in a weak and guilty shrug. I narrow my eyes at him.

"How do you know?"

"They do it sometimes," he tells me. "When mum and Mick are out."

"Since when?"

"I don't know," Joe shrugs again, and looks briefly away from me as Gremlin tears yapping across the fields, chasing a crow. "I saw them do it about two months ago. They just laughed about it. I didn't bother saying anything."

"Okay," I say, folding my arms across my chest and trying not to let it show that I am annoyed he has not told me this before. If I tell you the truth World, I am annoyed but also sort of excited again. I know, I know, it's wrong, so wrong. Joe is standing before me with this taut expression on his soft face, and all I can feel is tremors of stiff excitement careering through me. Part of my mind wanders off on its own, picturing Travis, the bad boy, doing drugs and not caring. I shake myself out of it quickly, momentarily sickened by myself. "So if it is cocaine in that bag, why have they got so much of it? Are they fucking dealers or something?"

"I have no idea," Joe says, and I believe him. He is almost incapable of lying. He is good at not telling you things, but he is hopeless at actual lies.

"They can't seriously think it's okay to just leave it there like that, with your brothers around. I'm getting really worried about that Joe."

"We should go back and move it," he nods.

"Where to?"

"I have no idea," he says again as we start to head back. He drops his head and his brown hair dances about across his forehead. I wait for Gremlin to catch us up, then put his lead back on. Joe walks with his hands inside his pockets and his back bent. For some reason a small giggle escapes me. He looks my way. "What's so funny?"

"Nothing," I clap a hand across my mouth. My stomach is growling at me and I rub it absent-mindedly, thinking about another coffee to shut it up. "Was just imagining Leon and Travis, that's all. Finding it gone." I snort again, and even Joe cracks a smile at this. "They'll shit themselves," I point out. "But what will they do or say? Without dropping themselves in it?"

Joe just smiles at me.

When we get back to his house, we go in the front way so we can avoid Mick. We hare up the stairs two at a time and then quietly open the older boys door. None of them have locks on their doors. They did once, I remember. But Mick unscrewed them all when the boys kept storming off to their rooms to avoid being lectured at. Now he can follow them into their room and carry on the lecture. I smile again, my devious side wondering what words of wisdom Mick would impress upon them if he knew they had shit loads of Class A drugs stashed in their wardrobe. I imagine his head exploding and it makes me chuckle. Joe digs me in the ribs with his elbow. He is crapping himself, I know it, but what choice do we have? Tell Mick what we have found and witness world war three tear his family apart? Do nothing and risk the little brats finding it and sticking their mucky fingers in for a taste? I feel the thrill of danger and fear galloping through my body, and it is enough to make my hungry belly shut up. In fact I feel kind of sick as we sneak into the dark room and open up the wardrobe again. We feel and look just like sneaky little kids, stealing biscuits from the tin, and I just hope to God we don't get caught. Joe grabs the bag and we scramble back to his room.

***

In contrast, Joe's room is light and airy, with the curtains drawn and the window wide open. He clutches the bag to his chest, fear making him look like someone from a film, wide-eyed and full of emotion. I smirk, thinking he never normally looks like that. Funny thing is World, he looks quite sexy really. I slap a hand over my mouth again and wonder what the hell is wrong with me. I am not normal. Really. Joe looks at me in desperation, and I can almost imagine him throwing me the bag, as if it is a bomb or something. But he doesn't. He just looks around for somewhere to hide it. There is nowhere.

"Your house?" he asks, white faced now. I shake my head.

"No fucking way!"

"Marianne?"

I think about this. Her house is huge and vast and rambling. She is an only child. It is probably our best course of action until Leon and Travis come home. Then they can fucking get rid of it. "Text her?" I ask. Joe shakes his head.

"No, let's just go." We nod in silent agreement, and Joe slings the rucksack onto his back. We leave the house as silently and sneakily as we arrived, and hear nothing from Mick and Tommy in the lounge.

Outside, the day is getting hot. The sun beats down on our hung over brains and my stomach twists itself in hunger and fear and excitement. I have never had a proper adventure before, I am thinking, as we start to walk quickly towards the fields again. We can cut across them to where Marianne lives. We walk fast, me dragging poor knackered Gremlin along on his lead, Joe swinging his arms up and down, sweat beading across his forehead. "This is like the fucking Goonies or something," I say to Joe, and feel instantly guilty when he looks at me, because he is not enjoying any of this at all. It is only me getting off on it, and I have no right to. Just because my own life is so dry and so full of mind-numbing tedium. Just because I don't have criminal older brothers, or a mad witch for a mother. It never ceases to amaze me how fascinating other people's families can be. You never find your own family interesting, do you? Nope, nothing to look at there. Boring, boring, a bit annoying, boring, boring. I want to giggle again, but I shut up and say nothing and we storm across the fields, and climb through the fence and come out onto Marianne's road.

She opens the door when we hammer on it. She is tiny and frail, like a bird, dressed in black from head to toe, and her green eyes light up when she sees us, but her smile is always devious. "To what to I owe the pleasure?" she asks as Joe pushes past her. She is nearly always alone, but Joe feels the need to check every downstairs room for any sign of her parents anyway. Marianne fixes me with a beady-eyed stare.

"What is wrong with him?"

"We need your help," I tell her, trying like hell to stop the smile from tugging at my lips again. "We need to stash something here for a bit."

Marianne licks her perfect little lips at me. "Well aren't I the lucky one?" she says to us.

3

Dear World, so let me tell you about Marianne Sholing.

Firstly, she is one of those people who gives very little away. I mean, she is really, really good at it. I have known her for a year and still have no idea what to make of her. In equal measures I feel both privileged to know her, and scared of her. She only moved to our school a year ago and she stood out right away. She is small and thin, fragile looking, with jet-black hair that she wears loose to her shoulders. She usually has a fringe. Sometimes it is growing out and she shakes her head to remove it from her eyes. Recently she had it cut into a straight blunt line just above her eyebrows. Marianne has a small, round face, with a delicately pointed chin. People at school laugh at he, and whisper behind her back. They think she is a Goth, or a witch, or a freak. The people in our school are like vultures when it comes to new students. You can see them standing around the edges, licking their lips and narrowing their eyes, the most vicious of them quickly working out the unfortunate persons weak spots. They will stand and watch and decide right away if the person is worth knowing or not, worth being friends with. I've seen it too many times. I've stood back and observed the way they work, and it's simple and shocking in its coldness. And you might not believe this, but the girls are the worst.

I've always hated school for this very reason. And you might think that it all starts when kids become teenagers, but you would be wrong World. It starts way, way before that. You see, people can't usually see it, because everyone thinks little kids are so sweet and innocent and cute, but the truth is, the bitches and the bastards start young. They really do. Watch them. Sweet and innocent, my arse. Obviously they learn how to be a bitch or a bastard from their parents, and once they figure out how to be mean, they go for it, they find out that is the way forward, and forward they go. I've been lucky mostly. Plenty of things people could pick on me for, but I've got Joe, and Joe has the hardest family around. Marianne didn't have anyone, and they went for her all right. Freak. Weirdo. Witch. And that was how we became friends. I'll be honest; we felt sorry for her.

What we didn't know then was that she doesn't need us to. She mostly wears black. When she first came to our school she fascinated me. I didn't understand her at all. She was obviously ridiculously clever and articulate, but more than that, she did not give a shit what the other kids said about her, or to her. Eventually they got a bit spooked by her, and stopped teasing her. They still hate her, believe me, but she doesn't need them, so that is that.

Just like Joe and me, Marianne will be starting the sixth form at our old school in September. I would have liked to have gone to college, and get away from it all, if I'm honest. Maybe meet some new people, recreate myself among kids who have not known me since I was a child. But mum said we could not afford the daily train fare, and what was wrong with the sixth form? Walking distance, she had pointed out, and you already know everyone. I hadn't the heart or the energy to tell her that was the main reason I abhorred the thought of going back there. Okay, so we won't have to wear school uniform anymore, and we will be able to come and go as we pleased, but what else will be different apart from that? There will still be Scott Taylor and his pretty blue eyes, the Mr Popular and handsome that would never look at me in a million years. And there will still be Christine Raymond and Stacey Winters, the two biggest blonde bitches known to human history. We will all just have to endure it, I suppose.

Marianne regards Joe and his rucksack with hungry green eyes. She nods through to the large kitchen. "You sure there is no one home?" Joe sees fit to ask as we walk through. Marianne looks at him quizzically.

"What the hell have you got in there? A gun?"

Joe and I swap a look which suggests to Marianne that it may as well be. She looks even more intrigued now. "No one is home," she rolls her eyes at his desperate face and shrugs at me. Then she sneers down at poor Gremlin panting and dribbling on his lead. "You can't bring him in here," she says. "My mum is allergic." I tut and tie him up outside. I think what a strange day the poor dog is having. I go inside and wander slowly around the large country style kitchen. Marianne's parents have lots of old oak furniture, and the large robust kitchen table is a particular feature. It is huge and would be more at home in a farmhouse. It looks like it was built for a huge ruddy faced family to gather around, not just Marianne and her mum and dad. She did have a twin, she has told us once. A twin that died at birth. Joe and I have yet to decide if we believe this or not. "It is just me, myself and I," she tells us, crossing her twig like arms across her black long-sleeved t-shirt. "So what's going on?"

"Do we tell her?" Joe looks at me and asks.

"Of course we have to tell her!" I snap at him. "We can't ask her to stash it if she doesn't know what it is!" Later, I come to regret this statement, but at the time it seems obvious. Joe nods and lets the bag slide off his back and into his hand. He places it on the kitchen table, and I notice that he has a large patch of sweat at the top of his back between his shoulder blades. Marianne walks up to him and peers into the bag as he unzips it slowly. She sees the bags, and her mouth falls open in surprise, and she claps one hand over it and looks from Joe, to me, and back again. Finally her shining green eyes settle on the bag.

"What is that and where the hell did you get it?"

"It's cocaine, I think," Joe tells her, and zips the bag again. He pushes his hair back with the heel of one hand. The sweat makes it stick straight up in dark brown points. "It's my brothers."

"Holy shit!" Marianne exclaims, her hand falling from her mouth. "Do they know you've got it? What are they, drug dealers?"

"No they don't know we've got it. And I don't know if they are drug dealers."

"But you would assume they are, right? With that much stuff?" Marianne crosses her arms again and shakes her hair from her shoulders.

"We just need to hide it somewhere until they come back," I explain to her. "We found it by accident in their wardrobe."

"*You* found it by accident," Joe corrects me. "Actually not by accident, because you were poking around in their wardrobe on purpose." I give him a look of pure disgust and he stares me down.

"Lou Carling! Do I detect you have a crush on one of Joe's dear brothers?"

I groan inwardly at Marianne and her incessant habit of speaking like an adult. Not even an adult actually, more like an old lady most of the time. I decide not to warrant her question with a response. She smiles at me wickedly. "Poking around in boys wardrobes eh? What did you *hope* to find?" I roll my eyes at her irritably, but it's too late to halt the creep of warmth that flushes my cheeks.

"It was after you guys left," Joe takes up the rest of the story. "We were just looking for a lighter. They'd gone out."

"Now we don't know where they are or when they'll be back, and we can't leave it in the wardrobe in case the brats find it!" I look at Marianne and see the concentration deepening on her face.

"You could have told your parents about it," she says slowly, not sounding as if she really believes this herself.

"My mum would go fucking mental, and Mick would throw them both out and probably call the cops," Joe replies. Marianne scowls slightly.

"So what?" she argues. "They're both worthless twats, aren't they? Why would you care? If they were gone there would be more space for you."

"Marianne," I speak up. "They might be twats, but they're his brothers. You can't just do that to your family." Joe says nothing. Neither Marianne nor myself can tell what he is thinking.

"So how long do you want me to hide it for you?" Marianne questions, dropping her head slightly and peering at Joe from under her fringe. Joe releases a long drawn out sigh and drops his shoulders.

"Give me a day," he says. "I'll try and find them."

"Are you sure you're okay with this?" I look at Marianne and see a gleam in her eyes. I have to look at the floor and bite my lip, because I can tell she is relishing an adventure as much as I am, but I just bet she doesn't make a stupid crack about the Goonies. "If anyone finds that stuff, we'll be in deep fucking trouble."

"You're in deep fucking trouble anyway. You've stolen their drugs!"

"We couldn't leave it there," I argue with her. "The brats get their paws into everything!"

"Are you even sure it is drugs?" Marianne gives a little laugh and walks back to the bag on the table. We watch dumbly as she unzips it again and actually lifts out one of the bags. It looks like something you would see on the telly or something, on the news, when you see the police handling mass quantities of tightly wrapped drugs. She holds it in both hands, giving away how heavy it is. Joe is watching her in confusion. She looks up at us. "It might be salt or washing powder or something!"

"It's coke, isn't it Joe?" I look at him.

"I've seen them do coke," he tells Marianne reluctantly. "A few times recently."

She nods at him, and pulls her bottom lip in with her teeth. She is thinking, I can tell. "Shall we try it?" she says. "See if it is?"

Marianne's question hangs in the air between all three of us. The scariest thing to me is that none of us immediately shoot her down. That must mean that all three of us are considering her question. I decide to be the sensible one, though God knows why, and fuck knows I don't want to be. "They'd kill you, don't even think about it," I tell Joe, and he nods solemnly. Marianne looks momentarily disappointed with us, and stuffs the bag back into the rucksack.

"I'll take care of this then," she announces, slinging it onto her shoulder.

"Where will you hide it?" asks Joe. She looks back at him over her thin shoulder as she leaves the kitchen.

"Trap door in my room." she says and is gone.

"Is she joking?" Joe asks me. "I can never tell when she's joking. Can you?"

"I just hope we're doing the right thing," I say, as a monumental sigh escapes me. I suddenly feel significantly less excited about all of this. I am beginning to wish we had left it in the wardrobe and minded our own business. So what if the brats had come across it? That would be Travis and Leon's fault, not ours. It would technically be Lorraine and Mick's fault too. "Any idea where to start looking for your brothers? And are they going to kill you when they know what we've done?"

"More like I should kill them," he replies, with a toss of his head, and we both know this is never likely to happen. Joe is the calmest, most grounded one in his tornado of a home. His family make mine look normal. I have known his family my entire life and the only one I like and trust is Joe. By far the best thing about him is that he just gets me, like no one else does. It has always been that way. When we were babies and toddlers, I suppose we were pretty much forced on each other. As we got older, our parents would comment on how well we got on. Look at Lou and Joe, they would say whenever they saw us together, aren't they sweet? They both have embarrassing photographs of us in the bath together, and running around outside with nappies on.

When I was a child, I can strongly remember Joe's mother terrifying me. She was always so loud, so screechy, and her lips so red and violent. I used to cringe and squirm if she ever tried to pick me up or kiss me. I felt like I had to pretend to like her for mum's sake. My mum defends her to this day. She says Lorraine has to be like that because of her boys, which would seem to suggest that she was completely normal and non-threatening before they come along, and I have a hard time believing this. My mum thanks God she only had girls, and Lorraine curses God that she only had boys. They still make stupid remarks about swapping some of us over. If you had that many boys, you would be the same, my mum says. Boys are hard work, apparently. I can vividly recall Lorraine hearing Leon swear once, when he was about nine or ten. It was someone's birthday party, but I don't remember whose. We were outside playing pass the parcel on a picnic blanket, when Leon said fuck because the music stopped on the kid next to him. Lorraine heard and waded through the children like a deranged monkey, screaming and huffing and snatching him up by his arm. She dragged him into their kitchen, while everyone stood about and stared and tried not to laugh, and then she came back with a bar of soap, and proceeded to wash his mouth out with it. You can see why she makes me nervous.

My mum still shakes her head and listens and sympathises whenever Lorraine comes over to whine about her boys. I am beginning to wonder if this says more about my mother as a person, than it does about the strength of their friendship. When I look at them sometimes I see two people caught in a friendship trap. Do you know what I mean World? There are people like it at school. They reach out to each other when they are desperate for whatever reason, and then they end up stuck together. You can see that neither of them really likes the other, or at least, they sort of wish they had more options. But not everyone does. Have more options I mean. Maybe my mum falls into that category. I think about it a lot. Anyway, Leon was always in trouble, and Travis was what they affectionately called a cheeky monkey, or what my dad called a little shit. I think Joe may have been troublesome at times, but by the time he reached about eight or nine, I think he just thought what's the point? He was always calmer than the other two, and they picked on him just for being the youngest. There is only fifteen months between Leon and Travis. As thick as thieves, Lorraine says about them. I agree with the thick part. And the thieves' part. I can remember about a million mean things they did to Joe over the years, and he never fought back. He never cried either though. He was as silent then as he is now. I don't think I have ever seen him lose his temper.

When Marianne returns, Joe announces that we better go and find his brothers before they find out what is missing from their room. Marianne tugs her long sleeves down over her hands and grimaces at us. "Well, good luck with that. You'll be back by tomorrow then?"

"Definitely," Joe promises her. "Thanks so much for this Marianne. I owe you a massive favour." He looks at me and jerks his head towards the front door.

"Thanks Marianne," I say, and follow Joe out. We untie Gremlin and start to head home, our heads hanging low, our thoughts dark.

"There is no way Josh or Ryan would have done that," I say, just to break the silence as we cross the fields again. Joe has his hands in his pockets.

"Christ no," he agrees. "Ryan would have wet his pants and Josh would have just told his mum or something. Marianne is really cool."

"This is quite a day so far."

"I know. Unbelievable."

"Do you just wish we'd left it there now?"

"Well, I don't know. You know what the brats are like." Joe shrugs his shoulders and looks at me. "What the hell are my brothers doing?" he says, thinking out loud.

"Leon has been heading that way for years," I reply. "Travis follows everything he does. It's not really that shocking if you think about it."

"Not drugs, no, but in the house! That is."

"They're not exactly gifted in the brains department," I remind him. "God knows what else they've got stashed in there!"

"Maybe Marianne was right. You know, about letting them get caught. Letting mum and Mick deal with it."

We walk on in a nervous silence. Gremlin is knackered, and his lead is completely slack and hanging at my side. As we get closer to Joe's house, I feel none of the excitement or giddy fear I did earlier. I wonder where it went, and wish I knew how to lure it back. It was nice for a while, feeling like something big was going to happen, and we were all going to get caught up in it, and in years to come I would look back and have a story to tell. Now I just feel a sick knot in my stomach, and my mouth is incredibly dry, and my mind starts to wander towards the tastes and smells of the food I have been avoiding lately. I am thinking it might be wise to grab something to eat from my house pretty soon. Just an apple and a coffee, or maybe some dry crackers. Something to keep me going. I think of Marianne and how much I admire her twig like arms, and I simultaneously curse myself for being such a fucking idiot, such a fucking sheep. I started the summer thinking how great it would be to lose weight, and then go back to school in September a new person. Stacey and Christine, The Stick Insects I call them, would not even recognise me. They would flock around me, gasping at the difference, asking me to tell them how I did it. Scott Taylor would look at me for the first time ever, and his blue eyes would run up and down my body, and he would think I was a new girl at first. He will look at me, he will finally look at me, and then he will smile. I won't be the fat girl anymore. I told myself that when I crushed that doughnut in my hand at the start of the exams in June.

The day is getting hotter, and I have no idea in hell what time it is as we trudge out onto Joe's road. The sky feels dark and low, and the clouds on the horizon are turning navy blue, building up to grey and black. There is that feeling of electricity in the air, of something about to happen, of a storm on its way. I love storms normally. I even like to stand outside in them. But this feels different, and I wonder if it is because we can both see Leon's beat up Ford Fiesta parked outside the house. We look at each other. Is it good or bad, that they are back?

As we near the house, the car door opens on the driver side and Leon gets out. He is nineteen years old, six foot three and spends most of his waking hours lifting weights. He looks like Joe, but his face is wider and his features heavier. He is wearing a Nike t-shirt and blue jeans, and he flexes his tattooed arms at us. Travis gets out the other side. He is smaller and thinner than his brother, but with the same light brown hair, cut short around the sides, and longer on the top. He has a lanky quality to him, flexibility in the way he moves and walks, very casual and slow, whereas Leon is very quick and hard and solid. They approach us immediately and fall into step with us as we walk towards the house. Leon on Joe's side, and Travis on mine. That ripple of fear and excitement and inexplicable longing is rampant inside me again, and my eyes are wide with it. "Inside," Leon says, and he sounds like a deeper voiced version of his mother, all clenched teeth and bubbling fury. "Now."

4

Dear World, you don't want to know how odd I felt then. If you try to imagine cold terror mixed up with a hot rumbling excitement then you might come close. I had this sense of everything happening all at once and it wanted to floor me. Sparks of intrigue, of being close to things I always wanted to know about, all stirred up in my belly with a dragging dread of fear and the urge to get the hell away.

I tie Gremlin up again and he sort of collapses on himself and stares up at me through his saucer like eyes, his pink tongue lolling out from his squashed up face. We go inside. Mick and Tommy are still in the lounge. Tommy is racing around in just his shorts, flying a plastic green aeroplane through the air. We go upstairs without a single word.

Once we are inside the older boys room, Travis closes the door and leans back against it with his arms folded. I just stand there feeling stupid and redundant. Leon seems almost breathless with anger. He is breathing heavily through his nostrils as he whips open the wardrobe door and points inside to the empty space where his Adidas bag should be. "There was a bag in there," he says in a low, tight voice. "Now it's gone. Do you know anything about it?"

Joe is silent. Our eyes meet in guilt and fear, and Leon automatically deduces that we do. He lets out a roar and grabs Joe by his t-shirt, spins him around and slams him into the wardrobe, and then down to the floor. It is a scene I have watched play out many times before. But I have never seen Leon so angry, so dark. There is no play in this. But I'll tell you World, I'm a big coward really, because he has always scared me, and I have never liked him. Not just because of the way he treats Joe though. It's more than that, but it's hard to explain. I start shouting and try to pull him away from Joe, and the next thing I know Travis has hold of my arms and is holding me back. There is thumping and thudding on the floor as the brothers wrestle, and before the fight can escalate any further, the bedroom door is kicked open by Mick. Travis drops my arms, and Leon swings his leg over Joe and gets up. His eyes flick dangerously between Mick and Joe, and I cannot determine who he would like to damage more in that moment.

"What the hell is going on?" Mick demands, hands on hips. He is shorter than Leon, but stocky and square, with a boxers face. He always wears his t-shirts tucked into his jeans. "Are you fighting?"

"No," says Leon, his voice without emotion.

"Bloody well keep it down then!" Mick tells him, turning to the stairs. He cannot leave without a stinging criticism however, because that is how he operates. "You boys are always up to no good!"

Travis says nothing as he pushes the door gently shut again, and we all hear Mick's feet thudding down the stairs. Leon immediately turns to Joe and smacks him on the forehead with the open palm of his hand. "All right faggot face, where the fuck is that bag?"

"In a safe place," Joe tells him, and I am amazed at how calm and controlled his voice is. "We'll go and get it."

"What the hell were you doing in our room?" Travis asks him, but he is looking at me as he says it. I feel my cheeks getting warm again.

"Looking for a lighter," I speak up, my voice slightly shaking. "It's my fault," I go on, as the silence stretches out. I hang my head in shame. "I was being nosy. I was a bit pissed. I looked in your wardrobe." Travis lets out a laugh for some reason, but Leon is not finding any of this remotely funny.

"If anything happens to that bag…" He shakes his head at Joe. He does not even see me.

"You shouldn't have just left it there like that," Joe tells him. "We only moved it because Tommy was in my room again, touching all my stuff, and we worried him or Will might find it. They could have found it easily." Joe looks at Leon and shrugs his shoulders, as if this should be enough. But Leon ignores all of this and pushes his face close to Joe's. I watch Joe physically recoil from the closeness of his brother.

"Go and get it back right now," he says slowly and carefully, his hands resting on his knees as he speaks to Joe with his nose touching his. "Because if anything happens to that bag, I am going to put you in the fucking hospital. Then when you get out, I am going to tell the people who that stuff belongs to, and they will find you and then they will put you back in the fucking hospital, right?"

Leon turns Joe by his shoulder and shoves him viciously towards the door, as Travis opens it. We go.

We clatter down the stairs, the weight of an unreal day pressing down on our shoulders and making our legs feel weaker with each step. Joe is reaching for the door handle when Mick shows his punched in face again. This time he is holding Tommy by the hand. "You off out again?" he frowns at Joe.

"Yeah."

Mick pushes Tommy forward. "Take Tommy will you? I've got to get on with Craig's car, and I can't get a thing done with him around."

The disbelief hits Joe between the eyes and he drops his shoulders and tilts his chin and his eyes up to the ceiling. "No way!" he complains. "Not now!"

Mick grits his teeth and pushes Tommy's small hand into Joe's. "I'm not asking you, I'm telling you," he says, and that is that. Joe shakes his head at me, screws his mouth up to stop himself from protesting, and opens the door.

I pull the door shut behind me and draw in breath as the intensified heat of the day slams into my eyes. I still have no idea what time it is. I untie Gremlin. He looks like he is suffering now. He is panting like crazy and staggers ungracefully to his feet, looking at me desperately for pity. Joe is running his fingers back through his sweaty hair. "I have to take Gremlin home first," I tell him, helplessly. "I can catch you up though," I add, when I see the horror in his eyes.

"No, come on, let's just do it," he groans, and starts stalking off back towards the parade of shops, dragging Tommy along with one hand. "This is just un-fucking-believable," he is moaning as he walks. I trot to catch up with him. He is walking so fast that I have to trot the whole way back to my house, and so does the poor dog. Tommy is still wheeling his plastic aeroplane through the air and making annoying meeeowwwm type noises, that we try to block out for fear of killing him.

Back home, I open the front door, unclip Gremlin from his lead and shove him through the door into the hallway. I am just about to close the door and join Joe and Tommy, when I hear my mum's footsteps pounding down the stairs in urgency. "Is that you Lou? Lou? Or Sara?"

"Me." I shout back, one hand on the doorknob. "I'm going out again. I just brought the dog back. He needs a drink."

Mum appears at the bottom of the stairs. She is wearing her plastic backed apron and clasping a feather duster in one hand. "Been cleaning your room," she announces, breathlessly, trying to peer around me and the door to see who I am with. I let the door move enough for her to see it is only Joe and his brother. She uses her hands to smooth down her apron and smiles lovingly at Joe. She is extremely fond of him, and I think at times she would like to adopt him. "Hi Joe! Hi Tommy!"

"We're in a hurry mum," I say, pulling the door again, "We've got to go."

"No, hang on, hang on, I need to speak to you!"

"Not now!" I say, glancing apologetically back at Joe.

"Les is going to move in."

"Oh fuck, not now! Does dad know?"

I can hardly believe this. I cannot deal with this now. She has no bloody idea how true the statement, 'this is a life or death situation', is for us right now. My mum tips her head to one side slightly, her lips pressed together. She has the same fair hair as me. It is not dark enough to be brown, but not really light enough to be blonde either. She wears hers short and sharp around her face, whereas I keep mine long and messy. She always has far too much eye make up on. Her eyes look massive. Her and Lorraine are hilarious really. Her with the massive black eyes, and Lorraine with the huge red lips. Neither of them knows a thing about subtlety.

"Lou please do not swear at me."

"Sorry, but mum, dad said…"

"I know what he said, that's why you can't tell him!"

I drop my head. I want to weep. I can't argue with her now. In fact I can't really ever argue with anyone. I just use the occasional slice of sarcasm to make me feel better, and write the rest of what I really think on my wall. It is all there for them to see, any time they want. But they never look.

"I have to go," I mutter and slam the door behind me.

I turn back to face the day, and the clouds are blackening fast, and skidding along the horizon. Any time soon it is going to break and piss down on us, and I look wearily at the half naked three year old that has been entrusted into our care. Joe looks at me with sympathy, and we head off again. I finally bother to pull off my hoodie and tie it around my waist. My armpits are slick with sweat.

We walk for a while in silence, me and Tommy struggling to keep up with Joe's frantic strides. Back across the fields again, back towards Marianne's road. I am thinking about mum and Les, and trying not to at the same time. It is making me feel close to vomiting, so I force my mind to the situation at hand. Joe and his mad family. For some reason, my mind keeps jerking me back to mum and Les, and I can't quite believe it is true, and I certainly don't want to believe that it is true, so I start to jog.

Joe laughs at me at first. Maybe he thinks I am trying to amuse him, to make him feel better. Tommy certainly finds it funny, and starts pointing his finger and howling at me. I am not jogging fast, not at all. Just enough to get my knees up, and my heart pumping. It works though. They may be laughing at me, but fuck them, it is working. "What are you doing, are you mental?" Joe calls to me. I keep jogging.

"No."

"You'll collapse, you spaz, it's too hot for that."

"I need to do my exercise at some point. Doesn't look like I'm gonna' get the chance at this rate."

"*That's* exercise?"

"What else does it look like?"

"Insanity."

It doesn't matter. It works for me. By the time we get across the sun baked fields to Marianne's house, I am so bone tired and drenched in warm sweat that I have completely forgotten about mum and stupid Les. My body is all that concerns and overwhelms me, and I like it. I listen to my heart thudding like hell through my chest, as we approach Marianne's long driveway. I feel far away from Joe and Tommy, as I watch them head up to the big door. I feel like there is a dense and spongy fog surrounding me, and I can hear my heart, I can hear it drumming in my ears. This might sound crazy, but I feel like it is trying to tell me something. I imagine it pulsing double-time, propelling the blood at twice the speed around my veins and arteries. I picture the globules of fat under my skin, being attacked by the energy particles, being eaten up and abolished. I am a smiling panting pile of wide-eyed shit by the time we knock on her door, and that is fine.

Joe knocks and waits. Knocks and waits. Looks at me in my mist of dumb happiness, and then knocks harder. Joe loses his cool and punches and kicks the door, but no one is home, and that much is horribly obvious. Marianne is not home.

Jesus Fucking Christ.

"Call her," Joe says in a small, clenched voice.

I scramble for my phone. My palms are sweaty so I drop it. I grab it and find her number. "It's ringing," I tell him. He is just staring at the door, with one hand still gripping Tommy's. To my horror, there is no answer, and the phone goes to messages. I shrug and hang up. "No answer. You can't go home," I hear myself saying in a hoarse, worn out voice. Joe turns to face me, and I see he is close to panic. "They'll kill you."

"Where the hell is she? Stupid bitch!"

I shake my head, and wince at the pain in my side. "God knows. She didn't say anything about going anywhere did she?"

"Idiot!" Joe says, letting go of Tommy's hand and covering his face with his hands. Tommy immediately wanders off towards what he can see of Marianne's back garden.

"We'll have to wait for her to come back," I shrug at Joe, still catching my breath. "Let Tommy play in her garden. Come on."

I am only calm because I am completely and utterly knackered. I started the day off with a mild hangover. I am now teetering close to hysteria or panic or tears, and I am not sure which one I would prefer. I take Joe gently by the elbow and lead him around to the back garden. Tommy has already discovered the swing set and is having a whale of a time by himself. Her back garden is massive compared to ours. There is a solid six-foot fence around the perimeter. There are Oak trees, and a summerhouse nestled between them at the bottom of the garden. I would have loved a garden like this growing up. I would have been out there all day. Pretending there were fairies at the bottom, climbing trees, making dens. It's perfect. It's beautiful. Instead I had a patio, a barbecue and a lawn that my dad used to throw fits over. I mean, he used to tell us to walk up it one way, and down it another way and I am not fucking kidding. He liked it short and green and fresh and untouched. He was the same with carpets. Walk one way; come back another, then you won't wear it out. I ask you. I fucking ask you. There were times I would have taken the insanity and violence of Joe's house, over that mind numbing soul destroying pointless shit any day.

Joe and I sink down onto one of the two garden benches Marianne has. Joe rests his elbow on the arm and covers his mouth with his hand. I lean back and fold my hands across my belly and try to take it all in, and this makes me smile. "What are you smiling about?" he asks me eventually. "Why do you find everything so funny all the time?"

"What else are you supposed to do Joe? I ask you. What else, in this kind of piss-taking situation, are you supposed to do?" I sit forward and my smile is reaching my ears now, and I feel so giddy with it all I wonder if my alcohol intake from last night, my sixteenth birthday celebrations no less, has come back to haunt me, come back to ravage me. My shoulders shake with the laughter. "Joe? Really? What else can you do? It is funny! It really *is* funny. It's one of those things like they always say, you'll look back and laugh one day."

"Really? You think so?"

"I know so. We'll be like, old and grey and wrinkled, sitting in our fucking rocking chairs in some manky old peoples home, going, oh wait, do you remember that day when we found the cocaine in your brothers wardrobe, and hid it at Marianne's so the kids didn't eat it, and then when we went back to get it, she had fucking gone out?" I laugh and laugh at my own excellent imitation of an old person's voice, and lean back again on the bench. "We so will, we so will. You'll be like, yeah, remember how you jogged across the field for no fucking reason? It will be one of those stories Joe. Trust me. You may be shitting yourself now, but in years to come, when life is so boring and tedious and predictable, you will look back on this day and feel glad."

Joe regards me patiently and scratches his eyebrow with his index finger. "At least you make yourself laugh," he muses, "You are insane, you do know that?"

"I'm sixteen, you know?"

"I heard what your mum said."

"Hey?"

"About Les moving in." Joe looks back at Tommy, who is swinging upside down, and he pulls his feet up onto the bench and wraps one arm around his knees.

"Oh that."

I feel my cheery mood take a nosedive then. It is almost like a comedown, and the only drugs I have ever taken are alcohol and pot, so I guess comedowns are really just a natural part of this disappointing life. I stare out across the beautiful summer garden. The birds are singing in the trees, and there are two squirrels chasing each other up and down the trunk of the largest Oak, and the shade of the fence behind us is a blessed relief on my sweat soaked skin. I think about Les and his mousy brown hair that just flops about on his head from one side to the other, and his ridiculous little moustache that can hardly endear him to anyone in life when it makes him look so much like Hitler. I feel a great chasm of loneliness open up inside of me, and my previous good humour takes a shaky dive and falls in.

"You don't like him, do you?" Joe asks me.

"I don't even know him," I shrug truthfully. "He can't be any worse that Mick."

"Fucking Mick," Joe sighs, shaking his head at Tommy.

"It's only because dad will go bloody mental, that's all," I say. "It's his house. He still pays the mortgage. Okay, he is allowed to move on and have someone else, but she is not. I would say go for it to her, go for it and show him, but honestly, *Les*! I ask you. What a prize piece of stinking steaming stupid crap."

I watch a helpless smile envelope Joe's face, and the tightened wrinkled look of despair eases off as he cracks up at me. "Did you write that on your wall yet?" he asks, snorting laughter at me. I grin.

"Not yet. But he's getting more than that, believe me."

"You're so funny."

"Not as funny as you."

"Ha ha."

"Fuck you."

"Fuck you twice."

"Dare you."

"Double dare you."

Honestly, Joe and I have barely progressed past age ten. Tommy is probably more mature than we are. Joe seems to suddenly remember the shit we are in, as he lets out an agonised groan and drops his head onto his knees. "Why did we take it?" he wails. "We should have just left it there! We should have ignored it. Pretended we never saw it."

"Joe, Tommy was in your room going through all your stuff," I stifle a yawn and lift up my arms for a stretch. "He could have been in their room next. He's only three. I know he's a pain, but you know. He's three."

"Why did they leave it there like that then?"

"They don't think," I shrug. "They don't care enough to think. Look, we'll get it back. She'll be home soon. If not, I'll go and take Tommy home for you and I'll just say I don't know where you are."

"They'll make you show them. Don't trust them. Besides, I can't stay out forever."

"Wait till your mum is home then. They won't do anything in front of her. They wouldn't dare."

"They'll find a way."

Before long, the day is growing dull and the rain is already spitting down upon us, and little Tommy is whining and wailing that he is hungry. There is no sign of Marianne or her parents. I try calling her four more times, but each time it goes straight to messages. I tap in a few abusive text messages just to amuse myself, but I don't send them. I wonder helplessly if she is doing this on purpose. If she is somewhere else, laughing and gloating at us. We drag ourselves from the bench and the beautiful garden, and start to trudge home. There is no jogging this time, you can believe me. The rain gets harder and harder as we cross the field, plastering our hair to our skulls. I can even feel my knickers are getting wet, that's how much it is raining.

We go to my house first, and I leave Joe rain soaked and miserable on my front door step, while I take Tommy by the hand and lead him home. He tightens his small hand on mine and I look at him. He is a little bare chested warrior in sopping brown shorts and trainers and I look at him and wonder what the fuck life is all about, really. It always feels like we are just traipsing from place to the other. Is that what life is meant to be like? World, is that how it will feel when we are adults too? When I get to his house, I knock on the door and thankfully it is Mick that answers it. He looks slightly drunk, and relieved, and grateful all at once. "Good kids, you are, good kids," he feels the need to tell me, as he ushers the dripping three year old inside. I just turn and go. I cannot see Leon's car anywhere, so I quicken my pace and make it back home, and open the door, and Joe and me go in.

We make it upstairs without any interruptions or surprises, and we close the door on my room, and collapse, both of us, onto our backs on my bed. We both close our eyes, and no doubt the un-fucking-believable day spins around like a horror show inside Joe's head, just as it does in mine, and finally I scavenge for my pen under my pillow, suck off the lid and scrawl lazily upon the wall, '*the sky turned black, the bitch was out, a bag of shit laughing at us, puddles, puddles and puddles of shit.*'

Joe reads it and then laughs and laughs.

5

Dear World, is it wrong that I am finding all this drama so intoxicating? Personally I think it says a lot about my own life. No one would want my life. My life consists of cynicism and traipsing around. I told you.

So anyway, we have no choice but to hide out at my house until we can get hold of Marianne. I get my mum to call Lorraine and tell her Joe is staying for tea, and having a sleepover. My mum's lips pull into a grimace at this part, because they all worry about us having sleepovers, of course. You know, in case I get fucking pregnant or something. I ask you. I just stare at her with big hopeful eyes, and I know she is feeling guilty about the whole Les thing because she picks up the phone and calls Lorraine. My legs are wobbly as I start back up the stairs. Mum hangs up the phone quickly and comes after me. "What shall I get you both for tea?" she asks me. "Sara is staying at her friend's house. It's just us."

I shrug at her. "Don't mind."

"Sausage chips and beans?"

"Can we have it in my room?"

"Of course you can," she sighs, and I turn to go. "Hold on Lou," she says. I can't hold myself up anymore so I just sit down on one of the stairs and wait for it. "Look," she begins gently. "I know you don't really know Les yet, but what's happened is his flat he was living in, it's his sisters, right? And they've had this awful fight, and now she wants him out, and it's just dreadful really."

"Yeah, it is," I tell her, but my sarcasm is lost on her. Her eyes are full of the pity she feels for Les. She is holding a tea towel and wrings it between her hands.

"So it's not forever," she goes on. "It's just until he gets sorted with another place, okay? That's another reason why there is no point telling dad. He'll go off on one for no reason, because it's not going to be for long."

"Does Sara know about this yet?"

"Not yet. I'll speak to her when she comes home."

I can't see my older sister liking this news any more than I do, but this is the least of my problems right now. I heave myself back up, and my mouth waters just slightly at the idea of sausage, chips and beans.

Joe is still lying on my bed, and sits up when I walk in. "Mum's bringing us tea up in a bit," I inform him, stretching back out beside him.

"Brilliant," he says, with a smile. "I love your mum."

"She's better than yours, that's for sure."

"We go back to Marianne's in the morning," he tells me, as if he has been thinking this over by himself. "If she's still not answering her phone. We sit there and wait till she comes back. It will all be fine. We'll get the bag back to Leon, and make sure he keeps it out the house. It will all be fine." He nods with the certainty of his own predictions and I frown at him from the bed. I have my pen again and I am doodling lazily on the wall.

"Is that what you do Joe, to get through life?"

"What do you mean?"

"Tell yourself everything will be fine, and believe yourself."

I hear him snort at me. He does that a lot. "It's better than what you do."

"What do I do then?"

"Expect everything to be shit so you don't get disappointed when it is."

"Ha ha, I call that being intelligent. Like this thing with Les, you know what's going to happen don't you?" I sit up suddenly; pen in hand, a flurry of unexplained aggression washing over me. He waits. "He'll move in, dad will find out, dad will be a prize knob, mum will cry, Les and dad will fight, mum will cry, Sara will probably throw a hissy fit and move out. Mum will cry. Les will stay, and dad will want to throw us all out of his precious fucking house. *That* is what will happen. And they should be able to see that too, if I can."

"And in all of that, what will you do then?"

I lie back down, and jab my pen at the wall. "I will get drunk with you."

Joe gives a little laugh. "Fair enough."

I feel grumpy and pissed off at everyone. I wonder if that is what not eating much does to you. I expect my body to react violently when my mum comes in with the food. I expect my mouth to water again, and my eyes to fixate on the food, and my stomach to growl louder than ever. But when she puts the tray down on the bed, and Joe picks up his plate, I feel a kind of disgust and loathing that takes me by surprise. I put my plate on my lap and push the chips around with the beans, and I see it for what it is, just like I did with the doughnut that day. It was not a tasty snack to fill a hole. It was a vile and lard filled trick. I eat one sausage, three chips and a forkful of beans, and then I feel like crying. I have no idea why. I have no idea what is wrong with me.

Joe tucks into his dinner like he has never been fed so well. I reach out and scrawl doodles on the wall behind me. Joe looks hungrily at the rest of my food. "Do you not want that?"

"No. Feel sick. You have it."

"Cool. Thanks."

"When can we get drunk again?"

"I don't know. Why?"

"It's fun. Takes your mind off things."

"I know, I'll trade Leon's bag for a bottle of cider. Reckon he'll go for that?"

"Possible. I think I like the sound of drinking cider in the park with my retard friends. How wrong is that?"

"It's not wrong. It's fun."

I sit up, resting my back against the wall and dropping the pen. I rub my arms and this brings back the memory of the rough warmth of Travis's hands closed over them. A shiver of what I can only describe as lust runs through me, and I smile. Isn't it meant to be teenage boys that get all horny and hormonal and hot under the collar at inappropriate times? I realise I have never witnessed this in Joe, and fleetingly wonder if he is gay, like his older brothers sometimes accuse him of being. I honestly do not know what is wrong with me. I think Joe would kill me if he knew what I was thinking right now. What I am picturing in my mind.

Leon scares me. I don't like being in his presence. He makes me feel uncomfortable, but I am unable to really articulate why. He wants to be a hard man; he wants to not care about anyone or anything, as if somehow he believes this to be the best way to go through life. It is what he seeks to achieve. Not giving a shit. Dealing drugs, if that is what he is doing, and we can strongly suppose that it is, is just his latest ploy to try to achieve this. He is bizarrely determined to live as crooked and brutal a life as possible, and you can see it in every inch of him – his empty, hard eyes, his lack of remorse or empathy for anything or anyone. The way his body ripples and bristles, as if every muscle within it has been injected with pure blind rage. I wonder whom he is trying to impress, and I can only imagine that it is himself.

You might be wondering about Travis, World. Well he is a bastard. All the girls say it. That's what I hear, so I don't trust him, but I can see some of Joe in him. Some. His eyes give away more than Leon's ever do. His voice reflects his emotions – his frustration when he loses at Grand Theft Auto to Leon. His humour when one of the little ones does something funny. Leon barely acknowledges their existence, but Travis sees them. He has human qualities, where Leon seems to have none. I wonder how far he would go for his brother. For either of them? I wonder these things World, because I am a curious person. You wouldn't believe how much of my life has been spent standing back quietly and just watching, just listening. It is a skill I have honed well over the years, and it means that I know far more about everyone else than they do about me. It only occurs to me in rare drunken moments that this is not necessarily a good thing.

When I finally look at my clock it informs me it is half past six. Why does it feel so much later? Joe and I stretch out on my bed and stare at the cracks in the ceiling. "I'm surprised you haven't written anything up there yet," he muses sleepily. We pass the evening feeling like we are on death row. When I close my eyes I can see redness behind my eyelids. It reminds me of blood, shifting and building, like a blood clot growing. I blink as I involuntarily imagine Leon's fist slamming into my face. I picture blood exploding from my nose and lips, and the bridge of my nose collapsing and folding in on itself. I am good at this. Picturing violent and bloody scenes inside my head. Sometimes when I look around me all I can see is all the potential for physical damage. Windows that could shatter on top of your head. Knives that could slip in your grip and plunge into your wrist. Cars that could skid and career towards you, helpless on the pavement, the brute force of the gleaming metal pinning you to a wall, pulverising your organs. Blood pumping like a fountain from your mouth. I do it when I am speaking to people sometimes. Especially people like teachers, and other grown-ups who are not my parents. I will find myself drifting off as they speak, and then picturing me smashing them in the face with something really heavy, like a brick or an iron or something. Once, in science, I imagined Mr Foster's eyeballs flying out of his face after I lifted a stool and cracked him over the head with it. They flew right across the science lab and splattered against the windows, sliding down slowly, leaving bloody snails trails behind. I don't know why I do this World, except maybe just for amusement.

Every time the phone rings we expect it to be trouble. We turn the music up and down, imagining we can hear the doorbell go. Mum drifts up the stairs again later, and starts shoving blankets and pillows through the door. You can tell she is on edge about Joe sleeping over, even though we have known each other since we were foetuses. It is a sad indictment of adult stupidity, that as soon as we entered puberty they all started acting like we ought to fancy each other. They had decided that we would, and nothing we could do or say would remove this idea from their heads. 'Watch them,' even my dad said to my mum once, and he very rarely has anything to say that involves thinking about me. 'They're getting too big to go around like that.' Luckily my mum ignored his insightful wisdom about my friendship with Joe. She retorted with the well-used, 'Oh they are just like brother and sister.' But you could see the worry in her eyes every time we went up to my room alone. You just know that if I were stupid enough to get pregnant, the first vicious words he would say to her would be; 'I told you so.'

That night, Joe falls asleep before I do. I can hear him snoring gently on the floor. I am lying awake, I am staring at the ceiling, and I am smoothing my fingers up and down the curves of my hipbones. I am savagely proud of myself for barely eating today. I tell myself it is the only way to get rid of the fat. It is the only way to get the body I have always wanted. In a strange and childlike way, I truly feel that when I am slim enough, everything will be different.

Dear World, well here we are again, and the saga drags on another day…

The plan was to wake up early and run over to Marianne's before she can do another vanishing act. But we do not wake up until the bedroom door is kicked open, and when I roll over to groan at the clock I despise, I see that it is nearly ten o'clock. Not good. It is Sara who has burst in on us. She is taller and slimmer than me. She has blonder hair. It is straighter and silkier than mine. She slams the door behind her, throws a bag onto her bed and looks as if she might explode. "Jesus *fucking* mum!" she growls, hands in her hair. Joe sits up on the floor, rolling the ball of his fist into his eye and yawning. I swap a look with Joe. You don't really need to bother speaking when my sister is around. She is very good at having a conversation with herself on your behalf, and filling in the blanks when you do not speak. "What the hell is she thinking? Do you know about this Lou? About her bloody creepy boyfriend moving in? Is she insane? Dad will go mental!"

I quite simply do not want to have this conversation. Joe is already looking alarmed about the time and hauling himself out of his makeshift bed. I pull my quilt around me so that I can get changed under it. Joe passes up my cut-off jeans from the floor, and I only have to rummage around in the mess at the foot of my bed to find a suitable t-shirt. Sara is ransacking the wardrobe for a change of clothes. "I cannot believe it," she continues to rant. "I cannot believe that woman. She knows how dad will react. She knows how he feels about the stupid house. And we're supposed to keep it a secret for her? Bloody hell! Great one. Nice one mum. Well done." She plonks herself on her bed to pull off her shoes. "When is this supposed to be happening anyway? Do you know?"

"No idea." I get out of bed and brush my hair in front of the mirror.

"Have you lost more weight?" Sara asks, frowning at me. I look myself up and down.

"I don't know."

"What size are you now anyway?"

"Twelve," I say, and smile at her proudly. "Fourteens are too big now. I had to get mum to get me some new clothes."

"Bloody hell, well done!" My sister is beaming at me for some reason. I mean, *really* beaming. It catches me off guard to tell you the truth. My sister and I have always got on really well, but these days I am old enough to recognise why this is. I was always the quiet, calm one, and she was the opposite. See? No competition there. Apparently when I was really little she used to pretend she was my mum, and choose my clothes and get me dressed and stuff. I used to play with her for hours and I loved it, but everything was on her terms you understand. She doesn't see life any other way. Her beaming takes me by surprises and sends a warm rush of something like pride through me. I smile, despite myself. "You've done really well. You're looking amazing you know. Isn't she Joe?"

Joe looks up with a start. He looks exhausted and confused. "Hey?"

"Oh trust you not to notice," Sara groans, rolling her eyes at me. "Men are all the same. Take Rich. Did he notice I'd had my hair cut and coloured? No he did not. And when I told him, do you know what he said? He said, oh it doesn't look any different to me!"

Joe has his trainers on and is hopping about impatiently. I tie up my hair and follow him to the door. "We've got to go," I say to Sara.

"Don't worry, I haven't finished with mum yet," she says, not looking at us as she goes back to the wardrobe. "She's not getting her own way that easily! I'm getting changed then going back down there for round two."

"Okay, good luck," I sigh, and we leave.

I pause in the bathroom to wash my face and brush my teeth, while Joe heads to the front door. When I come down the stairs, he has the door open a crack and seems to be scanning the street. "Really surprised they haven't come looking for us," he murmurs as I come up behind him. He tugs his phone from his pocket and frowns at it. "No calls either."

"Maybe they trust you to get it back."

"Lou?" Mum calls from the kitchen. I know what she is going to say. Take the fucking dog. I want to just slam out of the door and not even look at her, but something pathetic in her voice makes me turn around. She has been crying, there is no doubt about that. Sara does not mince her words or hide her feelings. She is the opposite of me in that respect. She has the unfathomable bravery to say exactly what she thinks at all times. I only have this bravery when it comes to my wall. As I suspected, mum is holding out Gremlins lead to me. "Would you mind?"

"No, course not," I mutter and snatch it from her. I clip the lead onto the dog and we go out of the door, leaving her in her own sad silence in the hallway.

Outside the pavement is wet from yesterday's downpour. There are puddles everywhere. But the sky is impossibly blue and vast and clear, not a cloud in sight. We head for Marianne's, and our legs feel heavy. Gremlin trots a jaunty walk alongside me; oblivious to the disgusted looks Joe affords him, and I bring up her number one more pointless time.

We start to cross the fields that surround our estate, and the grass is wet and squishy underfoot. A hell of a lot of rain must have fallen yesterday. The fields wrap right around the housing estate, enveloping it in green. There are two parks on the entire estate. A small baby one just around the corner from my road, and a bigger one for older kids on the fields. It has a slide built into a hill, two swings, a battered old paint flaked roundabout, a climbing frame and a wooden castle with another slide coming out from the top chamber. The bottom chamber is like a little hut, with a table and benches inside. You can choose either wooden steps, or a rope ladder to climb up to the bit where the slide is. We glance across, hearing voices from that direction. There are kids circling on their bikes, weaving in and out of the apparatus, and whizzing down the hill. "Park and cider," I say, more to myself than Joe. He nods grimly.

"You better fucking believe it Carling." I look at him and wonder if he was serious about getting his brother to buy us some cider in return for their bag. I wouldn't put it past him. He may not be a fighter in any way, shape or form, but Joe has guts. He may not be able to fight them back physically, but I know he is not as scared of them as I am.

When we reach Marianne's we breathe a collective sigh of relief, as both her parents cars are parked in the driveway. We are assuming, and hoping desperately that this means she is with them. Her dad drives a silver Renault Megane, and her mum has this nippy little black Jeep. Just as we approach the door, it opens and her mum comes out. She looks a lot like Marianne, small and delicate with black hair. She does a double take when she sees us there. I wonder morosely how scruffy and sleep deprived we appear to her. She is a nice lady, always polite and welcoming, but I can't help detect a bit of uncertainty from her about us. It's like she is too polite and well brought up to act on the instinct she has not to trust us. Funnily enough, that is pretty much how I feel about her daughter. "Hello there," she says, one pale hand falling back onto her own chest. She is wearing crisp white trousers and a blue and pink floaty, chiffon blouse. She is holding a small watering can in her other hand, and starts to water the many pot plants that surround her front door. She wrinkles her nose at Gremlin. "Marianne is in her room, go on up. But you wouldn't mind leaving the dog out here, would you? I am terribly allergic!" She gives a little self-deprecating laugh at this.

"Thanks," Joe says rather gruffly, heading for the door. I tie Gremlin up to one of the drainpipes.

"I would leave him at home," I feel the strange need to explain to Mrs Sholing. "But my mum makes me take him everywhere." I shrug at her. I suppose I want her to know it is not my fault I keep bringing my dog to the house of someone who is allergic to him. She smiles at me sweetly and we go on in. We remember to wipe our shoes on the mat and head up the stairs to find Marianne. I can sense the urgency in Joe now. I imagine he is thinking about what he will do if she doesn't have the bag for some reason. Either that, or he is repeatedly telling himself that everything will be fine.

Marianne's door is closed, so we knock on it. It seems to take forever for her to open it and I watch the sweat gathering on Joe's forehead. Eventually she unlocks the door and looks at us vacantly. She is rubbing at one arm and pulling her long sleeve down over her hand. She doesn't need to try to hide it from us, because we know exactly what she has been doing. Her face looks even paler than usual. Joe glances once at the drops of blood we can see on her palm, and then crosses his arms.

"Where the hell did you go yesterday? We came back for the bag and you were gone. My brothers wanted it back! And your phone's been off!"

Marianne holds the door open so we go in, and she closes and locks it behind us. "I lost my charger. You said to give you a day, so I went out. I am so sorry." She says sorry like it is the last thing she means. Joe looks around her room. It is huge. She has a double bed, a double wardrobe, and a massive wooden desk at the window. She has a view of the garden, so I walk over and stare out at the adventure playground beyond.

"Where is it?" Joe spins around and demands.

"Chill out," she tells him. I wince.

"Don't tell me to fucking chill out," he warns her. "I need it now. You have no idea what shit I'm in if I don't get it back right now!"

Marianne merely rolls her eyes and sighs and crosses the room to her vast wardrobe. She opens it, puts one hand in and comes back out holding the Adidas bag. Joe nearly collapses in relief and so do I. He snatches it from her and unzips it to check the contents. "I didn't try any, don't worry," she says to him. He zips it back up and slings it onto his shoulder. He runs both hands back through his hair and closes his eyes for a small moment.

"Thanks Marianne," I speak for him. "We've got to get it back now."

"You're welcome," she sighs again and sits down on the edge of her bed. "Do you want to do something later maybe? Go out or something?"

"We'll see how this goes," I say, glancing at Joe. "He had to stay at mine last night. We're both totally fucked to be honest."

"Well you know where I am."

"Thanks again," Joe says, and lets himself out of her room. You can tell he doesn't feel thankful at all, and he has not yet forgiven her for the panic she gave him yesterday, despite it not really being her fault.

"Are you all right?" I ask her tentatively, as I head for the door. She fixes me with a bright, brave smile, and her eyes are challenging me, but I do not understand why or for what reason. World, I do not understand her at all.

"Oh yes," she says, mysteriously. "I am now."

Joe wastes no time in getting away from Marianne's house, and I can't blame him. We grab Gremlin and run for it. We are half way across the field, and on our way to his house, drugs in tow, when I finally say something. "She was cutting herself before we got there? Wasn't she?"

"I saw blood."

"Me too."

"It's fucking gross."

"It makes her feel better."

"Better about what? How can it?"

I shrug, and think back to the first time we found out about her self-harming. It was at my house. We were up in my room drinking cider. Having a giggle. Marianne is a very controlled drinker though. She never lets herself get wasted like us. She will just have a few sips of a pint and make it last all night. You could tell the small amount she did drink loosened her tongue and her body, and made her pale face flushed with daring. But she never lets herself go overboard. I suppose she doesn't want to make a fool of herself, whereas we don't give a shit. We were playing monopoly. It was one of those phases, one of those things you get into as a group for a few weeks, and then forget all about. Monopoly is hilarious when you are pissed, take my word for it. I was getting ridiculously aggressive about having to pay extortionate amounts of rent to Marianne. Joe was just a giggling mess. I reached across to slam the rest of my money down in front of her, and knocked my pint of cider everywhere in the process. It mostly covered Marianne. She found it funny, and merely stood up and pulled her wet top off over her head. Joe had covered his mouth, and then his eyes, as she dropped the wet garment to the floor and stood there in her neat white bra, asking to borrow something of mine. It was not until I had fetched her something to wear and she reached out to take it, that I saw the scores of little white scars on the inside of her arms. Some were tiny. Just little nicks. Others were longer, more jagged. A couple were covered in scabs.

I think if I had been sober I would have pretended not to notice out of politeness and awkwardness. But I was pissed and I held onto her arm, lifting it up for Joe to see, which in hindsight was just horribly insensitive and vile of me, but she let me. She just smiled and let me. "What the hell have you done to your arms?" I asked her.

"It makes me feel better." She had taken the top from me and pulled it over her head, before sitting back down to our aghast faces. She had shrugged her tiny birdlike shoulders at us. "It's no big deal. Some people get pissed to feel better about life, like you do. Some people take drugs. I cut myself a bit. I just do it when I feel like I want to explode or kill myself or something. It makes me feel better. That's all."

She made it sound so normal, I remember now. So plausible. So every day. We had just accepted it. What else can you do? Marianne, in my opinion, is not the kind of girl who needs looking after or protecting. Marianne, in my opinion, is possibly the kind of girl who could eat you alive if she wanted to. But now Joe is looking at me as if I am somehow in on it. Just because I sort of understand her.

"She's not hurting anyone else," I shrug uselessly. He shakes his head. We are nearly at his house, and right away we can see no sign of Leon's car.

"It's warped," he tells me, his eyes scanning the road for the Fiesta. "It's not right."

"You could say the same thing about getting pissed in the park," I point out. "And you know that's exactly what you feel like doing right now. So you can forget all this shit when it's over, and release it. It's the same thing."

"His car's not here," Joe stops walking. "What the fuck is going on?"

6

Dear World, my guts are all a mess. As we approach the house several disjointed and unrelated thoughts hit me; the last one being *I don't want to grow up*. You would think the same World, if you thought there was a chance you might turn out like Mick

He is in the front garden leaning under the bonnet of one of the cars. Joe's expression is utterly bereft and bewildered as he walks up to the car, shifting the bag full of narcotics nervously on his shoulder. I keep just behind him, never keen on getting too close to Mick and his smacked in face. Joe taps on the bonnet, making Mick jump, lift his head too fast and bang it on the metal. "Ow! Christ!" he cries out, screwing up his face in pain and annoyance as his eyes settle on Joe and his pained expression. "Bleeding hell! What are you creeping about for?" Joe's eyes are nearly hooded by his frown, as they flit from side to side, and then up and down at the house.

"Are Travis and Leon in?"

Mick ducks his head back under the bonnet. "No."

"Do you know where they are?"

"No bloody idea."

Joe looks at me in desperation, so I beckon him away from Mick, because we both know that's about all the help he is capable of. "What now?" he asks me when we are out of Mick's earshot. He has pulled his phone out again and sighs at it forlornly. "My battery is dead Lou!" I am trying to think. We can't just carry that bag around with us all day, we just can't. The weight of it is going to kill us both before long. We can't leave it in the house, because that would just put us back to square one. I bite at my lip and try to remember all the places that Leon and Travis are likely to be in.

"The men's club?" I say suddenly, looking up at Joe. His eyes widen and he nods at me.

"Sunday lunch."

"That's it." We both drop our shoulders in relief, and start walking again with Gremlin. As we walk away from the house, Will passes by on his bike with two of his friends in tow. He looks too much like Mick for my liking. He has the same flattened nose and puffed up eyes, and he is only seven years old. He's okay though. He's preferable to Tommy and his sticky fingers.

"Where you going?" he asks Joe, skidding to a halt.

"Nowhere."

"Can we come?"

"No. Go away." Joe picks up his speed and marches on, and I have to jog to catch him up. I can feel Will's eyes watching our backs as we go, and a flashback careers through my mind, of Joe and me at his age, trying to tag along with Leon and Travis. They were always marching off, arms swinging; weapons in hand, up to no good and not letting us come. We used to whine and think it was so unfair. Now I am glad they didn't let us go with them. I am glad that whatever darkness taints them did not rub off on us.

The men's club is on the outskirts of our estate. It is not really just a men's club anymore, as that is incredibly sexist and probably illegal. Women are allowed in, but mostly they don't bother. For decades and decades the men had it all to themselves. They would go there to drink beer, play pool and watch sport. They would go there to get away from their women. When my parents were still together, it used to be my dad's favourite place. 'I'm going down the club,' he used to say when he had had enough of us all. You have to be signed in by someone if you are not a member, and you can't be a member until you are eighteen. Sunday's they put on a roast dinner at midday for just under a fiver. It's as good a guess as any that Leon and Travis will be found here.

It takes us ten minutes to cut through the streets and the back alleys to get to the club. It is a sagging one-storey building, painted white. The car park goes all the way around it, and there are some little kids kicking a ball about out the back. I look at them and can remember doing the same thing at their age with Joe and my sister, and his brothers. Passing the time. If you were lucky your dad would remember you were out there and bring you out a coke and a packet of crisps. The place makes me sigh and shove my hands into my pockets. It reminds me of a hundred hot nights, loud music, and being ignored by your mum and dad. They have a children's party every Christmas, and my mum still drags us along to it. Father Christmas comes, and everything. The only good thing about it now is waiting for your parents to get too pissed to notice, and then stealing their drinks. The first time I ever got drunk was at the club at Christmas. I was twelve, and I did such a good job of being less drunk than my parents, that they never even knew.

Joe drops a heavy hand onto my shoulder when he spots Leon's car parked out the front. I manage a strained, weak smile and we both exhale out deeply, although I'd had no idea I was holding my breath in so much. We traipse up to the doors and peep in. The place is busy, mostly full of men, and it takes us a while to spot Leon and Travis at one of the pool tables. To me, they look perfectly at ease, taking their shots and strutting around the table as if they own the place. Joe puts one foot inside the door, and is almost immediately accosted by a tall thin man known as Whitey. He is around seventy years old, impossibly gnarled and wrinkled, with a small scrap of startling white hair on the top of his long head. I have no idea if this is the reason he is called Whitey, or if it is just his sir-name. Men seem to have a real habit or either making up nicknames for each other that stick for life, or simply calling each other by their sir-names. He holds a shaking hand up in front of us. His other hand is wrapped around a pint glass. "Hey you young ones got to be signed in, you got to be signed in," he informs us, as if we don't already know this.

"Can you just get my brothers, over there?" Joe points to Leon and Travis. Whitey rubs his head and squints over at them.

"They're your brothers, over there? You want your brothers, over there?"

"Yes please."

"Oh all right then, all right then, hold your horses, hold your horses." He stumbles off towards them, and when Joe turns to look at me he frowns because I am pressing one hand against my mouth. I can't help it, I just can't. I so desperately want to talk to Whitey and repeat everything twice the way he does, just to see if it confuses him or not. Cruel, I know, but hey he's a drunk, he won't notice. Joe looks back inside the club. We watch Whitey chatting to Leon and Travis, who both turn their heads and see us at the door. I see Travis drop his shoulders and roll his head on his neck, as if a great weight has suddenly been lifted from him. He even smiles as he jerks his head towards Leon, and for a moment the smile lights up his face. Leon narrows his eyes, lowers his pool cue carefully onto the table, says something to a man waiting to use it, and starts to walk over to us. He struts more than he walks. When he walks towards you, you have the automatic reflex of wanting to back off. And so we do.

We back out of the door and wait for them in the car park. Leon is first out of the door, practically punching it open, and letting it fall back for Travis to catch. Joe has let the bag slip from his shoulder, and is holding it by one strap. "Thank fuck," Leon snaps, his eyes on the bag, as Joe pretty much throws it at him. He catches it, then digs into his pocket and drags out his car keys, which he then tosses to Travis.

"You guys were just about to become dead meat," Travis tells us both, with a twinkle in his eye, as he takes the bag from Leon and walks over to the car. Leon spreads his feet apart and folds his chunky arms across his puffed out chest.

"I hope you've learnt a lesson kiddies," he says to us, his head low, and his eyes moving quickly between Joe and me. "Stay out of our fucking room from now on!"

"What are you doing with it now?" Joe asks him. Leon raises his eyebrows.

"None of your business."

"You can't leave it in the house, Leon. Not with the kids."

"You think I give a fuck about those stupid kids?"

"You can't. That's why we moved it. You just can't leave stuff like that in the house."

Travis joins us, folding his arms just like Leon, but still smiling as if he is finding this all very amusing. "Don't worry about it, forget about it," Leon sighs and tells Joe. "It's gone, okay?"

"Didn't know you were drug dealers."

"Shut up. Go and play. Run along." Leon flaps his hand at us dismissively.

"You owe us," Joe tells him adamantly, and when I look at him I am amazed at how calm he appears. Leon and Travis could drag him around the back and give him a good kicking and there would not be a thing I could do to stop them. Leon shakes his head in amazement, glances at Travis for back up, and steps forward.

"How do we owe you? You stole our bag. You got it back. End of."

"We did you a favour and you know it. Sign us in the club and get us a drink, or give us some money for cider." Joe stares at Leon and does not back down. Travis is still smiling. In fact he is practically laughing. The silence drags on until Joe speaks again and hits them where it hurts. "Or we tell mum and Mick everything."

"You wouldn't dare," Travis says in hushed tones.

"Do you like the taste of hospital food?" asks Leon. Joe stands strong.

"I mean it," he says. Travis laughs then, and slaps Leon on the back.

"Oh fuck it, let them in, let them have a drink, who cares?"

Leon only has a moment to make it look like letting us in is as much his decision as Travis's. He steps back, grabs the door and wrenches it open. He then holds out his other hand, spreads his legs again and beckons for us to go in. "Go on then kiddies," he says, in a mock friendly voice, speaking to us as if we are ten years old. "Come and have a drinky with us."

I go first, dragging the dog with me. There is a collie that lives behind the bar and trots about freely, so they can't say a thing to me about Gremlin. Joe steps forward, but does not take his eyes from Leon. "You're just gonna' leave that out there in your car?" he asks, incredulously. "You're gonna' get caught with it you know." Leon claps him on the back and follows him into the club behind me.

"Haven't done so far," he replies with an arrogant shrug.

"Who are you doing it for?" is Joe's next question, and even I know this is one question too far. Leon only has to give him a look, and all the colour drains from his face.

"Shut it," Leon hisses, and the conversation is over. Travis signs us in, and we scurry over to a table and chairs in the corner. Once we are seated, the relief washes over us again. The bag is gone. It's over. It's their trouble now, their stupid business. Nothing whatsoever to do with us anymore. I smile widely at Joe and he grins back. Leon has taken a stool at the bar, and is hunched over a pint talking to the man next to him. It is Travis who gets us the drinks and brings them over. He places two cokes and a pint of cider on the table before us, and we both stare hungrily at the pint. "It's my pint, yeah?" he tells us with a wink, and goes back to the bar. We spend the next fifteen minutes drinking our cokes, and sneaking sips of the cider when we are sure no one is looking. We probably don't even need to worry. No one in here is going to give a shit if we drink or not. The only problem with sharing a pint of cider with your best friend is the thirst it gives you for more. I start to wonder how generous Leon and Travis might be feeling now that they've got their drugs back.

I slip into a bit of trance and watch them at the bar. I do that a lot World. I think of my mind sometimes as sort of perched on a slippery rock. It can hold on for so long, but every now and again it inevitably slips into oblivion. I can do nothing but stare. Leon, and his thick, tattooed arms folded on top of the bar. Exuding confidence and danger. Travis who is smaller and calmer, but equally as tough. I think about the bag in their car, and I wonder like Joe did, where did it come from? Who are they working for? Who do they deal it to? What strange and dark lives do they lead under everyone's noses? I look at them, and it occurs to me that I have known them my entire life, yet I do not know them at all. Not one bit.

"Do you think it's a one off?" I ask Joe, dragging my eyes away from them, and battling out of the fog of my trance. "The drugs?"

"Don't know," he shrugs. "I'll keep an eye on them now though. See if they start flashing money around unexpectedly."

"Mmm. Or do you think they found it, or stole it?" My imagination has gone into overdrive now that I am a getting a little tipsy. I cannot seem to tear my eyes away from the backs of Joe's brothers at the bar. Weirder than that, I can feel that surge again, you know the one I mean? Like a hot surge of a sort of yearning I just cannot explain, except that it's partly physical, and horrifyingly it seems to start down between my legs, and then spreads right through me, making me shiver. I wonder what the fuck is happening to me, and I wonder if Joe gets the same feelings and doesn't tell me?

"Yeah, maybe," Joe nods. "Hadn't thought of that."

"Your mum would do her nut, wouldn't she?"

"Oh she'd throw them out for sure. Because of the kids."

"You've got quite a bargaining tool then, haven't you?" Joe meets my eyes and frowns at me. I smile. "I mean, should you ever need it? If they piss you off, or whatever. You've got quite a hold over them really. Look how easily they caved in and got us in here."

"Are you suggesting I blackmail my own brothers Carling?" Joe is regarding me with mock disbelief and bites his lip, shaking his head at me. "Really, and I thought I knew you! You're pretty twisted under that innocent exterior, aren't you?"

"You don't know the half of it," I tell him, letting my eyes scan back to Travis. Almost as if he can feel me watching him, Travis turns slightly on his stool and peers over his shoulder at us. He winks. At me, or at Joe? I look away, just as my stomach emits a loud growling sound that causes Joe to put down his coke and stare at me.

"I hope that was your stomach and not your arse!"

"Of course it was my stomach."

"Right, I'm gonna' get them to get us some food," Joe announces then, wiping his mouth with the back of his hand and getting to his feet. "Let's see how grateful they are to us for keeping their secret, hey?"

"Go for it."

Joe marches up to the bar and squeezes himself in between his two brothers. Leon looks down at him, his expression displeased. He looks at everyone the same way, I realise. Like they are a piece of shit on his shoe. I wonder for a moment, has he ever been afraid of anyone, or anything? Has he ever been impressed by someone else, or wanted to emulate them? I shake my head at my own questions. Not that I can remember. He's always been like this. I can see Joe talking to him, and Leon scowling. Joe shrugs his shoulders, says something else. Travis laughs. Leon looks mad. I fidget in my seat. I want to be up there too, I want to know what is being said between the three of them. The next thing I know, Travis says something to the bar man, then gets up and comes over to me holding two packets of crisps. I feel a bit panicked and frown over at Joe. He is about to come over, but then Leon grabs his arm and starts talking to him again, with his face nearly in his ear. I see Joe's body tense, but he remains there, and slowly I watch his body relax again as Leon continues to speak to him. I am now thinking, what the hell?

Gremlin utters a pathetic slobbery sounding growl as Travis plonks himself down in Joe's seat, chucking the crisps down on the table. I feel my heart rate picking up pace immediately. "Shut it," Travis addresses Gremlin, and grins lazily at me. "Joe said you two hadn't had any breakfast."

"No, we were a bit too busy rushing off to get your bag back," I say this too quickly, too defensively, but fuck it, it is true. Travis raises his eyebrows at me and rests his arms on the table, pint in one hand. The way he sits is the same as the way he moves World. Loose and fluid, like his muscles never feel the need to tighten or clench, like he views life through a warm haze of indifference. He sits next to me like he is part of the furniture and part of everything.

"Yeah, thanks for that," he says, his tone dropping a level. "I know we were angry yesterday, but you probably did us a favour actually. Where did you hide it by the way?"

"Well I better not say," I shrug at him, and his grin widens across his face for some reason.

"Okay, fair enough. We've all got our secrets I suppose."

"Yeah, but some are bigger than others," I point out, and then decide to shut up and drink my coke. Travis is watching me carefully. I glance up at the bar, but Leon is still talking to Joe.

"You two doing anything tonight?" Travis asks me then, changing the subject, which I think is a good idea.

"Don't think so."

"Mate of mine is having a party."

"Oh yeah?"

"You know Hogan?"

I nod cautiously. I remember Hogan. His real name is Lewis Cross, but they call him Hogan because he is built like a tank and has lank blonde hair that he wears to his shoulders, making him look like the bastard child of the ageing wrestler Hulk Hogan. "He's got a place with his girlfriend," Travis informs me, relaxing back in his seat, and holding his pint casually on the table top. "We're all going over about eightish, if you two fancy it? He said more the merrier."

"You're asking me and Joe to come?" I look at him as if he is crazy. I am sure I have misheard him somehow. I am thinking back to a lifetime of being told to fuck off by him and Leon. *Fuck off and die,* they used to say to us.

"Why not?" he shrugs at me. "You're sixteen, aren't you? You're not little kids anymore."

"And Leon is okay with this?"

"Course he is."

"What are they talking about anyway?"

"No idea. Look, maybe it's just to say thanks, yeah?" Travis cocks his head at me and holds my gaze. I feel that shiver twist through me again, the same one from the night before, when I had relived the touch of his hands on my arms. I want to look away, to look down, anything, but I can't. "You two could have dropped us right in it, you know, with Mum and Mick, but you didn't. And you got it back okay. Call it a thank you. It's at 12a Wick Lane, yeah? You know where that is?"

I nod at him. I can see Joe is on his way over now. "Can we bring some friends?" I ask Travis, as he gets up to go. I am thinking of Marianne, and Josh and Ryan. Back up, if you like. Travis shrugs.

"Course you can," he says, and goes back to the bar to join Leon. Joe slides silently back into his seat and promptly drains the last of the cider. I look at him, feeling my impatience intensify with every second that he remains silent.

"Travis just asked us to a party," I say finally, lifting and dropping my hands in sheer exasperation. I do not understand any of this. Joe mostly keeps his gaze on his brothers at the bar. I sense that he is not really with me at all.

"Did he?"

"Yeah, at Hogan's new place, no less. Why would they do that?"

"Thanking us, I think," Joe says hesitantly, and opens one of the packets of crisps. "For not dropping them in it."

"What was Leon saying to you?"

"Oh nothing much. I'll tell you later." He gets up then, swinging his leg back over the chair, and nodding down at the other packet of crisps. "You gonna' have those or what?"

I nod and pick them up, and follow his lead by getting up from the table. "We going?" As I walk I feel like looking back over my shoulder for some reason. But at the same time, I don't want to, in case Travis sees me, and thinks I am looking at him.

"I've got to get home, do a favour for Leon," Joe is saying. "Do you want to go to that party then?"

We reach the doors and go back outside with Gremlin. I shrug my shoulders at Joe and blink my eyes at the bright sunlight. "I don't know. I suppose we could do. It's something to do."

"Ask the others?"

"Yeah. I might take Gremlin home and go over Marianne's actually. See if she's all right."

"Make sure she hasn't severed any arteries?"

"Joe, don't be mean. You can never know what is going on in a person's head. You can never even hope to understand how someone else feels."

Joe is looking at me, both amused and concerned. I feel tired and confused, without really knowing why. Part of it is Joe not telling me what Leon said to him. Part of it is everything else. I need to be on my own for a while, so I say goodbye to Joe and head off back to my house alone. The cider has made my head feel slightly fuzzy and full, but at the same time I feel the ridiculous urge to run. I am still clutching the crisps in one hand. As I walk along I open them, feed one to Gremlin, and eat three in a row. The salt and vinegar seems impossibly strong and reactive within my taste-starved mouth. The chewed up crisps feel heavy and distasteful as they slip down my throat, so I screw the rest up in my hand, feeling the satisfying crunch of them crushing to crumbs in my fist. When I walk past the parade of shops I hurl them into a bin. I walk on slowly, feeling the familiar regret and disgust that follows a fat person around after they have just eaten.

7

Dear World, I am such an idiot. What is simple for other people becomes so complicated for me. My mum has cooked vegetable stir-fry for dinner. This touches me somewhat. I know she has done this for me, for my diet. We never used to eat this kind of food. We used to basically just eat crap. Which is how I got as fat as I did. I have only eaten three crisps all day, so I am well and truly ravenous. I sit at the table, enduring the heavy silence that exists between her and my stony faced sister, and I tell myself that I am just going to eat half of it, or maybe even less than half of it. But before I know it, Sara and my mum are making snide comments to each other across the table, which leads up to my mum announcing that Les is bringing his stuff around tomorrow, which leads onto a full scale screaming match between the two of them. I bow my head, unhappily reminded of all the screaming rows my parents used to have over the dinner table. I suppose you can spend the rest of the day avoiding each other, pushing past each other and walking out of rooms. Unless you all eat separately, you are forced together at the dinner table.

I do not want to add to, or join in with their row. I have no personal views on Les, or his moving in, or nothing that springs to mind right now anyway. No doubt there will be plenty of sneering bile spilling from my pen later on, especially if I get drunk at the party. But right now I am silent, and I eat, and before I know it, I have eaten the lot. All of it. The whole dinner. I have not eaten an entire meal in over a month. I am sickened and horrified, and I want to jump up and shove back my chair and point to my empty plate and scream at them; look what you made me do!

But I don't do this, of course. I get up, guiltily and shamefully, and I wipe my mouth, and already I can feel the vile heaviness in my belly, stretching it out over my waistband, and I excuse myself, and leave them to it. I go up to my room and get changed, and only look in the mirror long enough to put mascara on, and a slick of lip gloss, and then I poke my head around the door and interrupt their fury long enough to tell them I am going to Marianne's and sleeping the night.

I leave the house, wretched tears in eyes, and decide right away that I better jog. It is my only hope. Try to burn it off. Try to cancel it out. I pick up my pace and jog across the estate and over the fields to Marianne's house. I feel like an idiot in every possible way. In fact I want to slap myself in the face, if I am honest World. I want to go back in time and be more disciplined. My body is full of violence as I tear across the fields.

Half an hour later, I am feeling calmer again, as Marianne's parents have left us to it, so we are helping ourselves to their well-stocked liquor cabinet. They have gone out, dressed up smart, to some dinner party somewhere. I want to laugh at this, and Marianne cannot understand why. "Don't think my parents ever went to a dinner party in their lives," is all the explanation I can give her. She frowns at me as she snatches the vodka from the cabinet. "Just piss ups and parties," I shrug. This means nothing to her.

"Drink up," she says, and pushes a glass of vodka and lemonade into my hand. We slump and sprawl across the sofas in the living room. She puts on one of her dads records. She is dressed for the party in black trousers, black vest, and a silver cardigan. "So where's Joe?" she asks me. "You two are usually joined at the hip."

"He had to go home for some reason. I think he's meeting us there with Ryan and Josh."

"Ooh, we have to enter the party alone? Could be scary."

"Well we'll be fashionably late," I suggest. "That way they'll be there already."

"So Joe's brothers invite us to say thanks? For not calling the police on them or whatever?" I shrug at her, because I really don't know.

"I think so."

"Weird," she says, narrowing her eyes, and she is right. I glance sideways at her and I really want to ask her about her arms, and tell her about my meal, but all I do is sigh, and look down at my feet. My ankles are crossed, and all I can think is that my trainers are in pretty shoddy shape, and when I get to the party I am going to kick them off somewhere and go barefoot. "I find it all very intriguing you know," Marianne says then, curling her little legs up under her on the sofa, and holding her glass in one hand, whilst the fingers of her other hand trace circular motions around the rim. "Joe and his family. You've known them your whole life, what do you think?"

"What do you mean?" I ask, and drink more vodka.

"Well the brothers of course, and the drugs, and the other brothers, and the parents and everything! Maybe my life is just totally dull, but it does kind of fascinate me. I have no brothers or sisters remember. I just can't imagine having that many, all in the same house. All that drama and testosterone!" She has this huge smile on her face World. Her green eyes sparkle and I realise for the first time how pretty she really is.

"Marianne, did your twin really die at birth?" I have no idea why I say this, or what I am thinking, but it just comes out. I think I am beginning to realise that in some ways, Marianne is a lot like Joe. You can say anything to her. I have known her for a year now, and I cannot ever remember seeing her get offended or upset about anything. Either my friends are excellent at keeping their feelings well hidden, or they are simply far more balanced and positive than I am. My feelings about everything are spewed out violently all over my bedroom wall. And Joe has not noticed yet, that I have started to write on the ceiling as well. I used a chair to reach and wrote '*I want to fly away, I want to run away, I want to go away, I want to fade away,*' up there, in a circle around the light bulb. Fucked if I know why.

"Yes, she really did," Marianne says softly, and looks at me carefully. "Why? Didn't you believe me?"

I shrug my shoulders. "I don't know. I'm sorry though." Sorry is the most useless, pointless, tedious thing you can say to someone when they've lost a loved one. Well, everything is really. In fact, most words are rubbish when humans speak them. Nothing ever conveys what you want it to; nothing ever gets across what you feel inside, or what you fear. There are never any words. I am beginning to realise this as I search and search to find ways to articulate how I feel. I remember when my Nana died, all the people saying sorry to each other, over and over again, that little useless word, as if they were all partly responsible for her getting old and just fading away. Sorry, sorry, sorry, what good did it ever do?

Marianne gets up suddenly with a little gentle smile on her face, and crosses the room. She snatches a photo frame down from the massive Oak bookcase that is next to the fire, and marches back to the sofa. She thrusts it at me as she dumps herself back down. "Melissa," she says.

I take the photo frame, and I have to concentrate to make my fingers hold it properly, because suddenly they do not seem to want to work at all, and it is heavier than I expect and I fucking nearly drop it. I almost don't want to look. The photo is of a new-born baby girl. She is wrapped tightly in a white blanket. Her eyes are closed, and she has thick black hair. You can see right away that she is dead.

I gulp, and swallow, and sort of shake my head, and I want to hand it back to her, and find some fitting, sorrowful words to say at the passing of this tiny child, who never knew life, never knew anything, but I can't say a word, and I can't stop looking at her. "I came out alive," Marianne tells me. "And she came out dead."

That just about sums it up, I suppose.

"I'm really sorry," I say again, and hurriedly pass it back to her.

"It's okay," she says brightly. "It's not like I knew her. It's not like losing someone that is totally part of your life. I just feel fucked off about it really, you know, cheated."

"I don't blame you. It's not fair. Did they know why?"

"No, no one ever knows why. Just life I suppose."

"Your poor parents."

"Oh I know. They act like everything is great and cool, and they do a pretty good job of it, don't you think? But they're not. They never have been. They missed out on her."

I feel the intense urge to cry. In fact I feel the intense urge to wrap my arms around Marianne and try to pass on my sorrow somehow, not that she needs it, for fucks sake. She is staring at the picture, and I wonder then how many times she has sat and held it like that, sat and stared into the face of her own twin sister, who she never even knew, yet was conceived and formed alongside. It's bizarre. It's soul destroying. It makes me want to take my glass of vodka and hurl it at the wall.

"We should go," she sighs finally. "Melissa won't mind."

Later, this strikes me as an odd thing for her to say, but right now, it is fine by me to get going. It is fine by me to put that picture back where it came from, where I had never even noticed it before. It is okay and great to be getting out of this empty, echoing home, and get our arses to a party where getting shit faced is an absolute given.

Wick Lane is just down the road from the men's club. Handy for Hogan, I think, as Marianne and I arrive. Flat 12a is a ground floor council flat. Hogan and his girlfriend, who I later discover is called Fiona, have the front garden and the driveway, and the first floor tenants, who are also a young couple, have the back garden and the shed. It seems a fair divide to me, when we show up and see the hordes of young people milling about in the front garden, smoking and drinking. Marianne takes my hand and squeezes it in excitement. I just feel bowled over.

I start searching for Joe. I don't want to bump into Leon or Travis without him. I don't really want to talk to anyone until I have Joe. They are all older than us, these people. They look like they could eat us alive. Some I recognise, but most I don't. I just slip through them, dragging Marianne with me. Inside the house it is stuffy and hot, and each room seems a stark contrast to the next. The lounge is too dark with the curtains closed and no lights on, and too many people bumping and grinding against each other to music. The hallway is cold and empty, with the front door hanging wide open, and a smooching couple taking up the whole doorstep. The kitchen is too light, too bright, with a huge window, and the lights all on as well, and a gaggle of people crowded around a makeshift bar. This is where I finally find Joe, and my immediate instinct is to wrap my arms around him and bury my face in his t-shirt, but I can't do that, I know I can't do that. Christ, they'll all start saying I'm pregnant or something. Instead I roll my eyes at him, letting him know I have been anxious without him and he smiles a big wide smile, a real *Joe* smile and reaches out to us. He is pleased to see us, I can tell.

Marianne and I allow Joe to hug and greet us. He is holding a bottle of beer in one hand, and uses his other hand to pull us close to him. "You look good! You look good!" he is saying to us excitedly, as if this has surprised him. "Let me get you a drink! I'll get you a drink!" He is obviously drunk already, which slightly unnerves me. I don't like being sober when my friends are drunk. Who does?

"Any vodka?" Marianne shouts over the music. Joe holds up a finger, as in I will have a look for you, and spins around to the table, the bar, behind him. I look around, rubbing at my arm with my hand. Ryan and Josh come bounding in at that moment, knocking into us and nearly sending Marianne flying. Ryan and Josh are in the same year at school as us, and apparently they are already drunk as well.

"How long have you guys been here?" I ask Ryan suspiciously, as Josh throws an arm around Joe and starts trying to get him into a headlock. Ryan is extremely tall and thin, with a host of amusing nicknames that have followed him about since infant's school; beanpole and lanky streak of piss being the most repeated ones. He has been learning to play the guitar for the past two years, and is now utterly convinced that if he, Josh and Joe start a band together, it will sound good. This is despite the fact that Josh and Joe have only just started having music lessons, and do not own any instruments. I know, pretty funny hey? Ryan has white blonde hair, a long, angular face and bright blue eyes. He lives with his mum and younger sister in a council flat and she lets him do whatever the hell he wants, and always has done.

"Got wrecked at mine first," he explains, lolling all over me, and I should have known this was the case. "But they got plenty here! Look, you can help yourselves!" he leans against me, hugging me to his bony side, and swiping his arm across the air in a gesture towards the copious amount of alcohol that has been laid out on the kitchen side. Joe finally shakes Josh off, and turns back to Marianne and I with our drinks. I taste mine and immediately grimace. There is way more vodka than coke. Joe holds up his bottle of beer.

"To a great night!" he roars, clinking his bottle into my glass and then into Marianne's. I smile, drink my vodka and try to ignore the uneasy feeling that rests in the pit of my belly.

"I'm gonna' pull tonight," Josh states, and necks the rest of his beer. I just shake my head at Marianne. Josh wears glasses, and reminds me of Harry Potter. He is just small, and gangly, and awkward looking, and his mother is extremely overbearing and overprotective; the complete opposite to Ryan's. If he thinks he is capable of pulling, when apart from Marianne and I, the rest of the girls here are older than him, I mean practically *women*, for Christ's sake, then he's drunker and more delusional than I first thought. I look around us, holding my vodka, and wonder for the first time what the hell we are all doing here. We look like twelve year olds compared to this lot. Worse than that, we look like we've been brought in as the entertainment or something, the fucking bait for when these animals get really hungry later. I shiver and drink more vodka and try to calm myself down.

We huddle together in the kitchen, feeling too small and young to venture further. We make full use of the supposedly free bar. No one seems to notice or care that we help ourselves. Marianne and I stick to the vodka, but Joe and the boys drink anything they can get their hands on, and it isn't long before all three of them are steaming drunk. Every now and again I spot Leon or Travis walking past the kitchen, or hanging around in the hallway. Leon, as usual, pays us no attention whatsoever. We do not even register on his radar, which is fine by me. But Travis looks over at us sometimes and gives the odd lazy smile.

"It's gonna' sound like REM," Ryan is leaning into Joe and telling him, in a loud, drunk voice that makes me cringe. Marianne and I have hopped up onto the side, as this seems safer. We are out of the way of the increasingly drunken people who keep bumping into us as if we are invisible, and we are up off the floor, which has puddles of alcohol all over it. "But rockier…like The Black Keys, but like REM, 'cause I really like REM, they're like my favourite probably, but sometimes they're not rocky enough for me, do you know what I mean?"

"So how's it gonna' sound like REM?" I feign interest and ask Ryan.

"Well," Ryan lifts his head, which looks like it is getting difficult for him now, and tries to focus his eyes on me. "Because Lou, because of the lyrics, that's how. The lyrics are gonna' be shit hot, 'cause they're gonna' really mean something, you know what I mean?"

"Will it make me want to dance?" Marianne questions.

"It will make you want to puke," I whisper to her.

"Yeah, dance," Ryan nods emphatically at us. "Dance around like you're in a mosh pit, yeah? Leaping around, that kind of thing. Not dance like fucking pop music, or anything. Not like that."

"Can we be your groupies?" Marianne asks him, and his eyes bulge and his mouth drops open.

"Oh yeah," he nods again. "Oh yeah, course you can. Only if you wear skimpy clothes though!"

"It's a deal," she grins at him, and drinks more vodka. I wonder if she is close to her limit yet. There is a line that she never crosses and it must be getting close.

"So have you got a name yet?" I wonder, rolling my eyes at Joe, who is leaning next to me. I start to run my fingers through his hair. This is not in a pervy way though World, just so you know, not at all, it's just something that I like to do. He has extremely soft hair for a boy, and you can really play with it. You can move the parting about, spike it up, and squash it flat, because it's thick, without being coarse or wiry.

"Crash Landing is one idea," Ryan tells us, looking to Josh and Joe for support, but they just look totally out of it to me. "What was the other one? Oh yeah, The Maggots."

I burst out laughing at this one. I just can't help it. The maggots? Do they have no self-worth? Surely it's for other people to judge them as maggots? Joe and Marianne laugh at the fact I find this funny, but in his drunken stupor Ryan seems genuinely hurt.

"Can you think of something better then?"

"No, stick with The Maggots," I tell him, giggling. "You're onto a winner with that one."

"I like Crash Landing," Joe tells me sleepily. I pull his hair back and frown into his face.

"Can you even play anything yet you slimy maggot?"

"Course I can. I'm the drummer."

"Oh trust you to get the easy bit!"

"Easy? It's not easy bitch. It looks easy. But it's not easy, is it Ryan?"

I just laugh and hop down from the side, because I am suddenly dying for the toilet. I pat Joe on the shoulder reassuringly as I pass him. "Sitting on your arse, and banging about, yeah, that sounds really hard to me!" He makes a face at me.

I am obviously drunk now, because I walk out of that kitchen and start hunting for the toilet, as if I fucking own the place. Being inebriated really does give you a unique kind of confidence. Ordinarily if you were to walk about in society, and suddenly couldn't put one foot in front of the other, or couldn't walk without having to hold onto the wall, and your clothes were all skew whiff and your hair was all a mess, you wouldn't exactly be glowing with courage, would you? You would think what the hell are they doing letting me out, and you would run home to hide. But when you are pissed, you're a bloody walking mess of pathetic human delusions and yet you feel great about it! More than that, you want to show it off, and you have the adamant belief that everyone else will think you are shit hot too. It's bizarre. But you can sort of understand why certain people become alcoholics World.

So I wobble and stagger out of the kitchen, and away from the safety of my little group, and I do not care one bit. I have to keep one hand flat against the wall as I walk, partly so I don't trip up, and partly so I don't get lost, because the place suddenly seems far more complicated now. I have to kind of stare at my feet as they walk, have you ever done that? Really stare at them to make sure they are doing what you tell them to do. I pass people, and I even touch them, which is something I normally loathe, but I have to touch them, otherwise I can't get past them.

I finally locate the toilet, but there is a queue. So I lean back against the wall and promptly knock a framed picture off its hook. "Oh shit!" I say, and bend over to pick it up. "Whoops sorry," I say to no one, and hang it back on its hook. The girl in front of me is smoking, and smiles at me.

"I just did that too," she says. That's okay then. We hear the toilet flush and another girl comes out of it looking a bit worse for wear. I vaguely recognise her from school, a few years above us though, and her blonde hair is all over her face, and she is wiping at her mouth apologetically.

"Sorry," she mumbles, but I am not sure who she is saying it to. "Bit of a mess in there."

The smoking girl just shrugs and goes on in. I move up. My turn next. Someone bumps into me, hard, as I am waiting, and I turn to glare at him or her, feeling my first wave of drunken aggression, and nearly tell him or her to fucking watch it. But it is Travis.

He is wearing a black shirt, which is open, and a white t-shirt underneath and for some reason I have to take an extra breath then, just looking at him like that. He is smiling at me, and holding two bottles of beer. "You all right?" he says over the music, which has got steadily louder. I narrow my eyes at him, and in that moment, for some insane reason, I want to tell him exactly what I think of him and Leon. How they've been shitty, shifty, no good brothers to Joe, and how unfair that is. How I'm glad he's not like them, because I can trust him and feel safe around him, and he's also funnier and cleverer than them.

"What do you want?" I ask him instead, in a tone that suggests I dislike him intensely. He looks slightly taken back, but also amused.

"Toilet," he says, nodding at the closed door. "Here. Take one. I'm gonna' drop it." He shoves one of the beer bottles at me. I don't need any more encouragement to drink, and that is just one of many things he does not know about me. I keep my eyes on him, on the lookout for danger, and lift the beer to my lips. He does the same then leans back against the wall, his elbow touching mine. "So you guys having a good time?" he asks me.

"Suppose so," I shrug. "Apart from the music, which is awful."

"You don't like dance music?"

"I don't like dancing, so why would I like dance music?"

"Oh. Okay. Fair enough. Lots of drinks though, eh?"

I nod and drink more beer just to show that I agree. "So why did you invite us?" I ask him. He scratches his stubbly chin and looks bemused.

"Just thought you guys would enjoy it. You know, why not? You're not little kids anymore, are you?"

"That's the second time you've said that."

"What?"

"That we're not little kids. Did you only just notice we're not three?"

"Well, yeah, maybe." Travis winks at me then, and I don't get it, so I just shake my head at him, fold one arm across my chest and drink more beer. I want to ask him about the bag and the drugs. I want to know what they've done with it, and where they got it from, and what kind of people do they think they are? I want to grab him and shake him, and call him an idiot, but I can't, so I don't. Is it my drunken imagination, or has he moved closer to me? I bite my lip and look away, only realising now how utterly hammered I am. But I am sure at first, it was just his elbow poking into mine. Now his whole arm is resting heavily against mine, and he keeps staring down at me and grinning like a lunatic. I assume he is laughing at me. I gather he is taking the piss, so I turn my back on him and reach out to tap politely on the toilet door.

"Are you gonna' be much longer?"

"Sorry!" comes the startled reply. "Got a bit sick!"

Oh no, not another one. I sigh, and shrug and lean back on the wall, and try to ignore Travis, so that he will get bored of laughing at me and just go away. He could, in all honestly, go and take a piss outside, couldn't he? I feel drunk and aggressive and pissed off, and out of patience. He taps me on the shoulder. "What?"

"Christ, why are so always so moody?"

"I'm not! What do you want? Why are you even talking to me?"

"Why is it such a problem? I've known you your whole life."

"Yeah, and you've never bothered talking to me before. Not unless it's to be mean."

Travis looks down at the floor briefly, looks to one side, then the other, while I frown at him and shake my head, and think hurry the fuck up in the toilet you dopey bitch, and then suddenly he puts his arm around my shoulder. I freeze. I am dumbfounded. I know I am pissed, but I am literally stunned into silence. I am so confused I could weep. For some reason I start to smile, and before I know it, my smile has stretched into a grin, and I am laughing. Well, good! See how he likes being laughed at for once! "What the fuck are you doing?" I laugh at him. He is smiling too, and he has a pretty fantastic smile to be honest. In that moment I kind of don't want him to open his mouth and speak, as I am pretty sure that whatever he says will ruin it. In that moment I feel bizarrely close to him, but it's the drink, you see World, it's the fucking drink. That's what it does to you sometimes. It encases you in these warm, yet fake, moments with people you barely know. With people you probably hate. You feel a warm rush for them, not of love, but of understanding and unity. But you have to remember World, it is a transient and passing thing. It is not real.

"I think you're looking pretty hot tonight, that's all," he leans forward and whispers in my ear.

"Really? You must be drunker than me."

"Why do you put yourself down so much?"

"To save other people the trouble."

"Well I'm not taking the piss Lou, you look hot. You really do. I'm just being friendly and telling you what I think."

I suck in a deep breath, and then let it out slowly. I think I must be dreaming or something. I do not know what the hell is going on here. Travis is looking at me in a dopey way, and there is a part of me that wants to believe him, there is a part of me that longs to believe someone like him could really like me, in that way. There are two parts fighting over my consciousness right then. The sober me, the negative me, the realistic me, poking me in the ribs and telling me to snap out of it, shove him away and storm off, because there is no way he is not taking the piss. Then the drunk and confident and brash me, doesn't give a shit and is telling me just to go along with this crazy unexpected shit and see what happens.

Travis keeps smiling, and so do I while I let the two sides of me fight it out. I am not quite sure who is going to win. He keeps one arm around my shoulders, pulls me in a little closer to his chest, and then uses his other hand to stroke my arm. Okay. That's kind of nice. But also kind of frightening to tell you the truth. Then he goes and ruins it all, just like my real self knew he would. "I have always fancied you," he says.

Fear shoots through me. My smile falls away. This is not true. This cannot be true. He has known me since I was born, and until recently I was always fat. Chubby. Unattractive. Whatever. I know it, and he knows it, and for him to say he has always fancied me, brings the truth of this crashing in. He is up to something. I am a pawn in something; I am the butt of a joke, or something! I feel suddenly horribly self-conscious and out of my depth, and wriggle away from him. "We can't do this," I mutter. "Sorry."

"What do you mean?" He looks confused. "You're sixteen. You're all grown up now, you know?" He strokes my arm again and I want to believe him, I want to think he could actually mean it, but I can't let myself believe a word he says.

"Joe," I mumble, looking around awkwardly, wondering where he is.

"What about him?" asks Travis. "It's time you two stopped acting like little kids, you know anyway?"

What the hell does that mean?

"This isn't right, I don't know what you think you're doing."

He suddenly moves forward, his face towards mine, and I jerk back, but not before I feel his lips brush my cheek. "What?" he asks again, throwing up his hands in exasperation. I just stare at him, blinking dumbly, like a rabbit caught in the headlights. I feel totally trapped and unprepared. I want to let him kiss me, but none of this feels right. "You're not doing anything with him, are you?"

I assume he means Joe, and I wonder what he means by *anything*? I feel resentful and I want to cross my arms and stamp my foot, and tell him that Joe and me do plenty of things actually. You know, like walking the dogs for our lazy parents, and drinking cider in the park for a laugh, and taking the piss out of each other and everyone else we know, just to make ourselves feel better. But somehow I don't think those are the kinds of things he means.

I want to cry suddenly. I am reminded of that fat little girl who just wanted to hide away, and not be seen by anyone. My mind jerks around frantically, piecing together images and voices from the last few days. My sister asking if I had lost more weight. Travis holding onto me in the bedroom, and how I had let him and not struggled. I look up at his face and try to read every part of him then. I so want to believe he means it. I so desperately want to be the kind of girl that boys like in that way. Like the stick insects at school. Flicking their glossy hair and making the boys trip over at their feet. I feel useless tears in my eyes, when suddenly I guess Travis gets bored, and he grabs my face and presses his lips down upon mine.

I let him. Just for a moment. A second. I allow myself it. I allow myself one moment of pretence. One moment where I believe I am worthy of this attention, and this is not just a cruel piss take, and not only that, I deserve this. And then I pull quickly away from him, slapping my hand over my mouth and dropping my beer all over the floor, and that is when I see Joe. He is standing a little way back. I can see his staring face over his brother's shoulder. He looks horrified, and he turns and runs into the kitchen.

Shit.

8

Oh World, what an awful moment. You hear people say it don't you? I wanted the ground to open up and swallow me. God, it is more than that though. I don't just want the ground to open up, I just want to not exist anymore World. "Joe!" I say, and Travis spins around, but Joe has gone. Travis looks back at me.

"Don't worry about it," he shrugs at me. "You can do what you want."

I have to go after him. This is all wrong. I pull away from the wall, and push past Travis, and the journey to the kitchen seems unbearably long and complicated, as people, so many people, get in my way, and I have to push and shove and squeeze through them, just to get to Joe. He is in the kitchen, leaning against the cupboards next to Marianne. There is no sign of Josh or Ryan. I open my mouth to say something to him, but before I get the chance, he lets out this angry noise and launches himself at me. Or so it seems. But it is Travis he is after. Travis has followed me, God knows why, and I have to move out of Joe's way as he goes for him.

Joe crashes into his brother and then they are both on the floor, scrambling and tussling, while everyone who is in the kitchen just moves back dumbly, watching them. I shout at Joe to stop it, and sort of dance around the edge of them, trying in vain to grab at Joe and pull him away. I am shocked by the viciousness that spirals and spins on the floor before me. They both look possessed. I have never seen Joe like this before. I assume he must be completely wasted to do this. I try again to separate them, calling Joe's name and snatching at his clothes. "Watch out," someone warns me, and true enough, I am going to get kicked or punched in a minute if I am not careful. That is when I feel a light touch on the top of my arm, and I look over my shoulder to see Leon just behind me.

"Let them get on with it," he tells me. I look at my arm, and he drops his hand and folds his arms across his muscular chest. I watch his eyes flick back to his brothers, punching the hell out of each other on the floor. As usual, his face portrays no emotion whatsoever, and yet his eyes are alive. I shake my head. I feel disgusted with all of them.

"Fine!" I shout, and storm out away from them all. I find myself out in the front garden, and suddenly I am throwing up into the flowerbeds. As my vegetable stir-fry makes an unwelcome reappearance, I am hoping miserably that Fiona had not planted these flowers herself. I hope they were here already. Anyway, they are ruined now. Just like everything else. I let my backside find the doorstep and sit down heavily. I wonder where Marianne is as I drop my aching head into my hands, and close my eyes to the carnage that is all around me. I still need the toilet, and I know I am drunk and probably overreacting, but I really don't think I have ever felt so utterly alone and afraid. I just do not understand what has happened. I just do not know what to do about it. I just feel small World, so small. I look up, trying to force myself to think, trying to clear my mind, but all of a sudden I have to leap to my feet again because the boys are coming outside now.

Egged on by Leon, whose eyes seem to be gleaming with excitement, Joe and Travis's fight spills out into the garden. I stand back, shaking my head from side to side in shock. I can only assume that Hogan or Fiona have ordered them outside, for fear of their new home getting trashed any further. This is disgusting. Both of them are bleeding. I have had enough, so I run off to get Mick. Fuck it.

It's either Mick or the police, I tell myself as I run. Mick, or the police? Mick or the police. What would Joe prefer? Surely his stepfather's wrath would be preferable to getting arrested? What the hell is Leon thinking? I keep running. I am surprised I don't trip over my own feet and go sprawling into the concrete, but somehow I keep going. I reach Joe's house and hammer upon the door. I have no idea what time it is, but it only takes a few moments for Mick to open up.

"It's Joe and Travis," I tell him breathlessly. "They're killing each other!"

"Where?"

"Wick Lane."

"Jesus," Mick grunts, and follows me out. I start running back, and he soon overtakes me, rolling up his shirtsleeves as he goes. I have no time to wonder if I have done the right thing or not, but I can see they are still fighting as we turn into Wick Lane. I can hardly breathe, I have run so much. I give up, and stand back and watch, as Mick wades in and breaks their fight up the same way I have seen him do it a hundred times before. He grabs each boy by the back of his shirt collar, yanks them apart, and then thrusts them back together again so that their heads clash in the middle. Next thing I know, he has them both on their feet, and is marching them home, holding one on each side of him. They both look stunned and exhausted, shoulders hunched, holding onto their heads. I remember that I had always thought getting your heads banged together was just a threat your parents used. I can remember mine saying it to me and Sara enough times. Just like, I'm going to wash your mouth out with soap. Threats are realities in Joe's family. The amount of fights Mick has had to break up, I am amazed none of them have brain damage.

It takes Leon a while to decide to go after them. I watch him chatting casually to Hogan, laughing even, as they shake hands and he makes some comment about a party not being a party without a fight, and then he throws down his fag end, and follows his family. As he passes me, he gives me the briefest of looks.

"Are you okay?" asks a gentle voice at my shoulder. Marianne.

"Not really," I tell her honestly. "I'm gonna' piss myself in a minute. Can we go?"

"I think we better."

"What happened to Josh and Ryan?"

"Got sick and went home. Joe was saying goodbye to them at the door, when he saw you and Travis."

I look at her quickly. "Don't," I warn her gravely. "Just don't."

"Okay," she nods. "It's okay."

We stagger back to her house, linking arms and weaving from side to side on the pavement as we go. At her house, I finally get to use the toilet and then we go to her room and climb silently into her double bed. She leaves her curtains wide open, and the bed is draped in moonlight. I just lie there on my back, breathing slowly, my eyes closed tightly, trying not to be sick.

"I am loving this summer already," Marianne tells me enthusiastically, curled on her side next to me. She has removed her silver cardigan and is lying with her arms wrapped around herself, and her knees drawn up to her chest. Even in the moonlight I can see the scores of white marks on her thin arms. It makes me feel so sad and I can't even explain why. "It's hardly even started," she says, as if to make her point. "Isn't that weird? Feels like so much has happened already since the exams."

"Like another lifetime ago," I say softly, echoing her own thoughts. I think to myself, that is one of those phrases that gets thrown around a lot, but now I can understand why. Sitting bowed over the exam papers in the hot, stuffy sports hall at our school, sucking the top of my pen and trying not to cough, does seem like a lifetime ago. It really does.

"Do you think you'll do well enough to get into sixth form?"

"I don't know. I think so. I suppose I hope so."

"What do you mean, you *suppose* you hope so?" Marianne asks with a little giggle. I wonder how much she has had to drink. She certainly seems more relaxed and less uptight than usual. "What does that mean?"

"I just mean going to sixth form, and all that, it's not like it makes me feel really excited or anything."

"You are funny Lou."

"But it doesn't. I'm not really that arsed if I get in or not." This is true World. I just haven't spoken about it to anyone before. "My parents would be annoyed, I suppose, if I didn't get in. They'd harp on about me getting a job instead."

"Yeah, and that would be a pain," Marianne yawns. "I'd much rather go back to school and muck about for two more years."

"I don't understand how they all expect us to know what we want to do with the rest of our lives at our age." I stare at the ceiling, not at Marianne, as I speak. I am relieved that we are talking about something else other than Joe and Travis. I had fully expected her to go into total meltdown about the whole thing, seeing as how she seems to find it all so fascinating. But now I feel a surge of words and thoughts crowding and pushing behind my tongue and inside my head. I am vocalising my thoughts as they come, and so I keep my eyes on the ceiling, and it is almost like I am totally alone in the giant bed, almost like I am writing on my wall. "It's bollocks and it's annoying. From about the age of twelve or thirteen for Christ's sake, whenever we had to pick our options for GCSE's. All those visits to the careers office. Work experience, all that pointless shit. How the hell does anyone know what they want to do at that age? I just want to be left alone, that's all. You know the truth is, the truth is, none of it appeals to me. None of the career options, none of the crap that comes up on the computer, none of it. I don't want to do any of it. It's become like this fucking mantra, this fucking chant that they all repeat endlessly, again and again, what do you want to do? What do you want to do? I just want to scream at them, actually I don't want to do anything, I just want to be left alone!"

Marianne is shaking with laughter beside me. "But what do you want to do?" she asks, pressing her small hands to her mouth.

"Ahh, see? Don't you get tired of it? I don't want to do any of those shitty jobs. I don't want to work in a fucking supermarket or corner shop, or clean toilets, or wait tables, or pull pints, or cut old ladies hair, or mend cars, or look after children, or deliver pizza, or anything!"

"Lou, you wouldn't be doing jobs like that."

"Why wouldn't I? Every grown up I know has a job like that."

Marianne is quiet for a moment and I can tell she is thinking about this. Then she sort of nestles her head into her pillow and smiles sleepily at me. "Lou, you are too clever for jobs like that."

"Being clever has nothing to do with it," I correct her sharply. "Are you saying that all the people I know who have jobs like that are stupid?"

"No, course not, not all of them, but…"

"Well they're not. That's just all there is. Boring, mind-numbing jobs. Getting up in the morning is hard enough, is it not? Without the joyless knowledge that the reason you are getting up is to go and stack some fucking beans in the supermarket?"

"Lou, calm down. There must be something you want to do."

I stare at the ceiling again. I don't want to tell her what the only thing that remotely appeals to me is, because she would probably laugh, just like everyone else has. Because the only thing I can think of, the only thing in the world I can plausibly imagine me hauling my lazy arse out of bed for, once all this education we're so keen on is done and dusted, is something to do with dogs. You know, looking after dogs. Walking them and stuff. Just feeding them, and caring for them. Something like that. Maybe.

There is a silence that lasts so long I am sure Marianne has drifted off. I feel pretty close to it myself, but then she shifts and yawns again into her pillow.

"They were fighting over you," she says, and I can feel her watching me. I shake my head. "Don't be stupid."

"They were. What happened with you and Travis?"

I don't know how to explain it to her, because I don't know myself what happened. "Nothing," I say instead. "Joe got the wrong idea. Or there's something else going on between them, I don't know."

"Why do you find it so hard to believe they would be fighting over you?"

"Because they weren't Marianne," I open my eyes and tell her. "There's more going on, isn't there? Stuff Joe hasn't even told me."

"I think you're wrong."

"Anyway, Travis was drunk. And probably taking the piss out of me."

I watch Marianne smiling ecstatically, as she rolls onto her back and stares gleefully at the ceiling. "Okay, think that if you want," she grins. "But wasn't that amazing? The way that man just strode in and separated them like that? Like they were animals."

"I had to get him," I say, closing my eyes again, and feeling wretched. "He's a prick, but I had to get him. No one was stopping them."

"You did the right thing," yawns Marianne beside me. "Christ, what a party. I suppose we should have expected it really?"

I don't answer her. I want her to think that I have nodded off. I stay quiet and still until I hear her start to breathe softly in sleep. Then I open my eyes and stare around at the moonlit room. Marianne was right. We should have expected it and we should have stayed away. I think about Joe and I hope that he is okay, and I think about Travis, and my body shivers involuntarily from head to toe. My stomach feels so empty and hollow that I run my hands down over it, and find it is concave. Just one small thing to smile about then.

***

I wake up feeling really light-headed. Really weird. When I push back the duvet and lower my feet to the floor, I can feel all the blood rushing to my head, and the room swings and shifts, and I have to close my eyes quickly and cover my face with my hands. I want to go home, but I feel strangely like I won't make it. I nudge Marianne awake. "Any chance of a strong coffee?"

"Sounds like a plan," she agrees with a yawn, and climbs out the other side of the bed. I watch her cross the room and pull her dressing gown down from the hook on the door. She pulls it around her clothes from last night and ties the belt, and then she shuffles slowly out of the door.

It's not nice being alone then, because it all comes rushing back. The party. Travis. Joe. The fight. I feel genuinely sick to my stomach. I wonder how much my best friend hates me right now. I wonder when, or if I will ever have the guts to phone him, or go around to call for him. Not today, that is for certain.

Marianne returns with a carefully laid out tray. She has made us both a coffee and there is a choice of Marmite toast, or cinnamon bagels for breakfast. I look at both and my stomach growls in protest. I am aware of the little spiteful voice that warns me to not to take anything except the coffee. One bite, it warns, just one bite and that is it. You'll eat the lot, you know you will. But the other voice, the sane one that wants my legs to be able to carry me home to my own dear bed, tells me to fucking eat something, so I do. I eat most of one of the bagels, and wash it down with strong, sugary coffee. The effects are almost immediate. My head feels clearer and less fuzzy, and I feel like I can trust my legs to hold my weight, and take me home. I thank Marianne for the food and the bed, and head for the door.

"Are you going to call Joe?" her little voice asks me, before I can leave. I look back at her and a massive sigh escapes me.

"I don't know," I tell her, and this is true. I really don't know.

I walk slowly, wearily home, craving my nice comfy bed, my squishy pillow, some soft music, and my pen in my hand. I crave being alone. Letting whatever wants to spin through my mind just go right ahead. I am sure I will feel a thousand times better once I have slept properly and just been alone for a while.

But when I get to my house, a chaotic scene greets me. I just stand on the front grass and try to take it all in. My sister is lugging a suitcase across the garden. Her boyfriend Rich is starting up the engine of his battered mini cooper. My mum is weeping on the doorstep, and Hitler's long-lost son is standing with his arm around her waist. I am struck dumb by it all. I just stand there with my arms hanging down at my sides, and my mouth lolling open, and my eyes shooting helplessly from my raging sister, as she huffs and puffs and hurls her case into the tiny boot of the mini, and my mum and Hitler's spawn on the doorstep. I don't think I can realistically be expected to cope with this at my age.

My sister is either too angry or too selfish to even stop and say anything to me, and to be honest this is probably for the best, because what exactly can either of us say? She just jumps into the car, slams the door, sobs melodramatically and then Rich drives off with her. Just like that. I look around at the street where we live, wondering how many neighbours are watching us. I raise my eyes just enough to see my mum take a step towards me, and I think oh no, oh no you fucking don't, because I know I can't let her, I can't let either of them speak to me, or look at me, or touch me, or even acknowledge I exist, because all I want, all I need is my own fucking bed.

I put my head down like a bull, and charge through them and past them. They might be speaking, but I cover my ears with my hands and thunder up the stairs away from their bleating. Inside my room I close and lock the door and turn and stare at the emptiness my sister has left behind for me, and think whoa, this is all mine then. I gulp back tears and go to my bed. I don't want to think about any of this fucking shit. I put on Bob Dylan, they all take the piss about Bob Dylan, but they can all go and die, because I've liked him since I was twelve, and I'm pretty proud of that actually. I put him on and crawl under my duvet and pull it right over my head, to block out the sound of my mother knocking and tapping up and down the blasted door. I lie there and screw up my eyes, trying to create the perfect blackness to disappear into. I want to take my fist and plunge it into my stomach. I want to feel some physical pain to blot out all this crap. I can totally understand why Marianne does what she does to herself. Fuck it.

What is wrong with these people?

I lie in my bed, under my duvet, and the tapping at my door comes and goes. I think I drift in and out of sleep, but I can't be sure. I try not to think about Joe, or Travis, or mum, or Sara, or anything. I don't want to see anything, or hear anything, but I realise I am not going to be able to keep this up for long.

"I'm not going to go away, you know," my mother tells me on perhaps her sixth or seventh trip up the stairs. "There is a lot we need to talk about young lady. Starting with where you and your friends actually went last night!"

Ha, she sounds cross! At me! Bloody hell, she's got a nerve. I throw back the duvet and my feet hit the floor with a thud. I open the door, and she is stood there with a tray. She has made me tea and toast. Bless her heart. I take the mug of tea and go to close the door, but she deftly sticks her slippered foot in the way.

"You should be at work," I tell her. She works in the 99p shop in town.

"Day off actually," she says, jerking her head towards the stairs, as if this is adequate enough to explain why. I am assuming she means Les.

"Right," I sigh, "well look I don't want to talk about any of that. You can do what you like. So can Sara. So can Dad. None of it is anything to do with me."

"But Lou, I just want you to know that…"

"No," I hold up a hand and stop her. "I don't want to hear it. Nothing to do with me. You want to talk about the party we went to?"

Mum frowns at me, attempting to look stern. "Yes, actually. Lorraine is downstairs as we speak."

"Is she?"

"Yes. She said you called Mick to break up a fight between the boys last night, and you were all at a party, drinking!" Her frown deepens at me. "You told me you were sleeping at Marianne's. I don't like being lied to by my own daughter."

"I did sleep at Marianne's."

"Louise!"

"Okay, okay, sorry. Look, tell Lorraine Leon and Travis asked us to go to that party." I have decided to drop them right in it, why the hell not?

"Oh did they now?"

"Yes, and they gave us loads to drink. Like loads. Totally free. Then they had a fight because they were all drunk."

"Oh my," my mother clicks her tongue and taps her slipper up and down. "Well I better go and talk to her then. But really, you should have known better! People can't force you to drink you know!"

"No," I agree, with a loose shrug. "But they can make it seem pretty attractive, can't they?" I close the door on her. I smirk as I head back to my bed with the mug of tea. I wish I could be a fly on the wall now, and listen to her give it to Lorraine. I bet she's trying to blame it all on me.

If I had my way I would stay in my room all day, and creep out at night to make myself some tea and toast and use the toilet. My phone is dead so I plug it in and sit and fear what text messages will or won't come through from Joe. I keep thinking about this Les bloke, someone I barely know, down there in my house. Probably with his feet up on the coffee table, watching TV in my lounge. I have only met him a handful of times, and most of those have been brief and awkward. I don't know what I am supposed to say to him. I don't even want to have to look at him. I just sit on my bed and seethe. It is only the thought of Joe, and how much he must hate me, that drives me from my pit of despair. I don't want Lorraine to leave without telling me if he is okay. So I creep down the stairs when I hear her loud cackling voice in the hallway. She immediately stops laughing and talking and regards me very seriously, as if she is my mother as well, for God's sake. She has her handbag on her shoulder and is on the way out. Mum is behind her, and just at the back I can see Les. He looks sheepish all right. I peer at him briefly, wondering if my original assertions of him looking like Hitler were correct. He is taller than mum, but not big built or stocky like Mick. He looks sort of weedy to be honest. His hair is thin and too long and flops around his face. He flips it about, from one side to the other, and you really just want to scream at him, fucking get it cut, it makes you look like Hitler! And as for the thin little moustache…oh dear Christ. How can I converse with someone like that?

"Finally showing your face, eh?" smirks Lorraine, her bright red lips pouting at me menacingly. I hold onto the handrail and tighten my grip.

"Is Joe okay?" I ask her, because that is all I care about. She raises her tiny little over plucked eyebrows at the question.

"Apart from having a monster hangover and being grounded, yes he's okay thank you. What did you all think you were doing?"

"Travis invited us," I shrug at her, just in case mum has neglected to tell her.

"I know, your mum said, and I'm on my way home to have words with him and Leon, I can assure you of that. But you and Joe are normally so sensible. It's not like you to behave like this!"

"It was all free drink," I tell her, again, just in case mum has not. Lorraine swaps a weary 'kids eh?' kind of look with my mum, who sighs and shakes her head.

"You should know better," Lorraine repeats, wagging a finger.

"Can Joe come over here please?"

"No darling, he's grounded."

"For how long? Well I can come over there then?" I'm not sure, now that I've said it, if I am really brave enough to do this, but the alternative is staying in my room forever, or starting the tedious process of getting to know Les. Lorraine and my mum swap looks again. "Please," I beg, coming down a few more stairs. "We'll do something to make it up to you." I know I'm onto something now, because Lorraine lifts those minuscule eyebrows again and smiles slightly. "Babysitting, tidying up, walk the dog…" I reel off a few possible ideas.

"Well I don't mind if you don't mind Lol," Mum says to Lorraine. I expect she is thinking it will be good to have time alone with Les. They've had a traumatic first morning as a co-habiting couple. "She's just worried about your Joe. You know what they are like. Like sister and brother, eh?" I don't give Lorraine a chance to think it over.

"I'll just get changed, wait for me," I tell her, and thump back up the stairs.

9

Dear World, it feels very strange walking over to Joe's with Lorraine. Like fraternising with the enemy or something. I am wondering as we walk, what age you have to get to before you start to feel on an even level with grown-ups. Seventeen? Eighteen maybe? I must be immature for my age. Well, I know I am. I just have to be near an adult to start feeling like a shy little kid again. Or maybe it is just that the adults I know have that effect on you. Lorraine certainly does. She has an amazing knack of making you feel about three years old. She clips along the pavement in her red patent high heels, clutching her handbag, and looking sideways at me. I am surprised she doesn't fall over, because I bloody would if I wore heels and looked sideways. She must be an expert. Finally she breaks the tense silence.

"What do you think of Les moving in then?"

I am surprised by the subject matter she has gone for. She has never asked for my personal opinions on family matters until now. She is from the 'like it or lump it' school of parenting. "I don't know," I tell her. "Sara's moved out."

"I know. Your mum said. She's in bits about it."

"She'll be back. Probably. She likes to throw a tantrum."

"But not you, eh?" I look at her and she gives me a little smile. "Just give Les a chance yeah?" she says then. "He's a nice bloke, I can assure you of that. I wouldn't let your mother anywhere near anyone who wasn't decent."

I just nod silently, but inside I am both raging and laughing at her. Raging, because what right has she to tell me to give him a chance? As if I wouldn't? If she knew anything about me at all, she would know that I am the least likely person to even give my mother my opinion, let alone throw a fit like Sara has. He could be a fucking axe murderer and I would just keep my thoughts to myself. And laughing, because does she honestly think her statement is reassuring? Considering that she married a bloke who is one step away from a Neanderthal and who treats her three sons like second class citizens compared to Will and Tommy? Christ!

Thankfully we are soon at her house, and that is when the nerves start to kick in big time. Honestly, it is a feeling ten times worse than before an exam. I think of Joe and feel sick. I think of Travis, and him trying to kiss me, and I am very nearly close to vomiting. I keep my eyes down and my head low as we walk up to the front door. Mick is in the front garden bent over a car again. He looks up and wipes his hands on his green overalls. Lorraine stops next to him and lights up a cigarette. She waves her hand at me. "Go on in, he's in there somewhere." I go on towards the open front door and hear Lorraine say to Mick. "It's all right, it's all right, they're just staying in. She'll keep him out of trouble."

I have to step over Tommy in the hallway. He is still wearing his Thomas The Tank Engine pyjamas, and has red jam smeared all over his face. He is lying on his belly, brooming toy cars up and down the hallway carpet. I glance into the lounge, which is darkened, with the curtains closed. This is because Leon and Travis are sprawled out on the sofa next to each other with the TV on. They have closed the curtains so they can see the TV properly. Leon is smoking, with an ashtray on his lap. He is bare chested, just wearing tracksuit bottoms. He barely looks at me, but Travis looks scarily like he is about to get up to greet me. "Joe upstairs?" I quickly ask, pointing weakly to the staircase.

Travis nods at me, and his expression is hard to read. "Yeah," he says, and sinks back into the sofa. I nod and hurry up the stairs. I find myself taking deep breaths outside my best friends bedroom, and wonder how the fuck it has all come to this. Finally I reach out with my clenched fist and rap on his door. "Who is it?" he calls out gruffly.

"Me. Your ex-best friend."

I hear him snort. "Get in here bitch."

I feel a sense of relief and open the door, but my relief turns to concern when I see what he is doing. Joe is sat up at his window, which looks down onto the back garden. He has the window wide open, and is sat there smoking a joint. My brow creases in confusion. "What are you doing?"

He lifts the spliff to his lips and takes a drag. "What does it look like?"

I close the door, remember that they have no locks, and lean against it instead. "Are you insane?" I hiss at him. "Your whole family are in!"

"I'm nearly finished," he shrugs. "You want some?"

"No I don't. I'm in enough trouble as it is, and so are you! Where did you get that from?"

Joe takes another drag, considers the joint done and stubs it out on the windowsill. He then takes the butt and hurls it as far as he can into the garden. I just watch and shake my head, mesmerised by the insanity of him. He slips down slowly from the window, smiles lazily at me and climbs onto the bottom bunk bed, which is his. There are dirty clothes and food wrappers and magazines in the way, but he swipes a hand at them and they all hit the floor. He lies on his back and laces his hands behind his head. "You are seriously freaking me out," I tell him, finally deeming it safe to come away from the door. I sit on the edge of his bed. I suddenly feel the urge to touch him. To hold his hand or something. To tell him how sorry I am. He is just smiling at me, and his eyes look fucked. His right eye is a little bruised and swollen, and there is another, bigger bruise on his forehead. "Where did you get it from?" I ask him again. I am thinking maybe Ryan; because it was him we smoked pot with once before. And I mean once. At the park no less, with our bikes dumped on the ground around us.

"Leon," he tells me.

"What? Why?"

"Owed me," Joe shrugs at me, still smiling sweetly. Oh Christ. I should have known.

"I ought to go down there and tell your mum and Mick!" I say haughtily, and instantly see the alarm jump into his eyes. He sits up and grabs my hand.

"Don't you dare."

"I've told her it was Leon and Travis that asked us to the party," I inform him, in case he doesn't know. "I've told her about all the booze they let us have. They can't just get away with things all the time. Arseholes."

Joe lets out his breath and lies back down again. "It's gonna' kick off down there in a minute then," he sighs. "I would say let's go, but I'm fucking grounded."

"How's your head?" I give him an apologetic smile, which he returns wryly, as he gently fingers the bruise on his forehead.

"Fucking Mick," he says softly.

"I'm sorry mate. I didn't know what else to do. Leon was just standing there, just encouraging you both. No one else cared."

"Don't worry about it," he tells me, with a yawn. "You probably saved me a trip to the hospital."

"Well I'm still sorry." I look around at his room, how he keeps all his things on one side, as if trying to create a physical barrier between him and Will. All his teenager things on one side, and all Will's kid things on the other. Will has a wooden train track laid out across his side, and the top bunk bed is covered in soft toys. "Your mum said you had a bad hangover," I say.

"Well I did. Until, you know." He means the joint. I nod.

"Oh. I see. I'm surprised it doesn't make you sick."

"Must be getting used to it."

This is a comment I really ought to pick him up on, but the time just does not feel right somehow. I think of Mum and Les, and Sara, and experience that immense and heavy sadness again, like falling into a pit. We both jump when we hear the front door slam downstairs. Moments later Lorraine starts screaming. I look at Joe and he shrugs. "Your fault," he tells me, and I am not sure if he is joking or not. I feel strange and uncomfortable, and I have never felt like that around Joe before. The silence between us is weighted with the one word we have not said. Travis.

"Travis was just pissed," I say, hardly able to look at him. "He was just pissed and being an idiot. You didn't need to worry."

"I saw him kiss you."

"He didn't really. Well, he did. But I was just taken by surprise. And anyway, he was just pissed and I don't know why he did it." I lift my hands and drop them uselessly back in my lap. I feel like crying. Joe seems so distant, so cold to me, and I don't like it, I don't understand why. I have this overwhelming urge to lie down next to him and curl into his side, but I can't can I? I can't.

"I don't know why I went for him," Joe says then, and I look at his face, and he is frowning, but not looking at me. His eyes are focused firmly on the wooden slats of the upper bunk bed. We hear Mick join in the shouting downstairs. "You can do what you want," he says. "You can let him kiss you, or whatever."

I don't know what to say to this. I don't want to say anything that might hurt him. I don't know why he attacked his brother either, but I just feel so sorry that I was the cause of all this. "I'm never going to do anything that upsets you," I say quietly, staring at his face, and I mean it. His eyes flick towards mine. He says nothing. I feel tears flood my eyes. My lip is trembling. I simply cannot bear him to be angry with me. Not now.

"You stupid twat," he says with a sigh, and I laugh and cry at the same time. I give in to the urge to be close to him, and pull myself up onto the bed, and lie down next to him, still crying. He drags one arm out from behind his head and wraps it around me, and I cry harder. "What the hell are you blubbing about woman?"

"Just all this," I manage to tell him, holding one hand over both my eyes, trying to halt the leakage. "And bloody Les has moved in. And Sara has left home. And I thought you hated me. You should hate me."

"You haven't done anything wrong, twat-face."

My shoulders shake against his arm with laughter. We lie still for a few moments, listening to the row downstairs. It is mainly Lorraine and Mick, screaming and bellowing in turn. "You're skating on thin ice with me!" we hear Mick shout. We cannot really hear either Leon or Travis, but they must be arguing back.

"Don't you dare speak to me like that!" Lorraine screeches. Joe pulls me closer and closes his eyes. I rest my face against his t-shirt and inhale the sweet smell of the weed he has smoked.

"One step away from throwing you out!" comes another classic from Mick. How many times have we heard that one since he moved in?

"This is the thanks we get!" Back to Lorraine. I am cringing now, and wanting to get out of this crazy house. I have caused this. I should have kept my stupid childish mouth shut. I prop myself up on my elbow and look at the door. The front door has slammed again downstairs, but I have no idea who has stormed out. I glance down at Joe and see that he is asleep. Or passed out.

There are sudden, steady footsteps on the stairs and they are coming towards Joe's door, and I feel a panic seize my heart, because I know, I can fucking *sense* who it is. The door opens and they both walk in, Leon a scowling dark faced menace, and Travis looking stressed and pissed off, and jumpy all at the same time.

"Well isn't this cosy?" Leon hisses at me. I scoot away from Joe, who opens his eyes groggily, but does not move. I lower my feet to the floor. Travis sinks his hands into his pockets.

"Thanks a lot kids," he says to us, but his eyes are on me. "You dropped us right in it there."

"That was my intention actually," I tell him, standing up and crossing my arms. They look at each other in surprise.

"Why?" Travis asks me.

"Because you're a pair of fucking arseholes, that's why. I don't see why we should always get the blame."

They look at each other again. Leon is frowning so deeply I can barely make out his eyes. He spreads his legs a little; his defiant stance, and his eyes shift to Joe, still lying on his bed. "You going to let your little girlfriend talk to us like that eh?"

"She's not my girlfriend," Joe yawns in reply. "And she can say what she likes."

"Last time we invite you losers to a party," Leon says. "You're obviously still just a pair of little kids. Go running to mummy over nothing."

Joe laughs at this. He folds his arms back under his head and giggles away. Leon glares at him silently. Travis is still looking at me. "It was him that attacked me actually," he sees fit to point out, nodding towards Joe.

"Yeah, because he was hammered." I sit back down on the bed then. I don't like the look on Leon's face. I feel the urge to stay close to Joe in case something erupts again. I think, that should be it, they've aired their grievances, now they should go, but they don't, although I can tell that Travis wants to. His gaze keeps shifting sideways to Leon, and then jerking back to me. He is frowning, and seems fidgety. "Is that all?" I ask finally, shrugging at them.

"No that's not fucking all," Leon snaps at me. "I need a word with my brother alone, if you don't mind." He nods towards the door, suggesting that I leave. I raise my eyebrows at him, and glance at Joe.

"I'm not leaving," I say.

"Look, I'm not asking you, I'm telling you," Leon says, sounding frustrated. I realise this is probably the longest conversation he and I have ever had. "We've got important things we need to talk about. Mick has gone out. Now is the time." His eyes are boring into Joe when he says this. I watch Joe struggle up into a sitting position on his bed. He folds his arms over his chest and smiles pleasantly at all of us.

"I'm not leaving," I say again. "If I leave you're just going to beat him up or something!"

"Christ, I'm not!" Leon says with a heavy sigh. "Joe will you tell her?"

"Let her listen," Joe shrugs, "I don't care."

"Don't be stupid, idiot."

"You best go," Travis tells me gently. I wonder if they have all gone mad or something! What the hell is going on?

"I'm not going," I tell them for the third time, and I stare back at Leon and I do not flinch, and for the first time I think to myself, you're not so tough after all, you're just a nineteen-year-old thug who thinks he's a hard man. You're just a kid, still living at home with your mum, even though you hate it. You're nothing. I watch his shoulders drop and he rolls his eyes up into his head. "So you either carry on with me here, or you talk to each other after I'm gone."

"Are you sure?" Leon asks, but he is asking Joe, who just shrugs at him in reply. "Okay then, but don't expect her to be very impressed with you."

"She won't tell anyone," Joe assures him. I frown at him.

"Won't I?"

"No," he tells me seriously. "Swear whatever we say in this room now, you won't repeat to anyone again ever in your life, or me and you can't be friends, okay?"

I am open mouthed and hurt and intrigued all at once. I blow breath out and shake my head at him. "Okay I swear," I tell him. "I'm just gonna' sit here and say nothing. Whatever it is has nothing to do with me."

"She won't tell," Joe tells Leon again, and I can see something between them, something that has never existed there before. Almost a kind of mutual understanding, not quite respect, but something more than the sneering resentment and annoyance that had always passed between them before. Travis just looks resigned to whatever is going on, and he leans against the closed bedroom door and keeps his hands in his pockets. I try hard not to look at him at all.

"Right," Leon says with another sigh. "I've got another address for you." He pulls a scrap of paper out of his back pocket and passes it to Joe. I watch in silence as Joe looks at the paper, nods vacantly, then pushes it into his own pocket. "About nine o'clock tonight, okay?"

"Okay," Joe nods again, and looks briefly at me. I sense he is enjoying this, this secret that they have between them; this new elevated position that he suddenly has with them. Me, I just feel a warning bell of churning dread within my empty belly.

There is an awkward silence as Joe looks at Leon, and Leon looks to Travis, and Travis looks at me, as if he wants to say something, but can't. I just look bewildered, and wait, saying nothing. "Okay," Leon says heavily, and drags something else out from his pocket. It is a small wrapped package and he passes it to Joe. Joe takes it quickly and puts it into his pocket with the piece of paper. Slowly but surely things are starting to add up for me. Not exactly quick, am I World? I give a slight nod of the head, bite down on my lower lip, and wait. "Cool," Leon shrugs at us all, as if we are all on his level now, whatever that is. He looks momentarily relieved, and almost smiles as he stuffs his hands in his pockets and shrugs his wide shoulders. "Cheers," he says, supposedly to Joe, and then he turns to go and nods at Travis. I watch them leave and close the door behind them, and then I turn my steely gaze on Joe, and expect him to shrink and simper beneath it, but he does no such fucking thing.

"Worked it out yet smarty-pants?" he laughs at me, sinking slowly down on his bed again, his eyes partly closed. I shake my head at him. I want to be angry, I want to be dismayed and horrified and disappointed. I stare at him in silence, wanting to feel all these things. I wonder miserably if I even know him at all. I consider simply standing up and walking out of there, not saying a word.

"Not really," I say instead, deciding to play dumb. "Why don't you spell it out for me?"

"Fuck you," grins Joe. "You're not going to tell are you?"

"I think you are insane. I think you have lost your mind completely."

"You don't want to make some money then?"

"What?"

"Come with me. Go halves."

"You're fucking joking. You've lost it!"

"I'm not joking. It's up to you. Come with me and make some money, or just forget all about it and don't tell."

"Don't tell anyone my best friend has turned into a low-life drug dealer?"

"More like a low-life errand boy actually," Joe corrects me with a self-satisfied smirk. I want to hit him.

"Who are you trying to impress?"

"No one."

"Why then? Why do you want to be their errand boy for fuck's sake? Are they forcing you to do this, or something? Haven't you got any dignity?"

Joe sits up then. He sits up hard and fast and thrusts his face towards mine, and his hazel eyes are so intense, so fired up so suddenly that I draw back from him instinctively and yet at the same time, if you can believe this, I feel the undeniable dual urge to both hit him and kiss him. What the hell is that about World? Wanting to hit your best friend at the same time you want to kiss them? "Why not?" he spits at me. "Why the fuck not eh? What else is there in life eh? You're always saying it yourself smarty-pants! Maybe I want to make some money! Maybe I want to have my own money for once, so I don't have to go begging to mum and Mick every time, and they always say no, because they need all the money for fucking Tom and Will! Maybe I want my *own* money. What's wrong with that?"

"You know what's wrong with it," I tell him softly.

"It's not forever," he says, lifting his hands and dropping them. "That stuff they had in the bag. It's a one off. They've never done it before and never will again. But we've got to get rid of it somehow. What are you going to do? Throw it in the river and pretend nothing happened? Or try to make some money out of it? Some serious fucking money."

Joe sighs slowly and lies back down again. I feel like the room is crashing down around me, like the walls are tumbling, brick by brick, such is the heaviness and the suffocation that surrounds and overwhelms me then. I think about the words Joe has spoken, and I think, those are not Joe's words, that is not Joe speaking. It is like Leon has crept inside his soul.

"You don't need to impress your brothers Joe," I tell him, watching his face closely as he shuts his eyes and screws them up tight. "You don't need to be like them. You never have before. You don't need to impress anyone Joe. You're amazing the way you are, don't you know that?"

"Go and look in my sock drawer."

"What? Why?"

"Just do it. Go on."

I wonder if this bastard of a day can get any worse. I get up from the bed and my limbs feel like clogged up pipes. I go to the bedside table and yank open the top drawer. There is a pile of tangled and mismatched socks, but at the back I can see one black sock that is bulging. I pick it up, part of me not wanting to know, part of me utterly hooked on the adrenaline that is swirling through me now. I only have to glance inside the stuffed sock to see that there is a lot of money there. More money than I have ever seen. I look at Joe and he is defiant.

"Plenty more where that came from," he says. I swallow. My throat feels like sandpaper.

"Oh Joe," I say. "I don't want you to do this. I really don't."

"Don't be such a wuss," he rolls his eyes at me. I stuff the sock back into the drawer and shove it back into place. He reaches out and closes his hand around my wrist. "Think about it," he says then, speaking very carefully and slowly. "What the fuck have any of them ever done for us Lou? Think about it. Your family. My fucking family. This shitting place. We can have some fun. Some real fun for once. If anything goes wrong, its Leon and Travis that get caught, not us. It's them that go to jail, or whatever. All we are doing is delivering a parcel, yeah? Delivering a parcel to an address and getting paid. We have no idea what is in that parcel, do we? We're just doing a favour. We're just taking back something for us, for once."

I want to say I have no idea what he is talking about, but the sad thing is I understand every word he has said. It is all up there on my bedroom wall. He is right about two things, I realise that right away. He is right to question what the hell any of them have ever done for us, because it has always been me and Joe, at the bottom, ignored, patronized, put down, pushed aside. Because we don't argue back, and we don't cause scenes, and we don't make trouble for anyone. We just fucking take it, don't we? And he is right about us having some fun, for once.

"How are you going to do it?" I ask him. "You're grounded."

"Sneak out," he shrugs simply. "You up for it?"

"I'm not even grounded."

"Cool then."

"Will it be dangerous?" I cannot believe I am even asking this. I cannot believe I am even anywhere close to considering this utter madness.

"Not at all," he grins at me. "You just knock on the door, or meet them somewhere, and give them their parcel. They give the money. That's it."

"How many times have you done this for Christ's sake?"

"Just once," he says. "Just yesterday. Well, twice technically. There were two places yesterday."

"Why don't they want to do it themselves?"

"They are. Some of it. They just want rid of it as quick as possible. Three of us is quicker."

I bite my lip and sigh. "Where did they get it from in the first place?"

"I don't even know that," replies Joe. "I think they stole it or found it, but they won't say."

"There must be someone out there somewhere who wants to kill them."

"I suppose." Joe looks at me expectantly. "You want to make some money then?"

10

Dear World, I am sat at the kitchen table in my house. I am staring at the fish and chips on my plate. It stares back at me, all fat greasy and pale. I am trying to figure out in my head how many calories there are. I am guessing maybe at least a thousand. Les has bought the fish and chips. Mum is gushing over this, as if buying fish and chips is the most admirable thing a person can do for you. I wasn't even allowed to go to my room with it. I could have taken Gremlin and fed the greasy shit to him. But no. I've got to sit at the table with my insane mother and her weasel-eyed house guest, watching them swap loving looks with each other. I present them with a steely silence that I am childishly determined not to break. My mother utters empty words about us all getting along nicely, and pretends not to notice the filthy looks I give her. As for him, I do not look at him at all. I am not going to be a stroppy bitch like my sister, but I am not going to fawn all over this stranger either. As far as I am concerned, he is a cheeky bastard, and no good is going to come out of any of this. What is she going to do when dad shows up? Hide the bloke under her bed?

I feel resigned to living with this joke of a situation, and push my fat wet chips around my plate with my fork. I am not going to eat any of this shit. I can hear Les gobbling away, and when I inadvertently glance up, I see he has chip grease smeared on his chin, and he laughs at something my mum has said, which is not funny, and he leaves his mouth open when he laughs, and I can see all the chewed up food in his mouth, and I want to kill myself. I get up abruptly, screeching back my chair and walk out of the room.

A perturbed silence follows me up the stairs. I go into my room and close the door. I feel sullen and angry and spiteful and irrelevant. I think of my mother, and I almost wish for Dad to find out about Les. To stand back and watch it all explode around her. To laugh in her face. But the prospect of Dad finding out is actually quite scary. I shiver and throw myself face down onto my bed, and I close my eyes and in my dark mind I can see Joe, and his fucked up eyes. Even though it is completely insane and dangerous, the more I think about it, the more I can understand what he is doing and why. His brothers have never asked for his help before. His brothers have never asked anything of him before, except for him to fuck off. Leon especially, has never needed or desired Joe to exist. Now suddenly he does. He needs him. He asked for his help. This proves to Joe that on some level, Leon trusts him, maybe even values him. I am concerned about him, but I can understand why he is doing it. I am not going with him obviously. I am too chicken, too scared, too childish and afraid. Joe is not afraid of anything, and I don't know why, or how that can be. Look at him. Throws himself at his older brother for a fight he would not have won. Sneaks out from a grounding, risking round two with his mum and Mick, to deliver Class A narcotics to a complete, and undoubtedly shady stranger. It is insane, I think, my face still pressed into my duvet. But he's not afraid to do it, is he? Why isn't he?

Then I think about the way he has been brought up. Lorraine is not one of those cuddly, touchy-feely mothers and she never has been. It has always been fend for yourself in their house. She has always worked, so she has always had to rush out of the door, leaving the kids to it. Secretly, I think she just wanted to get away from them for a few hours. When Joe was little, Leon and Travis would be left in charge. You can imagine the insanity that would follow. She would come home to chaos and a wrecked house. I can remember sneaking quickly out the back door more than once, so that she would not know I was involved. You could hear her shrieking half way down the street. That was her way. Scream, shout, smack, wallop. I have seen my own mother wince on more than one occasion when witnessing Lorraine chastise her sons. Luckily for me, neither of my parents has ever raised a hand to me, or to Sara. People are all different, my mum will repeat this every time I dare to question Lorraine's parenting skills. People are all different, and they all lead different lives, and you cannot hope to understand a person until you have walked a mile in their shoes. That last bit always makes me choke. I don't know how Lorraine manages to walk a mile in her own shoes, let alone me trying it.

I roll over onto my back and stare at the ceiling. I can hear the murmur of chat and laughter coming from downstairs. I try not to think any more about Joe. My mind, and its obsession with potential violence and gore, wants to think up all the many ways this could blow up in his unassuming face. Such as the stranger being a psychotic who takes the drugs, refuses to hand over the money and beats Joe to a bloody pulp when he protests. Or the true owners of the drugs catching up with him, mistakenly thinking this skinny young kid is the one who stole their goods. I press my hands against my eyes, willing away the images of fists and feet and weapons putting an end to my best friends short existence. I am going to have to talk to him again. I am going to have to spell out the dangers to him, the 'what ifs' he obviously has not thought of himself. How long is this going to go on for? How long does it take to get rid of that much cocaine? How the hell are they doing it? Oh Christ, I feel sick just thinking about it.

If I had any kind of mother I would go downstairs and ask to speak to her. I would probably cry in her arms and tell her about it, and she would comfort me and then do something about it. She would sort it all out. But I am beginning to realise that adults are not any better at sorting things out than we are. In fact, dear World most of the time they seem to be even worse at it. I mean, why doesn't my mother speak to my dad honestly about bloody Les? Why doesn't she offer him more money for rent if Les moves in? It's not so much him moving in that enrages and appals me, it's her stupidity and cowardice in not telling my dad. This is his house. He bought it from the council, so he likes to tell anyone who will listen; he bought it from the council. Yay, I feel like saying when he tells this story. Well done. Really proud of you dad. Now he technically has two houses anyway, I bet he tells everyone he sees in the street about it. He moved in with the woman he cheated on mum with, Maria. She already owned her house, so the greedy bastard bought in with her, and now owns half of that one as well as ours. Why does he need two houses I ask you? Why does anyone? Greed and stupidity. I am surrounded by greed and stupidity dear World. You and me both know it.

Anyway, just because he owns our house and mum pays rent to him, he thinks this gives him the right to show up whenever he wants to. He will never ever phone first. Bastard. I have told mum a million times that he can't do that. He can't do that as our landlord and he can't do that as our father. He just can't. When he left, he was all, oh we'll sort something out about the kids, see them every weekend, have them at ours, all that worthless shit. That didn't last long. I've been to Maria's house three times in three years, and I wouldn't go again if you fucking paid me. You would have to tie me up and drag me by the hair. So he shows up here whenever he feels like winding up mum on the pretence of caring about his daughters.

Right, I've had enough of this. I am so wound up I want to punch the wall. I want to pick up every single object I can see in my room and hurl it at the floor. I look at the desk and wonder how it would feel to just swipe it all right off. I have never done that before, but I bet it is fun. I jump off the bed and look at myself in the mirror. I turn sideways and then I turn the other way. I decide there and then to go for a run. It will make me feel better in so many ways. So I get changed into my jogging trousers, sports bra and t-shirt and drag my trainers out from under the bed. I do a few stretches, and then go downstairs.

My mum comes out of the kitchen automatically, tea towel in hand, hopeful expression on face. I totally blank her and go out of the door before she can even think to ask me to take the dog. I start running right away. I used to get embarrassed when I first started. I used to think people would laugh at me, so I would either get up early and run, or do it in the evening just before dark. I don't care now. Now you can see I have lost weight, and I feel proud of that, proud to show it off, and proud to show them how I have done it. I am still doing it. I get to the fields and run around the perimeter. The whole field is empty. The park is deserted. There is no one in sight, and this feels wonderful. I feel the freedom lift my vile mood slightly. It feels good to be running, to be charging along, my feet hitting the earth, totally and utterly alone. My mind starts to clear. The clutter starts to drop away. I lift my knees, and embrace the earth, my feet pounding on it, my arms pumping, my hair flying back from my face. Until I started jogging, I never understood how exercise could make you feel better. It seemed a bizarre concept to me. But I get it now. You feel kind of in tune with your body, with your physical self. I think I've always been ridiculously in tune with my emotional self, but not the physical, not until now, not like this.

I feel and hear my heart pumping, my breath forced around my body, blood careering through my veins. I think about my body as a machine now. I do not accept that my knees ache. I do not allow myself to consider that once around the field is enough. I want to control my body and make it do what I want. It is not going to let me down anymore. I force it on because I own it. I am in the driving seat. I am operating the controls. This brings a crazy smile to my face as I start to run around the field for the third time. I am amazed at how my body does it. I make it do it.

I only stop running because I trip over a fucking brick and go flying into the ground. I am fine. I am worried about twisting my ankle, or some such thing, because if I had to stop jogging for a while, then I would have to eat even less, wouldn't I? But I am fine and nothing hurts. I sit back on my arse and look wonderingly at the brick, and look around to make sure no one saw me fall. There is still no one in sight for miles around. I am panting and my chest is heaving quickly up and down, and now that I have stopped, I can feel a tight gripping pain down the right side of my chest. So I sit back and just breathe, and stare up at the sky, and think okay, maybe that will do. Of course, there is a part of me that says it will not do, so get up and run on. But the pain is getting worse, and I know I can't.

I do feel better though World. It was like every negative thought, every tensed and angry muscle, every piece of sadness, started to fall away as I ran. They just drifted away, they fell off me, they fell out of me, they backed off. I breathe in lungful's of summer air scented by cut grass, and think about going home. Not an attractive idea, but the alternative is staying out here on my own. Could get depressing.

I haul myself to my feet and walk slowly towards home. I am thinking about a large mug of coffee, followed by some mints. I have recently discovered that having packs of mints around when you are dieting is really handy. Next to no calories, and they give you a little rush of energy and make the thought of food go away again. I think about Joe, in his bedroom. I wonder how he is feeling, what he is thinking. I wonder what has been said, if anything, between Travis and him about me. My cheeks flush with warmth automatically at the thought of Travis. I have not really let myself think about what happened at the party. It still scares the shit out of me. I can strongly picture Travis and Leon talking and joking about me. Maybe it was a dare from Leon. I wouldn't put it past him. I shudder. That horrible bastard.

When I get home, my dad's work van is in the driveway.

I want to laugh. I really do. I want to throw back my head and roar with laughter right out there in the street. Okay then. Here we go. Here we go. He must be on his lunch break. He's a painter and decorator and has a couple of lanky lads working for him. I don't want to see him but I have to see this. I just have to.

I open the door and go in, and there is my dad in the kitchen, mug of tea in hand, wearing his paint splattered work trousers and shirt. I look at him and he looks at me, and I wonder as usual what he thinks or feels when he sees me. Because I am sixteen years old and I have yet to work out exactly what I think or feel about him. The only answer I can give you World is not much. Not much at all. When he lived with us, he made me feel small, so I kept out of his way if I could. After he left, I started to feel increasingly shy and awkward at seeing him. Now I realise that I have always felt this way around him, my own dad, like he is a stranger. Like he is a distant relative who shows up from time to time, and isn't really interested in kids, but has to make small talk with you to be polite. That's how it is. He is someone I am perpetually too shy to approach or talk to. He is someone who cares too little to ever ask me what I am doing, what I am interested in, or what I want out of this life. So we skirt uncomfortably around each other, and it is all an avoidance tactic.

"All right?" he says to me with a wink. He always winks. What does this mean? That we are somehow close, or share a secret? It's laughable.

"All right," I say back, and that is usually as far as it goes. My mum is leaning against the kitchen cupboard with her cup of tea. She gives me a strained, wide-eyed look, that I can only imagine is her way of begging me not to drop her in it. I look around and vaguely try to picture where Les could be hiding. It makes me want to laugh. I kick off my trainers and make a fuss of Gremlin, because my dad hates dogs, and would never let us have one when he lived here. I stroke and fondle his long ears, and even go as far as planting a loving kiss on his squashed up nose.

"Ah look at this," says my dad to my mum. "The bleeding dog gets more affection than I do!" This is his little try at humour, so I smile dutifully and head for the stairs.

"Sara is at your dads," Mum says then. I stop and look back.

"Is she?"

"Yes, you know, because me and her had that little fight?" My mum gives me that look again. Ah okay, I see. Dad does not know about Les. Even Sara, in her anger has not dropped Mum in it. I can't see her lasting long there though.

"Popped by to tell your mum," Dad shrugs at me, so I nod back.

"Okay."

"She's getting skinny," my dad says then to my mum, and looks back at me. I frown. This is what he does as well. Talks to you through someone else.

"She's doing ever so well on her diet," Mum says proudly, smiling at me. "I can hardly get her to eat a thing these days! And look, she goes jogging too."

"Bleeding hell," laughs Dad. "Who would have thought it? Right little porker she always was."

"Thanks a lot," I sigh, and start up the stairs.

"He's only joking Lou!" Mum calls up after me. "No one can call you that now, can they?"

I go into my room and resist the urge to slam the door. They can all fuck off and die. Seriously. Fuck off and die. I wonder if Les is hiding in her room, and I want to storm in there and shout at my dad to come and see. Why should I hide their pathetic secrets? I find I am now back at square one. I am seething with rage and indignation and hurt and I am mystified as to why. Why do I let their useless shit bother me? Why does Joe not care about anything? How does he do that?

I lie on my bed and close my eyes and let the anger fill me and consume me. There is no point fighting it or denying it, so I just go with it. I think vile and nasty things about all of them. I imagine my dad's brakes failing on his way home, and his van crashing into a wall, and his paint splattered body flying helplessly through the windscreen. Ouch. But eventually, inevitably I turn the anger on myself. I want to punch myself in the stomach, I want to smash my face into the wall and watch the blood run down. I slide my hands down onto my stomach instead. I search for the rise and the fall. I feel for my ribs. I calm myself down by thinking about fading away.

I hear Dad go an hour later. He calls goodbye up the stairs. I think of Les, crawling out of his hiding place. Mum comes up to see me. She looks pained and anxious and guilty, and so she should. I give her a withering look. "It's not for long," she tells me. "I know what you are thinking, and you are right, I should not be putting you in this position. But Les has lots of places to look at, you know, new flats. It's not for long Lou, it's really not worth upsetting your dad."

"Why don't you just tell him? Why can't you have a boyfriend move in if you want to?" I sit up and ask her. I have a blinding headache coming. "He left you for Maria. He cheated on you with her." I see the hurt in her eyes, but I cannot undone what I have said, and for God's sake, I cannot undo that it even happened, but it did. He did it. Plus, in case she has forgotten, he left her in the shit financially. I remember her sat at the kitchen table, head in hand, staring down at her own workings out on a notepad as she struggled to figure out how to pay all of the bills herself. I can remember us all hiding behind the sofa's in the lounge, when the bailiffs turned up one afternoon. How can she have forgotten that? How can she not hate him like I hate him?

"Lou," she says softly. "You know your dad."

"No I don't actually," I argue with her. "I don't know him at all. Never have."

"What does that mean?"

"You work it out. Well if you want to live your life this way, with him controlling you, with him acting like you're still his, when it was him that walked out on you, then that's fine, you do that." I lie back down and stare at the ceiling. "Just don't expect me to congratulate you."

"You think I should talk to him about Les?" She is leaning against the door frame. She looks tired and old and frightened. I cannot understand how people can live their lives like that.

"Nothing to do with me is it?" I retort in anger. "None of you care what I think. Just do what you like."

"Oh Lou, it is never as easy as that. I wish it was, but it is so much harder than you know."

"I don't know anything," I tell her. "Hadn't you better tell him he can come out now?" My mum sighs and goes out of the room, closing the door quietly behind her. I roll over and find my pen and start to spread swearwords and insults all over my bedroom wall.

11

Dear World, I wake up desperate to see Joe, to talk to Joe, to see how he is and tell him about the farce I am surrounded by. He will make it seem funny and we will laugh about it. But I do not feel very well. My head is killing and my stomach hurts. I know this is because I need to eat something. I am not stupid World, in case you were beginning to wonder. So I make myself some breakfast once I am dressed. I decide to go for a huge coffee, an apple and a yoghurt. The yoghurt is always a good plan, because it comes in a pot which tells you the calorie content on the side. I like this information. It makes me feel secure. I eat my breakfast in the kitchen alone. I am assuming Mum and Les are still asleep. Gremlin trots in for some fuss, so I decide to take him with me to thank him for his loyalty. I think about Marianne, and decide to call her or visit her after I've seen Joe.

My day mapped out in my head, I leave the house quietly, glad of the peace and glad that I do not have to see or speak to anyone. The morning outside is warm but fresh. I can tell it is going to be a scorcher once it gets going though. I eat my apple on the way around to Joe's house. I am hoping Travis and Leon will not be there, and I am immediately reassured by the absence of the red Fiesta. They are usually together, so there is no reason to suppose that only Leon is out.

As I approach the front door, I see Will and Tommy playing with cars on the doorstep, and I can hear the screaming from within the house. I stop and look around, and imagine the neighbours all hushed and waiting inside their own little boxes, rolling their eyes and whispering about the family next door. Will and Tommy look quietly shocked, but they keep playing, they keep pushing their little cars up and down on the doorstep. Will is in his school uniform, and has his book bag and lunch box sat neatly next to him. They have two pieces of wood propped against the step, and they are using them as ramps, so the cars go up one ramp onto the step, across to the other end and then down the second ramp. They do not look up at me or speak to me as I walk up to the door, where I stop again, and listen.

"You stupid useless bastard, get your bleeding hands off me!" That is Lorraine screeching. She sounds madder than hell, like she can't even breathe.

"What's your fucking problem? You're just never happy are you? Miserable bitch! You're just never happy!"

"Get your bloody hands off me before I call the police!"

I decide to go in. I am scared for Joe. I hate and loathe Mick, and Lorraine scares the shit out of me, but I make myself be brave, just like I did yesterday, and I step over the kids, pulling the dog in with me, and walk into the lounge. They stop screaming when they see me. The lounge is all messed up, furniture is overturned and it looks like someone has hurled a cup of tea at the wall. Mick has Lorraine by the throat, pinned to the wall, but she looks anything but scared, and part of me doesn't blame Mick for not letting her go. I can imagine those talon like fingernails slicing into his face the second he does.

"What do you want?" Mick yells at me. I look past him, to where I can see Joe in the kitchen. He is standing next to the sink, where it looks like he has been assigned washing up duties again. He looks blank and cold. Mick releases Lorraine and she immediately socks him in the chin. He staggers back, and she makes a run for it, past me and out of the house, slamming the door shut behind her. I spin around to the window, and see her marching towards her car, head held high, dragging Tommy and Will along with her. I hear a thud and spin back to Mick. He has started to kick the hell out of the kitchen door. I watch him in shock, my mouth hanging open as he lands strike after strike on the thin wood, and bits of it splinter off and land on the carpet. My eyes meet Joe's, and I can see the problem here. He is on one side of Mick, and I am on the other. I swallow, and take one step forward, thinking I am probably swift enough to nip around him, grab Joe and get the hell out of the back door.

But I don't have time to do this, because Mick gives up on the door, hurls a shelf loads of DVD's onto the floor and reels back into the kitchen towards Joe. "Get out!" he bellows, obviously wanting to be alone. "Go on get out! Get the fuck out, all of you!" Joe does not move. He seems rooted to the spot. Mick launches himself at him, grabs him by his t-shirt and hauls him out of the kitchen. "Get out I said! Get out!" Joe stumbles towards me. I snatch up his hand and pull him towards the front door.

"I'm grounded," he mumbles at me.

"I don't think you are now," I tell him, and shove him out of the house.

I pull the door shut behind me. Joe is just standing there in confusion. I push him again to get him moving. "Come on let's go to the park or something," I say, and propel him forward. He finally starts moving. He drops his shoulders with a sigh, puts his hands into his pockets, and walks. "Jesus Christ, someone should call the police," I say to him, glancing back at his house. "What was all that about?"

"They went out last night to the pub," he says, looking sideways at me with a frown on his face. "They got hammered. They started fighting when they got in, because he caught her flirting with another bloke or whatever."

"They've been fighting all night?"

"No they passed out, then started again this morning."

"Bloody hell Joe."

"Nothing new," he shrugs in reply. "Weekly occurrence, isn't it?"

"I don't know how you put up with it."

"Neither do I." I look at him and he grins at me.

"Well just wait till I tell you what's going on at my house," I say, as we head to the park with Gremlin.

"Oh yeah?"

"Oh yeah, I think it might trump yours."

"No fucking way."

"Yes fucking way."

We arrive at the park on the fields, and slink over to the bottom chamber of the slide. I let the dog off the lead, and we duck our heads and go inside the little hut. Joe sits down on the floor with his back against the wall. I sit on the tiny little bench and start to giggle. "What?" he asks me.

"Just got the image of your mum socking Mick in the chin in my head, that's all."

"Was pretty funny."

"Where are Leon and Travis?"

"Stayed out last night. You know, working." He looks at me and raises his eyebrows. I nod.

"Oh, right. Much more to get rid of?"

He shrugs. "Fair bit."

"Jesus, your family are unbelievable."

"Tell me about yours then. Make me feel better."

"Okay, okay." I settle back on the bench, resting on the wall, and cross one leg over the other. I watch Joe pull a small tin out of his back pocket, and realise that he is going to roll a joint. I hesitate for a moment, and then I think; what the hell, he deserves it, so I say nothing. "Okay, so you know Les has moved in, and Sara has moved out?"

"Yeah, mum said. How's it going?"

"Hilarious to be honest. I can't stand to be around either of them. It's all got to stay a secret because of Dad. I go out for a run yesterday, then when I get back, Dad's fucking there!"

Joe looks at me with widened eyes. "Ooh!"

"Yeah, you know how he just turns up like that? I go in and Les is nowhere to be seen. Hiding somewhere, the gutless prick."

"Oh my God, what are they playing at?"

"Sad, isn't it? So dad leaves, none the wiser. I say to Mum why don't you just tell him? He's not your husband anymore. It shouldn't matter. Not that I think much of Les, but you know."

"Your Dad's a cunt," Joe says and I smile at him.

"Thanks. He is, isn't he?"

"He's got Maria but your mum can't have anyone?"

"Well, exactly. I think she should tell him. I'm going to give them a week then tell him myself."

Joe is spreading tobacco along a cigarette paper. He roars with laughter at me.

"Are you really gonna' do that?"

"Why not? I would love to see the look on his face."

"But he won't like, try to kick you all out or something?"

I shrug at him. "Probably. Who cares? I don't want to live in his house anyway. My mum should just find somewhere else to rent."

I watch Joe run his tongue slowly and carefully along the sticky edge of the cigarette paper, before adeptly rolling the joint up. "But do you think Les is all right?" he asks me, his eyes on his work. "Or do you think he's going to be an arsehole?"

"I don't know," I sigh. "He seems okay every time I've seen him. Sort of weedy really. Seems harmless. Not like Mick. Not yet anyway."

Joe snorts at me. "Yeah well I remember him being a prick from day fucking one, so you'll probably be okay." Joe pulls a lighter out of his pocket, holds it to the end of his creation, and inhales deeply as the joint lights up. I lean back against the wall and watch him lazily. I wonder what time it is. Joe pulls his knees up and rests one arm across them. He seems thoughtful for a moment, lost.

"Why do you think your mum stays with him?" I ask then, watching him carefully. "When he does stuff like that to her?"

"Oh don't worry, she gives as good as she gets. She starts it half the time."

"I know that, but you know, it's not right is it? It's not how marriages are meant to be. It's not normal married behaviour to grab your wife by the throat and all that." Joe lifts his gaze to mine and holds the joint out to me. I don't know what to do for a moment, so I just make a face at him, so he knows that I am thinking. He waits, saying nothing, while I make up my mind. Finally, I lean slowly forward and take it from him. He wraps his other arm around his knees.

"Mick is like her match," he says to me. "They're exactly the same, if you think about it. Act now, think later. Get mad, lash out. Shout and scream the place down. They fucking love it don't they?"

"I don't understand why." I take a long drag on the smoke.

"It's just the way some people are," he shrugs. "It's why it didn't work out with my dad. Because they were too different."

"But I thought they say opposites attract?"

"I don't know. But he wasn't up to it. She obviously wanted someone who would stand up to her and fight her back." I hold the joint back out to Joe and he takes it from me.

"Weird," I say, resting my head back on the wooden wall behind.

"Messed up," Joe agrees. "I thought that was what women like. The bastards and all that."

"I don't!"

"Well not you obviously. You're some kind of freak."

I sit up indignantly, but Joe is grinning at me. The wall is too hard, my back is aching, and my head is getting fuzzy and tired. I slip down to the floor and lay on my back, with my legs hanging outside the hut. When Joe passes me the joint again I take it without thinking. "Do you remember that time the neighbours called the police on them?" I ask him, blowing out smoke and watching it drift slowly up to the wooden ceiling.

"Oh yeah," says Joe, nodding. "We were what? About twelve?"

"Think so. And it was Leon that got arrested!"

"Shit yeah!" Joe exclaims, smiling a wide amazed smile, as he begins to remember. "It was New Year's Eve, wasn't it? All your family were around, and Mum and Mick got into a fight in the kitchen about something. Me and you were out there with the phone I got remember?"

"How can I forget?" I ask him, laughing. "You were so chuffed you got a bloody phone for Christmas at last. You made me sit and listen while you showed me all the amazing things it could do!"

"Shut up! I felt so embarrassed when they started fighting right in front of you."

"My parents were just the same mate, remember?"

"Oh yeah. Fights or silence, right?"

"Yep."

Joe takes the joint and lies down next to me. We are both flat on our backs, giggling and staring at the ceiling, which is covered in abusive graffiti, some of which is our own work. "We just sat at the table, trying not to look at them," he says softly beside me. I can see it in my head like it was yesterday.

"She slaps him one. He slaps her back, then they start really grabbing each other, until Leon runs in."

"Yeah, he grabbed the frying pan and clocked Mick over the head with it. Jesus Christ there was blood everywhere. He had to have eight stitches."

"And the police turned up."

"And arrested Leon. Mum and Mick told them to."

I turn my head and look at the side of Joe's face. "Joe, I've never really thought about it much until now, but you do know that is really disgusting don't you?" I watch as Joe nods back at me. "He was about fourteen then? He was just trying to protect his mum. I've never ever felt sorry for Leon before, but thinking about it now, that was pretty harsh on him."

"He's hard to feel sorry for."

"Do you think your mum and Mick ever feel sorry about that? Letting him get taken away, when it was them fighting in the first place? I couldn't live with myself."

Joe snorts again. "They always think they're right," he replies. "Doesn't matter what you say or do. Doesn't matter if you prove them wrong or whatever. Neither of them are ever fucking wrong, ever. So no, I don't think they would ever feel guilty about that."

"Madness," I say.

"I'm really feeling messed up," Joe says quietly, and lifts his hands up to his face. He presses them down onto his eyes and groans slowly and softly under them. "Are you?"

"Yeah, a bit."

"I think I made it too strong."

"I think you did."

"I feel a bit sick."

"Me too."

"Just lie still," Joe advises. I have closed my eyes too. I close them and the darkness of my own mind surrounds me tightly. It is a relief. I do feel sick. I feel really really wrong. I try to fight it. I do what Joe said and just remain still. I feel totally and utterly detached from everything, like I am physically floating alone, separated from him, and the hut, and the hot July morning. In the end I have no choice but to open my eyes, roll onto my belly and vomit spectacularly. Most of it lands on the grass outside the hut. I am dimly aware of Joe patting me on the shoulder, and then on the back. "Sorry," he is saying. "Sorry mate."

"Ah, that feels better now."

"Sorry mate, I'm such an idiot."

I drop my head onto my arm and close my eyes and just breathe in and out nice and slowly. My stomach is empty and growls accordingly. But my head is already feeling clearer. I am coming back. "Bloody hell," I mutter. "You're trying to kill me."

"I made it too strong," Joe repeats pathetically, rubbing at my back with his hand. I can sense his sadness strongly. I laugh at him.

"Don't worry about it."

"I'm such a twat. They're all right about me, aren't they?"

I want him to lighten up. I want him to laugh. So I take the piss out of him, which usually works. "What, that you're gay?"

His hand drops away from me quickly. "I am not fucking gay!"

"All right, I'm only joking." I lift my head and look at his face. "Calm down you freak."

"Well I'm not! Fucks sake."

"Well I know that, don't I?"

"Do you?"

"What?" I am so, so confused.

"Nothing," he snaps at me, and sits up. He rakes his fingers back through his hair and leaves them there. He looks totally wrecked.

"Sorry," I say from the floor. Then; "I think I better go home."

"Oh no, don't." Joe looks back at me, biting at his lip. "Stay."

"Okay, okay," I say, and I reach out and pull him back down by his arm. He lets me and I snuggle into his side, like the other day on his bed. I close my eyes and feel the sleepiness rushing in. As I drift away, I am thinking about everything, you know, how *everything* can just pass through you all at once? Images, and memories, thoughts and feelings, and I feel pretty numb, so that is all okay, and I tighten my hold on Joe's arm, and I am warm and fuzzy all over as he presses his lips down on the top of my head, and I want to tell him that he is the one constant thing, the one thing that means anything to me, the one person that has never let me down or saddened or sickened me, the only one person who gets me, and that I love him. But I cannot speak. I open my lips very slightly, but nothing comes out.

12

Dear World, I have not written to you for the last two weeks, and I can't really tell you why, except for that I didn't have much to say. Maybe I thought I was going to be all right on my own. But things are still concerning me World, and my wall is still overflowing with it all, so if you could bear to listen a little longer, I will fill you in.

So guess what? I now weigh eight and a half stone, and I am a size ten. This is like a miracle to me. This is like a dream. A fantasy. Something I have yearned for my entire life, yet never believed would truly happen. My mum seems pleased when I tell her I have reached my goal weight and size, and she ruffles my hair and tells me how beautiful I am, and how proud she is of me. But she looks anxious when I tell her I really, really need new clothes again. She even rolls her eyes and lets out this big heavy sigh. It's as if she expects me to go around in trousers that keep falling down. Tops that hang off me like tents. How would she like that? She says she will have a word with my dad about some money, because she has none.

In the end though, I don't need either of their money. Joe takes me shopping in town, and we drag Marianne along for the fun. She always has money, but never seems to want to buy anything except music and books. Joe shoves me into New Look and stands about awkwardly, telling me to hurry up and choose something. I choose two new tops, both closer fitting than I would ever have dared to buy before, and a short denim skirt, and some khaki coloured shorts. I try them all on with Marianne, and for the first time in my life, when I look in the mirror in the changing room, I honestly, genuinely like what I see. I smile, and Marianne smiles at me smiling. "You look lovely in all of them," she tells me, and I feel tremendous. I feel on top of the world. I feel like I was right. Everything is all right now that I am slim.

I mean, it should be shouldn't it World?

Joe insists I have all of them. He pays the girl at the till with cash. I swap looks with Marianne, and she just grins. She knows what he's up to for his brothers, but typically, she gets off on the thought of the danger and thinks it's all cool. I thank him with a kiss on the cheek, and we all link arms and head to a café for a milkshake. Joe pays again, and Marianne spends most of the time fiddling with her phone and making us repeat the parts of the conversation she has missed.

After that we wander down to the quay, and this time Marianne puts her hand in her pocket and buys us all an ice cream. All the schools break up today, so we are reminded that this is the last time for six weeks that we will have all the parks, the fields and so on to ourselves. Soon enough there will be screaming brats and stressed out parents in our way wherever we go. Joe groans that he will be expected to watch Tommy and Will even more, and asks us to remind him he needs to be home by four o'clock at the latest, as his first babysitting duty commences at that time. We determine we must enjoy this last day of total freedom. "We'll do whatever it takes!" Marianne informs us brightly. Only six weeks left now until we go back to school. It's a horribly grim thought and drapes me in a momentary cloak of depression.

Marianne invites us back to her house, so my mood lifts again in curiosity. As usual, her parents are not at home. While she puts the kettle on to make us all a cup of tea, Joe spreads his cigarette papers out on the large kitchen table, and starts to roll a joint. "Yippee, great idea," Marianne enthuses. I say nothing. I think he has been getting his little tin out far too much lately, but who am I to tell him this? He has a lot he wants to escape from, I guess. He has a lot he wants to block out. We take our cups of tea out to the garden. Marianne grabs a packet of chocolate chip cookies and brings these too. She leads us down to the summerhouse, which is beautiful. "I could live in here," I tell her, as we pull out the deck chairs and set them up inside.

"I've kind of adopted it lately," she grins. She has certainly put her teenage stamp on it, I think, as I look around. There are posters stuck on the walls, and she has shoved all her dad's packets of seeds and gardening tools into a cardboard box on the floor. She has set up a little radio and she stands and fiddles with this, while Joe sinks into a chair and lights his joint.

"I could pay you rent," I say, sitting down next to Joe and gazing around me. The summerhouse is gorgeous; it is painted white, and looks like a little log cabin. Marianne laughs, finds a station she likes on the radio, and passes us our teas. "I am not joking," I tell her. "I really could. When the shit hits the fan at my house, I am moving in here, I'm telling you."

"Me too!" agrees Joe, smiling widely.

"We won't even tell you," I go on. "You'll just come down here one day and find us here. We'll claim squatter's rights and everything. You'll never be able to get rid of us."

"I won't mind that," Marianne says, shrugging her tiny shoulders. She has been brave enough to ditch the long sleeves today. She would have melted in this heat. She is wearing tiny black shorts, and a deep purple vest top. The scars on her arms stand out like tiny white and pink flecks, like her skin is mottled and covered in veins. I try not to look too long, but there is one new one on her right wrist that looks pretty nasty. The scabs are huge. She seems happy though, I think, looking at her face. She seems fine. Like nothing in this world can touch her. "I'd like the company," she tells us, and then she holds her cup of tea out to me, indicating that we clink cups. I oblige, and Joe holds his out too. "To you, Lou," Marianne says sweetly. "Well done on the new you."

"Yeah, well done," Joe agrees with a snort. "Though I still say you looked fine before."

I shake my head at Marianne. "Yeah, right."

"Well I thought that too," she says, "but it's what Lou thinks and feels. That's what important. It doesn't matter if other people tell you that you look great, does it? If you don't believe it yourself." I nod in agreement. Joe makes a face at us, drags for the third time on his joint and passes it my way. I take it.

"So this is a celebration?" he asks, sitting back in his chair, looking very chilled out and relaxed.

"Yes I think it is," replies Marianne, her eyes on the spliff and me. "A celebration of Lou's hard work."

"Well I think you're both stupid if you really believe any of that shit matters," Joe says to us. Marianne frowns at him and crosses her thin little arms.

"It matters to Lou," she tells him.

"But it doesn't really matter," he argues. "You know, in the grand scheme of things, that's all I'm saying. I think Lou looks great, yeah, but I thought she looked great before as well. I'm not going to encourage her to go along with all that superficial shit."

"I am here you know," I speak up, exhaling, and passing the joint onto Marianne.

"Not if you get any thinner," says Joe. I laugh at him, but I do feel slightly annoyed at him really. It's like he's pissing on my celebration, making a mockery of my achievement.

"Oh Joe," Marianne sighs, smiling lazily at him, and evidently enjoying her turn with the joint very much indeed. "We can't expect you to understand, being a male. You can't possibly understand what girls have to put up with."

"Oh yeah, like what?"

"The whole society that surrounds us! Everything! It's all geared towards looks and sexiness, isn't it? For girls. All the magazine, all the TV shows, the pop stars, everything. You're made to feel fat if you're any bigger than any of them."

Joe gives her a look of pure contempt and drinks his tea, shaking his head slowly. "Crap," he mutters.

"No, she's right," I butt in. "It is like that, you know. It's not like that for boys. You don't have to care what you look like."

"Neither do you! You don't *have* to."

"Oh he doesn't understand does he?" Marianne touches my bare knee with her little pale hand and smiles at me as if we share a secret.

"No, he doesn't understand."

"You're both so stupid," Joe leans back in his chair and tells us. He has his legs crossed at the ankles, and I look him up and down. He is wearing old jeans with grass stains around the knees and a Rolling Stones t-shirt that he's had since he was about fourteen.

"How are we stupid?" I ask.

"You're stupid if you think any of that stuff matters. All this weighing yourself every ten minutes, and starving yourself just so you can be a fucking size ten? What's that about you moron? You're you! It doesn't matter what anyone else thinks, you loser." The scorn that he drips onto me is never-ending and vicious and I can't help but love him for it. "Idiots," he tells us again. "Brainwashed. Think you're modern feminists, but you're not, you're sheep!"

Marianne stands up for me. I don't have to say a word. She launches a counter attack in her deadpan, emotionless voice, staring Joe right in the eye and refusing to release him. "It's not her fault," she says, neatly excluding herself from his insults. "She's a product of this male dominated, consumerist society. Look at every ideal that has ever been forced upon her, from Barbie dolls, to princesses in fairy tales, to all the famous people who are all skinny. Go to your mums shop now Joe. Look at the covers of the celebrity magazine. So and so and their magical weight loss! Diet shame! Who's lost and who's gained? People scrutinising every pound they lose or gain. Cut her some slack Joe. It's hammered into girls from the moment they are born. *It matters what you look like.* Boys can roll in the mud, and have torn clothes, and get their food all over their faces, but girls can't, because *it does matter what you look like.* Bollocks if you think any different."

Joe raises his eyebrows in calm surprise, looks to me, and starts to laugh. I start to laugh too. I can't help it. "I'm not saying you're not wrong," he tries to speak over his own giggling. "I'm not saying I don't agree with you on that."

"Shut up then," Marianne tells him curtly. "Don't try to have opinions on things you don't understand."

"I just don't want you to go along with it," he tells her, his shoulders still shaking with laughter. Marianne is smiling silently. "Don't fall for it!"

I am laughing so much, and I am not really sure why, or what at, that I lean back too far in my deck chair and the stupid thing suddenly collapses under me. I hit the floor with a bang, and they stare at me in amazement, before bursting into hysterical laughter. "What a bunch of freaks we are!" I say to them from the floor, where I am so weak from laughter that I have no chance of getting back up again.

"Speak of yourself!" Joe yells at me.

I point a finger at him. "You and your drugs you fucking stoner!" I point at Marianne, "you and your cutting, and me and my weight obsession. Bunch of freaks!"

"She's right," Marianne is smiling at Joe and nodding. The joint is on its way around again, and she opens the cookies up as well.

"I'm surprised we're not beaten up on a daily basis at school," I manage to croak, trying to pull myself together.

"Me too," says Marianne, holding out the cookies to me. I take one, thinking oh what the hell, it won't suddenly make me fat again. I am ravenous. I get onto my knees, give up on standing, or sorting the chair out, and eat my cookie.

"We should be dead meat every day," Joe agrees with me.

"It's only because of your family," I tell him. "Everyone knows how hard they are. No one will mess with you because of them."

"True," he nods. "That's one thing to thank them for I suppose."

I stay where I am on the floor. I realise I seem to be down here a lot of lately. It just seems easier that way. I finish my tea, take two more cookies from Marianne, and tell myself it is a reward for fitting into my wonderful new size ten clothes. The warmth of satisfaction fills me again, and I feel giddy, and girlish, and brimming with happy confidence. I know deep down that Joe is right. It is superficial to care about such things. It is sad to want to be like everyone else. But it is easy for him to say. He has good genes, looks wise. He has always looked good, damn him. Plus, he's a boy. He doesn't know what it's like to look in the mirror and see every little flaw. He doesn't know what it's like to be name called for being fat by your own stinking family. I feel a closeness to Marianne then, which I have never experienced before. I want to be alone with her, even. I want Joe and his good looks to sod off and leave us alone. She understands. She's tiny and skinny, but she is odd looking, and she cuts herself up, and I don't really understand why or what sadness drives her to do it.

I roll onto my side, and find myself gazing up at her strange, calm little face. I think we ought to get a bit drunk one night and have a conversation. Take things a little deeper. Right now is not a good time though. I feel sleepy again. I put my head down on my arms, and close my eyes, and listen to the conversation going on between Joe and Marianne.

I wake up suddenly when one of them kicks me in the backside. They start giggling immediately. I roll onto my back and glare at them. "You fell asleep," Joe tells me. He is on his feet; hands on hips and grinning down at me like an idiot. Marianne is stood next to him, looking even tinier from where I am lying on the floor.

"Really?" I ask, hoping my tone is as laced with sarcasm as I intend it to be. I feel groggy and light-headed. "Was I?"

"Been out for ages," Marianne giggles. "We thought we better leave you to it. You obviously needed the kip!"

"It's the lack of calories," Joe says, faking concern, nodding his head at Marianne. I roll my eyes and sit up.

"Shut it idiot. You could have left me alone."

"I need to go," he replies. "Back to look after the little shits, remember?"

I groan again, feeling rushed and irritable. "Is it that time already?"

"Nearly."

"Okay, okay." I haul myself slowly to my feet and pick up my shopping bag from the floor.

"You don't have to come too," Joe points out. "I'm just telling you I got to go."

"No, it's okay, it's okay, I'll help you," I say with a yawn, and we head out of the door together, while Marianne remains inside the summerhouse. "What else am I gonna' do? Go home?"

"Bye Marianne," Joe calls back to her. "Thanks a lot."

"Oh yeah, thanks," I say over my shoulder. She just watches us go, and nods her head once. It is not until I am on the front driveway that I realise what I bitch I have just been. Why didn't we ask her to come too? I flick my hand out at Joe, slapping him on the arm.

"Ow! What was that for?"

"Forget it," I say grumpily. I look back at the house as we leave. Why didn't I stay with her? God, I am a bitch. I could have stayed with her. Oh Christ. I decide to chat to her properly next time I see her. Or maybe text her later. I remember my thought about getting a bit pissed and grilling her about a few things, and I nod to myself. I am definitely going to do this. I am going to make more of an effort with her. She's actually pretty cool.

"Good day, wasn't it?" Joe says, as we start across the sun-parched fields towards his house. He links his arm through mine and I swing my New Look bag back and forth as we walk.

"Yeah," I grin. "It was a really good day. Thanks so much Joe, for the clothes."

"You're welcome Carling. You look good in them."

"You ought to spend some of the money on yourself though. You're the one earning it." He looks at me and rolls his eyes and shakes his slim shoulders with a little laugh.

"That's true."

"It doesn't scare you yet? Not at all?"

He looks down at the ground as he kicks along. "Not really, no."

"I don't know how you do it."

"I just get on with it," he grins at me, as if he is talking about mowing the lawn, or washing the car or something.

We turn into his road, and walk slowly up to his house. I am not relishing the thought of helping baby-sit Tommy and Will, but I am less keen on going home. Sara is not at Dads anymore. I knew that wouldn't last long. They are just as fiery and outspoken as each other. She has moved in with her boyfriend Rich, who she has been going out with for nine months. Mum and dad are both concerned and angry about this, and so poor Les is practically living under the bed. I just can't be witness to it World, I just can't!

We are grinning and feeling stupidly warm and fuzzy and at ease as we open the front door and go into the hallway. But almost instantly, that feeling changes. There is something wrong. My body knows it, and Joe's body knows it too. There are four silent faces staring at us from the lounge. Tommy and Will are nowhere in sight. Joe and I hesitate in the hallway, our smiles falling away, our eyes meeting, our bodies stiffening with caution.

It is Mick that moves and speaks first. He gets up from the sofa where he has been sat rigidly beside Lorraine. Leon and Travis are behind the sofa, Leon looking shifty and nervous, and Travis even more so. I feel the urge to reach out and hold Joe's hand.

Lorraine rises from the sofa behind Mick. Her face is pinched and scowling, her eyes are blazing. She cannot wait to explode. Mick thrusts his hand towards Joe and I in the hallway where we have frozen. We can see his open palm is full of what look like scrunched up fag ends. A horrible realisation floods me then. I feel my skin turn cold. I do reach out for Joe. I slip my hand around his arm, just above his elbow.

Mick's wrinkled up, bashed in face is a mask of barely contained rage. "Are these yours?" he demands.

13

World, for a moment or two it feels like time stands still, and not in a good way. I often wish I could freeze time, pause it so that I can catch up, catch my breath, but this isn't the kind of moment anyone would want paused, or dragged out. This is one of those moments you want to end as quickly as possible and never have to relive again. Joe does not answer Mick's question. Instead he takes a small step back towards the door that we have closed behind us. I look at his face and I can see he is shitting himself. Mick is holding a whole handful of the roaches Joe has been throwing out of his bedroom window. Mick looks wild. He comes forward. He thrusts his hand towards Joe's startled face. "I said are these yours!"

I look from Mick to Joe, starting to panic now. Joe nods his head ever so slightly. Lorraine is right behind Mick. I glance past her towards Leon and Travis, who are keeping quiet, just watching. Mick pulls his hand back and sniffs the ends. He narrows his eyes slightly. "Not just fag ends are they?" he barks at Joe. Joe has his back flat against the door now. His hazel eyes are getting wider by the second.

"Are they joints Joe?" Lorraine snaps then, coming up beside her husband, shaking her head at her son, as if daring him to say they are. Joe says nothing. He looks down, away from her accusing face, and he scratches at the back of his neck.

Lorraine's eyes shift to me. "Lou? Are you going to help fill us in?" I don't know what to say. I start to shrug my shoulders, but think better of it, and just look down at the floor instead. "They are aren't they?" she goes on. She jerks her head back towards Leon and Travis, lurking in the background. "Now we've grilled these two already. They say this is nothing to do with them. We found these in the back garden, Joe. Tommy was collecting them up and putting them in his dumper truck."

At the mention of his precious baby son, Mick's eyes widen in anger, and he folds his fist over the roaches and licks his lips slowly. He looks like he can't decide what to do first. Like there are a couple of possible solutions that would make him feel better right now, but he can't choose one quick enough. He lifts one hand momentarily and touches his own forehead, glancing down, almost as if he is attempting to compose himself. "Have you been smoking weed in your bedroom and throwing the butts out the window?" he asks, not looking at Joe. Joe swallows. Scratches his neck again. Looks at his mum. Looks down. He knows he cannot win here. He knows this is bad. I watch his nervous eyes flick towards his brothers, as if pleading them to step in and say something, but we both know that they won't.

"Joe," Lorraine says the word clearly and carefully. Her hands are planted on her hips. Her eyes are fixed on Joe in a stern and motherly way that traps him in her eye line, forcing him to look her in the eye. She knows he cannot lie to her face and she is using this to full advantage. "Tell the truth. Have you been smoking weed up there and throwing the butts out the window?"

Joe finally drags his gaze down to the floor again as he mumbles his almost incoherent answer. "Yeah."

"Where my fucking kids can play with them?" Mick roars, rushing forward then, coming at us with his fists up. I move back, nearly stumbling over my own feet, and Joe cowers against the door, ducking at the same time, and Mick's fist catches him on the back of the head. He crouches down, against the door, arms over his head, fearing more. I stare at Mick, and Lorraine in disgust and horror, but they look resolute and strong, and not embarrassed. Lorraine merely puts a hand on Mick's back, and he stops at that, but leans over Joe, shaking his head from side to side and pointing a finger at him. "You're smoking cannabis up there? You fucking little shit!"

I am close to tears. I look desperately to Leon and Travis, begging them with their eyes to stop this and help their brother, but they remain silent witnesses in the background. Leon has his arms crossed. He looks stern faced, but calm. Travis looks like he would rather be anywhere else in the world right now. Guilt is splashed all over his reddening face.

"Kitchen!" Mick barks into Joe's ear. Then he straightens up, as Joe stands away from the door, and he looks back at Leon and Travis, and points at them quickly, one at a time. "You two out. Now."

I move closer to Joe as he steps from the hallway and into the lounge. I reach out and grab his arm again, and I can feel his whole body shaking. I see him looking at his brothers, looking at them for help. His eyes are begging them, but they do and say nothing. They just walk past us and leave.

Joe heads for the kitchen with me in tow. But Lorraine holds her hand up to me. "You need to go too love." I feel outraged by the sight of her. I want to lash out and slap her pinched up, make-up plastered face. I step around her and follow Joe into the kitchen, where Mick has pulled a chair from the table. Joe stands there looking lost and helpless. Mick shoves him into the chair. He is a raging bull of a squat little boxer man, all thick pulsing arms and broad shoulders, and short stumpy legs. I hate him. I can feel Lorraine behind me, sighing angrily at me.

"What's the matter with you anyway?" Mick asks, slamming his hands down onto the table in front of Joe. "Running around with girls all the time like a little gay boy! Smoking drugs out the window! I ought to throw you out!"

Joe folds his arms across his t-shirt and stares at the table. "I'm not gay," he says, teeth clenched.

"Why you always with girls then?" Mick questions, his confused glare taking me in. "Unless you're girlfriend and boyfriend all of a sudden?" He straightens up and looks even angrier for a moment, as if being deceived by us about this would be even worse than having a gay weed smoking stepson. "Are you two girlfriend and boyfriend?" he asks, looking at me.

"No!" I say haughtily, my voice shaky and emotional. "And he's not gay either!"

Lorraine steps around me. "Are you smoking this stuff too?" she asks, peering into my face. "I'm going to have to talk to your mum."

"No she's not," Joe speaks up from the table, with his back to me. "She never has. It's just me."

"Go home then Lou," Lorraine says it again and this time her tone is gentler. "This is family business now, okay?"

I don't want to leave Joe there with them, but Lorraine takes my arm when I don't move and propels me back towards the front door. I can't stand it, but I don't know what I can do. One way or another they are just going to destroy him. As Lorraine pulls open the front door I hear Mick saying; "I can't cope with you kids much longer. There's always one of you causing trouble. If my Will or Tommy had fucking eaten those or something?"

I am pushed outside. I am still clutching my New Look bag. The sun blinks and glints off of all the cars parked in the street. I don't know what to do World. Then I see Leon and Travis leaning against the Fiesta and smoking cigarettes. I march right up to them. I am shaking with anger and disappointment by the time I reach them. "You're not going to stand up for him?" I practically scream at them. "They're tearing him apart in there!"

"Nothing to do with us," Leon gives me his usual unbothered shrug. I want to smack him in the face as hard as I can and watch his nose explode.

"Yes it is! Who does he get it from? You!"

Leon throws down his cigarette then and snatches up my arm, hissing into my face; "keep your fucking voice down!"

I try to pull away but he holds on. "I ought to go back in there and tell them the truth," I say to him, our faces barely an inch apart. "Why should he take all the blame? You got him into all of this!"

"He can handle it," Leon says to me, still holding my arm. "You know them. We're nearly rid. Then it's all over. They'll chuck all three of us out if you tell."

"He's right," Travis tells me, almost apologetically. I finally yank my arm free of Leon's grip.

"Unbelievable," I spit at them.

"Please," says Travis.

"It's not like we're not sharing the money with him," Leon points out, stepping back from me and shoving his hands into his pockets. "He's saving up for a drum kit, you know."

"Look, we're not going anywhere," Travis says, his voice falling softer, his teeth biting at his lower lip. He glances quickly up at the house and then back at me. "We'll stay out here. Make sure they go easy on him."

"You're a pair of scumbags. You're the worst brothers in the world. You just stand there and let Mick smack him in the head." I feel tears prick my eyes now, so I turn away. I start to walk away from them. "You make me sick," I say quietly, and I leave them there. I have no idea if either of them feel guilt, or concern, or indeed are capable of it. They say nothing as I walk away.

I have no choice but to go home. I feel so heavy as I walk; each footstep is a trial, a huge effort. I feel like someone up above has their hands upon my shoulders, and I'm being slowly pushed down into the ground. It really feels that way World, like you and all your troubles are pressing down on me, trying to grind me into the pavement. I want to shake it all off, but it clings to me as I walk, the heaviness of despair. I struggle on, anger fading away now, only to be replaced by sheer sadness. Poor Joe. None of them understand him. Poor Joe.

I let myself into the house and once again I am instantly met with solemn adult faces. My mum and my fucking dad, no less. I throw my New Look bag onto the stairs and kick off my shoes. My shoulders are slumped; my feet drag as I walk down the hallway to join them in the kitchen. It is plainly obvious that Lorraine has already been on the phone to them. They know everything; I can see that from their faces. My dad is smoking a cigarette, with one arm slung across his waist as he leans against the worktop. Mum is sat at the table, wringing a tea towel in her hands. Does she *ever* put them down? "Let me guess," I say to them, slipping weakly into the chair opposite my mother. "Lorraine has already filled you in."

My mum looks at my dad. He smokes his cigarette. Why the hell has she got him here anyway? I wonder where poor old Les is again. "She phoned me when they found the cigarette ends, or whatever they are," Mum answers me, holding onto the twisted tea towel with both hands as she rests it on the table top. She shakes back her short hair, glances nervously at my dad, and then back at me. "She wanted to know what I thought."

"Oh right," I say, looking away from her. "What do you think then?"

"Well, I don't know," she says, sounding flustered, and looking to my dad for help again, but he just remains silent and smokes his cigarette. "It's not you though is it love? It's just Joe smoking that stuff isn't it?"

I look back at her and sigh, and I really want to say, no it's not just Joe, it's me too whenever the hell I feel like it, but it is just Joe running around the estates at night delivering cocaine to people for his brothers. It all goes through my mind. It enrages me again. "I've tried it a few times," I tell her, watching her carefully, wondering what the hell she is going to say to this. My dad lowers his hand, the one holding the cigarette, and he cocks his head at me as if he has not heard me correctly. My mum has covered her mouth with one hand, finally letting go of the bloody tea towel.

"You better be joking!" my dad yells at me. I look at him, scowling in disgust.

"What?" I say to him. "Why would I joke? I suppose I could lie and say it's all just him, but that wouldn't be very fair on him, would it?"

"Oh Lou," my mum is shaking her head into her hand. "I am so disappointed in you. I thought you knew better than that. What has gotten into you two lately? First getting drunk and fighting and now this?"

"Getting drunk and fighting?" my dad practically explodes at her. "You never told me that! When was that then? What the hell is going on around here lately?"

I get up then. I do not want to hear any of this. "Stay there please Lou," says mum, holding up her hand. "We need to talk about this."

"There are lots of things we need to talk about Mum," I say viciously, raising my eyebrows at her, so that she understands what I mean. *Who* I mean. She closes her mouth quickly, biting back her words. I know I have won.

"This is a joke!" my dad yells at her. He is not even looking at me. He does not give a shit if I smoke weed or get drunk, he just relishes another reason to throw shit at her, to hurt her and humiliate her and ground her down even more than he already has done. "What kind of mother are you? Letting one daughter move in with her boyfriend, and the other one is just running wild!"

I leave them to it, which is really rather cruel of me, as none of this is my mum's fault really. But I've had enough. I could stand there and really get into it with them, really give them what for on their own fucked up little lives. I could turn it all around on them, and ask them to think about why Joe and me have let them down so badly. I mean, who raised us eh? But I can't handle this anymore. I need to be alone. I can't even look at my dad most of the time, let alone argue with him. What is the point?

Up in my room I hear them screaming at each other downstairs. It is so bad I have to cover my ears with my hands. I close my eyes and tell myself over and over again, that I will never be like them. I will *never* be like them. No one will ever talk to me like that. No one will ever treat me like that.

"You can never lay the law down can you?" I can hear my dad bellowing. "You've never been able to control them!"

"Easy for you to say!" my mother is screaming back at him. She can scream with the best of them when she's angry enough. "You were the one who walked out on them! I'm the one who stayed! You have no right to say a thing!"

I listen to them going at it, and I am reminded of every argument that filled my childhood. The screaming, the banging, the slamming of doors, the accusations, and the crying. I remember thinking, why are you even together? What are you doing married to each other if you hate each other this much? I could never work it out. I could never see where the love was. I could never see what the point was. Maybe I never will. My mum says I will understand everything when I am an adult, when I have grown up and been in love myself, when I am a parent. Maybe she is right. Fair enough if she is. But right now I want to tell them to shut the hell up. It's only a bit of weed. There are far worse things we could be doing. If only they knew.

14

Dear World, those bastards! For the last two weeks they have refused to let me see or speak to Joe. I can't tell you how evil this is. I can't begin to explain how depressed it makes me. He is about the only one who keeps me sane World! I feel I am falling apart without him, and I am not joking about this. Those evil hypocritical bastards have not allowed me to even phone him, or text him. They took my phone away and everything. The same goes for him. Our parents have got together and decided on this forced separation themselves. Tough love they call it, the idiots! After I admitted to smoking weed too, they pretty much all lost the plot. They can't quite decide who the bad influence is among us. None of them think to look any further than Joe and me. One of us led the other one into it; they just can't work out whom. I hear layers of shocked and outraged conversations between them, where none of them actually go as far as to point the finger at the other parents, but the insinuation is there all the same. The fact is, neither Joe nor myself have done anything to outrage or upset them before now, and they don't know quite what to make of it. In truth, the fact that we have barely focused on their radars before now, seems to make them come down on us even harder. It feels like they already have Sara, Leon and Travis to lose sleep over, and they simply will not entertain the idea of Joe and myself adding to it. It's just not going to happen. My dad tells my mum not to buy me any more new clothes, and my pocket money is suspended.

"I'm not having it," I hear him hiss his opinion, when the four of them are huddled in our kitchen one evening, no doubt sipping wine and beer and flicking fag ash all over the place as they discuss what do to with us. "Drink is one thing, that's one thing! I can handle that. We all did that. But drugs! Smoking weed! I don't bloody think so, I'm not bloody having that, that's bloody disgusting behaviour that is."

I am listening on the landing. They may be aware of this, but it does nothing to stop or hasten their enraged discussions. "Leads to more of it, more drugs, that's what happens!" my mum is freaking out about this. The opinions of others and the newspapers she devours have convinced her that next week her youngest daughter will be smoking crack cocaine, and most likely be injecting heroin by Christmas. "It's a gateway drug," she informs the other three adults. "That's what they call it. A gateway to harder things."

"Well I'm not bloody having it," my dad says again.

"Never even had this from Leon and Travis, did we Mick?" That's Lorraine, obviously. I can hear Mick grunting. I can just picture him screwing up his face and squaring up the way he does, even when there is nothing and no one to square up to.

"They're spoilt and lazy, that's the truth of it," he huffs and puffs in my kitchen, and the others murmur in agreement. "I had a bloody job at that age, I bet we all did! They just lie around all day with nothing to do, that's the problem."

"Well Joe's on babysitting and dog walking duties for the rest of the summer, isn't he Mick?"

"Too bloody right he is!"

"And no band practice either. We're coming down tough on this, Michelle, and we think you two should as well."

"Oh we are, we are, aren't we?" my mum says quickly. "Well, I'm letting her have Marianne over, because she's such a sensible young girl."

"Is she?" Lorraine does not sound so sure.

"Oh yes, oh yes, have you seen where she lives? Her parents are very well off you know. She's a lovely polite girl."

I don't know about Joe, but I get through it by keeping a low profile. I stay in my room, I go out jogging, or I take the dog for long walks around the estate. I avoid my mother because I do not want to have another drugs conversation with her. Les is still living with us, if you can call it that. He still has to run and hide every time my dad shows up. I am relieved that I am allowed Marianne over, or I would probably go insane. I soon learn that Joe has not been allowed the luxury of other friends at all. Josh and Ryan are banned, and Joe is under house arrest. He is forbidden from leaving the house at all. I think that if they are deliberately trying to drive him crazy, they are going about it the right way. Marianne comes over nearly every day during this punishment period. It amazes me that my mother has no qualms about this at all, based solely on the fact that she comes from a big house and her parents have good jobs. She has no idea that Marianne is so fucked up she slices into her own arms most days! She has no idea that Marianne was getting into the weed as much as us.

"Do you think they would let me visit Joe?" she wonders, when we are up in my room kneeling on my bed and gazing out of my window. I sigh, feeling like a prisoner in my home. I am wondering how the hell Joe is surviving it. At least I've got relative peace and quiet. He's got those bloody kids!

"I doubt it," I tell her, watching one of the neighbours little girls ride her bike up and down the road. "But you can try asking if you like. He must be going out of his mind by now."

"You can't even phone him?" she shakes her head incredulously.

"Nope. I did try on the land line. Mick answered and went mental. It's not worth it. They'll just add another two weeks on."

"Poor Joe."

"I know. It makes me sick. The bastards."

"You could have landed his brothers in it too." Marianne looks at me sideways. I stare dismally down at the street. Her younger brother has joined the little girl from next door. He still has stabilisers on and can't keep up with her, so he is crying and calling after her, but she won't stop, she won't slow down for him.

"I nearly did," I tell her. "But it's up to Joe really. They're his family. Apparently he's saving up for a drum kit. Leon reckons he would rather keep making money than drop them in it."

"Insane!" Marianne breathes, her eyes growing wide. I nod in agreement with her. "So is he still sneaking out for them then? Is he still, you know?"

"I'm not sure," I admit. "I wouldn't risk it if I were him."

"Oh my God," Marianne smiles. "Crazy!"

She pulls back from the window and lies flat on her back on my bed. She is wearing a long black skirt today. Her pale little feet just barely poke out the bottom of it. I look back out of the window, as my neighbours little boy crashes his bike spectacularly in his efforts to keep up with his sister. I watch him sprawled out on the concrete, knees bloodied and face wailing. I should feel sympathy but I don't. I look at his sister to see what she does. She stops her bike and turns it around. Then she looks up at her house to see if anyone is coming out yet. She makes no effort whatsoever to go to her little brother, or to help him. He just wails at the indignity and the unfairness of it all, as he clambers onto his shredded knees and throws back his head to the sky. Finally their mother, who is very overweight and always wears bright pink tracksuits, comes waddling out of the house. She shakes a finger and says something to the older girl, who just looks back at her blankly. The mother drags the little boy up from the ground, slings him onto her hip and grabs his bike with her other hand. I watch in awe as she staggers back to her house with both. He must be about five, and the bike looks heavy. I think to myself, well there you have it. Children are cruel. Siblings are born to outdo each other and tear each other to pieces in the scramble to be the best. Parents are simply adults who have been bumped to a higher status merely because of the fact they are physically able to have sex and squeeze out babies. This all becomes clear to me from my window. We live in a merciless world. This life is full of people who want to stamp you down into the ground to stop you getting past them. That is what it feels like World, at the moment. I am torn between wishing I was a child again, not having to worry about anything, except being allowed to play out, and wishing I was old enough to leave home like Sara, just pack my stuff and get the hell out.

I sigh again and look down at Marianne. I realise she has been a good friend to me this summer. I used to view her with suspicion. She intrigued me, but I did not trust her. I found her hard and abrasive, lacking in warmth. I could never tell if she meant the things she said. I could never quite work out if she actually liked me or not. But I feel differently now. She must like me and Joe, otherwise what the hell would she be doing with a pair of rejects like us? I feel bad too. I feel bad because she was right about us always being joined at the hip. We don't always think of her. We don't always think to ask her along, not unless we need something from her.

"You've been a good friend," I tell her then, surprising her with a rare compliment. She even sits up and gapes at me. "What?"

"Wow. It's just unusual to hear you say something nice, or positive!"

"Really?"

"Yeah. But I can't talk. I'm the same. What makes you say that?"

"Just, you know," I slump back against the wall under the window and shrug at her. "You've been keeping me company and stuff. Me and Joe probably leave you out a bit, usually, don't we?"

"Oh I don't mind that," she grins, waving a hand at me. "I know what you two are like. I'm used to my own company anyway, remember?"

"Well yeah, but you know," I shrug again. I am not comfortable with praising someone. It never sounds genuine, does it? It always just sounds like you are sucking up to them for some reason. "I'm sorry," I say instead. "If we have left you out ever. That's all."

"Forget about it!" Marianne laughs at me. "Don't be silly. Hey, when this punishment is all over, I'm getting you both over to mine for a piss up. And Ryan and Josh too. They can bring their instruments!"

"Your parents won't mind?" I feel brighter now she has said this.

"Course not. They like me having people over, because I'm an only child and all that. Anyway, we'll do it when they are out. It'll be brilliant. We need some good nights don't we? Before we go back to school and everything."

I groan at the thought. "Yeah, we do. Definitely."

"I bet you can't wait for the stick insects at school to see you." I look at her, and she is smiling a devilish smile at me.

"Oh yeah," I murmur. She stifles an excited little giggle.

"They probably won't even recognise you Lou. You're gonna' blow their tiny little minds. They'll be all over you like a rash." She leans forward then and puts her hand on my arm. "I think you've done amazing, by the way. Really amazing."

"Thank you."

"Has it been really tough?"

I shrug. I am not sure. I have not really thought of it that way. "Not really," I tell her. "Once I made my mind up, that was it."

"So many people fail, don't they? Fat people, when they try to lose weight. They can never do it normally. But you did!""

"Yeah," I say slowly, frowning slightly at her delighted little face. She seems particularly hyper today, I have to say. "I did, didn't I?"

"You should be extremely proud," Marianne insists. "You've totally changed your body you know. All by yourself! No one helped you."

"You're right about that."

"Yeah, I know. Amazing. Really amazing."

I have to admit, as odd as she is at times, I do enjoy Marianne's enthusiasms over my weight loss. It's really kind of her, I think, to encourage me all the time. Makes me feel less alone. She seems to notice every pound that I drop. Bless her.

I consider telling her how odd it seems to me that I never feel hungry anymore. That I really, truly cannot recall the last time I felt hunger. I did at the start. Bloody hell it was nothing less than torture at the start! I would find myself staring longingly at the food my mother and sister stuffed into their faces. The silky smoothness, and overpowering sweet scent of Cadbury's Dairy Milk chocolate; my mum's favourite 'sin'. But I don't do that now. I don't look at food like that anymore. In fact I kind of see it the opposite way, if that makes sense. I see the fat content and the spoonful's of processed sugar. I see the fat beneath my skin swelling and growing with every mouthful that I allow to enter it. It's great though, I think. It's great not feeling hungry anymore. It makes it so much easier to eat less.

I don't share this with Marianne. Probably because she might think I had lost the plot a bit. I don't know. I don't tell her about the photos my mum took of me recently either. I hate having my photo taken World. It does not matter what you dress me up in, or what you do with my stupid hair, or whatever, I still don't photograph well. I am not, what do they call it? Photogenic, that's it. I'm just not. Never have been. Well my mum has this old camera she's had for years. She must be the last person on earth to still take rolls of film to Boots to be developed. I keep telling her just to get a camera phone, but she seems to think the two things should be separate. Sometimes there is just no telling grown-ups. So anyway, she was snapping away over my birthday, like she always does, then rushes off to get them all developed. Shows me. Christ, I wanted to cry. Oh look, oh look darling, she waffled on, going all teary like she always does when one of us is a year older, oh you look so grown up, so pretty! I don't know what she sees when she looks at photos of me World, but it sure as shit isn't what I see! Would you believe World, even after all this effort, I still looked fat? I was gross in those photos. Really. I wanted to shout bollocks and screw them up, but she whisked them off to send them to obscure and uncaring relatives. So I don't tell Marianne this, as she already knows I always look down or cover my face when any of my friends snap me with their camera phones. But I do make a promise to myself to treat her more like a friend from now on, and not just an acquaintance, someone we call on from time to time. She deserves more than that after all.

After Marianne has gone home, my mum comes up and sits on my bed next to me. She has her hands in her lap between her knees. There is no tea towel. She seems lost and weary and I almost consider putting my arm around her shoulders and giving her a hug. I don't though. I don't know why she has come up here, and my cynical suspicions are aroused. "I have decided to tell your father about Les living here," she sighs eventually, and confirms that I am nearly always right. I nod, and wait for more. "You are right, Lou. I can't live my life for him anymore. He left me didn't he? He went to her. I should be over it by now. I should move on. And Les is a good man, isn't he? What do you think?"

"Well," I say, thinking on it for a moment before replying. "I haven't seen that much of him, seeing as how he's mostly having to hide under your bed, but apart from that, he does seem okay. I mean, he talks to you nice. Not like dad. He talks to you like you're a human being, not a piece of shit."

My mum looks at me with a stern frown. "Lou!"

"What?" I shrug at her. "It's true. Dad talks to nearly everyone like they're shit. Especially if they are female. Can't believe you've never noticed."

"Well, actually I have noticed. I was married to him, you know."

"When are you going to tell him?"

"I don't know. Give me time. It takes courage to work up to these things, you know Lou. Even when you're an adult. Life doesn't stop being scary. I'm not looking forward to it." She looks back at her knees and takes a deep breath, before exhaling again, as if to give herself some strength. "I will do it though, I promise you that. No more lies and secrets. Everything out in the open. Maybe Les and I will be happy."

"Well I hope so Mum." And I do. I mean it.

"I will tell your sister too. Next time I see her."

"Okay," I nod again. "Cool."

"Lou, you're not going to smoke that stuff again, are you?" She looks slowly at me, turning her head as if it pains her to do so. Her eyes are narrowed, like someone flinching from a smack.

"You mean, cannabis?" I ask her, and she physically squirms at the word.

"Yes, Lou. It's time we had a proper talk about all that."

"Course I won't Mum," I tell her with another shrug, that means so little, I wonder if she buys it any more than I do. How can she even ask me that, I wonder. How am I meant to know what I might do, or not do? The chances are slim anyway, so it seems easier to just say no. I don't tell her that I would take being hammered over being stoned any day. Though that might actually be a relief to her. Obviously alcohol is a 'safe' adult approved and tested gateway drug. "I only did it to keep Joe company. You know."

"Well no, I don't know actually, but if you promise you won't do it again…" she looks at me pleadingly.

"You were a teenager once Mum," I point out to her.

"And my mum would have clipped me round the ear if I'd even thought about doing something like that!" she tells me incredulously. "It was very strict. You did what you were told or else."

"That's not so different from today," I mutter, thinking about Joe. Mum blows her breath out through her teeth, and lifts one leg to cross it over the other. She tugs her skirt down towards her knee.

"What do you mean by that?"

"I don't know really."

"You mean us punishing you and Joe, don't you?"

I shrug in reply. She puts her arm around me then, taking me by surprise. She wraps it around my shoulders and pulls me into her side, and I let her. I rest my head on her shoulder, and feel her hand rubbing up and down gently on my bare arm. "You two," she says, and I can feel her smile. "You're just like sister and brother, aren't you? Always have been. Always been joined at the hip you two. Never seen anything like it. Me and Lorraine always say it, you know. The rest of the kids never bothered much with each other, but you two…You two are so sweet."

"Mum, why are they so horrible to him then?"

"I don't think they are horrible, Lou. They just think it's best to be tough. To nip these things in the bud. Boys can be a handful you know. Lorraine was on her own for a while with the first three. I know how tough it was for her." She is still rubbing my arm slowly.

"But Mum, you don't understand. When I was there, Mick just waded in and smacked Joe in the head. He has no right to do that!"

"Oh Lou, Mick is very fiery, he acts first and thinks later, you know that."

"That's no excuse. He's vile to her kids! He thinks his two can do no wrong!"

"Well they are only little, darling. It's different. Three teenage boys in the house is hard work for anyone. I don't think I could do it!" She holds me a little tighter and leans in to kiss me on the top of my head. "I've always been glad I had two little girls, you know. But Mick cares about those kids really, he does. He wouldn't do a thing if he didn't care. He would let them do whatever the hell they liked, wouldn't he?"

"Well I don't like him," I say, petulantly, and I pull away from her hug, dismayed at her allegiance to him, determined to not ever feel empathy for him. "He's always horrible. Always has been." I cross my arms over my stomach. Mum sighs a little and gets to her feet.

"You might understand more when you are an adult and a parent Lou," she says, looking down at me calmly. "That's all I can say. It's the hardest job in the world being a parent, and I imagine being a step-parent is even harder."

"Whatever."

"Okay," she sighs, this time it's a huge one, and she walks to the door. "I'll leave you to it. You can go and see Joe tomorrow, okay? Lorraine said. But you two are on thin ice, remember? Best behaviour or else!"

I could say whatever again, but I don't. I just turn my back on her slowly, making a feeble effort to hide my disappointment, and I lie on my belly on my bed. I hear her open the door. "Lou, I don't want you getting any thinner either," she says suddenly, and the way she says it I can tell it's not just an afterthought, but more like something she has been building up to saying. "You're lovely as you are now okay? I don't want you taking this diet any further." I don't answer her, so she goes out and closes the door behind her. I am left alone with my own jumbled thoughts. I lie flat on my belly and experience a whirlwind of contrasting emotions. I feel the familiar stab of pride at my weight loss. Even the fact my mum has mentioned it the way she has makes me feel proud and defiant. I feel excited and yet nervous about seeing Joe tomorrow. How has his two weeks been? What are we going to say to each other? I feel a little warmer towards my mum, and relieved about her telling dad the truth for once, but still…she always has to stick up for Lorraine and Mick, doesn't she? Makes me sick.

15

Dear World, when I am finally allowed to see my best friend again, it is not a reassuring sight. Neither is it the happy reunion I expect it to be. Instead, Joe slouches out of his house, Will and Tommy flanking him on either side, and Rozzer on the lead. He gives me a look, which tells me this has been his existence for the past fourteen days, and I swallow and grimace, and the words I hope to find to make light of it do not come. He comes out of the front door stony-faced and dark eyed. Despite the heat wave, his face looks pale, with large dark shadows hanging beneath each eye. "You look like shit," I tell him bluntly, hoping to raise a smile. He takes the strain as Mick's dog launches into his panting, heaving death walk, and does little more than raise one eyebrow at me.

"Haven't had a smoke in two weeks," he grumbles, yanking Rozzer back on his lead, to no avail. "Leon won't risk giving me any."

"That's why you look like shit?"

"Can't sleep," he snaps at me. "I was always having a quick one before bed. It was nice." He walks along with one arm stretched out in front of him, and the gasping, lurching dog on the end of it, half strangling itself. Tommy and Will walk politely behind him, as if sensing how unwanted and begrudged their presence is. I glance back at them in guilt. They are holding hands, and talking to each other. Tommy has a little plastic truck clutched in one grubby paw. We head silently to the park. All the things I want to say to him, to ask him, I cannot say in front of a three year old and a seven year old. The atmosphere is heavy with Joe's anger and resentment. I am so relieved when we make it to the field, and he unclips Rozzer from his lead. "Go on then fuck off!" he shouts to the dog, as it races off across the grass, barking at nothing. "Bloody thing, bloody hound from hell," Joe mutters in disgust.

"I should have brought Gremlin," I say, watching as Tommy and Will run on their little legs towards the park. "They would have worn each other out."

"Can never wear that bastard out," Joe spits. "Take him out all day and he's still a bloody nutter at home. Stupid thing."

"So how have you been?" I ask, now that the little one are out of earshot. I look at him and he shoves his hands into his pockets and walks along to the slide. He sits down and I join him. I look back inside the hut, and remember how we had stretched out there after our smoke that day, after I'd thrown up. Joe just sits and glares out at the world. I feel like I am walking on eggshells with him. I feel like everything I want to say is going to annoy and enrage him, and this upsets me. This is not the Joe my mum and me were talking about yesterday. He looks both haunted, and rigid with rage at the same time. "Joe?" I say softly, prompting him. He does not look at me. "Are you okay?"

"Just brilliant," he replies, his tone cold. "Had a brilliant two weeks thanks. Haven't left the house unless it's to come here and do this. Fun times."

"But it's over now," I remind him, "we can have fun times now."

"How?" he asks, glaring at me. "I've still got *them* twenty four fucking seven. I'm still being punished."

"They can't make you have them the entire summer!"

"They can," Joe disagrees, "They've both taken on extra hours at work. They say they need the money." I look into his eyes then, and all I can see is the pain and the fury that has been spinning in his mind for weeks. I swallow quickly and I drop my hand onto his arm.

"Look, it's okay," I tell him firmly. "I'll help you. We'll do it together okay?"

"Push me on swings!" Tommy is yelling suddenly. We both look up at him. He is over at the baby swings, clinging onto one with all his might, legs dangling and kicking as he tries desperately to launch himself into it. I feel Joe tense and stiffen beside me. "Joe push me on swings!" Tommy yells again.

Joe tries to ignore him. He looks down at the ground and digs the heel of his trainer into the dirt. "I've been so bored," I tell him, trying to lighten the mood. "Had Marianne round a bit. Mum likes her! Thinks she's sensible or something."

"Oh yeah?" Joe snorts with vicious laughter. "Sensible hacking her arms to bits eh?"

"Well obviously she doesn't know about that."

"Push me on swings Joe!"

"*Fuck off*," Joe hisses under his breath.

"She's been cool though," I go on, although I am horribly aware that anything I say could push him over the edge. He is glaring down at the dirt and taking deep breaths in and out. "I feel bad actually," I witter on, "you know, 'cause we never really like include her or anything. She's been really cool."

"Good. Brilliant. Any other news?" Joe is still staring at the ground.

"Push me! Push me! Joe push me on swings!"

"Well, sort of. Mum is going to tell Dad the truth about Les. At some point. Kind of a good idea I think."

"Cool."

"Have you seen much of Leon and Travis?"

Joe finds a stick lying in the dirt and picks it up. He holds it by one end and stabs the other end back into the dirt. "Swings!" Tommy is now yelling at full volume. There is a mother near the swings, pushing her toddler in a buggy. I see her looking awkwardly at the hanging Tommy, and then over to us, as if expecting us to do something about it. "Joe swings!"

"Hang on a minute Tommy!" I call out, more for the mothers benefit than Tommy's.

"Just ignore him," hisses Joe. "And no, I haven't. They've been busy."

"I bet they have."

"Don't start," he sighs at me, dropping his head into his hand.

"What?"

"Just don't."

"Joe, I could have killed them that day," I tell him, glancing up at Tommy, who has fallen back from the swing, and is now sat on his bottom on the ground, wailing angrily. Will hovers near him wondering what to do. "The way they stood back and let you take the blame."

"It was my blame to take though."

"But they gave you the weed! It was their fault too."

"No point us all getting in trouble."

"So what do they ever do for you?"

"Oh shut up, forget about it, shut up," Joe looks up then, and catches sight of his two half-brothers, one crying in the dirt, and the other stooping down to comfort him.

"Push me on swings Joe!" Tommy wails again.

"No I fucking won't!" Joe screams back at him suddenly. I am shocked. The mother with her toddler is shocked. Even Tommy is shocked. Because he stops asking, and shoves his thumb into his mouth to stop himself from crying.

"I will Tommy," I say then, getting up. I do not look at Joe as I walk away from him, over to Tommy. Will scuttles off. The mother with her toddler has unstrapped him from his buggy and hauls him into one swing. I pull Tommy up to his feet and lift him into the one next door. He stops crying and sucking his thumb and starts to giggle instead. I stand there and push Tommy back and forth in the swing, while Joe sits and sulks in the hut.

I don't look at the mother with her child, as I push Tommy on the swing, because I know that my cheeks are red with embarrassment. She looks well dressed, with poker straight blonde hair, and subtle make-up on. Her little boy is clean and wearing expensive Clark's trainers. I sigh, and imagine she comes from Marianne's side of the fields. It seems like I have only pushed Tommy for a few seconds, before he changes his mind and starts demanding to get out. I stop the swing and lift him out and he runs over to where Will is climbing up the ladder to the slide, right above Joe's head. I drop my shoulders as I walk slowly back to Joe. He looks bored and angry. He does not even thank me for pushing Tommy. I sit back next to him.

"Have you still been helping them?" I ask softly, meaning Leon and Travis. Joe stares at the dirt and does not look at me.

"Sometimes."

"But how?"

"Sneaking out when they're all asleep."

"You're insane," I tell him, shaking my head. "Can't they do it themselves now? Haven't they got you into enough trouble?"

Joe shrugs at me, uncaring. "Think I would go crazy if I didn't get out the house anyway," he tells me. "I don't mind doing it. I need the money."

"Joe, how are you going to explain to your parents where you got the money for a drum kit from?" I wonder what the hell he is thinking. What the hell is going through his head right now. He looks up, past me. Tommy is wailing again, this time because he is in pain. It looks like Will has given him a pretty hard shove down the slide, and he is now lying face down in the dirt at the bottom. Joe stands up, huffing with frustration. He goes to Tommy and wrenches him up by the arm.

"Did you shove him down?" he demands, looking up at Will who is just about to come down the slide. Will lifts and drops his hands apologetically.

"He wasn't going down! He takes too long!" Will slips slowly down the slide towards Joe, just as Tommy's wailing reaches a painfully high pitch in his ear. Joe lets go of Tommy and grabs Will by the neck of his t-shirt. I can only stand and watch in horror as Joe punches Will in the head, just as Mick did to him that day.

"Joe!" I practically scream at him. He doesn't look at me. Will starts to cry and tries to pull away.

"You're mean! You're mean!" he yells. I look up helplessly. The mother by the swings is staring at us with her hands over her mouth. Joe does not see. His face is ruined by rage. He looks like he wants to kill his brothers.

"Joe, stop it, stop it," I tell him firmly, and I reach for Will and grab his arm. Joe swats at him again as I pull him away, catching him on the ear. "Joe *no!*" I shout, and I pull Will and Tommy away from him, and the staring, horrified mother. I pull Will to my side and wrap my arm around his shaking shoulders. He has balled his fists up into his eyes and is really sobbing. Tommy is just screaming for the sake of it. It really is a horrible grating sound. "Get the dog!" I hiss at Joe as he glares at me silently. "Get the dog, we're going!"

Joe stomps away finally, swinging Rozzer's lead in one hand. I have an arm around each boy, and start to lead them gently away from the park. I keep my back to the woman staring, but

I can sense her accusing eyes on me. I feel red faced and ashamed and angry. I want to shout back at her, what are you looking at? It's not his fault, that's what they all do!

"He's mean to me! He's mean to me!" Will chants behind his leaking eyes. I have to keep my arm around him, as he is not looking where he is going. I pat his shoulder in a clumsy way. Part of me feels genuinely sorry for him. He is only seven, and he didn't deserve that. But part of me feels more sorry for Joe. I don't even like to think what will happen when Mick finds out. I almost want to tell Will and Tommy to shut the hell up and be good for once. I want to tell them how lucky they are to have both their parents together, and on their side. I feel like telling them they will never understand how it is for Joe. But I say nothing, except for the odd pointless 'there, there' and 'it's okay'.

Joe has called Rozzer back and clipped his lead back on. The dog is not tired out in the slightest, and pulls and gasps the whole way home. We walk in a cold stony silence, Joe staring at the ground as Rozzer hauls him along. Tommy and Will manage to stop crying, and just utter the odd pathetic whimper instead. I decide to get them something to eat when we get in. Something they can go in the garden and stuff their faces with. Anything to keep them quiet, and out of Joe's way for ten minutes.

We get back to the house. Joe drags out his key and unlocks the door. Will heads inside and disappears. Tommy immediately trips over the doorstep and hits his head and starts to scream again. Joe has no patience left to lose. He lets Rozzer go, and reaches out for Tommy. "Just fucking shut up will you!" he hisses at him, grabbing his little arm and pulling him to his feet. I see Tommy staring up at him, his face red and glistening with sliding tears. "Shut up for once! I'm sick of you!" Joe releases him, but can't help giving him a little shove into the lounge. I've had enough. I follow Joe in and close the door, and I pull him back by his arm.

"That's enough," I warn him. "Seriously. They're just kids."

"They're *his* fucking kids," Joe corrects me, eyes blazing. "Spoilt little brats. They get away with everything. I *hate* them."

"It's not their fault, Joe," I tell him, still holding onto his arm. "They didn't ask to be born, any more than you did."

"Tough luck."

"You're just passing it on to them. Like Leon and Travis did to you."

"Leon and Travis are my real brothers," he says, and pulls away from me.

"This isn't like you," I say helplessly, following him through to the lounge where he drops down onto the sofa and sticks his feet up onto the nearest coffee table.

"Good," he replies, "I'm glad."

"Well I'm not! I like the old you better!"

"Tough shit," he tells me with a shrug of his shoulders. "Don't care."

I can see that. They have done a good job on him all right, I think then, staring at him in disbelief. They have taken away nearly everything that he cares about, and ruined his summer by lumbering him with two whining kids and a dog that never tires out. And here is the result. He is acting scarily like Leon. Blank and uncaring, simmering rage just under the surface, no empathy or concern for anyone. I lower myself onto the sofa, as he gets up and sets up the X-box. I have no idea where the little ones have gone, but I don't blame them for totally vanishing. I watch in silence, trying to find the right words to say to get through to him, as he plugs in the X-box and starts to play a game, slumped back into the sofa, with his thumbs waggling the controls. His face goes totally blank, his eyes dead and unseeing. I get up with a sigh and go into the kitchen to make us both a coffee.

I find cups, put the kettle on, and lean against the table while the water boils. I fold my arms around my body, and find the bumps of my ribs against the palms of my hands, and I find it comforting. There is a cardboard box on the table, full of broken biscuits. I smile slightly, remembering the excitement of broken biscuits, and I think, only poor people can find broken biscuits exciting. I find a clean plate and pile it with chocolate ones for the little ones, in case they reappear. I am just pouring the coffee, and starting to feel a little bit calmer, when I hear Joe start to swear in the lounge. "You little shit!" he is cursing. "I told you to stay out of my room! Damn it!"

I run in, holding the plate of biscuits. Tommy is standing in the middle of the room holding one of Joe's records. He only started collecting them recently, since he decided being a drummer was a genuine career move. Apparently if you are serious about music then you buy records. Off Ebay. I think Tommy must have a death wish. Will has reappeared too. But he is keeping his head down, and is crouched on the floor in front of the TV where he has his Lego spread out. It looks like he has been busy building some sort of fort. There are heaps of little plastic soldiers mixed in with Lego, lying all over the carpet. Joe snatches the record from Tommy and checks it over. It looks okay to me, but Joe is searching for damage his face screwed up, his eyes scowling. "Just stay out of my stuff!" he growls. Just then Tommy picks up the X-box control from the sofa and starts to press the buttons. "Get off that!" screams Joe, shoving him away. He loses his temper completely then. I have never seen him so wild, apart from when he attacked Travis, and then he had been very drunk. "Touch my stuff and I'm gonna' touch yours!" he starts to yell loudly, and brings his foot down on Will's Lego. Will moves back, eyes wide in horror.

"No!" he screeches. "My fort!"

"I'm gonna' break all your stuff and see how you like it!" Joe is shouting, and now he is stamping again and again on the Lego. The fort is destroyed, and little pieces of coloured plastic start to splinter and fly about the room. Will covers his face with both hands and just sobs uncontrollably. When Joe has had enough, he sits back on the sofa, picks up the controls and goes back to his game. Just like that. I feel like I am in some kind of nightmare, where Leon's warped soul has infiltrated Joe's sweet one.

"I'll help you build it again," I say quickly, kneeling down next to Will and putting the plate of biscuits on the floor. Tommy sits next to me and helps himself to half a bourbon. I only look briefly at Joe, as I start to sweep armfuls of bricks towards me. Will takes a biscuit, but carries on sobbing. "We can build an even bigger, better one," I try to tell him. "A massive one! One with towers and everything!"

Five minutes later, Joe is totally engrossed in his stupid football game, Tommy is eating his own body weight in biscuits, and Will is still crying about his fort. I am not that good at Lego. Everything I try to do just seems to make him cry more. He is still whimpering when the front door opens and Mick storms in. I stare up at him in horror, my eyes frozen on his heavily lined, boxers face. He slams the door behind him and squints down at his two little sons. "Daddy!" Tommy cries out gleefully, a biscuit in each hand. Will just stares up at him, eyes wet with tears.

"What's the matter with you?" Mick asks, in that unbelievably soft tone he uses for his boys.

"My fort!" Will tells him, starting to really sob again. His whole face has gone red with the effort. I look apologetically at Mick.

"I'm helping him fix it," I say uselessly. Mick frowns.

"Oh look at that!" he says, kneeling next to Will and stroking his back with one hand. "What a mess!"

"My fort daddy!" Will wails again, sobbing into Mick's shoulder. And then I hear him say it; "Joe did it! Joe did it daddy!"

My glance flicks nervously to Joe on the sofa. His eyes register the accusation, but he says nothing, and keeps his eyes on the TV, his thumbs still waggling madly on the control. Mick's face hardens and he gets back to his feet.

"Is that right?" he asks Joe, nodding at the Lego. "Did you break his fort?"

Joe does not answer. I watch as his bottom jaw juts out slightly in defiance, but he says nothing. "He stamped on it all daddy!" Will says, adding fuel to the fire. Mick's eyes widen.

"Oh yeah? Is that right? Did you stamp on it? On purpose?" He does not wait for an answer this time. "Right, that's it," he snaps as he reaches for the control in Joe's hand and snatches it away. He throws it down, and hauls Joe to his feet by his arm. I feel sick. I can't look. But I have to. Mick holds Joe by the top of his arm and drags him towards the stairs. I see Joe resist slightly, but other than that he does not put up a fight, or yell, or even say a word. Mick drags him up the stairs. "Let's see how you like it eh?" he is yelling furiously. I stand in the hallway, feeling utterly helpless, biting at the knuckle of one hand. I hear Mick kicking open Joe's bedroom door. "Picking on little kids, are you? Let's see how you like it!"

I can hear stomping, and more stomping. Next thing I know Mick hurtles back down the stairs and seems to be shoving a ten-pound note at my face. "Bloody hell I only came home to check on things! I can't trust him, can you look after these two?" I just stare. He looks stressed out, running one hand back through his short hair, waving the ten-pound note under my nose. "Come on," Mick prompts. "I'm desperate. I've got to go back out. You kids have no bloody idea the shit us adults have to put up with, you know. I can't deal with this now. Please?" I have never heard Mick say please before. I take the note and put it in my pocket.

"Okay," I say.

"Good. Great. Thanks." He pats me softly on the shoulder and goes back out the door, slamming it shut behind him. I glance at the kids. Will has picked up the control for the X-box. Tommy is on the biscuits again. I take a deep breath and head up the stairs to Joe's room.

His door is open, so I walk in. He is lying face down on his bed, sobbing into his pillow. When I step forward my foot crunches on something on the floor, and I look down and see his small record collection in a smashed up pile there. Mick has thrown them down and it looks like he has stamped on them repeatedly. "Oh Joe," I say quietly, looking back at him. He stays on the bed, and tries to control himself, tries to stop crying. I am heartbroken. I cannot remember the last time I saw Joe cry. We must have been very little.

I go over to the bed and sit down next to him. I place my hand on his shoulder, and he lifts his head and looks back at me. "You can't say anything, you can't do anything, in this house, they don't let you!"

"Joe..."

"You can't do anything..."he says over his sobs. "They don't let you! You can't even breathe!"

"Joe, I'm so sorry, we'll try to sort them out, they're probably not all broken. I'll sort them out for you." I squeeze his shoulder and he sits up suddenly then, turning towards me, and wiping with his hands at his eyes, wiping the tears away. "It's okay," I try to tell him, even though it so obviously isn't. I don't know what else to say, I really don't. I don't want to make things worse. I am scared of saying the wrong thing, so I just wrap my arms around his shoulders instead, and I pull him in for a hug. He lets me, and he rests his wet cheek on my shoulder and I feel and hear him sigh heavily, a juddery shaking sigh, his final sob. I am rubbing his back and telling him it will all be okay, when suddenly he pulls back, looks at me strangely and then kisses me on the mouth. I am so shocked that I automatically pull back away from him, and I straight away see the hurt in his eyes, and before I can stop him, he jumps up from the bed and runs from the room. "Joe!" I cry after him, but all I hear are his footsteps thundering down the stairs, and the door slamming after him.

I sit on the bed in stunned shock for what seems like an age. I try to take in what has just happened. Every time I try to figure it out, the shock just smacks me in the face again, and my jaw hits the floor. Part of me wants to laugh out loud; it's so strange, so crazy. Part of me wants to run out after him, grab him and tell him to stop being so fucking stupid. Part of me wants to run home and hide in my bed, and stop being sixteen, with all this confusing shit going on all the time. I am shook from my daydream by the sound of Tommy and Will fighting downstairs. I get up, step over the broken records and yell out at them; "stop fighting, and I'll be down in a minute!"

I can't leave Joe's room without at least trying to sort out the records, so I kneel down slowly next to the mess. I should have reminded him that he can just download them again, but it probably would not have made him feel any better. Joe loves his music. The anger trembles through me then. This isn't the same as breaking Lego, I want to shout out to whoever may be listening. Lego is just fucking bricks! You can make it again, for Christ's sake. Just then Will appears cautiously in the doorway. "What you doing?" he asks me. "Where did Joe go?"

"He got upset because your dad smashed his records," I reply, not looking up.

"Joe smashed my fort," says Will, hanging onto the door with both hands.

"I know," I say. "That wasn't very nice of him. But Lego can be put back together again. Records can't."

"Where did he go then?"

"I don't know Will. He's not very happy at the moment, living here."

Will chews at the nail on his thumb for a few moments, watching me while I sort them out. "Are you looking after us now then?" he says eventually. I sigh, thinking of the tenner in my pocket.

"Looks that way."

"Can we have something to eat then? Can we have some crisps?"

"In a minute," I tell him. "When I've done this for Joe."

Will seems happy with this, and goes away. When I have finished cleaning up the mess, the ruined pile is twice the size of the okay pile, and I feel devastated for Joe, looking at it all. I remember his money then, for the drum kit, and go over to his drawers. I open the top one and feel around until I find the fat sock at the back. It is even fatter now, jammed tight with ten and twenty pound notes. I hope it will be okay there, and close the drawer again.

I wonder where he is.

16

Dear World, I am sprawled on the sofa with Tommy nodding off on my lap, and Will snuggled up next to me, when the front door opens and Travis and Leon come in. I narrow my eyes at them, as usual wondering where they have been, what they have been doing, who they are. Will yawns and rests his head back on my shoulder after looking up to see who is home. It is nearly five o'clock. I was really hoping it would be Lorraine or Mick back to take over. I am shattered. Utterly exhausted. My mum was right when she said having kids is not easy. It fucking isn't. I'm never having any, if this is what it is like. I have spent the last three hours running around after them, telling them off, distracting them and tidying up the mess they make. Why anyone would want to do that in life, I have no idea.

Leon walks through the lounge, barely giving me a look, and disappears into the kitchen. Travis lingers in the doorway, looking confused. "Before you ask," I say to him, stifling a yawn. "Joe is out and I have no idea where. I got asked to baby-sit these two by Mick."

"Oh right," Travis shrugs, smiling slightly before looking confused again.

"Joe broke my fort," Will announces, his eyes on the TV, his little body loose and relaxed next to mine.

"Yes and daddy paid him back for that, didn't he?" I say, looking back at Travis. Travis raises his eyebrows in question. "Mick trashed most of his records," I inform him. "Stamped on them all."

"Fucking prick," Travis says under his breath, and I have no idea if he means Joe, or Mick.

"I have to go home," I say, and start to ease Tommy from my lap. He is nearly asleep, and rolls onto his side to bury his head in a cushion. Will moves slightly as I get up from the sofa, then leans back and yawns again, eyes totally fixated on the TV.

"Quite a day then?" asks Travis from the hallway. I approach slowly.

"You could say that."

"Things have been tense round here lately."

"Joe's a mess," I say, sinking my hands into the back pockets of my shorts. I yawn, and glance at the kitchen, where I can see Leon at the back door, smoking a cigarette. "He's not himself at all. He was vile to these two today. That's not like him."

"Yeah, he's been stuck with them constantly," grimaces Travis. "That's probably why."

"Still doing his little trips out for you two though, hey?" I ask, dropping my tone lower and looking quickly at the back of Leon again. Travis looks at his feet, crosses his arms over his t-shirt and shrugs his shoulders.

"Nearly there," he practically whispers. "Honestly."

I step closer, and Travis looks at me, his eyes slightly alarmed. "For some reason," I say very quietly, looking up at Travis, who is at least a foot taller than me. "Joe is incredibly loyal to you two. Like you're the only real family he has, or something. I just hope you two are worth it, that's all." I step carefully around him and slip out of the door.

I get home. I feel totally wiped out physically, like I need to sleep for a week to recover from babysitting. Mum meets me in the hallway. "Tonight is the night love," she tells me, hanging onto my arm and squeezing it.

"What?"

"Les is working late. Your dad is coming over. I'm going to tell him."

"Oh right."

I pull away from her and head for the stairs. I can't think about this now. I am still trying to digest Joe's kiss, and everything else. "You are pleased aren't you?" she says, sounding desperate.

"I don't mind," I tell her, one foot on the bottom stair. "Just don't involve me, okay? Don't go calling me down, or sending him up or anything. I don't feel very well."

"Why? What's the matter? Have you been with Joe? Have you two been behaving yourselves?"

I pull away from her incessant questions. I try to plant another foot on the stairs, but all of a sudden, the staircase is moving and blurring, and I can feel my head, somehow it is falling past me, it is like I can see it going, I can see it plummeting like a stone towards the stairs. There is nothing I can do to stop it. I am going down.

***

I think I am out for a matter of seconds, if that. Mum is freaking out big time. She tried to grab me and stop me going, but I hit my head on the stairs anyway. She gets me up to my room, practically drags me there. "You've never done that before!" she keeps saying, as she sweeps back my duvet and pushes me into my bed. I fall in easily. The mattress sags under my weight. I sink into my Lou sized hole and want to smile. My head hurts. Everything still seems fuzzy, like when you are pissed. She plants a firm hand across my forehead. "You're not hot," she tells me. "Do you feel sick? What happened Lou? You've never fainted before in your life!"

"I don't know, do I? Can I go to sleep now?"

"I'm so worried about you," she goes on. "I think you've not been eating enough darling, that's what it is. You can't keep this diet up anymore Lou. I'm serious."

"I have been eating," I lie easily. "I ate loads today. I'm just not feeling well. I need to sleep now."

"I'll let you sleep," Mum nods at me. "But then I want a serious chat with you young lady."

"Not another one," I groan, closing my eyes against my pillow. "There's nothing to chat about. I'm fine."

"You don't look fine to me. You have never done that before!" She shakes her head. She looks like she is cross with me, though I have no idea what I have done wrong apart from keeling over when she wanted my attention and approval. I close my eyes, and she finally leaves me alone and shuts the door behind her. I am left alone with my dark mind, my headache and my pleasantly empty belly. I think to myself, I don't care what she says, I don't care what anyone says, I am not stopping my diet and getting fat again for anyone! Because that is what will happen. If I go back to eating like that, if I stop jogging, I won't be slim anymore, will I? I'll get fat again, World, that's the thing. That's the fear. But they won't understand that, will they? I'll be the little porker again. I'll be that person I despise, the one that no one noticed, the one that lived in the background. It's not like that now I am slim, is it?

I smile a triumphant smile to myself, while I curl my arms around my body, and place my hands over my ribs, ribs that never used to be there. No, I think, it's not like that now you are slim. Travis notices you. Travis tried to kiss you. Joe tried to kiss you. I am, for a sick little moment filled up with self-satisfaction and vanity. I have never had the luxury of either before. The thought of them both wanting me, of fighting over me, over *me*, is kind of funny and delicious and sexy all at the same time. It's wrong. But fuck it, I think. I have lived my life the *right* way for too long, trying to please them all, trying to be good. This is way more fun. This is dangerous and scary and wild and wrong, but this, all of this, is way more fun.

I must sleep for a while, because it is the familiar old sound of my dad raising his voice that brings me out of it. I sit up slightly and listen. I have no idea what time it is, or how long they have been talking, but it sounds like my mum has finally told him about Les. I don't want to hear it. I don't want to know about it. I pull the duvet over my head and disappear into the dark. That is their world, I think. This is mine.

I sleep again. I really sleep. I sleep like I have never slept before, and it is wonderful. I drift in and out of dreams that run away from me every time I creep close to consciousness, and then I feel myself go back under again. It's amazing. I never ever want to leave my bed and face the world again.

***

So World, listen to this. My mum wakes me up in the morning by telling me that she has made me breakfast. I am gutted. I had every good intention of grabbing my usual coffee and an apple and going over to Marianne's. I need to talk to her about Joe. But my mother has other ideas. She has the table laid out and everything. Tablecloth, full English breakfast and huge mugs of tea. My stomach does a little nervous flip just looking at it all. "Mum," I protest. "I'm never really hungry in the morning, you know. I can't eat all that."

Mum is sat at the table with Les. He has a newspaper, and does a good job of hiding behind it. Mum is frowning at me, so I slip into a chair and pick up half a slice of toast. For fucks sake. I hardly ever eat bread these days. Doesn't she realise? I feel a surge of panic then, which confuses and alarms me, because I have never experienced it before, but I know it is panic about the food, which is really stupid if you think about it World. She expects me to eat all that. She wants me to eat all that crap! She wants me to get fat again, I think then, glaring back at her. That's what this, I know it. I've been in too much trouble since I got thin, got too cocky, eh? Now she wants to fatten me up and shut me up again. I take a bite of the toast as my anger and paranoia intensify. "You need to eat properly," she informs me curtly, and I want to throw the toast at her. "I'm not having you fainting on me again!" She looks at Les, disguised as a newspaper. "She scared the life out of me, you know!"

"I told you, I was ill. I slept for ages, now I'm fine."

"It won't hurt you to eat a proper breakfast for once, young lady. This is all healthy, good food. Let me get you some sausages and bacon?"

"No, I only want toast." I turn and look at the front door at the end of the hallway. I feel the longing to run out of it. I use my fingers to tear another piece of toast off and put it in my mouth. It feels so stodgy and hard to swallow. I try to remember if bread always felt like that? I can feel it slipping slowly down my throat, even though I have chewed it for bloody ages. I want to be sick. I drink some tea to wash it down. "Mum, I have to go out now," I say then, pushing back my chair. She looks alarmed and reaches out for me.

"But you haven't eaten much! And I want to tell you how it went with your dad!"

I hold the toast, so it looks like I am going to take it with me. "Is he going to throw us out?"

"No, of course not. He was actually very reasonable in the end."

"Great. That's all I need to know. See you later." I turn and head for the door. I hear my mum shove back her chair and race after me.

"Lou!"

"Okay, okay, I'll take the dog."

"No, it's not that. Where are you going?"

"Marianne's."

"Oh okay." She has no choice but to let me go. I slip out the front door, holding toast and I am gone.

I am going to Marianne's, but I cannot go without checking on Joe first. He has not text or called me, so I just want to see if he is okay. I kind of want to see him, but don't want to see him at the same time, if that makes sense? Luckily for me, he is not even in. Leon answers the door with a face like thunder. "You seen Joe?" he barks at me before I can ask him the same question. I take a step back. I always have the urge to move back, to move away when I am near him. I try to peer around him to see if there is any sign of someone else, anyone else inside.

"I came to see him," I say, feeling lost. "Where is he then?"

"Wouldn't be asking you if I knew that, would I?" Leon snaps back, looking bored now.

"He ran off yesterday, after Mick trashed his vinyl," I explain. "He didn't come back after that?"

"He came back," Leon nods. "Then he left again, and he's meant to be grounded and looking after the brats. Guess who's got stuck with the brats now?"

I have to stop myself from smirking. "Oh," I say instead.

"He's got his phone turned off. They're gonna' kill him when he gets back. You've no idea where he is?"

"No idea," I say, honestly. "But I'll look for him." I step back and turn to leave.

"Hey, wait a minute," Leon says then. "Any chance you could take the brats with you? I'll pay you."

"No chance," I tell him, and walk off smiling.

I stroll over to Marianne's house, feeling full of myself again. I send her a text to let her know I am on the way. Fuck Leon, the stupid nasty bastard. See how he likes looking after those annoying kids all day. Hope he has to walk the dog too! It is only when I knock on Marianne's door that I remember Joe is missing, and I start to worry. Why is he doing this? Why is he getting himself into even more trouble? I don't understand it. Marianne lets me in. "Got so much to tell you!" I exclaim breathlessly as I jump into her hallway. She closes the door, smiling calmly as always. "You're not gonna' believe what happened yesterday! Plus Joe is missing! Just saw Leon and they're all going insane!"

"It's all right, it's all right," Marianne says then, placing a soothing hand on my arm and leading me through to the kitchen. "He's here. He's in the summer house." I am stunned.

"What? Why? Since when?"

"I don't know, I only just discovered him there this morning. Think he slept the night or something. Come on." She opens the French doors and goes out into the garden. I feel a sickness in my belly then. A nervous ache that starts to spread. I had not planned on seeing him yet. I wanted to talk to her first. And why do I feel a sharp stab of what I can only describe as jealously, as she leads me down to the summerhouse?

I say nothing. I try to work it out, as I follow her down. Why did he come to her, and not to me? Marianne stops outside the summerhouse, looking as calm and relaxed as ever, and I wonder if she still looks that calm and composed just before she cuts herself up. I bet not. I can see Joe inside, and he looks up from where he is slumped in a deck chair with a cup of tea in his hands. "Is it okay if I talk to him alone for a minute?" I ask Marianne, guiltily.

"Course it is. I'll go and make you a tea, or coffee?"

"Coffee please. And sorry Marianne. I did come here to see you, really."

"I know," she grins as she turns away. "We'll catch up in a bit."

As she heads back to the house, I open the door and enter the summerhouse, pausing to close the door softly behind me. "All right?" I say to Joe, and he nods at me in reply. He looks thoroughly miserable. Part of me is relieved though. At least he's not brimming with rage anymore. I sink into the second deck chair, with my hands in my pockets. "Just saw Leon," I tell him. "He's not happy."

"None of them are ever happy," Joe sighs, truthfully. I swing my legs back and forth under the chair. All I can think about, all I can see in my head, is his tear streaked face coming towards mine. The surprising touch of his lips against my lips.

"So what are you doing here?"

"Hiding."

"What did you do, sleep here?"

Joe leans back in his chair and runs one hand back through his hair. His eyes lift to meet mine briefly, then hit the floor again, as if he is finding it difficult looking at me. "I was out anyway," he says. "You know."

"Working?"

"More or less. I got a bit freaked out. This one guy was a bit funny with me."

"What happened?"

"He just started getting angry about the price. He said it was meant to be less, but it wasn't. I didn't know what to do."

"Another good reason why you need to stop all this Joe," I say, leaning forward in concern. "You're gonna' get yourself beaten up, or worse."

"I know," he sighs again, "I had to let him have it cheaper in the end. I wasn't going to argue with him."

"So that's why you didn't go home? Because Leon will be mad?" Joe meets my gaze again and nods slowly. "Christ's sake Joe," I complain bitterly. "What the hell is wrong with you these days? Are you purposely trying to mess your life up or something?"

"I'm trying to save up for a drum kit," he murmurs, looking down.

"You idiot!" I say, and I really do feel close to smacking him one. "Why don't you get a paper round of something, you retard? Anything but this!"

"It's nearly done," he says, and I am getting so sick of hearing that from all of them. I growl and throw my hands up in the air, then drop them back into my lap, shaking my head at him and his unique stupidity.

"So you're gonna' keep doing it? You're gonna' keep risking it?"

"What am I risking, Lou?" he looks at me then, frowning.

"More shit with your parents!" I cry in exasperation. "Getting thrown out by Mick! Ending up in the hospital or worse!"

"Those things are nothing new," Joe replies, his eyes still on mine. "I was living with those things anyway, if you hadn't noticed."

"Don't be so dramatic!"

"It's true. I was just going along with it all. Like you. Like you do with your messed up family." He sits forward again now, elbows on knees, hands on either side of his face. "Just taking it all. Taking all their shit. Doing what I'm told. Never causing a fuss."

"I know that Joe," I tell him. "I feel the same but…"

"Well why should we? What do they do for us? They fuck things up, that's what they do!"

"I don't know Joe, I just think…"

"If they're not careful they're gonna' drive me insane," he says then, closing his eyes tightly for a moment, before opening them and staring right at me. "I'll end up doing what that Danny kid did over in Redchurch, if they're not careful."

I am silent for a moment, licking my lips slowly. He keeps his eyes on mine and I do not look away. "Don't even joke," I tell him softly. "That was different. That kid was *tortured* for fucks sake. And he went to jail for years!"

"Just don't blame him, that's all," Joe shrugs at me. "If people push you that far…"

I remember Joe had been very interested in the story the first time someone told us it. Back in 1996 or something, a boy from Redchurch, which is the estate on the other side of the bypass, stabbed his stepfather to death in his own home. It's become one of those myths I guess, an urban legend, told and retold so many times in the area, the truth of it was probably distorted long ago. He went to the same school as us. Apparently there is graffiti on a bench over there, his name carved in a bench or something. It made the national news, and everyone at school; all the teachers were up in arms at the time. Some of them took time off work they were so traumatised by it. It was all over the newspapers when it went to trial, and in the end the boy got ten years in jail, even though it came out in court that his stepfather had been beating him up for years.

"He must be out of jail by now?" I ask Joe and he nods.

"Bet he wouldn't come back here though. Not this bastard place where no one helped him."

"You shouldn't say things like that Joe. Mick may be a stupid prick, but it is different. That boy ran away from home and everything to get away. I think in his own way, that Mick cares about you."

"I'm just saying," Joe shrugs again. "People like Mick should watch out. Bullies."

"Look, I know he treats you like shit compared to his own kids, but he's no worse than your mum, is he? She's just as tough. Maybe he just follows her lead."

"Yeah, they're all fucking scumbags," he says bitterly, folding his arms across his chest. "And now they're wondering why I'm playing up. Makes me laugh."

"Well just calm down," I tell him, pleadingly. "Just relax. You're scaring me lately, you know. You're like a different person. You don't want to end up in jail too, do you? What kind of life would that be?"

"I'm sorry about yesterday," he says then, and I frown at him, not knowing if he means the way he treated the little ones, or the fact he tried to kiss me. I cross my own arms, mimicking his defensive stance.

"What part?" I ask cautiously.

"All of it. I was a twat."

"Hmm."

"What does 'hmm' mean, Carling?"

I can't prevent the small smile that pulls at the corners of my mouth. "'Hmm' means you were so retarded you tried to kiss me." I let the smile run. I grin at him. He grins back, and his cheeks immediately redden.

"Sorry Carling. I won't do it again."

"Too right you won't. I was so shocked I didn't have time to punch you."

"Sorry mate. I was…I don't know what I was."

"So why did you do it then? I need to know."

"I don't know," he shrugs. "I was sort of thinking about Travis kissing you at that party. That pissed me off."

"Why did it?"

"Because you're my friend, not his. He doesn't even know you. He just suddenly likes you now you're all skinny. How fake is that?"

"I don't know," I laugh, my mind whirling.

"Well it is," insists Joe. "He never noticed you before did he? He really likes you apparently. He wants to ask you out or something."

"No fucking way!" I explode, and laughter seems to be my only chance of saving face. "Shut up!"

"I'm not joking, it's true. Just wait and see."

"Whatever!"

"Would you though?" Joe looks serious again for a moment. "If he did ask you out? Would you? If he tried to kiss you again, would you let him?"

"Course not!" I tell him, although I am not entirely sure if I am lying to him or not. It just all seems so ridiculous. I want to change the subject. I put my hand on Joe's arm and give it a squeeze. "Look, you retard, you are my best friend in the world, right? I never want to do anything to upset you. I'm here for you whatever shit happens. I'll even start helping you get shot of those bloody drugs if you want."

Joe's eyes widen in disbelief. "Carling, are you insane?"

"Probably," I shrug. "But two things just occurred to me. One, if I help, you'll get rid of them quicker, then this will all be over, and two, you are right. You are right about everything."

Joe grins the kind of grin I have missed on his face. His hazel eyes shine with warmth, and all the anger seems to vanish. "You're a legend," he tells me. "And I am right, aren't I?"

"Well not the bit about wanting to stab Mick to death and go to jail. You can forget about that."

"Okay then," he laughs. "I will."

When Marianne comes back with the coffees, we are smiling and laughing and all sanity seems to be restored. I feel like I have my friend back again, even if he is in a shit load of trouble. Marianne sits herself down on the floor between us, and is smiling knowingly as she pulls something out of her back pocket. "What's that?" Joe asks, leaning forward. She is holding a little metal tin, like the one Joe has.

"Anyone fancy a smoke?" she asks us, placing it on the floor in front of her and tapping the lid with the nail of her index finger. Joe and I exchange amazed looks.

"Where did you get it from?" Joe breathes softly, his eyes widening in hunger.

"That's for me to know," Marianne replies with a trace of smugness.

"You're a legend!" he tells her, and I look at him and think, hang on, that was me a minute ago. But it does not matter. We are soon pleasantly removed from our troubles and giggling on the floor, with a cloud of smoke swirling gently above our heads.

17

Dear World, I think we all sleep for a while. Joe peels himself up from the floor around mid-day. He looks a mess, I think, gazing at him from my deck chair. His hair is getting too long, and it is all stuck up everywhere. His eyes look a bit red and his clothes are crumpled. "Better go home then," he mumbles dejectedly. I am not capable of saying much in way of comfort.

"Probably a good idea," I tell him instead. Marianne does not move from where she is lying on the floor, with her eyes closed, and her hands laced together on her stomach. Her top is riding up enough to show us her belly button. Joe yawns as he opens the door.

"You still gonna' come meet me like you said?" he asks me, in a lower tone. I nod at him in reply.

"You bet I am. See you then. Good luck."

"Yeah. Thanks."

When he has gone, Marianne's eyes snap open and fix on mine. "You're going with him?" she asks, incredulously. "You're gonna' help with the drug deals?"

"I'm just going with him," I shrug irritably. "I don't want him going alone."

"He's a big boy, you know."

"What's that supposed to mean?"

"Just saying," she sits up then, and shrugs. "You do baby him a bit, you know." I just stare at her, wondering what the hell she means and where this is coming from?

"No I do not!"

"Okay, calm down," she says, holding her hands up apologetically. "Don't bite my head off. I just meant that he's managed this far on his own, so why do you suddenly feel the need to go with him?"

"Because he nearly got his arse kicked by someone the other day. I don't want him to get hurt do I?"

"So what are you going to do? Protect him?" I glare at her angrily, trying to let her know she is pissing me off, but all she does is smile in that calm controlled way of hers, as if nothing touches her, nothing breaks through.

"Come too, if you want," I say to her, wondering if this is what upsetting her. She just wrinkles her nose at me.

"No thanks. I'm not doing the dirty work for those idiots."

"What's your problem then? What's the matter with you?"

"Nothing is. Don't be so touchy. You are so unbelievably touchy. Especially when it has anything to do with that family. Do you want some lunch?" Marianne pushes herself up from the floor, and shakes back her dark hair. I look up at her, and feel totally confused.

"No thanks," I tell her. "Just a coffee."

She rests one hand on the door and smiles at me sweetly. "Oh well done you. Still on the diet, eh?"

I bite my lip for a moment. "Sorry," I say then, looking at her carefully. "I probably am a bit touchy about Joe. He kissed me yesterday. On the lips." I see it then. I see it in her face, and there is not a damn thing she can do to hide it, though she tries fucking hard, I can tell you. Her face changes. Her face falls. Her eyes harden. It pisses her off. Then she cracks a massive smile. And I wish I hadn't said it.

"Well aren't you the popular one?" she asks, opening the door. "First one brother, now the next? Bet you've got your eye on Leon, really, though?"

"Don't be disgusting," I tell her. "I haven't got my eye on any of them, least of all that moron."

"Look, I'll be back in a minute. You can tell me all about it." She goes out, closing the door with a gentle bang behind her. I sit back, slightly triumphant, but also weakened. She's cleverer than me. There is something about her, I think then. Something that lets you know she could destroy you if she wanted to.

While she is gone, I sit in the deck chair and seethe with paranoid insecurities. I feel like a dick for telling her about Joe kissing me. I really wish I hadn't said it like that now. Why the hell did I do that World? Say something that I immediately wished I hadn't? What is wrong with me sometimes? I wish I hadn't smoked the weed either. That was stupid too. Suddenly I feel horribly self-aware, almost transparent in my crapness. Why did I say it like that? Like a fucking brag? *Idiot*. What is wrong with me? I sit there and wait for her to return, and fear what is running through her tidy little mind right now. I see myself sat in the deck chair, a wasted, gibbering wreck of a person. I tell myself that apart from Joe, who is a boy, I have no real friends. I've never had any real friends who are girls! I realise this with a crushing pain in my belly. Idiot. Loser. Freak. Now I've gone and pissed off the one girl who could have been my friend. Christ World, what if she secretly hates me? What if she is really one of those, what do you call them? *Frenemies*, that's it, that's what they call them! I don't think I could deal with that. I *know* I couldn't.

I try to shake myself out of it when Marianne returns with a bag of crisps, a Mars bar and a massive salad sandwich. She passes me a huge coffee silently, and kicks the door shut with her foot. I take the coffee gratefully and wonder if she has spat in it. She tucks herself up on the other chair with her feast of a lunch. I look at it, my mouth dry. I wonder helplessly if she is doing it on purpose. Lucky bitch can eat whatever the hell she wants and never put on weight. She doesn't even have to exercise either. She was born tiny and will always be tiny. I sigh, and drop my head into one hand. "You okay?" she asks me. I nod and groan. "Bit wasted?" I nod again. That's for sure.

"Shouldn't do it really," I tell myself, speaking out loud.

"Sorry I said that, about you babying Joe. You've known him your whole life. I suppose it's like looking out for a brother or something."

I raise my eyes from my hand to look at her. She is nibbling delicately at her sandwich. "Mmm," I say, half of me wanting to giggle for no reason whatsoever, half of me wanting to just cry.

"So," she says, opening her crisps up. The sharp smell of salt and vinegar hits my nose, and makes my tongue sweat. "Tell me all about this kiss then. The kiss from Joe, that is. Not Travis."

I can't tell if she is being sarcastic or not. Feigning fake interest. I rub viciously at my temples with my hand. I swear I can feel her bright eyes piercing right through me. Just paranoid, I tell myself desperately. "Oh forget it," I sigh. "I don't even know why I mentioned it."

"Because you were dying to tell me, obviously! Bet you couldn't wait to get the chance." Again, I feel like she is angry with me, but I am not sure why.

"Well it was nothing. Just a kiss. He took me by surprise. He wasn't thinking straight. He was upset because Mick stamped all over his records." I lift my shoulders in a weary, half-hearted shrug.

"Mick stamped on those records he's been buying?"

"Yeah. Long story."

"So he got upset and tried to kiss you?" Marianne asks, holding a large crisp up to her lips, and then flicking her tongue at it. I nod slowly.

"Stupid idiot," I say, with a weak grin. Marianne lashes the crisp with her tongue again.

"Well, maybe he actually likes you. Maybe both of them actually like you." I just look at her. I can't work out the expression on her face, and it unnerves me, or am I just getting incredibly paranoid? I'm not going to tell her what Joe said about Travis, no fucking way. I decide to change the subject. That seems the best plan.

"Well anyway, I'm going with him tonight. I'm fed up of being such a good girl the whole time."

"Ooh listen to you!"

"Well, it's true. It's always been the same. Me and Joe have always been the quiet ones in our families, you know? The rest cause all the drama and we just stay good and quiet." I take a sip of the scalding coffee. She has made it good and strong, just the way I like it. I try not to look at the half eaten sandwich on her plate.

"Hey if you can't rebel when you're sixteen, when can you?" she asks.

"Exactly."

"So what's the plan? How does it work?"

"I don't know really. I'm going to sneak out at eleven and meet Joe at the end of his road. Don't know after that."

"You don't know where you're going? Who you're meeting?"

"He says it's someone he's met before, so it should be okay."

"Christ," grins Marianne, slowly licking another crisp. "You are brave Lou. I don't think I would want to mix with people like that."

"So who the hell did you get the weed off then? You haven't told us that."

"Oh it was just Ryan, you idiot," she laughs at me scornfully. "He always has weed, you know that."

"Didn't actually. Didn't know he *always* did."

"He says it helps him be more creative," Marianne shrugs. "You know, with the band or whatever."

"Really should listen to them some time," I murmur.

"You should," she nods. "They're not too bad actually."

"Since when have you seen them?"

"Oh I don't know, just sometimes, you know when you two are busy." She meets my eyes with a sunny smile, and again I can't read her. It's her voice you see. She generally says everything in the same sweet, calm voice, as if everything just sort of thrills and pleases her, as if everything is just great. But her eyes give it away. If you look at her eyes you can just about tell when she is being sarcastic, or ironic, or whatever. "We need another party," she tells me then. "You need to sort that out."

"Me? How am I meant to?"

"Another one like the one Leon and Travis asked us to. That was the best night. This holiday is getting dull. We should be at parties every week!"

I shake my head at her, frowning. "That was not the best night, that was a fucking horrible night." Marianne giggles at this. "Anyway, you're the one with the big massive house, can't you have one here?"

"Hmm," Marianne touches her chin thoughtfully. "Maybe. I'll have a think. It could be done, couldn't it?"

"Don't see why not."

"And I could invite Leon and Travis."

"Okay. But why would you want to?"

"I told you before," she laughs, finishing her crisps and screwing up the empty packet. "They intrigue me! They all intrigue me. Doesn't anyone intrigue you Lou?"

"Yeah, you."

"Really?" she throws back her head and laughs deliciously at this. "Now that is funny! But true?"

"Course it's true," I tell her warily. "You're a fucking enigma."

"I can never tell when you're being serious you know."

"I can't with you either."

"Oh well, maybe we will just *intrigue* each other then!"

"Yeah, maybe. Look I better go actually. Got to squeeze a jog in somewhere today." I get up from the chair, drink the last of my coffee and place the mug down on the floor. Marianne is just silent for a moment, curled up in her chair, with her feet tucked under her and her fingers stroking her chin. In my wasted state I see her as some kind of evil genius, plotting extreme damage.

"Well off you go then," she says sleepily. "Can't get in the way of Lou Carlings bid for the perfect body, can we now?" I just raise my eyebrows at her. "Have you got a new target weight in mind then?"

"No, just want to stay like this," I say, trying not to sound as defensive as I feel. "I don't want to put it all back on again, do I?"

"God no," she agrees quickly. "That would be awful. And so many people do that, don't they? Pile it all right back on again as soon as they relax."

"Well, not me. No way."

"Good for you. You go for it. You're looking so amazing now. Didn't have all these boys after you before did you?" I stare at her. I bite my lip. I feel hurt and anxious and I want to get the hell away from her, but she just smiles up at me, that sunny sarcastic smile.

I wander back home in a dreamlike state. World, how can I explain that I feel hurt, somewhere inside me, but I don't know why? For some reason this feeling makes me want to find my mum and crawl onto her lap. Then I get even more worked up and insecure in my own company, and that is not good. I walk along, and I am sure I can feel the fat of my thighs rubbing together as I do. That can't be good. I place a hand against my belly every now and again, picturing Marianne's hard flat stomach in my mind. I may have lost weight, but I am still all flabby and wobbly everywhere, how do you get rid of that? Oh Christ. I feel like shit. I feel like I want to shrink down small so that no one can see me.

I push open the front door and pause immediately. The kitchen door is closed. The kitchen door is never closed unless people are having private conversations in there, and true enough, I can hear the murmur of voices coming from the other side of the door. Curiously, I close the front door quietly so that they don't hear it. I tiptoe towards the kitchen door. I can hear my mum and my sister, which totally freaks me out and confuses me. Is she back? What the hell? I reach out to open the door, but freeze when I hear my mum say; "she's taking it too far now Sara. Jogging every day. Hardly eating at all." Oh right. Okay then. It's back to this again, is it?

"Okay, okay I'll have a word with her about being sensible," my sister agrees reluctantly. I press the side of my face against the door and try not to breathe too loudly. I am outraged, but also enthralled. I have never, ever overheard a conversation about myself before now. I would have a hard time believing that anyone talked about me ever, before this. What would there be to say?

"What with the drugs and everything, I'm at my wits end!" my mum is exclaiming to my sister. She does sound anxious, I'll give her that. Funnily enough, this does not make me feel guilty, which is odd, because it should do really shouldn't it World? My mum is a good person, and I have caused her stress. For some reason though, I just feel vicious and smug and snarly. "Her and Joe seem to be running wild at the moment, or that's what your dad thinks anyway. I don't know. I don't know what to say to her."

I decide that is enough. I don't really want to hear anymore through the door about what a delinquent I suddenly appear to be. I open the door and they both look up in surprise from the table. "It's okay," I say. "You can carry on."

"Lou…" my mum says, her hand reaching across the table for me. "I am just worried about you. I thought Sara could help." I look coldly at my sister.

"Are you back then?"

"No, no, I'm still living with Rich. Just came to see Mum."

"Oh," I nod, and turn out of the room. "Okay then." I head up the stairs, and become aware that someone is following me. It is Sara. She follows me into what used to be our bedroom, and closes the door behind her.

"Don't worry about Mum," she says warmly, perching on the edge of my messy bed. "She's just being a huge drama queen as usual. I've spent the last few hours convincing her that all is fine with Rich and me, and so now she's turned her anxiety onto you. Sorry."

"What's she even on about?" I complain, looking around the floor for my running clothes. "Bloody bollocks. I eat loads!"

"You sure? You're definitely looking slimmer again."

"Well fucking good!" I explode at her suddenly, facing her. "Who wants to be fat their whole life? Jesus Christ. It's got nothing to do with her at all."

"Okay, okay," my sister makes a face and holds up her hands. "Calm down. Don't shoot the messenger. I just said I'd make sure you were being sensible."

"Oh God," I groan, holding my hands over my eyes for a moment. "You lot are priceless. None of you gave a shit when I was too fat did you? No one worried about that being healthy or sensible, which it wasn't!"

"True," Sara nods at me. "Okay then. Calm down."

"Well it's all right for you," I tell her. "You've left. You don't have to be surrounded by all this pointless shit all the time."

"She says Dad was okay about Les?"

"She says that. Who knows? Who cares?"

"Well, if you ask me, she's just looking for trouble…"

"Sara do you mind?" I find my jogging trousers on the floor, pick them up and shake them off. "I've got to go for a run before she tries to force feed me a fucking doughnut. You can go and tell her I'm fine."

"Okay, okay," my sister says, getting up. "Do you want to come by the flat and see me and Rich some time? I gave mum the address and number."

"Yep," I say, not looking at her. "Whatever."

18

Dear World, it is far easier than I imagined sneaking out at night. Ha! Makes me wish I had tried it before! I had been getting worked up about creaking stairs, and shimmying down drainpipes and the like. But in the end, all I do is come out of my room, creep quietly down the stairs and go out of the front door. Mum and Les are still up. I can hear the TV on in the lounge, and the door is shut. Brilliant. Easy.

I walk quickly down the road, past the shops and on to Joe's house. He is already there and waiting for me on the corner of his road. He looks pleased to see me, and a huge grin envelopes his face. We link arms automatically and you know, I just feel good again, despite what we are doing. The nerves and the tension are gone from my belly. My face just wants to smile. "Well that was piss easy!" I tell him with a giggle. I feel wired. I feel alive, and brimming with fear and excitement. He looks at me, still grinning.

"Told you. Piece of piss. Parents are too wrapped up in their own lives to notice half the stuff that goes on."

"Everything okay at your end when you went home?" I check. He grimaces.

"I copped it from Leon. He was majorly pissed off after babysitting the brats all day."

"He can't complain!" I argue, amazed at his audacity. "You're doing this aren't you?"

"I know. I did remind him of that before he could lay me out. Seemed to work."

"Stupid arsehole."

"Fucking dick brain."

I laugh at him. "Useless twat faced moron."

"Vile cunt."

We carry on like this for a few minutes, before it occurs to me to ask where the hell we are going. "Just the bridge," Joe says, his arm still through mine, and his hands in his pockets.

"The bridge to school?" I ask, and he nods. Our estate Herton, is separated by a dual carriageway from the Somerley estate, where our school is. Somerley is next to Redchurch, and the kids from all three estates go to Somerley Secondary. We have to cross the pedestrian bridge over the carriageway to get to school each day. "Why there?" I wonder.

"Just easy," he shrugs. "It's not near anyone's houses, or shops. Police aren't likely to spot you up there, are they?"

"I suppose not. Bit creepy though."

"Oh this guy is okay," Joe reassures me as we walk on through the night. "He's like Leon's age, or whatever. A real stoner. Bit stupid actually. It won't be scary I promise you."

"Hey," I dig him in the ribs. "I came to protect you remember?" Joe laughs.

"Oh yeah, I forgot. My bodyguard right?"

"That's it. I'm coming every time from now on."

"Really? Why?"

"Why not?" I reply. "Who cares?"

"My thoughts exactly," says Joe, with a nod.

***

Five minutes later we start climbing up the steps to the bridge. I squint into the darkness and can just make out the figure of a man, loitering up there already. I know Joe said he was okay, but I can't help looking down at the road beneath us as we climb higher, and imagining how easy it would be for a psycho drug user to hurl us to our deaths. I swallow and cling to Joe's arm, and up we go. The cars roar by in the darkness under us. We approach the man casually. I try not to look at him. I try to look unconcerned and bored; as if this is the kind of thing I do every day.

"All right mate?" the guy calls out in a gruff voice, as we get closer. "Brought a friend?" I look at Joe in fear. He seems relaxed.

"My bodyguard," he says, and the guy laughs out loud.

"Oh right yeah! I get you!"

We stop in front of him, and it is all done very quickly and politely. Joe hands over a small taped up package, and the guy, who I can just make out, has long blonde hair under his hood, hands Joe a note, and that is it. "See you later man," the guy says, and slopes off towards the other end of the bridge. Joe pockets the money, turns around, and back we go. I look up at him and feel a weird, unexpected surge of pride.

"Well that was easy."

"Told you. That's it."

"You are kind of cool, you know."

"What?" Joe looks at me, wide eyed with disbelief. "What did you say Carling? Was that a compliment?"

I lean into him and punch him in the arm. I want to tell him I love him, you know, as a friend, like girls tell each other all the time, but I can't really do that, when he's a boy can I? It would sound wrong. "You're just cool," I say instead. "The way you deal with everything. I'm proud of you. I like you being you."

"Oh okay," Joe smiles at me and laughs as we walk along. "Whatever that means!" I want to tell him it means that I can only really be myself around him. That I feel different around everyone else, like I have to watch what I say, and think about what I do. Not with him. I'm just me. He's just him. Why can't it be that easy with other people? "Anyway," he says then, breaking into my thoughts. "Thanks for coming. It was nice to have the company."

"No problem. I want to be the first to listen to you when you get this drum kit, you know."

"Deal."

We walk on in comfortable silence together, arms linked. Joe tries to give me some of the money when we get back to his, but I refuse. I don't need it. He does. He needs his bloody drum kit, doesn't he? We say goodbye and I head home, feeling better than I have in ages.

***

Dear World, it's my mum doing her bloody tap tapping at the bedroom door that wakes me up the next morning. I am rolled up in my duvet, warm and snug. I do not want to move. "What?" I call out to her.

"Your mobile keeps going off! It's Marianne! Did you leave it down here on purpose?"

"Oh Christ." I close my eyes for a moment, and wonder why my guts clench at the thought of speaking to her. "Okay coming." I throw back the duvet, my feet hit and floor and I open the door. Mum is on the landing, holding a cup of tea, and my mobile phone.

"I made you this."

"Oh thanks."

"Have some toast or something with me in a minute?" she asks hopefully, as she goes into the bathroom. I nod at her and go downstairs with my phone in my hand. I am starting to wish Dad would kick off and give her some grief. At least that would get her off my back for a while. I go into the kitchen with the phone.

"Hiya?"

"Good morning Lou," Marianne sounds as cheerful as ever. "I don't suppose you are off out for a jog yet are you?"

"Just got up," I tell her, with a yawn. "But probably soon I will, why?"

"Thought I could come with you?"

I am perplexed. "Why?"

"For exercise," she replies chirpily, "and for fun, and for company! I thought you might get lonely on your runs. Or do you prefer to be alone? Just say if you do, I won't be offended." She has given me a chance to say no and get out of this, but I am too groggy and heavy headed to work it out.

"No it's okay," I tell her like an idiot. "You can come. Shall I meet you on the fields then?"

"Yes, what time?"

"What time is it now?"

"Ten fifteen."

"Bloody hell. Okay. Say eleven fifteen then?"

"Brilliant!" she cries happily. "See you then!"

"Okay. Bye Marianne."

I chuck the phone on the table and sit down with my cup of tea. Just then Les shuffles in, hiding behind his newspaper. I wonder if he is ever going to have the guts to speak to me. "Morning?" I say to him. He lowers his paper hesitantly and looks at me as if he is surprised to see me, or hear me there. He tucks the paper under one arm and gets a cup down from the cupboard.

"Morning Lou," he says, flicking back his hair. "How are you today?"

"Wonderful," I tell him dryly, and he smiles and turns his back to make his tea. What a great conversationalist he is! Incredible. I am blown away by his social skills, and I'm a teenager for Christ's sake! What is his excuse? Luckily Mum reappears then, or the silence would have become unbearable. She starts making me toast. Does she never go out anymore?

"What did Marianne want?"

"To come for a run with me."

"Oh. Right." Mum is silent for a moment, while she scrapes margarine and Marmite onto my toast. She turns and places it in front of me, with this strange pinched look on her face. She looks tired I think. "But she is so skinny!" she says then, clasping her hands together under her chin. "She doesn't need to lose weight either!" Oh God, now she probably thinks we are in a strange pact or something, a twisted version of Weight Watchers.

"Mum, running is not just about losing weight. It's about keeping fit and healthy. Keeping supple."

"Oh," she says. "Okay." I see her eyes flick down to my toast. I shake my head. I pick it up and eat the lot. Every last crumb. Just for her. It's okay, I tell myself as I chew it down. I will do a longer run. I will show Marianne what I am made of. She has no idea what a fucking machine I am.

"Can you take Gremlin when you go for your run?"

"No Mum. It will kill him. I'll take him out after."

***

An hour later I am on the field, doing my stretches as I wait for Marianne. I see her walking slowly across the field towards me, and when she sees me she lifts one hand in an excited little wave. I just don't understand her.

"Ready?" I ask her when she gets to me. I am thinking about that toast. I can see it sat in my stomach, starting to digest.

"Oh yes, I'm ready," she enthuses. She is wearing a tight pair of immaculate black jogging trousers, and a tight fitting black vest top. "Can we talk and run at the same time?" she asks, as I take off. I nod at her. She can talk if she wants to talk. "How far do you normally go?"

"Two or three times around the entire field, depending on how I feel. Was aiming for four times today actually."

"Ooh why?"

"Don't know. Just to push it."

"Oh, I see. Hey guess what?"

"What?"

"I've sorted out a party! We *are* having a party!" I look at her sideways and frown. She is bursting with this, I can just see. She is extremely pleased with herself.

"Seriously? Where?"

"My house! Like you said! My parents are away next weekend, from Friday until Monday. They've said I can stay in the house, as long as you keep me company." She flashes me a secretive smile. "And if we behave ourselves too, of course."

"Oh right. I see. Bloody hell."

"So we have this week to organise it," she goes on breathlessly. So far she is doing a good job of keeping up with me, which is pissing me off. "It's got to be the best party ever. It's going to be amazing."

"Brilliant," I say. "Can't wait."

We are on our second loop. I don't talk to her, because it gives me a stitch to speak. She carries on though, nattering on about this party of hers, and who she is going to invite, and what music they are going to have. She seems to think Josh and Ryan can play their music for us. Hmm. I just smile and run. I run faster. God damn it, she is like a bloody robot. Keeping up with me on her tiny little matchstick legs, chatting away, barely breaking a sweat. Unbelievable. On the third loop I really go for it. I think of the stupid toast and I picture me as a size eight, and I run faster and faster. I would normally collapse by now. Three loops equals a forty minute run nearly. But I keep going. "Round again?" Marianne questions. I look at her long enough to see the sweat shining on her forehead. She runs neatly, I think, little arms bent and pumping up and down, little legs hammering along. Her black hair tied up in a high ponytail.

"See if we can," I mutter, and press on. Marianne keeps up with me. At one point I swear she even tries to overtake me. I don't let her. I keep up the pace; upping my speed every time I think she is getting ahead of me. This is madness; I realise and grimace as I run. We must look like lunatics. Why are we doing this?

"Oh I give up, I give up!" she finally cries out, and stops running. She leans down over her knees, hair hanging. "Christ Carling! You're trying to kill me!"

I run on a bit longer, then turn around and run back. She has plonked herself down on the grass, and is panting heavily. "Sorry," I shrug at her. She grins.

"Bit of a pro these days, aren't you?" she says. "Not like at school. You really hated P.E, didn't you?"

I sit down next to her, red faced and sweating intensely. "That's different."

"Can't wait for this party," she says, pushing her damp hair back from her face. "How cool is it gonna' be?"

"Your parents will go mad if the house gets wrecked."

"It won't get wrecked. I'm gonna' lock loads of the rooms."

"Oh."

"We'll have the lounge and dining room, conservatory and garden. That's plenty. Want to come to town with me and buy some decorations?"

I shrug. "Could do. Have to bring the dog though. I told Mum."

"That's okay."

"How are you going to get booze?"

"Parents have loads," she says. "And don't you think Leon and Travis would get us some if we paid them?"

"You're going to invite them?" I ask her.

"Of course," she laughs, looking me in the eye. "Wouldn't be a party without them, would it?"

Is she insane? *Is* she?

I watch her curiously as she lies back on the grass and folds her arms behind her head. "Need to make a list," she says, eyes closed against the sun. "List of food, you know, party nibbles and stuff, drinks. Probably need paper plates and cups, because I'm gonna' lock all ours away."

"Good idea," I say, and lay down next to her on my belly. I pick a piece of grass and stick the end in my mouth for a chew. "What about big burly men to do the door?" I ask her, my tone serious. She snaps open her eyes and frowns at me.

"Are you serious?"

"Depends who you're inviting," I shrug at her. "Depends if things kick off. You saw what happened at Hogan's party."

"Yes, and we all know whose fault that was, don't we?" she smiles at me, licking her lips, as her eyes narrow to slits. I roll my eyes.

"Ha fucking ha. I did nothing wrong."

"I am only joking," she giggles, touching my arm briefly. "I won't really need security will I?"

"Just call the police if things get out of hand," I suggest. "Or have a word in Leon's ear if you're so determined to invite him."

"Oh yes I am," Marianne rolls neatly onto her side, props herself up on one arm, and grins at me. "Well you can, can't you? You can tell him, or get Joe to tell him. They'll all come won't they?"

"I expect so," I sigh. "And I expect you will end up regretting it."

"No chance," Marianne shakes her head at me. "Come on Lou, we need to get showered and changed and get shopping! So much to organise!"

That afternoon is a strange one, World. I meet Marianne again when we have both been home to shower and change. She is adamant that we do not invite Joe on our shopping trip. We are having 'girly' time apparently, whatever that is. We catch the bus with Gremlin, and spend the rest of the day traipsing around town. Marianne keeps her arm linked through mine the whole time, which I cannot help but find slightly unnerving. I keep thinking back to when we were all stoned. How her face changed when I told her Joe had kissed me. How sarcastic she was after that, going on about my diet and stuff. I can't relax, as we shop. I keep expecting her to change again, and come at me with her smiling sarcasm. She doesn't though. She is like the best girlfriend I never had at school. Friendly and attentive, excitable and genuine. I would have really enjoyed it if I hadn't been so on edge the whole time. She buys paper plates and cups, tons of frozen pizzas and crisps and dips. I wonder where she gets the money, but don't ask. I am just mystified by her as we shop. She even buys plastic tablecloths, balloons and bunting for fucks sake. I can see her having a career as a party organiser when she leaves school. She would be great at it. But I don't like to tell her that the balloons and bunting will be totally lost on most of the people she is intent on inviting. Bless her. Let her discover that for herself.

Obviously it falls to me to invite Joe's brothers. I have to break the news to him first, which I do later that evening, when we meet up for another walk across the bridge. This time we have to go right across the other side, and knock on the door of the first block of flats on the Somerley estate. A skinny girl in tiny shorts and a huge hooded jumper, opens the door smoking a cigarette. She wears her hair in a high ponytail, and is plastered in make-up, but I have a horrible feeling she is actually about forty-five or something. She has vicious eyes, so I hang back behind Joe as he passes over the package wordlessly. She takes it, unwraps it right there in the doorway, sniffs it, and then stuffs it in the pocket of her jumper. She looks Joe up and down, and for a terrible moment I fear she is just going to slam the door in his face and not give him the money. "Bit young for this kind of shit, ain't you love?" she asks him, as she presses the money into his waiting hand. "I got a boy your age. I'd have a fit if he was doing what you're up to."

Joe just smiles and turns away. "Night then," he says to her as we leave. I try to stifle my giggle until we are far from the flats.

"Oh but it's okay for her to be taking that shit?" I ask him, laughing, as we head back to the bridge. "Her poor kid!"

"She looks familiar," Joe says with a shiver. "Bet he goes to our school."

"Fucking hell. Hey at least our parents aren't druggies Joe!" I am still giggling.

"There are many things they could be that are worse, I suppose," he agrees, with a wry grin. "We should look on the positive side. Hey, how is the infamous Les anyway? My mum keeps raving on about what a gentleman he is!"

I snort with barely contained laughter. "That is so ridiculous. Typical of your mum. Anyone who is not a stocky dwarf with a smashed in face is obviously a gentleman!" We both look at each other and laugh again. "Oh he's all right," I shrug, when the hilarity has subsided. We are crossing the bridge again. "He just keeps to himself. He's like the invisible man or something. He has nothing to say. No opinions or questions. He just has the paper in front of his face the whole time."

"Weird," nods Joe, hands in pockets. "But he's nice to your mum and everything?"

"If you can call being an utter dullard nice, yeah."

"At least he stays out your business. He's not trying to tell you what to do or anything."

"Oh no. Think he's scared of me actually. Think teenagers freak him out, or something. I should probably have some fun with him. Start telling him all my intimate problems, or something."

Joe digs me in the side with his elbow. "What fucking intimate problems have you got Carling?" he demands. I look at him in mock anger.

"Oh you mean besides being a secret drug dealer, and having a best friend who may very well be my worst enemy?"

Joe looks at me, open-mouthed. "You better not mean me!"

"Course not dumb arse. I mean Marianne."

"Oh right. Why? What's she done?"

"Oh nothing," I sigh, looking down at the bridge as we cross back over to our side. "She's just hard to read sometimes. I can never quite tell if she is taking the piss out of me, or not. You know."

"Well I think she's a nutcase. She gives me the creeps half the time."

"She's got some sort of crush on your brothers," I tell him then, nudging him with my own elbow. He frowns down at me in confusion.

"You're joking?"

"She's having a party," I nod at him. "On Friday night at her house, and it is her explicit instruction that I invite you, and you bring your brothers. Her explicit instruction I tell you."

Joe is frowning deeply at me, walking along with his hands inside his pockets, and shaking his head in disbelief. "That's insane," he reasons. "Why the hell does she want them at her party? Is she mad?"

"She's intrigued by them, apparently," I tell him with a shrug. "Don't ask me Joe, I have no idea what goes on in her mind. I only know she's having a party and she wants them there."

"She's asking for trouble," he says then, looking back at the bridge and the steps as we approach them. "One way or another."

"It's up to her. I have tried to warn her."

"Who else is she inviting?"

"Well us, and Josh and Ryan, and people from school I suppose."

"Hmm. Should be interesting. Okay, I'll tell them. Count me in. Definitely count me in."

I nod okay and we go down the steps on the other side. "This must be nearly over by now?" I ask Joe then, looking up at his face in the moonlight. I have stopped growing, but he is getting taller. He makes a face.

"They say so."

"But what does that mean? Like, how many more trips?"

"I don't know Carling. You don't have to keep coming you know."

"I like coming, stupid."

"Well they say it's nearly all gone." He lifts and drops his shoulders before releasing a huge yawn. "So it must be. Then that is that. Thank fuck."

"Will you miss the money?"

"Nah. I'll get another job."

"Will you miss them needing you? Being nice to you?" I smile wickedly at Joe as he glares sideways at me.

"They don't know how to be nice to anyone Carling," he reminds me. "So don't worry about that."

"It's not really their fault," I tease him. "They weren't brought up properly. They can't help being total turds. Blame your mother."

"Oi."

"Oi what? It's true! People are not born bad you know. We all start off the same. Innocent babies."

Joe snorts at this. "Mum says Leon was never innocent. She says he had an evil glint in his eye when he was a baby."

"I can believe that actually. So anyway, what was all this crap you were saying before, about them being your *real* brothers and that?"

"Well they are," Joe shrugs. "They are my real brothers. The others are half-brothers."

"So what though?"

"I just meant that if I had to choose one pair over another, I would choose my real brothers."

"Even though they've always treated you like shit?" I ask incredulously, unable to understand how he could choose two thugs over two sweet little boys.

"Yeah but they're my real brothers," Joe says again, as if it is not getting through to me. "They might be pricks most the time, but they are my real brothers."

"Yeah but Tommy and Will are just little kids," I argue with him. "They're sweet, and innocent and all that."

"No they are not!" Joe cries back vehemently. "They're just as vile Carling! Just because they are little does not make them sweet and innocent. They're conniving little shits! You have no idea. They'll do anything to get us in shit, I'm telling you."

"All right, calm down idiot," I tell him, grinning, but I reach out and touch his arm as well. "You don't need to tell me."

"Sometimes I think even Mum would wish us older three away so she can just have her nice *new* family," Joe says this sneeringly, and I feel awkward, and get the feeling he has thought about this a lot over the years. "She says she can't wait for us to move out, often enough."

"She doesn't mean it, you idiot," I say, shoving my arm through his and leaning my head on his shoulder. "She loves you really. Come on, cheer up. Think about this party on Friday!" I jog him and he looks down and rolls his eyes at me.

"Ah don't even…that party is going to be a fucking nightmare."

"It's going to be hilarious Joe," I tell him, resting my head back on his shoulder. We are nearly home. We have walked past his house, as he insists on walking me home first. He is silent and subdued, his hair hanging down over his eyes, as we stop next to my front garden and I pull my arm free from his. For some reason then, I just cannot bear the sad look on his face, so I reach up; I go up on tiptoe, and plant a kiss on his cheek. He looks instantly embarrassed and shocked, so I turn quickly, smiling, wondering what I have done. "Night Joe," I say, and he says nothing. Just stands and watches me go in quietly through the front door.

19

Dear World, well the rest of the week is a shitter. I only get through it by thinking about Friday. About me and Joe and Marianne, alcohol and a huge massive party. My mum watches everything that I eat, and clicks her tongue and rolls her eyes every time I go out of the door for a jog. "Don't get any skinnier," she warns me time and time again, as if it is somehow up to her how thin or fat I am. "Size ten is small enough. You don't want to be any thinner than that." I don't know what to say to her half the time. How does she know what I want to be? Why does it matter to her? I just want to be healthy for God's sake.

The strange thing is, I have reached my target weight, my target dress size and all that. This is where I am meant to be, this is who I wanted to be. But somehow it doesn't exactly fill me with joy. Instead I feel restless and on edge. I feel like I can't relax, or take my eye off the scales, or the fat will find its way back to me. Insane I know, but I can't seem to help it. I am starting to panic about every little thing I eat. I am starting to worry if my runs are long enough to cancel out what I have consumed. I am starting to view all meals with suspicion and caution. It is getting harder and harder to satisfy my mother, without panicking myself into a right old state. Instead of feeling happy, I am wound up and tense. I am verging on an argument with almost everyone. I feel a kind of anger and frustration spinning around inside of me that I just cannot pinpoint or understand. The only time I feel good, the only time I feel truly at ease and free, is when I am running. I feel like I am running away from it all World, that's how it feels, but you know what? I'm not really am I? I'm just running in circles.

Food is increasingly disgusting to me. Especially the remnants of it. The leftovers. The smears and crusts on last night's dinner plates. It's just vile. It gets to the point when I can barely stand going into the kitchen in case I see an unwashed plate, or a cereal bowl filled with uneaten brown mush. Ugh, it's awful. That's when you realise what you have really eaten, when you see the remnants of it like that. The way tomato sauce darkens and hardens, and you have to scrape it off the plate. It makes my stomach turn over. Takeaways are even worse. I won't go near these anyway, but Mum and Les designate Friday as their takeaway night, and Saturday mornings now reek of stagnant curry, or cold fish and chips. I can barely stomach the hallway, let alone the kitchen, where I can see the stained plastic containers, and the plate all the leftovers have been shovelled onto. Looks like a plate full of worms and maggots. It makes me heave.

I feel like I am going privately insane. I start to scrawl longer and longer ramblings on my wall, none of which make any sense. They just serve to express the way I am feeling. I write about food I have eaten and how it has looked, smelt and tasted to me. I don't know why I do this World. I feel alone and scared when I think about how much I used to love chocolate as a child, and how much it horrifies me now. I bury my head in my arms and sob more than once that week, I can tell you. The misery of it, the panic and the fear, the self-loathing, it makes me want to punch myself in the face. It makes me want to smash my fist into the wall, just so I can feel something else for a change. More and more I think of Marianne and her razor blade, and wonder what it is she is escaping from when she does it to herself.

Joe is busy with the brats, the dog from hell, and housework. He is looking forward to letting loose on Friday as much as me, so he does it all for them, he keeps his head down and gets on with it. He goes back to being their servant, their whipping boy, and their good middle child who never complains nor gives them reason to worry. I seethe on his behalf. I cannot wait until Friday night. I feel like it will somehow be ours. We will get ours. Whatever the hell that means.

Marianne sails through the week on a cloud of excitement. She buys more food, more decorations, more everything. She spends hours on the Internet downloading the perfect playlist for the night. She even considers hiring a DJ, just to get it right, but I remind her that there is no way her neighbours would not complain about this. I find myself at her house almost every day that week, just watching her, just taking her in, trying to work her out. I have a lot on my mind, so I don't say much, but she doesn't seem to notice. She just swans about and chatters constantly, and rings lists of people to check and recheck that they are still coming. She helps me decide what to wear, and we spend one bizarre afternoon straightening our hair together. I have to say World, I don't ordinarily bother with all this shit. I really don't. Call me a tomboy or whatever, but I've never gone in for the polished look. Just never saw the point. But I must admit that straight hair makes me look totally and utterly different. For some reason, I almost smile at my reflection in the mirror when she has finished experimenting. My hair looks longer, thinner, straighter and glossier. It looks blonder. I struggle to recognise myself, and even this makes me want to cry. Where did I go, I wonder, where did I go?

Thursday night I receive a phone call from Joe. "Got to make a delivery tonight," he hisses down the phone at me. "Are you up for it?"

"Why not?" I sigh back at him. "Usual place, usual time?"

"Yep. Thanks Carling."

After the phone call I find myself lying on my bed, staring at the ceiling, while my hands caress my hip bones, my stomach, my ribs. It has an almost hypnotic effect on me. I go through what I have eaten today, like a list in my head. Breakfast, coffee and an apple, and a flapjack that I took from the tin to please Mum, but then fed to Gremlin when she went out to hang out the washing. Lunch, Mum was at work so I just had a yoghurt, a coffee, and two mints. Dinner, mum cooked Les's favourite; shepherd's pie. I joined them, but sulked. I pushed my food around, and I dropped bits under the table for the dog. I ate about half, then felt grotesque, and came up to my room for a cry. I punched my pillows and pretended they were my mum's face, for making me eat that much crap.

Now I feel calm, stroking my fingers across my pelvic bone. I close my eyes and try to see the old me in my head. The chubby one. The chunky one. The one who liked her food. Oh she loves her food, Mum used to say proudly to relatives. Never have any trouble feeding her; she's not fussy at all, no. You're bigger boned than your sister, people used to say. You've got puppy fat. You'll grow taller and stretch out. You've just developed earlier. It's puppy fat. You're just a different build than your sister. Last Christmas, Maria's oldest son James, looking at me like I was a piece of shit on his shoe and saying; is that arse all yours, or have you borrowed someone else's? Fuck them, I think now. Fuck them all. I clench my teeth. It serves me well to remember these things.

That night I meet Joe and we head to the bridge. "Someone you know?" I ask him as usual. He looks unsure.

"It's the one who got funny."

I shoot a dark look at him. "What?"

Joe looks troubled and embarrassed, and has difficulty meeting my gaze. "Well I think it is," he shrugs. "I kind of forgot his name."

"Oh Joe," I say, slipping my arm through his, and automatically looking around me into the darkness. "Is this a good idea? What if it is the same one? What if he gets funny again?"

"I'm not handing anything over until he gives the money," Joe replies, nodding his head at me, as if trying to convince himself. "That's what Leon said. Make them pay first. Any one of them could take the stuff and leg it."

"Oh God, I'm worried," I tell him, helplessly. "I don't think we should do it."

"I can't back out," Joe shakes his head. "But you don't have to come. Or you can wait at the bottom of the steps?"

"I can't let you go up there alone," I argue. "Oh Christ Joe, are you sure about this? Are you really sure this will be okay?"

"It's okay," he tells me. "It will be okay."

I have no choice but to believe in him. We keep our arms linked; we keep close together, and start to head up the steps. Joe is peering into the darkness, trying to distinguish the figure we can just make out up on the bridge. I can see it is a bloke, a bit on the weighty side, and taller than Joe. He is smoking a cigarette and walking across the bridge towards us. "That him?" I whisper to Joe.

"Still not sure," Joe whispers back. I look back at the bloke on the bridge. He has that way of walking that makes me think he is trying to look hard. That side-to-side swagger. Leon does it. All tough guys do it. Mick does it too. It's a 'don't mess with me strut', and I find it menacing and a bad omen. He shows no sign of slowing down as he comes upon us, and sucks the last drag from his cigarette before hurling the butt over the side of the bridge and onto the road below. I look tentatively at Joe and see him swallowing nervously. I think again; why does he have to do this? Why? Why is he so hell-bent on putting himself through this? Is it really for the money, or is it all just to impress his brothers? The bloke stuffs his hands into the pockets of his dark tracksuit top. He has a hooded top under it, and the hood pulled up over his head. He instantly sticks his hand out to Joe, practically thrusts it aggressively into his face. Joe moves back slightly.

"All right mate?" he asks.

"Yeah," the man says quickly, irritably. "Come on then," he nods at his own hand, stuck out towards Joe. Joe swallows.

"Money first mate," I hear him say. It all kicks off then. It happens so fast I am shocked into a dumb stupor. The man on the bridge kind of grunts a laugh at Joe, then seizes him by the front of his top, and shoves him back into the railing, pushing him back as far as he can go. "Hey!" Joe calls out in surprise, but there is nothing he can do to free himself. I am frozen to the spot in fear. I watch the guy search Joe's pockets quickly and expertly, and it becomes horribly obvious to me then that he knows exactly what he is doing, and has in fact planned it all. "Oi!" Joe shouts again, and I see the guy shove something into his own pocket. He then thumps Joe in the stomach and lets him fall. He turns and walks away without even looking at me. I am stunned and horrified. I watch him go. Then I look back at Joe, slumped against the railing, grimacing and gripping hold of his belly. "Fucks sake!" he is grunting at me. I kneel down next to him. I can feel tears in my eyes.

"Oh my God, are you okay?"

"We have to get the money!" he hisses, grabbing hold of the railing and hauling himself up to his feet. I stand in front of him and hold him back.

"Joe no!"

"Lou, he didn't give the money!"

"I know that, I bloody know that, and you are not going after him!" I have one arm around his waist, and my other hand holding onto his arm. If he decides to run after that psycho, he is going to have to drag me along with him. He rubs his belly and pants in pain, and wipes his hair back from his forehead angrily.

"Fucks sake!" he cries again. "Bastard!"

"It was gonna' happen sooner or later," I tell him, and start to shove him back towards the steps. "Let's just get out of here, let's go. Let's never do this again!"

"Lou!"

"Joe, no! He could have thrown you over!" I scream at him suddenly then, giving him a harder shove towards the steps. "I thought he was going to throw you over!"

"Jesus Christ," I hear Joe mutter, as he stumbles reluctantly down the first few steps. I am in a panic. I am looking back over my shoulder into the darkness, totally convinced that thug is going to come back and have another go. I cannot get down those steps fast enough. I just cling onto his arm and drag him along. He looks properly pissed off, never mind scared like me, just really pissed off.

We reach the bottom step and I start to breathe a little easier, but all the same, I have had enough of this shit. I keep hold of Joe's arm, and march us towards home, looking back over my shoulder every now and again. I try to remember the guys face, in case I need to, but his hood and the shadows mostly hid it. I can feel this awful, tight knot of dread in my stomach. It is making me feel ill. I keep looking at Joe, and maybe he is trying to save face, being male and everything, because he is just slouching along, hands in pockets, face dark. "Fuck's sake," he says through his teeth as we round the corner to his road.

"Was it the same guy as before?" I ask him then. He shrugs and nods at the same time. "Guess he saw me coming, hey?"

"You didn't stand a chance," I sigh, trembling now. "And I don't even like to think about what could have happened if I hadn't been there!"

"It's all right," he says softly, and stops walking. He turns to face me, and looks utterly bereft. "What a pain in the arse. What a stupid prick." I am not sure if he means the guy on the bridge, or him. He rolls his eyes up to the night sky for a moment. "Can't believe he did that."

I glance over to his house. Leon's car is parked out the front, and the headlights are gleaming. Joe follows my gaze and releases a heavy sigh. "Oh great. Now this is going to be even more fun."

"I'll come with you," I say quickly. "I'll tell him what happened. It's his own fault! He should be doing his own dirty work!"

"Come on then," Joe says and starts walking towards the car. I squint into the glare of the headlights. I cannot tell if Leon is alone or not. As we near the car, the engine shuts off and the lights fade. The driver's door opens and Leon climbs out, lighting a cigarette. He slams the door shut and nods at us as we approach.

"Hard night at it?" he asks, amiably enough for him. Joe and I look at each other, and the knot of fear in my stomach tightens. I almost feel that I cannot breathe.

"Shit," Joe tells him, stopping next to the car. I keep my arm linked through his, and watch Leon's dark eyes flick down to me, then back to Joe's face. He sucks on his cigarette and breathes the smoke over his brother's head. He is waiting. "Really shit," Joe says then, biting his lip.

Leon does that thing where he spreads his legs, and squares up. He is frowning at Joe, waiting. "What?" he prompts when Joe is reluctant.

"That guy that was funny last time," Joe tells him, hardly managing to meet his eyes. "It was him, and he didn't pay. He robbed me."

I watch Leon's eyes grow wider, and his mouth tightens, his forehead creases.

"He nearly threw Joe over the bridge," I speak up quickly, and Leon's dark eyes switch to meet mine. "He just grabbed him and punched him."

"He took the stuff and ran," Joe shrugs sheepishly. Leon blows out his breath, shakes his head and narrows his eyes.

"You fucking prick," he mumbles. Joe makes a face and nods.

"Sorry."

"That's all right, I know who the bastard is. I'll go and pay him a visit."

"He could have thrown him over if I wasn't there," I feel the need to point out angrily, glaring at Leon, who simply raises his eyebrows at me.

"Lucky you were there then."

"You can't blame Joe."

"What's with you two lately?" Leon asks, looking back at Joe and gesturing towards me with his cigarette. A suggestion of a smile tugs at his lips. "Why's she always speaking for you? Something we don't know about, eh?"

Joe sighs and rolls his eyes and says nothing. Leon looks back at me and smokes his cigarette. "My friend Marianne is having a party tomorrow night," I tell him. "For some reason, she wants you and Travis to come."

"Really? Okay."

"I'll tell her then," I say stiffly, and I want to get away from him as quickly as possible. I slip my arm out from Joe's. "You don't have to walk me home," I tell him, but he shakes his head at me.

"Don't be stupid. You haven't stopped shaking. Come on." He steps around his brother, who is merely smiling at us, and takes my arm again. We walk on like that, and I feel the strange and enquiring weight of Leon's eyes on our backs as we go. I cannot speak. I can barely breathe. Everything is just too much sometimes. Sometimes World, I think this life just makes a big churning mess of my stomach. A big churning mess. Just about sums it up, I think, and decide to write it on the wall when I get back. I'll draw a picture of me next to it.

"See you tomorrow night?" Joe asks me when I am at my house. I nod at him silently, wondering if I am in shock or something. Joe smiles at me tenderly then. "It will be a cool night," he suggests, and I nod again. "Don't worry so much Carling," he tells me then, as he turns to leave. "You worry too much. Everything always turns out all right, you know. Always."

I release a shuddering, near tears sigh, as I watch his back walking away. Hands in pockets, shoulders down. I wonder how the hell he can say that, or believe that, after what just happened, but that is Joe. That is Joe.

20

Dear World, Friday is here! Marianne insists I get ready for the party at her house. I have no choice. I take over the minimal make-up that I own, and the two outfits that I can't decide between. When I get there, Marianne's parents have already left for their weekend away. I gaze around at the big empty house, feeling lost and confused, as Marianne takes me from room to room, showing off the decorations and the food all laid out. As promised she has locked the rooms she wants to keep intact, but there is still plenty of space for the guests to mill about and mingle. Marianne is breathlessly pretty in a simple black dress and sparkly cardigan. I wonder if the cardigan is to disguise her cuts, but I do not ask. I let her bask in her glory. I actually feel proud of her. She has certainly gone to a lot of effort.

She ushers me upstairs to help get me ready. "Are you okay?" she asks me more than once. "You seem totally out of it Lou."

"Just tired," I keep telling her, while the image of Joe practically hanging from the bridge remains imprinted in my mind's eye. Marianne looks at my clothes and tells me to go for the dress. I am unsure.

"You look stunning for Christ's sake," she tells me firmly, gripping me by the arm and staring daggers into my eyes. "Show off all your hard work, Lou. Let all the kids from school see how amazing you look." I stare into her eyes and just want to cry, but I have no idea, no idea why at all. She lets my arm go and drapes the dress carefully over my knees. "Come on woman. Do it. Then I'm going to do your hair and make-up."

"Because it matters what girls look like?" I ask her weakly, recalling our conversation with Joe in the summerhouse that day. Marianne meets my gaze and smiles vividly.

"Exactly," she triumphs, her eyes glittering. "Now come on. Do it."

A short while later I am wearing a dress, and Marianne has straightened my hair to within an inch of its life. She kneels before me and painstakingly applies layers of mascara and eye-liner to my eyes. "You have the most amazing eyelashes I have ever seen," she says as she does it. "People pay to have lashes this long and dark, and you have them naturally."

"From my mum," I shrug apologetically. "Sara's are the same."

"They look amazing now," she tells me and holds the mirror up to my face so I can see what she has transformed me into. I was always such a nobody before, I think as I stare at the girl in the mirror. I swallow. She enchants me. She is not someone I recognise. She is not me.

"Thanks," I tell Marianne, pushing the mirror away. "How about a drink to steady the nerves?"

"What are you nervous about?" she frowns at me, getting up and walking to her large desk, where an unopened bottle of wine stands.

"I meant you," I lie. Marianne laughs.

"I'm not nervous! Why would I be nervous?" She opens the bottle and fills two glasses.

"I don't know. You're not ever nervous, about anything?"

"You have to care about stuff to get nervous," she says flippantly, thrusting a full glass towards me. I take it and consider her careless statement.

"Okay."

"We need some food now too," she says then, as if she has just remembered this is important. I try not to let my blind panic show. "Before the party starts," she explains, heading for the door. "You know, to line our stomachs!"

"What food?" I ask, my mouth like sandpaper.

"Toast is best," she assures me. "Otherwise you'll be on the floor after the first few drinks, don't you know that? Have some toast, then you'll be able to drink more."

"If you're sure," I say hesitantly, and drink my wine. Marianne stops and grins back at me just before she goes through the door.

"Don't freak out about it," she says. "You'll only throw it up again later."

"Oh," I say, lowering my glass and staring at her intently. "Oh yeah, I suppose."

After another glass of wine I am feeling more relaxed. Marianne has put some music on and Josh and Ryan have arrived first. They make a beeline for the drinks she has displayed on the kitchen counter. "You've thought of everything!" Josh tells her, as he makes himself a whiskey and coke. I watch from the doorway, drink in hand, wondering if Josh has ever tried whiskey and coke before, and if Marianne's dad is going to notice. What does strike me is the free and easy way Marianne has with them. I'd had no idea they were all so close. I had always thought of Josh and Ryan as Joe's friends, more than mine. They were there, you know, at school and at people's houses, but they weren't people I called up by myself to meet up with, or vice versa. I watch them all and feel a stab of jealousy and confusion. I lift my glass to my lips and drink steadily. I feel like something is unfolding around me slowly, but I have no idea what, or why. I can only watch Marianne, the star of the show, and wonder how I never noticed it in her before. I had always thought her strange. Confident and spiky in her own way, but I had never had her down for a social butterfly.

She plays the perfect hostess for the first hour of the party, as more and more people drift in. The doorbell seems to be ringing endlessly. Marianne floats around, serving drinks, embracing people she barely knows, and pointing them in the direction of the party nibbles. Everyone looks so grown up and glamorous, I think, as I watch from the side-lines. It has only been a matter of weeks since we saw people from school, but somehow it feels like months, and it seems like everyone has changed in some way. I don't look at myself this way, until the stick insects, Christine and Stacey spot me and come over. Christine holds her hands up and flaps them about excitedly, while Stacey sort of circles me, in this threatening sort of way, eyeing me up and down, smiling greedily. "*Oh my god*!' they both squeal at exactly the same time. I just smile awkwardly.

"Hi guys."

"Lou Carling! Is that really you?" Christine, the taller stick insect places her perfectly manicured hand gently on my shoulder, as if to steady herself, as if she is about to keel over or something.

"You look *amazing*!" Stacey echoes her, hands on her chest, mouth open, eyes wide. I nod at them, and want to kill them.

"Yes, yes, it's me, it's really me."

"*Oh my god*!" Christine cries again. It's like she is close to orgasm or something, I can barely stand it. "You look amazing! Doesn't she look amazing Stace? I just can't believe it!"

"You look so amazing," Stacey is still running her pale blue eyes up and down my body, which makes me feel queasy to be honest. I am not used to this, and wonder if I will ever feel comfortable with it. "How much weight did you lose? How did you *do* it Lou? You have to tell us!"

Yes, I think, glancing away for a moment and searching for help, because you two really need to lose weight, don't you? I shrug at them politely and try to fight the urge to claw their eyes out with my fingernails. "Oh you know," I tell them pleasantly. "Healthy diet and exercise basically."

"God you look stunning, you really do," Christine flicks her long blonde hair back over one shoulder. She has poured her perfect body into a skin tight dress which makes her breasts look huge. I smile politely. "You lost loads of weight last term, but this, *this* is unbelievable!"

"Thanks," I shrug, and drink more wine.

"And your *hair*!" Stacey cries suddenly, pointing at my newly straightened locks, with a look of childlike happiness on her freckled face. I would like to feel touched that I have made them both so ridiculously happy, but the only thing I am feeling is pure pent up rage. I wonder if now is the time to remind them of how vile they were to me in years eight and nine? When I was supposedly part of their little click? When I tried to be? When I tried so hard to please them, to be like them, that it kept me awake at night, that it tied my stomach in knots before school, never knowing if today they would be kind to me or cruel to me. I look at their admiring faces and wonder if they have really forgotten? Stacey reaches out and strokes my hair, and I feel like slapping her hand away, and then slapping her face.

"You look *so* beautiful," Christine tells me assuringly, and the look on her face suggests that she is trying to convince me of this. Let me know I have passed a test, or something. That I am all right now, in her book at least. I scratch at my neck and stare past them, wondering where the hell Marianne is.

"This party is totally brilliant!" says Stacey, gazing around at the kitchen, which is now pretty full. "It's so nice to see everyone!"

"So nice of Marianne to do this," Christine leans towards me, speaking to me as if we are suddenly great friends again. "This house is amazing."

"It is amazing," I murmur, and want to go and find a big fat thesaurus and shove it in her slightly too wide mouth. "It's all amazing," I say again, look back at her and smile.

"She looks great too!" Stacey says suddenly, as if this fact also amazes her too. "She looks *amazing*!"

"I always thought her a total freak," Christine leans in again and says. Stacey nods emphatically in agreement.

"Total freak at school."

"But not now?" I ponder. "Not here? Here she is amazing?"

They look at each other, a flicker of confusion passing over their bland Barbie doll faces. "Totally amazing!" Stacey says suddenly, looking relieved. I smile at her pityingly.

"Well let's just hope she is still amazing, when school starts," I say to them, moving away from where they have trapped me against the counter. "Let's hope she doesn't go back to being a total freak hey? I've got to get another drink." I walk away from them, in search of alcohol. What I would really like to search for is a blunt knife.

I am pouring myself a vodka and coke when Marianne suddenly bumps into the side of me. She immediately giggles and bends over her knees, pointing at the puddle on the floor where she has spilled her drink. I frown at her curiously. "Are you drunk Marianne?"

She straightens up, throws her skinny arm around my shoulders and wags her empty glass at me. She is drunk all right. Drunker than I have ever seen her, anyway. "I might just be, a little tiny bit!" she laughs, and pulls me closer with her arm. "I'm going to get myself some food now," she confides in me, "to soak up the booze. And I'm going to have a big pint of water too!"

"Really?"

"Oh yes! Oh yes. That's what you ought to do. You can slow it down a bit. That's my plan."

"How much have you had anyway?"

"Oh a few, a few!" she giggles against me and waves her glass about. I start to expect her to drop it at any moment and cover our feet with glass. "How about you? Have you had a few? Lou?" She instantly creases over again, bent double in laughter at herself. "That rhymes, that rhymes!"

"Yes it does," I nod at her patiently, looking over her head. "And guess what? It looks like your guests of honour have just arrived."

"What?" Marianne jerks herself up violently, and stares around, dramatically flicking her silky hair back out of her face. I nod towards the hallway, where just above the group of people milling there, we can see Leon's head. Marianne gasps, and then hides herself behind me.

"What the hell are you doing?"

"Oh like I said," she says quickly, "food, water, all that." She scampers off, and I shake my head, utterly bemused. I look back towards the hallway and see Joe pushing through the crowd toward me, with his brothers just behind him. Joe is looking excited but incredulous, staring around at the masses of people, and the extremely successful party our strange little friend has pulled off. He is holding a huge bottle of cider and thumps it down on the counter beside me. I look about, but there is no sign of Marianne now. "Good to see you," I tell him with a sigh. He nods. He has no idea. I glance at Leon and Travis, who are both clutching their own booze. They look like they have made an effort at least. Freshly shaven and wearing clean shirts.

"Where's the party girl then?" Leon enquires, spreading his feet apart, setting his shoulders, and claiming his space, as if anyone here would dare consider entering it anyway. Travis leans against the counter, crossing his legs at the ankle and smiling at me pleasantly.

"Who knows?" I shrug, picking up my own drink. "She was here a minute ago." I lift my eyebrows at Joe. "Right little socialite she is these days you know."

Joe snorts. "Really?"

"Well let's get these open," Leon says, dropping his six pack of Carlsberg next to Joe's cider, and yanking one free of the plastic wrapping.

"This house is fucking huge," Travis comments, looking at me. I nod at him.

"You should see the garden."

"Really?"

"It's got a summerhouse," Joe tells him. Leon rests his back against the counter next to Travis, folds one arm across his thick middle, and raises his can of beer to his mouth.

"Some people," he rolls his eyes. "They don't know they're fucking born."

I am not sure what this really means, but it is one of those sayings I've heard my parents say a million times. Whenever someone they know gets a bigger TV, or a new car, or moves to a better house. Apparently they don't know they're born.

"Lucky bastards," Travis says, with a lazy grin. He scans the room then, nodding and frowning in turn at the people he can see. "Loads here though."

"I've just spotted the food," Joe says to me, nudging me with his elbow. "Shall we head over there?"

"I'm not really hungry," I shrug. "Josh and Ryan are here somewhere."

"Are you okay Carling?"

"Yes, I'm fine," I snap at him. "Why do people keep asking me that?"

"Sorry," grins Joe. "You just seem weird, that's all."

"You would seem weird if you had to spend an entire afternoon being primped and prepared by Marianne!" I hiss at him. "And then be accosted by the stick insects, having fucking orgasms about how *amazing* I look!"

Joe snorts again. He has poured himself a huge pint of cider and has the plastic glass in one hand, and his other hand in the pockets of his jeans. He is wearing an Arctic Monkeys t-shirt. "Calm down woman," he says to me, grinning. "Don't let the vipers get to you. They're just jealous. You have a personality as well as looks!" He looks me up and down and raises his pint at me. "You do look hot, by the way. I was scared to react, because I know what you're like. Thought you'd kick me in the balls or something!"

Travis leans forward then, over Joe's shoulder. "You do look gorgeous Lou," he says to me sounding scarily sincere. I just stare at him blankly. "You really do."

"All grown up, all of a sudden," Leon comments, with what passes for a smile on his face clearly visible behind the rim of his beer can. I shake my head slightly, wanting it all to stop.

"Oh shut up, all of you," I say in disgust and finish my drink. They are bloody laughing. At me. I could kill them, but then I start to laugh too. I laugh back, and loosen up a little, and then I get the coldest feeling, tingling across my skin, and when I look back over my shoulder, Marianne is staring right back at me. From across the room. They have not noticed her, but she is there. So tiny, and so dark, maybe she has been creeping in and out of the crowd the whole time. Maybe she has heard everything. I swallow down a smile. I turn back to Joe, and his brothers. Joe has filled my glass up for me.

"Let's get wasted Carling," he says to me then. "To make up for last night. You with me?"

I feel somehow naughty and brave, as I let the smile slide across my face, and flick back my straight, glossy locks. I allow my mischievous gaze to sneak quickly to Travis, and then back to Joe, as I hold up my glass. Joe chinks his against mine. "Too right I'm with you," I tell them, and that is that. I am drinking with the boys.

After that it all starts to get a bit messy.

We drink steadily. We converse with the crowd. Josh and Ryan join us. Marianne keeps her distance. I am shorter than all of them, so I end up hopping onto the side so that I can hear them better above the music. Before I know it I am pretty fucking wasted, and brimming with that obnoxious self-love that only drinking indulgently can bring on. I feel wonderful, I feel beautiful, and I feel funny. I feel I am all of these things, as I perch on the side, with all three handsome Lawrenson brothers surrounding me. Joe is leaning heavily against me. Every now and again he places his hand on my leg. It is fine. We are just friends, and all that. Like brother and sister remember? So I take no notice, and I flick back my glossy hair, and laugh out loud at everything they are saying, and I do a fine job of hiding the strange and forceful desire that burns inside me every time he does it.

***

For the next hour and a half I only spot Marianne in the distance, through the crowd. I try in vain to call out to her every now and again, to get her over. But she either cannot hear me, or is pretending not to. Every time I spot her, she is making the rounds, playing the hostess to perfection. Good on her. It is a great party.

I find myself laughing with Joe when he retells the guy on the bridge story to Leon and Travis. Now that I am drunk it does not seem horrible at all, only funny and wild, and a tale to tell for years to come. "Back over there tomorrow," I hear Leon say to Joe after this, and I see a look go over Joe's face that tells me he is not so sure. I reel myself in then. I am so so drunk, but I saw that look. He doesn't want to do it anymore, and I know it. I find myself slinging my arm protectively around his shoulders and resting my head against him. I hold my glass up to my cheek. It is cold, and I am so hot. I breathe in and out slowly. I am suddenly almost incapable of speaking. So I loll into him, and just watch them, and listen to them.

I watch the easy rapport that passes between Travis and Leon. They are on the same wavelength, I realise. They have an obvious mutual respect that Joe by default of being the youngest, does not receive. Not that they are cruel to him tonight. They are at his friend's party after all. But as I watch them I become aware that they really only see him as a little kid. Someone to boss around. Someone to get doing what they want. I watch them, and I wonder if they love him at all. If they know him, like I know him. I wonder so many things World, and it's worse when you're drunk isn't it? Everything crashes through me like a runaway train. Feelings colliding with thoughts, my mood wrenching one way and then the other. My heart trembling within me.

My eyes meet with Travis' more than once. In fact, nearly every time I look at him, he is already looking at me. Talking to Leon, and looking at me. I still don't get it. I'm nothing special. Surely he could have any girl he wanted? But in my drunken state I get off on it hugely. I look back at him, daring him. I wait for him to make his move, determined to prove Joe wrong.

I am totally hammered by the time Marianne finally decides to join us. In contrast, she suddenly seems refreshingly sober. She squeezes sweetly in-between all the boys, asking them if they need a refill, or any food. "This is Marianne," I jerk my head away from Joe's shoulder and announce, with an accompanying hiccup. "This is her fucking party!" I say this too loud, and Marianne frowns at me smilingly. I point my glass straight at Leon, who I deem to be the villain in everything. "So you better give her some fucking respect right?"

They all crack up laughing, even Leon. Marianne slips in between him and me and looks up at him with a quizzical expression, that lets him know she knows nothing about his reputation. Except, of course she does. She has a glass of wine held delicately between her fingers. She still looks immaculate, and I can see Leon's eyes giving her the once over. I drop my other arm around her and give Leon the evil eye. "Best party ever Marianne!" I tell her, pulling her close. She smiles at me patiently. She looks at me as if I am three years old.

"Oh dear Lou, how much have you had now?" she says with a laugh, rolling her eyes at Joe.

"Not enough actually," I say defiantly, shoving my empty glass at her. "What else you got for me Sholing?"

"Ooh how about I make some cocktails?" she says suddenly, looking instantly back up at Leon. "Are you boys up for that?"

"Fucking right," Leon nods at her, a faint grin pulling at his lips. He nods at his empties, lined up along the counter. "Just finished all my beers."

"Right then!" Marianne puts down her glass and claps her hands. "Give me a minute. We need a load of stuff."

She scoots around the counter, grabbing bottles and glasses and plonking them next to us. She then pulls open one of the lower kitchen cupboards and drags out a huge glass bowl. "Do you want something tried and tested?" she asks us breathlessly. "Or something completely experimental?"

"Experimental!" I say loudly, before anyone else can speak. "Just chuck in a load of stuff, and we won't look! We promise!"

"Are you sure?" Marianne looks over her shoulder at the rest of them. They all nod back or shrug.

"You might want some water first," Joe whispers in my ear then. I look him in the eye accusingly. I realise that I simultaneously want to punch him in the face and kiss him. I don't know what is wrong with me. I let his sweet face warm my heart and smile at him lovingly.

"It's okay my sweet. I am going to just have one cocktail and then go outside and vomit spectacularly okay?"

"Okay," he laughs, crossing his arms. "If you think that is wise."

"I think that is very wise. One cocktail first. Then I will go."

"You really feel sick?"

"I think I really feel sick. But one cocktail first."

"Okay," Joe laughs. "If you are sure mate. I'll come out and hold your hair for you. Wouldn't want you getting carrot chunks in your new do, would we?"

"No we would not. We certainly would not."

"You're well and truly hammered."

"I am."

I can feel someone nudging me then, and when I turn in their direction, I find Marianne pushing a glass of red liquid into my hands. I frown down at it, and lift it to my nose to smell it. "What's this?" I ask and for some reason they all laugh at this. "What?"

"Mystery cocktail you idiot!" laughs Marianne, passing them out. "It was your idea!"

"Oh yeah. Let's give it a try then."

I only manage to drink half of it before I experience the undeniable and forceful urge to vomit. I slip ungraciously to the floor, dragging Joe with me, and find myself bumping straight into Travis, who spills his drink and stares at me.

"Need fresh air, excuse me!" I mutter and push past him. I feel Joe pull free from my grasp, and it occurs to me to turn back, beg him to come like he promised to, but I can't hang about. If I turn back I am going to throw up in their faces. So I plough on, pushing urgently through the people, ignoring the school friends who call my name and try to talk to me. I head for the conservatory, and that is where I feel a rough hand close around my bare arm, and I think thank God, it's Joe, he will hold my hair for me after all. I let myself be pulled into his side, and he helps me get out of the French doors and into the blissful fresh air of the back garden.

It is only once I am out there, that I realise in foggy confusion that it is not Joe. Joe is smaller. It is Travis holding me up. It is Travis helping me walk. I kind of pull away from him, feeling stupid and embarrassed and angry all at once. I head for the flowerbeds and kneel down. "Leave me alone, you don't want to see this!" I call out, waving my hand at him, before I hurl my guts up in Mrs Sholing's flowers.

I sit there for some time. It feels like ages. Travis held my hair out the way when I was sick, and then let it go once I had stopped. So I sit there and wipe my mouth, and breathe in the cold air, and feel my head start to clear, and I stare at my sick, and hope to God he has gone. When I turn around, I hope he is not there.

21

Oh dear God, dear World, he is! What the hell does he want?

I am angry now. I easily switch to anger when I've been drinking. I can be overloaded with happiness one moment, and seething with rage the next. It can really switch that quickly. I sit back on my arse and hug my knees and scowl at him. "You can stop watching me be sick now," I tell him. Travis smiles at me awkwardly. He is on his knees, and sits back on his feet.

"Joe dropped his drink."

"What?"

"He dropped his drink, that's why he didn't follow you."

"Oh." I blow out my breath and look back at my vomit steaming away in the flowerbeds. "You didn't have to come. I'm quite capable of being sick on my own actually."

"Wasn't sure you would make it out here okay."

"Why do you even care all of a sudden?" I shout at him. It takes him by surprise. Good. He can get up and fuck right off and stop messing with my head like this. He closes his mouth and looks away from me.

"Sorry," he says then. "I just wanted to make sure you were okay. I'll leave you alone, if you're sure you'll be okay."

"Why don't you answer the question?"

"Hey?"

"The question! Why do you care all of a sudden? I've known you my whole life Travis. Why all the attention suddenly?"

"Um." That is all he can say. Um. He scratches his nose. Then he searches his pockets for a cigarette and finds one.

"You're giving me the creeps," I tell him, staring back at my sick. "That's all."

"Well sorry." Travis lights his cigarette and smiles at me. I want him to stop smiling at me. "That cocktail was toxic by the way."

"What?"

"She put double in yours mate. She topped it way up."

"Did she?" I stare at him in confusion. "Why would she?"

"I don't know," Travis shrugs at me and puffs on his cigarette. "Maybe she wanted you out of the way?"

"What?" I just stare at him. I am sobering up now I have spewed, but I am still horribly confused by my entire life.

"Think she has the hots for Leon," Travis shrugs again. I roll my eyes at him, as if this is old news to me.

"Think she has the hots for all three of you," I tell him. "But I don't care. I feel better now anyway. Time for another drink."

"How about some food?"

"No thanks."

"Come on. Let me get you something. It'll soak up the booze."

"You sound like her." I groan, getting slowly to my feet. Travis stands up beside me and places his hand gently on my shoulder.

"You okay?"

"Yes thank you." I am lying. I am not okay. I am feeling better, but I am still extremely drunk. I suddenly start to make my way waveringly over to the garden bench. Travis follows me hesitantly. "Thought you were going back in?"

"Just need a little sit down first," I tell him, and drop myself down on the bench with a huge sigh. "A bit more fresh air." I wave my hand at him. "Go on, you go. I'm fine now. Go and enjoy the party."

Travis looks at me, and then looks at the house. It is heaving and throbbing with people and music. Why wouldn't he want to be a part of that? I watch his shoulders drop slightly and then he says; "I'll be back in a minute." He turns and goes into the house. I nod at his back, saying nothing, but inside I am thinking 'yeah right', and I am also relieved. I am on my own now. I breathe in huge mouthfuls of fresh night air, and rest my head in my hand for a moment. I recall the day, which seems like years ago now, when Joe and me sat out here watching Tommy play on Marianne's swing set. We had no idea where she was, and Leon wanted his drugs back. I remember how for a moment or two it had felt like our entire world had crashed down around us. And then I had started to laugh.

I am having a little giggle to myself at the memory when suddenly Travis reappears. I groan inwardly at his persistence, and curse him for being so stupidly handsome. And I remind myself that even if I did once have a teeny weeny crush on him, that was just on his looks, *not* his personality. No way. He passes me a pint of water and a packet of crisps and parks himself on the bench beside me. I just look at him quizzically. "You'll feel better," he says with a nod.

"Why do you keep doing this when I'm drunk at parties?" I ask him, my drunken state making me far more brazen than I would be otherwise. When I am sober I think so many things that I keep to myself, or write on my wall. I am glaring at him with an inviting smile. He smiles back. He shrugs at me.

"I don't get the chance in normal life. You're always with Joe."

"Oh." I look away and drink the water for a moment. I even open the crisps and consider eating some. I recall Joe suddenly kissing me on his bed that day after Mick had trashed his music, and it is on the tip of my tongue to just blurt it out. To see what Travis' reaction would be. But I bite down on the urge. I eat some crisps and drink some water, and we sit in silence until I look back at him and say; "You never bothered with me when I was fat, did you? You didn't like me then. How superficial is that?"

Travis looks momentarily stunned and amused. "I just never noticed you, that's all," he says in reply. "You were just Joe's friend. You were both just these annoying little kids." He grins a wide grin that reminds me of Joe, and looks me up and down for a moment. "Now suddenly you are all grown up."

"So let me get this straight," I say, dropping my eyes to my pint of water. I run my index finger around the plastic rim. "If I did let you kiss me, the only time it would ever happen would be when we're drunk at parties?"

"No of course not," Travis says more urgently, sitting forward, pushing his face towards mine. "The only problem we would have is Joe. It's like he thinks he owns you or something." I look at him, and suddenly he leans in and goes for the kiss. I duck away giggling, and he frowns. "What?"

"You can't really want to kiss me when I've just thrown up!"

"I don't care."

"It's disgusting!" I insist, keeping back from him. "Look at the bloody state of me!"

"Why are you always so hard on yourself? I said I don't care."

I stand up then, with my water and my crisps. "I'm going to go and brush my teeth," I look down at him and announce. "I bet that when I get back you'll be gone."

I don't give him a chance to reply. I storm away across the grass and into the house. I feel giddy with excitement, disbelief and alcohol. I slide through the crowd, not looking for anyone, just minding my own crazy business. I run up the stairs to the bathroom, and luckily no one is in it. I lock the door behind me and take five minutes to sort myself out. I find a pack of spare toothbrushes in the bathroom cabinet and brush my teeth. I splash cold water onto my face and neck and run my fingers through my hair. I check my clothes for splatters of vomit, and there are none.

I leave the bathroom, feeling oddly womanlike and conniving, and slip back downstairs. It is only as I slide through the kitchen crowd that I spot Marianne with Leon in the corner. She is sat on his lap, her face turned to his, her black hair hanging down over one shoulder. I wonder where Joe is, but can't see him anywhere. I run back outside, half expecting Travis to be gone, but he is not. He is still sat there patiently. I make a mental decision to use him just as I am convinced he is using me. Fuck it. You are only sixteen once. Who cares? It's not going to matter, is it?

I drop down onto the bench and Travis immediately moves closer to me, and stares into my eyes, biting down on his lower lip. I shiver. "Better?" he whispers. I nod. And then it happens. He slides his hands onto either side of my face, holding it like it is made of china. I feel my entire body tremble. I have broken out in goose pimples everywhere. He closes his eyes and presses his lips onto mine. I give in to him. It is the gentlest, softest kiss I could ever have imagined.

As we kiss, I wonder helplessly if this is what being a woman is really like. If this is what being attractive is really like. Beautiful, stolen kisses. Discoveries. I melt into his arms, and feel alive, like I am made of electricity. A part of me keeps expecting Joe to show up and interrupt us, for some horribly awkward scene to unfold, but he doesn't.

We pull away from the kiss at the same time, which is a relief. I feel stunned and wide open, utterly vulnerable, but I find myself resting my cheek on his shoulder and closing my eyes, waiting for him to say something. I feel him breathing next to me. I feel like I am in a fucking movie, or something.

"You okay?" he asks me finally, so I pull back and that is when the reality slaps me in the face; when I sit back and look at him. He stares back at me expectantly, and I think oh my God, you are Joe's brother. I have known you my entire life. You've never been anything more than an annoying twat until now. I want to laugh, but that would be awful. I glance nervously towards the house, suddenly convinced that I will see Joe's betrayed face staring back at me from the French doors. But I can't see him anywhere.

"I think I better find Marianne and make sure she is okay," I tell Travis, looking back at him shyly. He nods at me.

"Okay, good idea. I wouldn't trust Leon if I were you either."

I frown at him. "Or you!"

Travis laughs. "Oh. Yeah, right."

I slide off the bench and get to my feet before things can go any further. I feel the strong desire to get away from him and find Marianne to talk to. I feel the strong desire for another drink. "Think I'll get another drink," I say then, so it does not sound so much like I am abandoning him. "Do you want anything?"

"I'm coming," Travis says with a sigh, hauling himself to his feet. We walk towards the house, and just before we reach the conservatory, Travis stops me with a hand on my shoulder. I look at his hand and then look up at him. "You're not only beautiful and funny," he leans towards me and whispers next to my cheek, "but you're a fucking good kisser too." He kisses me once on the cheek, and goes on into the house. I stand and stare in bewilderment and pure joy, and watch him go. He has his hands in his pockets, which makes me think of Joe again. He slips easily through the crowd, and disappears. Well, I think, that is that then.

I do not see Travis again for the rest of the night. For all I know, he walked from one end of the house to the other and left through the front door, right after he kissed my cheek. I decide to look for Marianne. I *need* to speak to her. The party has descended into drunken chaos by the looks of it. People are drunk and falling over, or huddled in corners kissing people they never thought they would. I feel my cheeks growing warmer by the second as I try not to think of the kiss with Travis, and push my way through people to search for Marianne. I am getting quite desperate to find her. I really, really need to speak to her.

In the kitchen I find a legless Ryan leaning all over Josh. It looks like they have drunk nearly all of Marianne's punch by themselves. I wonder how long I have been gone. "Where's Marianne?" I ask them, looking around for a fresh drink. There is a can of unopened cider on the kitchen table, so I grab it, and when no one nearby protests, I open it and drink a mouthful.

"She went off with Joe's brother," Ryan tells me, trying like hell not to fall off the stool he is balanced on. I stare at him intently.

"What, Leon? Where did they go?"

"No idea," he shrugs back at me. "But they were snogging the faces of each other for a fair while down here!"

I am quite stunned. "Really? Were they?" I nearly go into a rant about how gross and out of order that is in so many ways, but then I remember what has just happened between me and Travis outside, and I shut my mouth up. I sit with Josh and Ryan for a while, digesting all of the information, and drinking my stolen cider. "So where's Joe?" I ask, just as he walks into the room. "Oh."

He slides in with his back to the counter, cider in hand and vacant look on his face. I think of Travis, and I feel sick. I feel so many things that I almost cannot take it, and seriously consider running back outside under the pretence of needing to vomit again, just to be alone. Just to take it all in, because right now World, I feel a bit like I am going crazy. I look at him, and then I can't look at him, so I look away, but then I need to look at him, just to work out what the hell is going on. Jesus Christ, what am I doing to myself? "You all right, you freak?" he bumps me with his shoulder and asks me, grinning. I grin back.

"Oh yeah."

"Been sick?"

"Just a bit."

"Loser."

"Fuck you."

"Lightweight."

I punch him in the arm and he groans in mock pain. "You can't even punch properly anymore, you're too fucking skinny!"

"Oh shut up twat face."

"You're too weak," he laughs, and I think he has that lovely happy sloppy drunk look on his face, and his body is all loose and silly as he picks up my arm and tries to make me punch myself. "Look, look! There's no strength in that!" He holds my fist and wiggles it around. "What is that? What is it for? You pathetic little specimen!"

"I could kick your skinny arse any day of the week," I retort, pulling my hand out of his. Josh and Ryan start to laugh.

"Come on then!" Josh tells me. "Show us what you're made of!"

"She's not made of anything, look," Joe picks up my arm and waves it about stupidly, while giggling like an idiot. "She's fading away!"

"Stop it," I pull my arm away from him, and he picks up his cider and drinks it, grinning broadly. "Where has Leon gone with my friend, by the way?"

"What?" he lowers his drink. "I don't know. What do you mean?"

I nod at Josh and Ryan. "They said Leon and Marianne were kissing. Then disappeared somewhere."

"Oh." Joe closes his mouth and looks confused for a moment. Josh and Ryan are nodding at him. They seem to have lost the ability to speak.

"Just a bit worried," I add, watching Joe closely. "I don't want him taking advantage of her."

At this statement, Ryan and Josh swap amazed, wide-eyed looks and then snort loudly with laughter. I look at them indignantly, and then at Joe. He looks just as confused as I feel. "Something funny?" he asks them.

"It's just I wouldn't worry about *him* taking advantage of *her*," Josh tells us, wiping his eyes with his hand, his shoulders still shaking with laughter. "That's all."

"Man, that is funny," Ryan sighs beside him.

"You're idiots," I tell them both. They just laugh at me. I look back at Joe and poke him in the ribs. "Think we should find her."

"Oh God, do we have to?" he groans, closing his eyes and wiping his hand slowly down his face.

"Yes, we have to. Just to check on her."

"Oh I don't want to. You go. She's your weird friend, you go. I'm having fun here."

"Joe," I say firmly, taking his arm in both of my hands and pulling him away from the counter. "I am not confronting your evil brother on my own. Come on. Don't be a wuss all of your life."

"But I *am* a wuss," he protests, as I drag him away. "That's what I am! I like it! I like being a wuss! Let me just be a wuss please!"

"Come on, stupid. She might need us."

"She doesn't need anyone!" Joe laughs, as we reach the large hallway. "She'll be fine!"

"Not with Leon she won't," I tell him, although I can't really explain why I think this. Maybe they are all right, I wonder, as we check the downstairs rooms for her. Maybe she is okay with Leon.

"God I really don't want to do this," Joe groans again, as I start to head up the stairs, pulling him with me. "Leon won't like it."

"It's not about him. I just want to see she is okay, that's it. You don't even have to say a word."

"But he'll be pissed off. He'll be pissed off anyway. I really don't want to piss him off, Lou."

"Oh stop being such a baby," I snap at him on the landing, as I try to think where to look and what to do. "I'm here to protect you aren't I?"

"He wouldn't not smack you just because you're a girl!" Joe cries out at me in exasperation at the top of the stairs. He is still smiling slightly, but I can tell he is worked up too. He is still happy drunk, but bordering on the paranoid drunk. I sigh and walk over to Marianne's closed bedroom door. Joe stands behind me, huffing and puffing with his arms crossed. I tap on the door nervously.

"Just going to check she is okay," I repeat again, glancing back at Joe. He rolls his eyes at me angrily.

"Tried to warn you," he says softly, just as the door is opened. I am face to face with Leon, and Joe was right, he does look pissed off. This is alarming enough, but even more alarming is the fact that he has no top on. I find myself swallowing anxiously, and trying not to let my eyes wander down to his naked chest.

"Hello?" he snaps at me in a typically unfriendly voice.

"Is Marianne with you?" I ask him, trying to peer around him into her room. "It's just that I can't seem to find her anywhere."

"She's in here." He raises his eyebrows at me and closes the door an inch. I push my face forward.

"Can you tell her I need to speak to her please?"

"What the fuck?"

"It's urgent," I plead, as the darkness spreads across his face. "It's life and death. I'll be so quick. I just need to talk to her."

"Not now, okay?" Leon tries to close the door, but I am too quick and get the entire left side of my body in the way of the door. He looks at me like he would like to kill me, and then flicks his hard eyes to Joe. "Fucks sake!" he yells. Joe steps forward.

"Just want to see she is okay," he explains softly to his brother.

"Marianne!" I call out then. "Can I talk to you quickly?"

"Look fuck off right?" Leon hisses then, his breath reeking of beer as it smothers my face. "I'm not kidding."

"Why won't you let us speak to her?" I ask him. "Just let us speak to her and we'll go!"

"She's busy," he snarls, holding onto the door as I try to press through it. "And I am getting seriously pissed off now. Come here!" He says this to Joe, beckoning him forward with a curled finger.

"We only want to check she is okay," Joe says, not moving.

"Why wouldn't she be?"

"Because she's with you, you fucking bully!" I shout into his face. "Because we don't trust you! Because you're probably some kind of maniac and she is my friend!"

Leon points at Joe. "Get this bitch out of my face right now or I'm gonna' lay you out," he says to him. I feel Joe slide his hand around my elbow.

"Come on," he says to me.

"No, no way. I won't be bullied by this prick. Lay *me* out!" I glare up into his hard-set face. "If you want to punch someone, why don't you try me? Then Marianne will see what you're really like. Or why don't you stop being such a fucking dick for once in your life, and just let us speak to her?" I am angrier than I thought possible. He does not scare me. I am drunk though. This is what happens when you drink. You get ridiculously aggressive and sure of yourself, when ordinarily you would just not bother. I punch the door with my fist, wishing it was his face, wishing he would just let us see her, I mean, what the hell is wrong with him. I am starting to think he has raped or killed her or something!

Leon calls my bluff then. He doesn't punch me, but he does shove me hard. I nearly land on my arse, but Joe is there to stop me. Now that he has moved me on, Leon closes the bedroom door behind him and claims his space the way he always does. He looks like a bear poised to attack. "Get her out of here," he says this softly to Joe, who looks like he is about to shit himself.

"Come on," Joe says to me again. "I'm sure she's fine."

"How can you say that?" I stare at him and cry. "When he acts like that? I want to know what the hell he's done to her in there!"

Joe looks worriedly back at Leon and tightens his grip on my elbow. "Forget about it, let's just go." He doesn't even look drunk anymore, just miserable and scared, and this angers me even more. I pull my elbow out of his hand and flick my hair out of my face and glare viciously at Leon. It is like years fall through me then, years of fearing and loathing him, years of seeing the way he treats Joe. It all falls through me and builds me back up brick by brick.

"Let me speak to my friend," I demand through clenched teeth. My fists are curled tightly at my sides. I don't recall ever feeling this enraged before. It is the sheer arrogance of him. The sheer stubborn stupidity that he exists in, day after day. Can't he see that if he just let me speak to her, I would leave them to it?

"You're always interfering aren't you?" Leon sneers at me, one side of his mouth pulling upwards slightly. His eyes move to Joe. "Can't you keep your girlfriend under control?"

"She's not my girlfriend," Joe sighs, with a roll of his eyes. He crosses his arms and shakes his head at me. "Come on."

"No," I say again. "This is ridiculous. What has he got to hide? Just let me speak to her and I'll go. How hard is that to understand? What is the problem?"

"I don't like being told what to do by bossy little bitches, that's what the problem is," Leon informs me calmly as I seethe in front of him. I take a step towards Marianne's door and he moves to block me.

"Fucking idiot!" I shout at him, incensed with frustration. "You just enjoy being a total prick, don't you? Your whole life! A total and utter prick!"

"Okay," he says then, his voice reasonable. "Let's put it this way. You shut up and go back downstairs and carry on necking your booze like a good girl, *or* for every second that you remain in my eyesight shouting the odds, I'm going to give your boyfriend here a good smack." He raises his eyebrows and smiles at me triumphantly. He even laughs. "What do you think about that?"

I swallow hard. I do not want to let him beat me. I have to speak to Marianne. I just have to. I narrow my eyes at him and look him up at down. "I think you are the biggest tosser in the world. I think you are a dumb, mindless thug. I think you are an ungrateful shitbag of a brother, and I think I am going to speak to my friend!" I take another step towards the door. Leon grabs Joe by the shirt, yanks him forward and cuffs him around the head. I stop.

"Ow!" Joe complains, with both hands on the back of his head. I blow my angry breath out through my teeth. I have seen worse. Joe is okay. I duck around Leon suddenly, taking him by surprise, and reach Marianne's door. I don't look back when I hear the sound of Leon slamming his brother back into the wall behind, or the noise Joe makes when all the breath has been punched out of his guts. I swallow again and wrench open the door and go inside her bedroom.

She is sat at her dressing table wearing little more than her silky black dressing gown. The gown is tied loosely at the waist, exposing one breast, and her entire right leg all the way up to the thigh. I can see the dozens of tiny scars that stand out across her creamy skin. She looks up at me in alarm, and at first I see guilt and fear etched across her face, but then her face relaxes, and she just smiles. She is chopping up lines of white powder across her desk with her own special razor blade. How fitting. I let the door close softly. I can hear the thumps and thuds of Leon punishing Joe on the landing, and a chant has started up of '*fight, fight, fight, fight!*'

I just stare at her. I am drunk and angry, and she is drunk and reckless, and I shake my head, at her, and at the white powder she is playing with like a child with matches.

"So that's why he didn't want to let me in," I say to her softly, my shoulders dropping. Marianne throws her head back and laughs, and then looks back down at the powder and continues to chop it up, organising it deftly into neat, white lines.

"I told him you wouldn't exactly care," she laughs and shrugs.

"Well then you don't know me at all," I tell her, my voice emotionless. "And it looks like I don't know you at all either."

"Well isn't that the truth about everyone?" she answers, looking back at me with a wide and hungry smile, her eyes shining with delight.

"Maybe it is."

"Oh it is," she laughs. "It really is. You want some?"

"No chance," I say bitterly, looking at her in disgust. "I wouldn't touch that shit if you paid me. You have no idea the shit Joe and me have gone through because of that crap. We're both sick of it."

"No one forced you," she says easily. "No one put a gun to your head. Everyone makes their own choices for their own reasons Lou."

"Yeah, and Leon is beating the crap out of Joe right now out there, because of you!" I say this angrily, but also guiltily, and I know I have to go. "I'll talk to you later," I tell her, my hand on the doorknob. "You're obviously completely fine. I don't know why I even bothered worrying."

"Because you are a good friend Lou," Marianne tells me in a sunny voice, her eyes on the desk. She does not look up as I leave the room and close the door behind me. On the landing there is a crowd of kids watching and cheering as Leon and Joe roll around on the floor together. I wade through, telling them all to get the hell out of the way, and I reach in to the blur of fists and red faces and grab Joe by the arm. The fight breaks up as Leon gets to his feet, grinning and panting. Joe stays on the floor, and drops his head into the space between his knees. I look up at Leon with all the fury and disgust I can muster. I am glad to see his bottom lip is bleeding.

"Go on go back to her you stupid bastard," I hiss at him from the floor. "Go back and leave us alone if you want us to keep your secrets for you!"

Leon just turns slowly on his heels, broad and arrogant and full of himself as always. He laughs, and his wide shoulders shake with it as he heads back to Marianne. The crowd breaks up too. Slouched shoulders disappear down the stairs, murmuring and chuckling. I sit on the floor and put my arm around Joe.

"I'm really sorry," I tell him quietly. "I had to see she was okay."

Joe snorts a little laugh through his nose and lifts his head to look at me. His nose is bleeding, and there are two little tracks of red running down into his mouth. I look into his eyes then, and I want to grab his poor face with both of my hands, just the way Travis did with mine. I want to hold his face as if I am holding china. I want to press my lips onto his and taste his blood. "And was she?" he asks me, and I can see the genuine concern in his eyes and my heart lurches against my chest and smashes into tiny little pieces yet again. I wonder how many times I can go through the same endless confusing emotions and urges. I wonder helplessly if I will ever make any sense of it. I lift a finger and use it to gently push back his hair, which is covering his eyes. I watch him smile.

"She's sat at the desk," I sigh. "Cutting up lines of coke. That's why he wanted to keep us out."

The realisation hits Joe, and I can see he is as surprised as me. "Oh," he says slowly. "That's why."

"I know," I say, and drop my arm away from his shoulders. "How stupid are we?"

"Pretty fucking stupid."

"Pretty fucking drunk."

"Me too. Oh man…" Joe rubs the heel of one hand into his eye, and then slides it around to the back of his head where he rubs it back and forth. "My head really hurts."

"Need more booze?"

"That might help, yeah."

"He's such bastard…" I shake my head at the closed bedroom door. "For so many reasons. I could write out at least one hundred reasons why he is *such* a fucking bastard." Joe looks at me and laughs. I nod at him. "Latest editions to the list being him seducing a sixteen year old girl and plying her with illegal drugs."

"Well I don't think she needed much seducing," Joe says, still rubbing slowly at his head. "You didn't see her all over him like a rash."

"Do you know that really surprises me?" I ask, looking at him. "I just never saw her like that before, you know? All sexy and seductive. I never thought she was like that."

"I don't think we know her very well."

"No, we don't, you're right. I've been thinking that a lot lately." I get up then and hold my hand out to Joe. He takes it and climbs awkwardly to his feet. He looks wrecked and knackered and yawns widely. "Let's leave them to it then," I shrug at the closed bedroom door. "She obviously knows what she's doing."

"Yeah, come on, fuck 'em," he agrees and heads for the stairs. "They deserve each other."

22

Dear World, I fall asleep on the wicker sofa in Marianne's conservatory, with my head in Joe's lap. I just cannot keep my eyes open any longer. The party is over. The guests have all gone. There are a few random people still milling around and making coffee in the kitchen, but in the conservatory, there is just myself and Joe, and Ryan and Josh. As I start to drift away in Joe's lap, I listen to the boy's conversation about their band. They sound so enthusiastic, so worked up and into it, that I smile to myself, and think how utterly sweet they are. Josh sings a few lines from a song he is working on. Joe taps out the drumbeat with his hands on his knees. I have both my hands folded under my cheek. They are still talking and laughing softly as I slide into the blackness.

I am woken up by own dribble. You know how it is. You feel the drool start to escape and you suck it back in quickly, and realise that your hand, or your pillow is already wet. I lift my head and wipe my mouth, and check my hand, which is already fizzing with pins and needles. I sit up slowly, and the room moves in that horrible, still drunk way, and I pull back from Joe's lap and lean against the back of the sofa, yawning. He has his head thrown back and is fast asleep. I peer forward to check his lap for dribble but it is dry. Phew.

I glance at the floor. Josh is lying on his back, with his head on a cushion and his arms folded across his chest. He is snoring softly. Ryan is curled up in the wicker armchair, also with his arms crossed tightly around himself. I listen for voices and movement in the kitchen, but they are all gone. I sit still for a while and the memories of the night swim in and out of my mind, jostling for attention. I don't want to think about any of them really. But I do need a wee.

I get up carefully, not wanting to wake any of the boys. I have no shoes on, and tiptoe cautiously across the floor towards the kitchen, dodging broken glass, and puddles of unidentified liquid. The kitchen is empty and bears the scars of the party like no other room. The counters are strewn with food and drink, and bottles and cups. There is vomit blocking the sink, and vomit under the kitchen table. Someone has ransacked the food cupboards, as the doors are all hanging open, most of the food gone. I don't know what the hell Marianne will tell her parents, but I suppose that's her problem, and anyway, knowing her, she will most likely already have a plan.

The downstairs toilet is in the hallway. I find myself sitting down on the loo, whipping down my knickers, and closing and locking the door at the same time as the piss streams out of me in an urgent gush. I fill with physical relief. I drop my head into my hands, my elbows digging into my bare knees. I seem to stay like that for ages. It is probably the longest wee I have ever had in my life. I start to wish I had timed it.

When it is finally over, I pull up my pants, pull down my dress and wash my hands. There is a mirror over the washbasin and I look at it accidentally. I try to avoid mirrors most of the time, the same way I try to avoid cameras. But every now and again I come across my reflection by accident, and usually this totally ruins my mood. I always look fatter in the mirror than I feel in real life. I can be feeling really good, having a drink, having a good time, and then come across myself in the mirror and the next thing I know I want to punch myself in my stupid ugly face. I always feel the life and the joy slide right out of me. It's like, oh. Oh, so I look like that, do I? That's me, is it? And I thought I looked good earlier. Oh well, looks like I was wrong.

But this reflection takes me by surprise for a different reason. It takes me by surprise because for a fleeting second I am confused, as I do not recognise the face in the mirror, and in my still drunken state, I momentarily think I have bumped into someone else in the loo. But then

I realise that it is me, it is my face I am staring back at, and how very peculiar not to recognise myself? I do not know whether to feel glad or sad, and I suppose that I feel plenty of both. The face in the mirror looks far too thin to be me. The face in the mirror looks almost glamorous in its ruined state. The mascara is smudged around my eyes. My skin is pale, almost translucent, which makes my eyes stand out even more. It is like all there is are my eyes. Huge, dark blue eyes, and masses and masses of thick, long eyelashes. I frown at the cheekbones I never knew I had. I feel my hands grip the basin, steadying myself as a kind of fear washes over me, a shivering realisation of what I have done to myself. The face in the mirror looks beautiful, but only in a haunted, wrecked kind of way. I lick my lips, which seem very red, despite my lipstick being long gone. I toss back my hair, which is a mess, but still straighter than usual. I nod at myself. I nod at her.

I am still drunk enough to feel recklessly proud of what I have done to myself, and I come out of the toilet looking forward to curling back up on Joe's lap, and wrapping my arms around my body, feeling for those ribs. I realise what a pointless fuck up I am, what a quivering mess of humanity I am turning out to be, and I don't give a shit. I come out of the toilet feeling brave and careless, and I bump right into Marianne.

She is still wearing her silky dressing gown, and she looks both pleased and excited to find me there. She grabs my hand with both of hers and squeezes it tightly. Her face is pale, her eyes are alive, and her smile is unnerving. "Leon just left," she informs me in a breathless tone. "*What a night!*"

My hand feels small and heavy between hers. "What happened?"

"Come and have a drink with me," she breathes, and pulls me by the hand back through the kitchen. She seems totally unfazed by the state of the place, and searches the room for any unused alcohol. Eventually she settles on a bottle of whiskey which has a few shots left in it, grabs it by the neck, snatches my hand back up, and pulls me through the conservatory and out into the garden.

"Why outside?" I ask, tugging my hand free to wrap my arms around myself as I start to shiver. She sits on the bench where Travis kissed me, and crosses her legs.

"I'm hot!" she cries, unscrewing the cap from the whiskey bottle. "Aren't you hot?"

"No, I'm cold," I say, sitting down beside her and pulling up my knees to hug.

"You want my gown?"

"Have you got something on under it?"

She looks at me and raises her eyebrows. "No!"

"No thanks then," I say. "I'll be fine."

"So what you been up to?"

"I just woke up. I woke up and needed a wee."

"Before that, I mean. How was the party for you?"

"Oh, good." I nod at her slowly. I wonder how much she remembers herself. "Not bad. Could have done without the big fight, but you know. Boys."

"Oh yeah, I heard about that." Marianne takes a big swig of whiskey, and then hands it to me. I take it hesitantly.

"We should have got some coke."

"Ooh it's okay like that. It'll warm you up."

"Okay." I take a mouthful and very nearly spit it back out again. It burns as I force it down my throat. I shudder from head to toe. But she is right. It starts to burn a fire from the inside.

"See?" she says. I hand her back the bottle and nod.

"Yeah."

"Fucking *amazing* night," she says then, but when I look at her, I see no joy behind her eyes. Only aggression and frustration, and I don't get it. She drinks the whiskey, wipes her mouth and shoves it back in my lap. I have to ask her what happened. I have to get it out of the way.

"So, did you sleep with him?"

Marianne bites her lip as she looks into my eyes, and nods her head. I don't know what to say. Congratulations, you had sex with a cunt? Well done on bedding a total bastard? So I just nod back, drink some whiskey and give it back to her. There is a silence as she knocks it back. I look out at the dark garden and a million thoughts and feelings fill my head and my soul and I want to swallow them all.

"Was he nice to you?" I ask her then, eyes on the garden. "I only ask because that's why we were worried about you and came to check on you. He's not the nicest person in the world."

"He was lovely," she says beside me. "It was lovely."

"Lovely?"

"Amazing. Lou, have you had sex yet?"

"Hey?" I look at her, taken back. She hands me the bottle.

"Are you still a virgin?"

"You know I am. I'd tell you if I wasn't. So you're not one anymore."

"I wasn't one anyway, stupid."

I swallow another mouthful of whiskey and the warmth fills my belly as the confusion fills my mind. "Oh? I thought you were."

"I thought we already worked out we don't know much about each other." I look at her and she is viewing me very sceptically. It reminds me of the way my older sister looks at me when she is trying to give me advice.

"I just thought you were."

"Nope." She is not smiling, as she looks at me expectantly. She takes the bottle out of my hand and throws another huge mouthful down her tiny neck. I wait. I feel like she is preparing to eat me alive.

"So who then?" I ask finally.

"Josh and Ryan for starters."

I stare at her. My jaw hits the fucking floor. "*What*?" I practically scream at her. She leans back on the bench, holds the nearly empty bottle of whiskey between her legs, and releases a huge burp.

"Yeah," she says.

"Josh and Ryan?"

"Yeah."

"Oh *what*!" I just cannot believe it. I want to laugh, but somehow that seems uncalled for. I smack myself on the head, and then leave my hand there, shaking my head at her. She curls her lip at me.

"What's the big deal?"

"I don't know! When was this?"

"A while ago. I don't know. Some time."

"Who was first?"

"Josh."

"Oh my God,"

"Lou, grow up," she snaps at me then, and there is no more excitement in those eyes of hers. They are flat and cold and empty. Only contempt spills from her face when she looks my way. "You sound about twelve."

"I'm sorry," I say with a nervous laugh. I look back out at the garden, because I am increasingly unnerved by her mood. "I'm just surprised that's all. It's a lot to get my head around. You never said before."

She shrugs her shoulders. "Oh well."

"So was it good? I mean, did you enjoy it? I wouldn't know, would I? Being a virgin?" I am almost deliberately acting like a twelve year old now, just to get her to spill the beans. She can look at me like I am a retard if she wants.

"Leon was the best, obviously," she sighs, and lifts the bottle to her mouth, even though it is my turn. I say nothing, I just watch her. She finishes it off and then hurls the bottle into the grass.

"You got a lot of cleaning up to do tomorrow," I say.

"Whatever."

"Are you okay?"

"Why do you ask?"

"You seem weird. Kind of angry." She looks at me then, releases a slow sigh and then wipes her mouth with the back of her hand. "*Are* you okay?" I ask again.

"I'm fine," she says, and a faint smile touches her lips. "What else do you want to know?"

"Um. Does it hurt? You know, the first time?"

"Oh not really. Just a bit. If he knows what he's doing then it will be okay."

"Did Josh and Ryan know what they were doing?" I ask, and cannot believe I am even asking, but hell, how can I not? She looks at me kind of wearily and I smile at her indulgently, feeling more and more like a child.

"Course they didn't," she sighs. "I had to show them."

"Marianne!"

"What?"

"Just…I don't know. I am just so shocked. Practically speechless. You are like two people, or something. I never knew you were so…" I look around, searching for the right word. "You know…*sexual*?"

Marianne laughs at me. "You are so funny."

"Am I?"

"Oh yeah. You'll never know how funny you are."

I frown at her. "What does that mean?"

"Huh?"

"You. You're like, talking in riddles. You must still be hammered. Or high." I look at her and make a face. "I forgot about that. How was that? Was that the first time?"

"I'm not going to sit here and answer all your dumb questions," she complains and yawns at me. I roll my eyes.

"Well you dragged me out here!"

"Oh for God's sake."

"Marianne!"

"What?"

"Why are you being such a bitch?"

She leans towards me then, with a tight smile on her lips, and a knowing look in her green eyes. I have the urge to move back, and in that second she reminds me horribly of Leon. The way he steals the space. I don't move back. I stare her down.

"I'm not being a bitch at all," she retorts. "I just wanted to have some adult conversation with someone, that's all. But then you go and get all silly and girly, and it does my head in."

I am appalled with her. "I'll go then shall I?"

"Don't be such a baby."

"Don't be such a bitch! I stood up to that tosser you shagged earlier, I'll stand up to you too, you know!" I am suddenly aware that I have leant towards her, so I am effectively shouting right into her face. The neat whiskey was probably not a wise idea on top of everything else I have consumed. She stares at me, giving nothing away. "He's a nothing but a nasty twat by the way," I tell her spitefully. "Although obviously you don't care. But he is. He's an animal."

"Maybe I like animals," she purrs at me then. "Better than little boys anyway."

"Nice."

"Look," she sighs then, finally moving back. "You can think what you want. I had fun with Leon. You hate him. Whatever."

"Are you expecting to see him again? Because I wouldn't get my hopes up if I were you."

"Course I'm not!" she snaps at me, and in that instant I can tell that she is lying. Her cheeks redden slightly. She looks furiously at me. She *is* hoping to see him again, and there is nothing she can do to hide it from me. She wants to see him again, and she knows there is not a fucking chance. "Don't be an idiot," she says. "It wasn't like that anyway. One night of fun. That's how I work."

"Oh lovely. That's really nice. Really romantic."

"Anything else is a joke."

"Really? Is it?"

"Yep. Relationships. Marriage. All that shit." Marianne lowers her feet onto the grass, stretches out her spine and stares indignantly at the dark shadows of her garden.

"So your own parents are a joke then?" I ask her. She nods, not looking at me.

"Yep. They're a joke all right. So are yours. So are everyone's."

"Well aren't you feeling cheerful? So you had a great night then? It really did you good? Sleeping with Leon and taking coke? Because you really seem happy about it mate."

Marianne turns her head to look at me. "What about you then?" she asks.

"Hey?"

"Tell me about your night then. See if yours has filled you with the joy mine so obviously hasn't."

"I got drunk and came to see if you were okay," I say to her. "Joe got beaten up by Leon, while I checked on you. Then we went downstairs and got more drunk. Then I fell asleep."

"And what about Travis?"

I feel something that resembles a knife, slicing through my heart. Not my heart again. This time it is sliced into two pieces of meat that slip and slide, trailing damp blood down the inside of my rib cage. Travis.

"What about him?" I try like hell not to let anything show up in my voice, but I know how astute Marianne is. I know I have no chance.

"He was here. Then he left."

"So?"

"He followed you out when you went to be sick."

"Did he?"

"He tried it on again, didn't he?" She turns her body towards mine, and I can't help but notice her left breast showing again. I want to tell her to tighten her gown, but what is the point? If I draw attention to it, and let her know it makes me uncomfortable, she will probably just whip it off and run around the garden naked or something.

"Don't be stupid," I groan at her. She laughs at me.

"He did! I *know* he did! I can read you like a book Lou Carling! He did, didn't he? Come on, tell the truth. I told you."

"For Christ's sake," I groan, burying my face in my hands for a moment. Marianne laughs and rocks beside me. I don't get her at all. I have never met a person more complicated and strange than Marianne Sholing, and I think she is just warming up. She is only just starting to reveal herself to me.

"Come on, spill," she demands, slapping my leg petulantly. I drop my hands into my lap and stare at the ground. The whiskey is hitting me harder and harder. It is like someone taking random and savage pot shots at my brain. "Your silence says it all Lou Carling. Your silence says it all. So you finally let him kiss you then? Out here somewhere?" I look at her and bite my lip, and my eyes fall momentarily to the bench we are sat on, and then I look quickly back at her, but it is too late, she knows. Her green eyes widen greedily. "Out here on the bench," she states it like a fact. "He kissed you right here where we are sat."

"Yeah, so what?" I stretch and yawn. Try to play it down. I have the distinct urge not to give her any ammunition. "That's all. Not like you and Leon."

"Ah bless," she smiles at me, her head tilted to one side. Patronising, I think.

"Yeah, well, I was drunk," I shrug at her carelessly. "It won't happen again either."

"Have you told Joe?"

"No," I look at her quickly. "And don't you either. Not yet."

"And why not?"

"I don't know." I frown wearily, and pull my legs up again, wrapping my arms tightly around my knees. "It's just complicated. You know how it is with his brothers. I don't want anything kicking off."

"You don't want them fighting over you again, you mean?" she asks. I shake my head.

"That's not what I mean. I just mean, Joe is my best friend, okay?"

"Yeah, so?"

"So I don't want to upset him. Anyway, forget it. It's boring. I do not fancy Travis."

Marianne leans back and folds her hands together in her lap. She watches me quietly, and her expression is peaceful and serene, and I wonder what the hell she is thinking when she looks at me like that. "Okay," she sort of sighs. "Let's forget it. You're right, it is boring. Do you want one more drink?"

"What?"

"I fancy one more drink." She jumps up energetically and starts heading for the house.

"You're crazy," I tell her back. She laughs.

"Oh yes!"

When she returns moments later she is carrying two glasses of white wine. I take mine reluctantly. My head is spinning out of control. I feel a bit nauseous again. Marianne sits down and takes a sip of her wine. "Ahh," she says. "That's nice."

"I'm surprised there is any booze left in there."

"I knew where to look," she says and winks at me. I look down into my wine and try to take some slow, deep breaths.

"What are you doing?" she asks me in amusement.

I look up at her through my messy hair. "I am just really, really pissed," I tell her sombrely, and she throws back her head and bellows laughter. Well at least she seems cheerful again, I muse. I think I have seen her swing between every conceivable emotion tonight.

"You're so sweet," I hear her say. I nod helplessly. I can feel my eyelids trying to drop down. I try to fight it. They want to close down for the night, they want to slam the shutters down on my brain, and I don't blame them, because my brain is totally fucked. In the end I let my head drift back towards the back of the bench, and rest it there. I watch the garden. I wonder what the hell the time is. I wish I were still curled up with Joe. I feel sickness spreading through my body and my soul and it saddens me. I want to cry. Alcohol is such a dangerous thing. Getting drunk is a risky and vicious thing to do to yourself for no reason.

"Didn't mean to ruin your fun," I hear myself murmur, as my mind takes me back to the fight outside her room. I am leaning against her now. I can feel the glassy smoothness of her silk robe against my bare arm. I feel her sighing.

"You didn't. We had our fun."

I close my eyes. Just for a moment, I tell myself. "Good," I reply. "I'm glad you had fun because we all deserve to have fun. We all need to have fun."

"That is very true Lou. And have you had fun? Tonight?"

"In the confusion of it all," I open my eyes and try to consider it. "Maybe. Yes. In a weird way."

"Everything happens in a weird way."

"Especially when you are pissed."

"You are probably my best friend, Lou." I look at her then. Her face is very close to mine. Her green eyes are startling in their colour. They remind me of cat's eyes. They sparkle with all the hidden thoughts that flow through her mind.

"Really?" I ask her. "I sometimes think you sort of hate me."

"Don't be stupid," she giggles, and nudges me. "I don't hate you. You are lovely. And very funny."

"Okay then." I close my eyes again, because my eyelids are winning, because they are tied down with weights. My eyelashes bump down upon each other, top meeting bottom, then batting back open again as I struggle to stay awake. Then she rests her head on my shoulder, and I rest my head on her head.

I jerk awake, God knows how much later. I am totally disorientated and confused, and there is a glass of wine in my hands that I don't recall being there, and as I jump out of my sleep I drop the glass, and it shatters into tiny pieces on the ground. I gasp and sit forward, staring with one hand over my mouth at the shining shards of glass on the grass. I look at Marianne, and she is not there. I look up. How is it possible that I feel even more pissed than I did before I fell asleep? I rub my eyes. How the hell is that actually possible? Where does the phrase 'sleep it off' come from then?

Marianne is not sat next to me anymore, and I suppose her moving away was what woke me up. She is not sat next to me, because she is on the grass in front of me, sort of dancing around. She is flapping her robe about, revealing one side of her tiny naked body, and then the other. She is staring at the black sky, scarred with twinkling stars, millions of years away from us and our pointlessness. I feel my eyes widen at the sight of her there, like that. I have to shake my head, and then rub at my eyes, and still I cannot believe I am not dreaming the sleep of the drunk.

She is laughing, and swaying, and whipping her open gown to one side, and then the other. I feel embarrassed, but also mesmerised, because her little body, it is so fucking beautiful. I feel a deep sinking sadness then, far down inside my weak little belly, because something tells me that no matter how skinny I get, I will never feel like that about my own body. I will never dance around like that, showing it off, revelling in its perfect and unique beauty. I only want to hide it and cover it up. I only view it as a means of transport.

She sees me looking at her and laughs at me loudly. She does not even attempt to pull her gown around her body. I sort of grin in embarrassment and lower my eyes. I feel a bit like a pervy teenage boy, spying. "Wakey, wakey," she laughs at me. "Want to join me for a dance?"

"I just broke your glass."

"So what? So did I. Look!" She points dramatically at the ground near her feet, which when I strain my eyes, I can see is sprinkled with shining glass.

"Watch out you idiot!" I hiss at her, as she carries on dancing.

"I don't give a shit!" she shouts back, throwing back her hair. She looks wild, I think. Untamed and fucked up. I shiver.

"Just be careful!"

"*Careful*!" she howls at me, laughing but angry at the same time. She shows me what she thinks of this by dancing in a crazy circle, even faster and harder on the glass. I cannot watch, so I cover my eyes. I imagine her little white feet getting sliced and diced upon the hidden shards of glass, lying in wait for her among the damp blades of grass.

I hide in my hands. I stretch my shaking fingers around my cold face, caressing my skin, comforting myself, and as I do I realise that this is what I need most right now, someone to comfort me, someone to look after me, not mess me up. I drop my head into the palms of my hands, and my hands press against my raised knees. I can hear her laughing. I wonder, and I wince, at the thought of her dainty feet covered in nicks and cuts, like her arms. I do not know what to do. My friend, (is she my friend?) is dancing on broken glass. Is dancing on broken glass. For *God's* sake.

"What do you think pain is Lou?" I hear her asking. I lift my head drowsily as she bounds back to the bench and sits down next to me. She pays no attention to her open gown, as she pulls her foot up onto her other knee and inspects the sole of her foot. I watch her, as my brains swells and throbs inside my head. I think, I don't know, I don't know what pain is. Except for my entire fucking life. I just shake my head at her, because I am barely able to speak. She is bent fiercely over her foot. I do not want to know if there is glass in it or not. "What do you actually think pain is? Have you ever really thought about it?"

I blink at her. "I don't know. No."

"Really? Haven't you?"

"No."

"It fascinates me. Really, it does." I look at her then, and she is pulling a slither of glass out of her heel. I feel my stomach turn over.

"Oh bloody hell, Marianne."

"Shut up. Don't be silly."

It is then that I remember her arms. I force myself to look at her. At her face. Her eyes are gleaming as she extracts the glass and holds it aloft triumphantly. I watch a fat droplet of blood swelling at the tip of the glass, before stretching and falling. I watch it land, fat and red on her naked thigh. I am breathless.

"Look," she says, and moves the bleeding glass closer to my eyes. I feel like I cannot breathe properly. "Look," she says. "It's just blood. It's just what we are all made of, Lou. Look at it."

It means so much to her, so I look at it. My eyes focus in on the blood-smeared shard of glass that trembles between her fingers. I don't know what to say. I do not know what she wants me to say.

"Ouch," I say.

"No," she says, quickly. "That's not ouch. Ouch is for children. Ouch is a stupid reaction. You can be braver than that."

"What?"

"Look," she says, and she brings the glass back down towards her exposed thigh. She whips it across the surface of the white flesh and I wince, and draw back in shock. I see her smiling. Laughing. I look back at her thigh. The bubbles of blood are pushing up along the lines of the white slash on her skin. I watch. I am transfixed. I watch the red beads forming along the line. I can hear her breathing get faster, and she sounds excited. The red beads grow fatter and fatter, and start to blend into each other, absorbing each other, and growing hungry. I watch the beads form an orderly line. A soaking wet red line.

"Marianne," I hear myself whisper at her. "Don't do that."

"Why not?" she says, matter of factly. "Why shouldn't I?"

"Because you'll hurt yourself," I say, stupidly. "You'll get hurt…"

"Hurt?" she questions, not looking at me. "What's hurt? It does not hurt." She pushes the glass towards my face and I move back fearfully. She laughs, and then whips it back down to her thigh, slashing at the flesh a second time.

"Marianne!" I cry out at her. "Don't!"

"Why?" she laughs at me. She is laughing at me. I want to cry. I watch a second line of blood beads stand to attention on her thigh.

"Marianne," I say. "*Please* don't do that do yourself."

"Why not?"

"Why not? Because I don't understand it Marianne. I don't get it. Why would you do that to yourself?"

"It feels good," she purrs at me, smiling from ear to ear. She seems oblivious to the pain. I watch the new line of blood springing to life next to the first one. The blood runs faster this time. She has cut deeper. The blood pours out from the cut, and down her thigh, zig zagging down past her knee. I gasp uselessly. "It's okay," she tells me. "It really doesn't hurt. It really doesn't. It stings a bit the next day, that's all."

"That's all?"

"Yeah. That's just to remind me. I wake up and think oh yeah. I did that. I would forget otherwise."

"And what do you think?" I ask her then. "What do you think when you wake up and realise what you have done?"

"I don't mind," she shrugs. "I think, oh well."

"Marianne. It's not right."

"It makes me feel better. Lou, do you know what pain is?" She is leaning very close to me now. I can smell the wine on her breath. I want to move back, to pull away, but I don't. I shrug my shoulders weakly. I am weak. "Lou," she says. "It is something you can easily conquer. It is nothing really. It is only what it is. It is only what you allow it to be. Once you realise that, life becomes a whole lot fucking easier, believe me."

I feel the sigh dropping out from my chest. I am so beaten down by everything. The alcohol has thrashed me. I keep my eyes on hers. Her smile. "Really?" I ask her. "Is that so?"

"Yes," she promises softly, and she moves closer. I feel her wet, bloody thigh press against mine. I know, that in a less drunken moment, I would pull away in disgust and make my excuses and leave. But excessive alcohol pins me to the inevitable spot and I cannot move. "Once you conquer physical pain," she is saying to me softly, slowly. "You can easily conquer emotional pain."

"Can you?" my voice asks her. "Really?"

"Let me show you." I look down. Marianne picks up my arm. She is still holding the weeping shard of glass. She holds my forearm with both of her hands and I see her staring at my waiting flesh. Then she looks into my eyes and smiles, and I know, that she knows, that I am totally fucked. "Lou," she says to me. "You are very open minded. That's what I like about you." She presses one thumb against the skin on my wrist. She moves the thumb higher, pressing softly towards the fold of the elbow. I think again; pull away. She has the glass and she moves it down towards my arm, and she lines it up, and drags it along my skin, just softly. When she hears my alarmed intake of breath she looks up at me. "Lou," she says to me. "It doesn't hurt. Open up your mind. Let your body take it. It only hurts if you let it hurt. If you think in those terms." I don't understand. I am locked within her eyes. She stares back into mine. I feel the glass pressing into my flesh and I don't know what to do. She is holding my arm gently. I could pull away at any moment, but I do not, and she takes advantage of this, and she scrapes the glass against me harder. I hiss at the pain. I pull my arm out of her hands and bring it up to my eyes.

"Marianne!"

"There you go!" she cries, and I watch her hurl away the glass. And then she is up again. Dancing. Spinning. Laughing. Throwing her robe to one side, and then the other. I let her, and I look down at my arm. On the inside, halfway between the wrist and the elbow, she has made her mark. I stare. I watch the beads of red bulging and spreading. I watch them join forces and march a straight savage line across my weak flesh. She is right. There is no pain. What is pain?

I would probably be all right if I wasn't such a fucking thinker.

I start thinking, what is this? What does this mean? The booze lends me to paranoia, and paranoia does a real good job with me, and tells me this bitch is actually trying to kill me. I feel my body lurching, without my permission, lurching to its feet. I am lurching up. Reeling. That is another good word. Reeling. Because you do not walk normally when drink has done this much to you. You reel. So I reel and lurch towards the conservatory. I run away from her. It is my body moving me on, and not my mind. My body wants me out of there. My body has had enough.

I hear her laughing and dancing, and I glimpse my bloody arm, and I want to scream out; 'you dumb bitch!' but I don't. I hurl myself through the open doors of the conservatory. I straight away see Joe, still lying where I left him. I want to get the hell out of there, and I feel an awful drunken panic consuming me. It is terrible. I seize Joe by his arm and wrench him away from his dreams. He opens blurry eyes and sees me. "What?" his sleep slurred voice questions me.

"Joe," I hiss this urgently into his ear. I am pulling at his arm. "Joe, we need to go. Take me home. Now. Please take me home."

He wakes up quickly, alarmed by my closeness and my panic, and I tighten my hold on his arm, and try to drag him from the sofa, because I am so mortified, and so confused, and I just want to get the hell out of there as quick as I can. I keep pulling at his arm. I can feel the wetness passing between us. My arm is bleeding into his.

"What have you done?" he asks me, climbing out of groggy sleep. I pull and pull at his arm. I just want him to get the hell up. "Why are you crying?" he asks me. I did not realise I was crying, but he is right, I am crying. There are fat hot wet tears sliding down my cheeks.

"Joe," I beg, pulling him harder. "Take me home. Please, please, you have to take me home."

"Okay, okay," he says, and thank God, finally, he gets up from the sofa and stretches. I have no time for stretches. I want him to get me out of there. So I keep pulling him. "What have you done you stupid bitch?" he is complaining at me. He is holding onto my sticky wet arm. "Jesus," he breathes then. "What have you done?"

"Joe," I beg, "Please take me home. Please, please, please."

He is staring at me. I have to get him moving. I pull him, I yank him, I force him away from the sofa, from his sleeping friends, and out of the conservatory. I say nothing, just become resourcefully adamant in my desire to get out of there, and I do not give up anything until I feel the cold air of the night again and I let the front door slam behind us. I feel the crunch of gravel under my feet and a grim determination takes over me. I can hear Joe moaning and protesting and worrying, but I do not slow down, or give in to him until I can feel the hard black pavement under my bare feet, and I am sure that she is not following us. And then I start to cry.

"Lou, Lou, Lou," he is saying to me, over and over again. He has his arm around my shoulders, and he is squeezing me, trying to get me to calm down. I cannot calm down. I am a complete and utter wreck of a human being. I can feel my shoulders heaving and lurching with every gut-wrenching sob. Finally Joe has enough, and he holds me by my shoulders and stops me. "Lou!" he shouts this into my face. "Lou stop it!"

I am beat. I hide my face in his chest and keep crying. I feel him lift my arm and I hear him swear. "Lou, what is this? What the fuck have you done to your arm?" I hide in his chest and cry and cry, and it is not all Marianne's fault. It is not. It is everything. I cannot speak, because I am crying too much. I let Joe lead me home. "Can I sleep at yours?" I ask him at one point. I just know that I do not want to be alone.

"Course," he tells me, rubbing my arm. "Course you can."

Somehow we make it back to his. I have vague memories of crossing the black, silent fields. Leaning harder and harder on Joe. I think I sleep.

I am subtlety aware of entering Joe's house. Of the shush noise he makes at me as he turns his key in the lock. I obey. I shush. I let him shuffle me in. I stare at the patterns on the carpet. He leads me up the stairs. They seem so huge and vast.

He pushes me towards the bottom bunk bed. The saggy old mattress is a welcome relief to me. I throw back the duvet. My head hits the pillow. I close my eyes, and I am dimly aware of Joe moving around the room, doing things. Finally I feel him climb into bed beside me. He pulls the duvet over both of us. He has something in his hand and he presses it against my wet arm. I hiss. Pain. I think of Marianne, and I examine the reality of the pain. She is right about one thing. It is only what you think it is.

"It's okay," Joe is whispering this to me in the darkness. How the hell did I get here? "What happened?" he is asking me. I am cold and black and my closed eyes press against his soft chest, and I want to love him.

"Marianne did it."

"*What*?"

"Marianne did it. She cut me."

"Oh Jesus Christ, that is mental! Jesus Christ, Lou." I can feel his hand rubbing my shoulder. His arm is around me, rubbing me. I close wet eyes upon his t-shirt.

"I'm sorry," I tell him in the darkness. "I am such a twat…"

"She's a mental bitch Lou! You stay away from her! Fucking hell!"

He sounds angry, and so he holds me closer. I try to remember our journey through the darkness together, but I can't. I am just suddenly here. I am here, and Joe has pulled the duvet right over us, and I bury myself in him.

I am sobbing again. But it is not Marianne's fault. It is only because I hate myself so much.

"Stay away from her," Joe rants to me in the darkness. "Stay the hell away from that mad bitch!"

"I let her do it," I sob uselessly into his soaked t-shirt. He is still pressing the towel, or whatever it is, against my arm. "I could have stopped her."

"You're hammered," he tells me firmly. He sounds like he is talking through gritted teeth. "It is not your fault Lou. She shouldn't be going round doing that to other people! It's sick."

I cannot stop crying. I am not just weeping silent tears, I am really crying. My whole body is rocking with them. They are coming faster and harder, and I am not in control of them, and I start to get frightened, because it feels like they are trying to consume me and take over me from the inside. They just keep coming and coming, and I just don't understand it, and I can't stop it, I can't escape. Joe holds me tighter.

"Lou, shh, shh, it's okay," he is telling me, and his voice sounds worried. He rolls onto his side and I push my head in towards his chest. I curl up into a ball.

"I can't stop, I can't stop," I try to tell him. I can feel the horrible drumming panic rising inside my chest, and I think I will probably die, I will just die, because soon enough I will be crying so much that I will not be able to breathe.

"What is wrong with you?" he holds my face in the darkness and pulls it up to his. "You're scaring me Lou," he whispers.

"I don't want to eat anything," I blurt out at him then. "I just don't want to, I don't want to eat anything…I don't want to get fat again." I close my eyes and the tears keep coming. Joe holds me against his chest and his arms are all the way around me.

"Don't be silly," I hear him telling me softly. "You're being so silly. You're just really, really drunk, and Marianne has scared you, and you're going to be fine in the morning."

"Keep telling me that," I shudder and beg him. I am trying to empty out my mind, and shovel away all of the thoughts that are driving me crazy. I don't want to think them anymore. I just want to be normal for once. I just want to be happy.

"You'll be fine in the morning," Joe whispers into my hair. "You're gonna' have one hell of a hangover, but you'll be fine, just fine. You are the loveliest person I know. You should stop worrying about everything all the time. You are just fine the way you are. You are lovely the way you are." He repeats this over and over again into my hair, until his words, and my breathing start to hum a regular pattern. It has all slowed down. "I love you the way you are. Just be the way you are. There is nothing wrong with who you are."

23

Dear World, I have strange disjointed dreams where I start to believe that Joe is right. That everything will be okay. That when I wake up in the morning, everything will be okay again, and so will we. But Joe is wrong. When we wake up in the morning, everything gets even worse.

I am vaguely aware of Will's feet hitting the floor beside us as he jumps down from his bunk. I have the duvet pulled over my head and I don't move. I can feel Joe breathing softly and slowly beside me. His arm is around me. The next thing I know, the bedroom door is crashing open, and heavy, angry footsteps are filling the room fast. "*Joe Lawrenson!*" I hear Lorraine shrieking, and suddenly the duvet is whipped away from us, and Joe awakes in total confusion, his hair stuck up at every angle. He sits up in alarm, and so do I, and Lorraine and Mick have invaded the room and are breathing heavily through their equally flared nostrils. It takes me a while to work out why they are so angry, but then Joe looks at me, and I look at him and I get it.

"What the hell is all this?" Mick demands, hands on squat hips, eyes bulging angrily. I catch a glimpse of Will in the background, dancing around on his light little feet and I think the next time I see him I am going to punch him in the head.

"Joe Lawrenson!" Lorraine barks again. "What the hell is going on here?"

"Nothing Mum, nothing," Joe starts to say, lowering his feet onto the carpet and rubbing the sleep from his eyes with his hands. I do not know what to do. I am still wearing my party dress, and I am suddenly aware of the tight sensation of crusty blood gathered along my forearm. I quickly spread my hands out on the sheet, my fingers searching for the towel Joe had pressed against me last night.

"Doesn't look like nothing!" Mick accuses, stamping his feet. I can see his eyes moving quickly between Lorraine and Joe, trying to work out what she wants him to do. He reminds me of an angry little troll. Lorraine snatches the duvet away from us and it falls to the ground, and her eyes zoom in on my arm and then all hell really breaks loose. She pounces on me, grabbing my arm and holding it up for Mick to see.

"What the hell is this?" Her voice has gone up another octave. She is really shouting now. I hear movement in the other bedroom, and I imagine Travis and Leon lurking in there, listening and wondering. I try to pull my arm away from her, but she holds on tight, and her raging eyes move between Joe and I, as she pieces things together in her mind. "What is this? What have you been doing?"

"It's nothing," I tell her quietly. "I fell on some glass last night. I got upset and asked Joe to bring me home. It's all my fault."

"Nothing happened!" Joe tries to defend himself then, as their accusing eyes bear down on him thunderously. He keeps his head low, as he looks up at his mum and his step-dad. Mick is right there next to him, standing over him, hands cocked on hips. Lorraine looks back at me, and I suppose I must look a right pathetic state, because her eyes soften, and her shoulders sink a little bit. Then she looks at Mick and jerks her head towards Joe.

"Get him out of here! I'll deal with you later young man. Sneaking girls in your room behind our backs, I ask you!" Her voice rises again towards the end of the statement. Mick takes his cue and grabs Joe by the neck of his t-shirt.

"You people are being ridiculous!" he shouts, and it is the first time I have ever heard him answer his mother back. Her face darkens automatically. She is looking at him in pure disgust, as Mick manhandles him towards the open door. "She's my best friend!" he cries. "We didn't do anything you idiots!"

"Don't you call your mother an idiot!" Mick shouts back. Joe holds onto the door frame as he gets pulled through it.

"Just leave her alone!" he tells his mother. "I want to walk her home!" Lorraine drops my arm then and strides towards her son like an army major marching towards an unruly recruit. I can smell her confusion and it only adds to her rage. Joe has never shouted at her before, *ever*. Joe would never dare. Joe was always like me, I think, watching from the bed as she bears down on him. Scuttling around in the background, trying not to annoy anyone. Joe is angry with them and I don't understand why. He tries to pull free from Mick and face his mother. I have never seen his face look like that before. Twisted with scorn and knowing.

"How dare you speak to me like that!" Lorraine barks into his face. "What is wrong with you?"

"You're just so bloody stupid Mum!"

She slaps him. Really hard. Right across his face. I cover my mouth with my hands. The sound of it. I see his head rock back. I start to cry. Joe does too. I see his face crumple. He drops his hands from the door frame and he lets Mick pull him away. But not before I hear him say to his mum; "I *hate* you…I hate all of you."

She slams the door in his face. She takes a second, breathing heavily, staring at the carpet, before she finally spins on her heel and looks at me. I just want to get the hell out of there. Away from her. She looks dark and scary, and God knows what terrors lurk behind that slash of red lipstick, so I crawl to the edge of the bed and lower my feet and look desperately for my shoes, before remembering that I left them at Marianne's. Tears are falling down my cheeks steadily and silently. My head is a mess of pain and foreboding. "Lou," I hear her say, and her tone is gentler again. "This is not like you. Not like either of you. Please tell me what happened to your arm. How am I going to explain this to your mother?" She comes to the bed and leans towards me. She attempts to lift my chin to make me look at her, but I turn my head away from her grip and stand up. The room spins and shakes. I just need to get home. To get into my room. I don't have to speak to her. I don't have to do anything for her. "Lou," she says, more urgently. "Look at me please. Talk to me!" I push my hair back behind my ears, take a deep breath and head for the door. She takes my arm, holding me back. "Lou, wait!"

"What?" I stare at the closed door. I can hear the thumps and thuds downstairs, and I close my eyes briefly and a weary sigh escapes me. "You shouldn't always do that you know," I hear myself say. "Just hit people. That's the whole fucking problem, you know."

"Don't you use that disgusting language with me young lady!" Lorraine snaps, pulling me round to face her. "What the hell has gotten into you kids? Are you on drugs? We're getting seriously worried, you know!"

"I need to go home."

"Yes, you do, and I'm taking you. Come on."

There is nothing I can do. I feel so weak and powerless. So beaten down and ashamed. She opens the door and leads the way down the stairs. I just go limp and let her take me. I wonder where Joe is. If he is still crying. And this is the way it always is. He tries to do the right thing, he helps me and this is what he gets for it. I wonder dully why he bothers at all. I think he was right to act like Leon a few weeks ago. I think, he was damned right punching Will in the head at the park, and stamping on his stupid Lego. What else do they deserve?

***

I cross my arms as we walk to my house. Lorraine keeps a motherly arm around my shoulders the whole time. I walk with gritted teeth and stiff legs. "Your mother is going to be beside herself," she says more than once. "And you better be telling the truth that nothing happened with you two!" I do not bother answering. What would be the point? Let them think whatever disgusting thoughts they like. Perverts. "I don't know what's gotten into that son of mine," she goes on. "He never used to be so defiant. He was always so good!" She looks at me, as if hoping for an answer or a clue, but I give nothing away. I stare straight ahead and keep walking. She sighs, and tightens her arm on my shoulders. "Oh my Lou, you are getting so thin these days. I can feel it. You know, your mum is worried sick about that too, don't you love? You were fine before you know. You know that, don't you?" I roll my eyes and want to be sick right there on the pavement in front of her. Yeah, right I think scathingly. I was perfect before. Gorgeous. And you're a stupid liar. "You kids," she says. "You kids will drive us to an early grave. Sleepless nights, I tell you, worrying about you all. Worse than when you were babies!"

We are home, and she opens the front door and walks in, calling out as she always does; "Coo-ee it's only me!"

"Lorraine?" My mum comes out of the kitchen holding a tea towel. I can see Les is sat at the table with his newspaper spread out before him. Nothing ever changes. You would think my mother was surgically attached to the sink. Sewn to it by her apron strings. She immediately catches sight of me, and throws the tea towel onto the table and marches towards me, her face a mask of concern. "Darling, you look awful!"

"Just found her in bed with my Joe," Lorraine tells her with a heavy sigh and a look on her face that lets me know she is enjoying being the bearer of this news just a tiny bit. She stands back so my mother can reach me. "Thought I better bring her home. Lord only knows what they've been up to."

I want to punch her in the fucking face. Really, I do.

"Lou!" my mum says breathlessly, shocked. She takes me by the shoulders. I keep my arms crossed tightly. The last thing I need is for her to see my bloody arm.

"I'll say it one more time," I reply, my eyes locking with Lorraine's. "We didn't do anything. Nothing happened. We are just friends. He was looking after me. If you choose to believe something else, that's up to you." I shrug, and look down at my feet, while my mum and Lorraine swap concerned looks with each other.

"Lou, there is no need to be so cheeky," my mum says. "I thought you were staying at Marianne's?"

"Changed my mind," I shrug again. "Is that against the law?"

"Lou!"

"Can I go to my room? I need to go to my room."

My mother drops her hands down to her sides. She looks at me, confused and unsure. She looks at Lorraine. I make my move and squeeze past her in the hallway.

"I'll be up to speak to you soon," she calls after me. I can hear the relief in her voice as I go. She is as unnerved and uncomfortable as Lorraine was when Joe called her stupid. She wants to talk to Lorraine. She wants to put the fucking kettle on and make cups of tea, and discuss us over the kitchen table while Les reads his stupid newspaper.

I close and lock my bedroom door. I feel angry and vile as I yank my dress over my head. I am just in my pants and bra, pacing the room, searching for my pyjamas, because I have a thought in my head, I have a plan. I have a plan to hit my bed and never get out of it again. Not until all this insanity ends. I catch my reflection in the dressing table mirror and stop pacing. I see that strange girl again. The one that surprised me in the mirror at Marianne's. I stand sideways, and run one hand over the bumps of my ribs, and for some reason this just makes me collapse in tears, because when I look at her, when I look back, I can still see fat where it shouldn't be. It disgusts and enrages me. And my face…my face…I throw back my duvet and climb into my bed in just my underwear because I cannot bear to look at myself anymore. I curl into a tight ball within my dark little cave. My only wish is to be left alone.

24

Dear World, I try to be left alone, but it is not easy. It appears in this life, that if you want to be left alone with your own thoughts, that gives the people around you full rein to interfere with you pretty much constantly. Wanting to be alone is not normal apparently. Just trying to withdraw from the world for a little while is cause for great concern, it would seem. I know what I am doing, and it makes sense to me. I am home in the darkness, curled up small. I feel a peacefulness wash over me that I have not experienced for a long time. I just stay there and listen to my body breathing. I slip in and out of bewildering dreams. I listen to Bob Dylan again and again.

My mother is at her wits end with me. Or so she informs me about twenty times a day. She bustles in and out of my room, mostly carrying trays of food. "You have to eat, you have to eat," she says repeatedly, and I just ignore her. As far as I know there is nothing she can do to convince me to talk, or to eat. I am hoping my silence will get through to her in the end. I am hoping it will encourage her to realise how much I just want to be left alone. She piles these stupid trays up all over the room. Toast, and ham sandwiches, Jaffa cakes, and endless cups of tea. Piles of shit basically. She is filling my room with shit. She cannot let it go. She cannot accept that I do not want any of them. So the food sits around my room, stinking it up. I think I will go crazy.

"I believe you that nothing happened with Joe," she sits on my bed and tells me in a weak, wobbling voice. "I know you are just like brother and sister." That is what she wants to believe, I think, listening to her. "It was just such a shock for Mick and Lorraine to find you in bed together like that. You can understand that, can't you? Just wait until you are a mother one day, love, then you will see, you will see how impossible it is." She says this a lot over the next few days. "It's harder now, if anything," she echoes the sentiments of Lorraine. "At least when you were babies, we could pick you up and cuddle you if you cried. We knew what was wrong with you. We knew how to fix it. Not like now."

She even gets Sara round to talk to me. She is less gentle. She gets frustrated with my silence within ten minutes and tries to pull the duvet from me. I hold on tight and refuse to answer her as she yells; "what the hell is the matter with you anyway? Are you just doing this for attention, or what?" I want to laugh, because nothing could be further from the truth. I want to tell her that if they would just leave me alone, I would be fine. I would come out in my own time. Eventually she calms down again and sits and talks to my huddled shape. "Well if you don't sort it out pretty soon, Mum will be calling the men in the white coats Lou, I'm serious. Is that what you want? You want to be carted off to the loony bin?"

"Marianne keeps calling for you," my mother comes to tell me sometimes in a hopeful voice, as if this information could just be what makes me get out of bed. If only she knew. "She's worried about you too now. Do you want her to come round?"

"No," I croak from under the duvet. It is the first word I have spoken in two days. I can imagine my mother's face filling with wonder, as she sees this as a good sign.

"Okay," she responds gently. "Okay then. Okay love. Shall I make you a sandwich? Bring you up some soup?" I do not answer. I hear her frustrated exhalation of breath. "Lou, this is not funny you know. This whole thing. If you don't at least sit up and eat something, then I am phoning the doctor and I mean it. You cannot just stay under there and starve to death!" I hear her voice break on the last word. Shit. She stands by the door and starts to sob.

I am forced to question just how selfish I really am. I don't think I can listen to her crying a second longer. "Okay," I say. "Okay, then. I'll have some soup."

She inhales this time. She inhales hope, and I imagine her smiling and drying her tears on her tea towel. "Okay darling," she says quietly. "Good girl. I'll be right back."

When she comes back, she finds me sat up with my back to the wall. I am still wearing the same pants and bra from the day of the party. My hair is a greasy tangle stuck on my skull. She tries to disguise both the alarm and the hope on her face, as she slides the tray towards me and then sits carefully down on the edge of the bed. I eat the soup as fast as I can so that she will leave me alone again. My stomach reacts with shock as the food curls down towards it. It clenches tightly and unclenches again. I force it down. My mum bites at her lip. "I want you to come and see Doctor Fielding with me love," she says eventually, not looking at me. "I've made an appointment for tomorrow. I want her to check you over. I'm so worried about you, love."

"No," I say, looking down at my soup. "I'm eating this, isn't that enough?"

"Lou, you must be able to see, this is not normal behaviour!" she says this in exasperation, lifting her hands and dropping them again. Her expression is pained. She is trying hard not to cry. "I'm your mother, it's my job to protect you and look after you, and how can I say I am doing that right now?"

I finish the soup, slide the tray towards her and lay back down. "I'm just tired," I tell her, my eyes on the ceiling. "A lot has happened lately."

"A lot that you don't want to tell me."

I look at her face. "You wouldn't want to know mum."

"I want to know all right," she argues, her eyebrows frowning down at me sternly. "Of course I want to know! I mean, that party, whatever it was. Going to a party is fine, having a few drinks I can accept, but coming home in the state you were in, refusing to tell us what is wrong, and staying in bed for nearly three days, is *not* okay Lou!"

I don't want to have this conversation with her now. I fold my arms across my face. Maybe one day, I think to myself as she sits there and waits. Maybe one day we could have a talk, and I really could tell her everything. I could tell her everything that I think and feel, and she would listen and understand. But not now. Not today.

I hear her release an enormous sigh. "What am I going to do with you?" she murmurs to herself.

"I'm okay," I tell her from under my arm. "I'm sorry."

"Look, either you come to the doctor tomorrow or you let one of your friends come and speak to you. Maybe Joe can shake you out of this, whatever it is."

I have tried not to think about Joe for the last few days, and I am surprised and dismayed at the hot tears that fill my eyes under my arm. I press my arm down harder against them. "Okay," I say, for her benefit. "Okay then."

"Okay doctors, or okay Joe?"

"Joe."

"Okay." She finally gets up from the bed, lifts the tray and walks towards the door. "But Lou, I will be getting the doctor to come and see you right here if you don't stop this dieting nonsense, I mean it."

Anger pricks at me. I tense. "O*kay.*"

She leaves me alone. She finally leaves me alone. Oh God, I think, pulling the duvet completely back over my head. Oh God. I have been trying like hell not to think about Joe these past few days. I wonder how quickly my mum will call Lorraine. I wonder how long it will take

Joe to get around here. I wonder what he has been up to since I last saw him, and what happened after Lorraine walked me home. I wonder a lot of things. I curl up under my duvet and wonder why I am such a waste of space. I am literally taking up space that someone else could have. I am using up oxygen and contributing nothing positive to this world. I am wasted. I am a waste.

I am listening to old music, and I wonder why this is still all I listen to. It's like I refuse to move on. There is so much more out there, but I just ignore it all, I just ignore all the potential for knowing more, learning more. I told you, I am a waste of a person really. I could be so much more, but I can't seem to be bothered. I want to do nothing. Be nothing. Have nothing to say. Have no one ask anything of me. I do not want to get out of this bed and *do something*. I do not want school to start. I do not want to finish school and have to get a job, because that scares me. I don't know what the hell I want to do, except nothing. I just want to be left alone, but this is proving impossible and highly unlikely. I don't want to even grow up. I really don't. I'm not like all the other kids who just want to be adults, so that they can do all the stuff that adults do. I don't want to. I don't want to do any of those things anyway. I'm the opposite, because I want to slow it all down, I want to stay like this. I am stuck I suppose. I am jammed. I am unable to move on. I am oddly incapable of development. But I am very good at shrinking. Going backwards. Oh Christ.

Doctors, or Joe. What a choice.

I am left with an unfortunate dilemma. Stay where I am, and let Joe discover me in bed, still wearing the underwear I had on at the party. Let Joe see who I really am. Or get out of bed and sort myself out a bit. Have a shower and put on some clothes. Pretend I am okay. Make out it is just my mother being melodramatic as usual. In the end I don't actually end up thinking about it a lot more, because I fall asleep.

I fall asleep for hours. I wake up once and hear the neighbours' children screaming outside my window. Then I fall back asleep again. The next time I wake up it is early evening, the street is quiet, and someone is tapping at my door. It is Joe. I hear him snort. He opens the door a crack and pokes his face into my room. "Safe to come in?" he whispers. "I'm on a mission."

I tug the duvet up to my chin and brace myself for humiliation. It's all right, I tell myself. I can take it. "Hi Joe," I say. He comes in and closes the door behind him. I look at him as he crosses the room. Weird. He looks taller. He looks older. Holding his head up. He looks pleased with himself. He grins at me as he lifts the duvet and scoots in fully clothed beside me. I wait for him to cry out in embarrassment when he realises I am just in my undies, but he does not seem to notice. He pulls the duvet up to his neck and folds his arms on top of it.

"So," he says. "What's going on?"

"I don't know," I say, honestly. "I don't know what the hell is going on."

"Well, neither do I. They sent me round to get you up. Otherwise I've been grounded."

"What happened after I left?" I ask him, with a sigh. His shoulder is pressed onto mine. I wonder how he cannot realise I am partially naked. I wonder if he cares. His grin stretches.

"I got into a fight with Mick."

I turn my face to stare at him. "No! Oh my God! You didn't!"

"Well, I did. I'd had enough. I punched him in the nose. Look at my hand!" He delights in showing me his right hand, where the knuckles are all bruised and swollen.

"Oh my God Joe!" I exclaim, my hand sneaking out from the cave to touch his knuckles. "What did he do?"

"Nothing! Leon and Travis appeared out of nowhere. He didn't dare take us all on."

"Oh my God!" I realise that I cannot think of anything else to say other than oh my God. Terrible.

"Yeah, I know. He stormed out. Left Mum to it."

"What did *she* do? What did she say?"

"She ranted and raved for a bit, then she calmed down. I told her no one in that house is gonna' hit me ever again. No one." I look in wonder at his face. He is glowing with a strength I'd never thought possible. His eyes are shining, and his mouth is firm. He is wriggling with pride in himself. I can barely believe what I am seeing and hearing. He normally always looks so beaten down, so resigned.

"Oh my God Joe," I say. "You are amazing. What's happened to you?"

"I don't know," he says, grinning at the ceiling. "I just snapped. I just woke up like that, then I was just so worried about you, and I wanted to walk you home. Then they all come in interfering, fucking ruining things as usual, blaming us." He rolls his eyes at the memory, and shrugs under the duvet. "I realised that's all I care about. People like you. People who get me, and care about me. That's why I wanted to walk you home and make sure you were okay. That's what set me off when they just got in the way again."

I don't know what to say. I am touched, and proud of him, and want to hug him. I don't want to cry. I could pat him on the back or something. I don't want to say 'oh my God' another time. "Travis and Leon stood by you?" I ask instead, coming back to this other amazing transformation.

"Yeah!" he beams. "Amazing, right?"

"About bloody time."

"I know. I know it. But I mean it. I'll behave myself. But if any bastard in that house lays a finger on me again, they're gonna' get it back."

"I never knew you had it in you."

"Neither did I."

"And you won't smack the little ones either then?"

He shakes his head firmly. "No, I won't. I won't. I'm going to be a decent brother to them."

"Even though it was Will who dropped us in it that morning?"

"Yeah. Even though. I'll show him the way to behave. I'll be decent to him, then maybe he will look up to me, or whatever."

I feel warmer with him next to me. Our body heat mingling. I feel the urge to throw back the cover, but then I remember I am partially clothed, so I don't.

"What about the deliveries?" I ask him. "Are you still gonna' do that?"

"No," he says quickly. "No way. I told them. It's over. Leon was not happy."

"I thought it was nearly all gone anyway?"

"Yeah, I thought so. But Leon got all funny and twitchy, so I don't know. Anyway, I'm out of it. We're out of it. One less thing to stress about, eh?" He nudges me with his elbow.

"Yeah, I guess so. Well done."

"So how are you?"

"Ahh," I say, knowing it was going to come to this eventually. "Tired."

"Tired of what?"

"Good question! I don't know. Everything. Nothing."

Joe blows his breath out slowly and shakes his head. "That was one messed up night."

"You don't even know the half of it," I warn him.

"Go on. Tell me then."

"Okaaay. Well, first of all Travis tried it on again." I wait for him to react, and feel his body stiffen next to mine, but he says nothing. I don't know why I am telling him this. Only that he is lying here next to me, trying his best to be a decent human being. Trying not to be a total waste. I feel like I should at least try to do the same.

"He did?" he asks. "When?"

"Near the beginning," I sigh. "Outside. After the cocktails. I let him kiss me. Then we had a chat. Then he left. That was it."

"And so what now?"

"Nothing now," I shrug. "Nothing. Really."

"Oh."

"I'm sorry, Joe."

"You don't have to be sorry. You can kiss who you like." He turns his face to look at mine, and he grins. I am thinking; I would rather kiss you. Just to see what it is like. But I do not say it.

"And then there was you and Leon, and Marianne and coke," I go on. He sighs at this.

"Ah yes. Not good."

"No. Not good. Then I wake up and go to the loo, and you and Josh and Ryan are all asleep. And I bump into Marianne, and she insists we drink neat whiskey in the garden."

"Oh Christ. You idiot!"

"Who me?"

"Yeah! Both of you!" Joe sort of laughs and rolls back to stare at the ceiling. I do the same. Fixing my eyes on the stained and cracked aertex patterns.

"I don't know what happened," I say, and I mean it. "I don't understand. She was very strange Joe."

"Well I phoned her," he says then indignantly. I stare at him. "I would have gone round there but I was grounded."

"You phoned her? Oh God, Joe." I groan and cover my face with my hands. "What did you say to her?"

"I had a go at her. She deserved it," he says. "I can't stand that girl. I told her to get some help. And to stay away from you."

"Oh Joe, you didn't?"

"What? Don't tell me you feel sorry for her?" He is staring at me in amazement, with his mouth open.

"Well, yes. Sort of. I can't help it. Joe, she must be so messed up! Worse than us."

Joe snorts in disgust. "Well funnily enough I don't see her spending three days in bed with no food," he retorts, and I flinch, and long to hide under the duvet away from his accusing eyes. "Lou, I don't think she gives a shit about anything, or anyone."

"Well, that's even worse," I argue. "That's sad!"

"She didn't sound sad on the phone. She talked a load of shit. She said you wanted to understand what pain was, like she does. Stupid *fucking* bitch!"

I shake my head and stare at the ceiling. I don't feel comfortable with Joe being this angry with Marianne. I think, he doesn't understand, because he has never understood why she cuts herself, and he probably never will. He is simply seeing this in black and white. "Joe," I say to him softly. "I can't even remember what I said, or didn't say that night."

"Doesn't matter," he says adamantly. "You didn't cut your own arm, did you?"

I look down at my arm lying on top of the cover. The cut has a thin trail of scabbing over it. It is about three inches long. I worry it will scar. I lie under my duvet and worry that people will see it there forever and think that I did it to myself. I shake my head. "No, I didn't."

"You were drunk, and then she got you even drunker. It's just totally sinister Lou."

"I'm probably going to have to talk to her at some point," I sigh heavily.

"Well if you do, just make sure you are sober yeah?"

"Course I will."

"And don't let her wriggle out of it with all that weird shit she talks. I know how you fall for it. She twists you around her finger mate."

I raise my eyebrows. I am too tired and fraught with confusion to argue with him. I don't understand what he means by this. He decides to change the subject by briskly clapping his hands together. "So what now?" he asks me.

"Hey?"

"Are you gonna' lie here wasting any more of your precious life, or are you gonna' get up and come and walk the fucking dogs with me?"

I frown. "Dogs?"

"Rozzer is down there," he grins. "I'm back on dog walking duties."

"Did Mick come back after the fight?"

"Yeah, he came back."

"What happened then?"

"Nothing," Joe shrugs and throws back the duvet. He gets out of bed and stares down at me. "We did the other thing we always do in my family. Pretended nothing had happened and carried on as normal."

I find myself smiling a little. "Oh yeah."

"Come on then," he tugs at the duvet but I hold onto it tightly.

"Joe, give me a chance. Go and have a cup of tea with my mum or something. I need to have a shower and stuff."

I see the light grow in his hazel eyes; he nods twice at me and goes to the door. He tilts his chin to the ceiling and grins. "Okay, off I go to let your mum know I have saved the day yet again. Hope she has biscuits too."

When he has gone I climb out of my bed slowly, wincing at the pain in my muscles and joints. I am not sure if the pain is do with lying in bed for three days, or not really eating for three days, but there it is. I find my dressing gown lying on the floor and put it on. My mobile phone is lying on the dressing table, dead and silent. Good, I think, it can stay that way. I have no desire to know what strange messages Marianne has been sending me. In the bathroom, I turn on the shower and let it fill the room with hot steam. I climb in and get myself cleaned up. I have to admit, it does feel good. Like I am washing away all of the confusion from that night. Like I am revealing myself again slowly. When I am done, I climb out and wrap a towel around myself. I use both my palms to rub a hole into the steamed up mirror, and my hands make a squeaking noise against the glass. I brush my teeth, watching my reflection. I look at myself, and I feel like I am sort of outside of myself, looking in. I tell myself I am a stupid young idiot, who needs to grow up. I am better than this, I tell myself. I am stronger than this. I try to believe it, because I desperately want to believe it.

When I am dressed and ready, and my hair is combed and towel dried, I leave my room and descend the stairs. I can hear the huge sigh of relief from my mother when she makes out my footsteps coming down. She is sat at the kitchen table with Joe and three cups of tea. I slip in beside her and pick mine up. Mum is staring at me, and when I look at her, her eyes are all shiny like she has been crying. "Well thank God," she says to me, one hand touching her chest. I nod at her. I don't know what I am supposed to say.

"You can pay me later," Joe jokes. I smile at him. Mum reaches across the table and squeezes his arm.

"You are a special young man," she tells him. "You always have been." Joe blushes a deep red and shifts uncomfortably in his chair. "Are you okay?" My mum turns to me and asks. I drink my tea and raise my eyebrows in reply.

"I think so," I say eventually. She smiles a brave smile.

"Growing up is not easy for anyone," she tells me. "Believe me. I was a teenager once too, you know. I still feel the same half the time. You know, your body grows older, but you still feel the same inside, even with all the responsibilities." She nods her head at the kitchen surrounding us. "It's not easy love," she goes on gently. "Because nothing ever is."

"My dad says 'nothing worth having, comes easily,'" Joe informs us brightly. "Or something like that anyway."

I just look at him and shake my head. "We should go."

"Breakfast first?" my mum enquires quickly. I am almost expecting her to follow this with a threat of 'or I call the doctor', but she doesn't. She doesn't have to because the threat is there. I roll my eyes and get up and grab a yoghurt from the fridge.

"Before you say anything," I tell her, pulling a spoon out from the drawer. "Yoghurts are fine for breakfast. Yoghurt and an apple are fine."

"As long as you are actually *eating*, I don't mind what it is!" my mum says with a slight laugh, swapping looks with Joe. I feel irritated. I feel hemmed in, and watched over. My head is pounding too. I eat the yoghurt, and take the apple with me. My mum lets us go, smiling sadly from the table.

Joe unties Rozzer outside, and I clip Gremlins lead on. I can't think of anything worthwhile to say, so I just breathe out heavily, and get walking. Rozzer starts pulling instantly and Joe rolls his eyes at me. "You'd think that would hurt him, wouldn't you?" he wonders. "Choking like that! That's how stupid a dog he is."

"Has anyone ever taught him *not* to pull?" I ask with a sigh of misery. "It's not his fault. He thinks that's how you walk." I nod down at Gremlin. "See, look at him. Because I trained him to walk to heel when he was a puppy."

"Well you know Mick," Joe responds. "He's never got time for the dog apparently!"

"He should have got a lap dog then," I say, feeling sulky, and sorry for Rozzer. "That would have suited better."

We get to the field and let them both off. Rozzer tears off at top speed, barking at nothing, and scaring the mothers with small children in the park. Gremlin tries to follow him, but soon gets out of breath and gives up. "Maybe you could be an animal trainer or something, when you grow up," Joe says to me. I look at him sideways and take a bite out of my apple. "What?" he asks. "I'm only saying. You would be good at it. You would enjoy it wouldn't you?"

I look away, munching on my apple. I have no idea why Joe suddenly seems so interested in my future employment. "Don't talk about it," I tell him quickly, when I see him open his mouth to say more. He laughs at me.

"What? Why not?"

"I don't want to hear about it," I tell him, and I mean it. "I don't want to have those depressing kinds of conversations thank you." This makes Joe laugh louder and longer, so I glare at him.

"Tell me what is depressing about that?" he asks. "I thought you'd enjoy something like that!"

"No," I say to him, and hurl my half eaten apple across the grass. "I don't. I *hate* having conversations like that. They are so depressing. I don't want to think about getting older, or having a job, or anything like that."

"Well it's gonna' happen, so you might as well get used to it mate."

"I know that, don't I? I am well aware of the inevitable passing of time and the result that has on our ages, but I don't particularly enjoy talking about it, okay?"

Rozzer is racing back across the field towards us with a huge stick between his jaws. He drops it at Joe's feet, but when Joe goes to pick it up, Rozzer leaps forward and snatches it up again, almost severing Joe's fingers in the process. He races off again and Joe shakes his head and swears at him. I can see Gremlin trotting along in the distance, close to the hedgerow with his nose to the ground. I cross my arms tightly across my chest and keep them there. I feel foul. I really do. I feel so angry I could easily smash someone in the face. I want to be alone, in my bed and none of them will let me. I want to be thin and get thinner, but they won't let me do that either. Joe is looking at me for too long. "Are you all right?" he asks me.

"I don't know," I shrug at him. "Not really."

"Well what's the matter then? I mean, really. You can tell me. It's not really normal to stay in bed for three days."

We are at the park, and the last mother is leading her child away by the hand, whilst casting anxious looks Rozzer's way every time he runs past her with the stick in his jaws. Joe climbs the little hill with the slide built in, and flops down on the dead brown grass there. I sit down next to him with my knees bent and my arms resting on them. "So?" he prompts me. "You can tell me, can't you? Was it just the whole thing with Marianne?"

I rub my forehead with the heel of my hand, because my head really hurts. "I don't know," I tell him honestly. "I was just so tired, Joe. So, you know, fed up. Just wanted to stay there."

"Marianne's fault," he nods at me.

"No. You can't blame her for everything."

"She *cut* your arm!" he sees fit to remind me angrily, and I can see that his disgust towards her is never very far from the surface. "What kind of friend does that, Lou? That's totally weird and psycho!"

"You don't understand. You don't understand her."

"I don't want to understand her. I think she's a spoiled stuck-up bitch with a fucked up mind and I haven't got any time for her now." He stares out across the field, as Rozzer charges after a pigeon, barking ferociously.

"It wasn't just her," I say, dropping my aching head into my arms.

"What was it then?"

"Everything."

"Everything?"

"Yeah, all of it. I don't like the thought of stuff, that's all. There's so much I don't like the thought of." I keep my head in my arms, my eyes closed tightly. I feel like I am on my own, back under my duvet, talking to myself. I know that if I look up and see his face, then I won't be able to say any of the things I am thinking. Is that the way it is for everyone? Or are there some lucky people who are able to voice their exact thoughts and feelings in such a way, that everyone understands them instantly?

"You don't like the thought of getting a job one day?" Joe asks me patiently.

"Or going back to school," I add. "Or eating meals. Or talking to people and pretending to like them. Or traipsing through each day, not knowing anything, not having a clue."

"Lou," I feel him place a hand on my shoulder. "I don't know what you mean. I mean, the school and job bit I get. I feel the same sometimes, but you just got to get on with it, you know? How about you think about all the fun we should be having? How about we just have more fun? You know, more parties and get togethers, and laughing and stuff? We haven't done enough of that lately."

I don't answer him because my train of thought has hit a crossroads and gone two ways at the same time. It's gone. It's all gone, I realise. I was close, I had it on the tip of my tongue, how to explain to him how I feel. But now it's gone, it's slipped away from me like a dream. I sigh and lift my head and rub my eyes, and he squeezes my shoulder once and then drops his hand.

"I don't like seeing you like this," he says. "This isn't the real you."

I look at him, frowning. "Isn't it?"

"No. The real you is cynical and sarcastic and hilarious all right, but not down and dopey and depressed. The real you is on the verge of an argument most the time, and the real you stands up for people even when it's not good for you."

I don't know what he means, but I feel warmed and touched by what he is saying, and I think, oh I wish I could see myself like that! "Thanks," I smile at him.

"It's true," he nods. "That's why you are my best friend, you idiot. All those times you've stepped in and spoken up for me at home. You've never just stood there and said nothing, never."

I nod at him and smile. He looks so sincere, so serious that I almost want to laugh. I bump him with my shoulder, and then pull away, although part of me wants to stay close to him. I lie down instead. I stretch out on my back under the sky. I fold my hands together on my belly and watch the streaks of white cloud rolling along above us. Joe lies next to me. He is silent for a few minutes, and we watch the clouds and listen to Rozzer barking far away. "Are you going to be okay?" he asks me then.

"Course I am."

"No, but I mean really. You're going to start eating again, aren't you?"

I suck in breath and feel my stomach muscles tightening under my hands. I just wish I could tell him how I really feel about eating and getting fat or thin, but I am scared to. I am scared now that he will report back to my mum and she will send me to the doctor. "Course I am," I tell him.

"But properly I mean? Your mum is really worried about you."

"I just have to be careful, that's all," I explain to him. "I don't want to get fat again."

"You never *were* fat!"

"That's easy for you to say Joe. I *was* fat. I was a fat pig. And I don't want to be that ever again. I can't be that ever again." I feel my breath hitch, my voice break, oh crap, I don't want to cry in front of him again. I have these awful fuzzy memories of sobbing endlessly under his duvet. Oh Christ. I stop talking and take some deep breaths and close my eyes for a moment. Joe stays silent beside me. So many thoughts are rushing through my head; you know all the things you think but never say, all the things you cannot say, all the feelings you have no words for. It is so frustrating, I think. "Let's talk about something else," I say finally, opening my eyes.

"I don't want to talk about anything else until I know you're okay," says Joe softly. My heart feels crushed. Does anyone else ever feel like that World? How do I explain that, without sounding insane? Maybe I am insane.

"It's so hard to explain Joe," I say instead. "I just can't explain."

"Maybe you need to try. Try and explain. You always keep everything to yourself. You put on a brave face and everything. You don't have to do that with me."

I sigh heavily yet again. "I wish I could get drunk with you."

"Why?"

"I don't know. That's what I feel like doing."

"We can do that if you like."

"Maybe."

"As long as it's not with Marianne, and you be straight with me for once."

"Might not be a great idea," I say then. "Drink and me don't seem to mix well lately."

"I'll look after you."

I want to turn to him then. I want to turn my face to his and find a way to thank him for being so amazing, for always being on my side, for being *him.* I want to take his face in my hands and kiss him. I want to snuggle up with him, like we did under the duvet in his bed. I want my head to be on his chest, and his arm around my shoulders, because those made me feel better, made me feel okay. I felt safe. Tears rise to the surface of my eyes yet again, so I cover them with my arms. Why? Why do I hide them?

"Okay," he says then, propping himself up on one elbow. "If getting drunk will get you to spill your guts, then so be it. We'll do it. I don't care if you cry or whatever. Are you up for it?" I nod glumly in reply. I feel heavy and repulsive in my own body. I feel trapped and submerged and weighed down. I can't imagine ever having the will or the strength to get back up again. What the hell is wrong with me? Joe sits up just as Rozzer arrives panting at his side. He pulls the dog in for a wrestle, but Rozzer breaks away and tears off again, barking. "When shall we do it?" he asks me. "Tonight? I can come to yours on the pretence I am helping sort you out?"

"How will we get away with it? They're watching us like hawks."

"Dog walk," he smiles. "Park. Cider. Simple as."

"Okay," I agree, and force myself to sit up and wipe my eyes. "I better go home then, and make my mum feel better. Then we might have a chance."

"Result." Joe gets to his feet and holds his hand down to me. I look at it for a moment before grabbing it and letting him help me up. He slings his arm around my neck, and we walk down the hill from the slide. "You know I've seen a drum kit for sale in the paper? One I can afford?"

"Really? That's so cool Joe."

"I know. Going to phone them later."

"Nice one. I can't wait to hear you play."

We walk back across the sun-parched field. The blue skies rolling above us, the clouds watching us go. I don't like the thought of going home. I don't like the thought of talking to anyone, about anything. But I don't want to let Joe down. We arrange to meet back at the park at seven o'clock.

"It's a date," Joe grins, and walks off towards his house.

25

Dear World, when I get home I go straight back to my room. I think my mum must be at work. The house is silent as I climb back into my bed. I am just so, so tired. I wonder helplessly if this is normal. If I am a normal teenage girl, or just a complete freak? I put Bob back on and this time he is singing 'Positively 4th Street.' I listen to it under the duvet, the irony of the lyrics not lost on me at all. Weirdly, it is probably my favourite Dylan song. It makes me think and wonder about Marianne. Who is she really? Is she my friend or my enemy? I mean, Joe gets it that I like this music, but her, I don't tell her. If she knew I was hooked on music from another century she would take the piss. I *know* she would, so why am I friends with her? I don't particularly feel like seeing her again, but I know I need to speak to her. Maybe it will straighten things out in my own head. Maybe I will feel better. Or maybe she will be the way Joe sees her, and I will end up feeling even more confused.

I drift into sleep for a while, and when I wake up my headache is even worse. Mum has been at work all day, so I have not eaten lunch. I sit up in bed and hold my head in my hands for a while, just letting it drum, feeling it throb. It is like humming waves of pain that make me want to close my eyes. I have no idea what time it is, and as usual I have no desire to find out. My mouth and throat are incredibly dry, so I decide what I need is a big drink of squash, most likely followed by a large coffee. I get slowly out of bed, feeling just like a little old lady. I hobble to the door and go out onto the landing. I listen there for a moment, in case anyone else is home, but the house is still quiet, so I go slowly down the stairs, holding onto my head as I go. I stumble weakly into the kitchen, ignoring Gremlin as he trots out from his bed and tries to greet me. I make myself a pint of blackcurrant squash, and put the kettle on. Shit my head is really spinning. I sit down at the table when I have made my coffee, rest my forehead in one hand and take slow sips of the coffee.

I only realise what time it is when the key turns in the lock and Mum comes in. She smiles at me gently as she comes through to the kitchen. "I stopped by to see Sara," she tells me brightly. "That's why I'm a bit late from work."

"Oh. Is she okay?"

"Oh same as ever," Mum sighs and drops her handbag onto the table. "Fighting with Rich. Had a good moan!"

"Oh."

"Did you enjoy your walk with Joe?"

"Um yeah. We're meeting for another one later."

"Another one? Why's that?"

I think fast. "Well it was too hot for the dogs, so we didn't keep them out long. They didn't run around much. It's cooler later."

"Oh lovely," Mum smiles and goes around the kitchen, opening and shutting cupboards. She is trying to decide what to cook for tea, I can tell. She has a very thoughtful look on her face, and shoots the odd glance my way, and pulls at her bottom lip occasionally with her finger and thumb. I decide to make it easier for her.

"Can we have chicken salad or something?"

She looks at me quickly. "Is that what you want? We could have that."

"Les won't mind?"

"No he won't be home. It's just us love. Just you and me. Chicken salad it is then. That will be nice and quick and easy anyway!"

"Thanks Mum."

I relax for a bit then. I even go in the lounge and watch a bit of telly with Gremlin stretched out on my legs. I look down at him twitching restlessly in his sleep, with his tongue lolling dramatically out of the side of his mouth. He is knackered, and I feel a little surge of guilt about my lie. He's got to go back out and run around with Rozzer again, the poor mite. My mum makes the salad and brings it into the lounge for us to eat. She puts a plate loaded with buttered granary bread on the coffee table between us. "This is nice, isn't it?" she questions, forking a cherry tomato from her plate. "Us alone? Having dinner in here?"

"I suppose so," I force a smile at her and eat some lettuce leaves. "How are things with Les?" I don't ask her this because I really care; I just want to deflect the attention from me before she starts it up again.

"Oh fine, I think, fine," she replies breezily, and grabs a slice of bread from the table. "Have some bread Lou. Salad alone is not enough unless you have bread."

I sigh in misery and pick up some bread and drop it on my plate. "So has he moved in for good then?" I ask her, trying again to get her mind off my eating.

"Well we haven't really discussed it in depth," my mum says, her eyes moving between the telly and me. "I suppose we should. Your dad has been a bit funny about it again though, that's what worries me."

"Why what has he said?"

"Oh you know, the usual. Moaning about how much this place costs him, how it's bleeding him dry and he'd be better off if he could sell it. You know." She raises her eyebrows at me and I nod. I do know. And I do appreciate the fact she never really slags him off or runs him down to me. She could if she wanted to. It would all be true, and I would even join in. I feel no loyalty towards him whatsoever. I could care less if I never saw him again. But she always bites her tongue and keeps it in, whatever she really thinks about what he did to her. I look down at my food and poke it around a bit, trying to break up the chicken so I can flick little bits onto my lap for Gremlin. I realise this is probably the first time I have looked at life through her eyes. My mum. When he left I was shocked and disgusted and angry, but I was also relieved. We had never got on and it was a relief to see him go. I had never considered it from her point of view, because as I remember, she had really loved him. They had rowed loads, but it was always him starting it, it was always him having a go at her and her just defending herself. I wonder how it must feel to love someone so much, that you will take anything from them, let them treat you like dirt and then have them just walk out on you. Just go off with someone else like you don't matter at all. Just grind your heart into dust and spit on it.

"Maybe you and Les could buy it off him?" I look at her and suggest with a shrug. "If you two are serious, that is."

"I'm not sure about that," she answers with a thin smile. "I would rather keep renting. Neither of us earns very much darling."

"Why don't you rent another house then? Be out of dad's control."

"Yes, there is that. We could do that."

"Talk to Les then," I tell her. "I won't care."

"We'll see what happens," Mum says, and I know that means she does not want to talk about it with me anymore. She still sees me as a child, I think, a child that needs protecting. "What do you really think of Les then?" she looks my way and questions.

I lift my knee a little so that she can't see Gremlin snuffling up bits of chicken. I take one bite of the bread just to please her and console her. I wait for it to go down, which seems to take forever. "He's okay," I say. "He doesn't talk much. He doesn't have conversations with me or anything."

"He's very aware Lou," Mum says this slowly and carefully, her eyes on her plate as if she is trying to choose her words wisely, "of, you know, being my partner, and not your dad or anything. He is very aware that he has no children of his own, so no experience with kids. He doesn't want to overstep the mark, if that makes sense."

"Well he is allowed to talk to me!" I say with a laugh. "I don't bite!"

"I know, I know, but he is a shy man Lou. He is a gentle kind of man. He feels very awkward really. Moving in here. He is very aware of how it could make you feel."

"Well that's nice of him but he doesn't need to worry. Tell him to stop worrying. I don't care he's here, but it's weird him not talking to me."

"Okay," Mum smiles at me warmly. "I'll tell him."

"Apparently Lorraine is his biggest fan. Joe says."

"Oh yes, you know Lorraine, she had to check him out for me. She thinks he's lovely. We're all off out on Friday by the way. Me and Les, and her and Mick."

I try not to smile or smirk, and eat some more lettuce instead. "I can't imagine Mick and Les getting on."

"Well you know," Mum laughs. "Men just play darts and drink don't they? Talk about the football and all that!"

"Did you hear what Joe did that morning Lorraine brought me home?" I put down my fork and ask her then. I think this is probably the longest and most adult conversation we have ever had. I know how easily it could slip into misunderstandings and an argument, so I pick my words carefully too. I am curious to know what, if anything, Lorraine has said to my mum.

Mum wipes her mouth on the tea towel she has on her lap. She looks at me for a moment, and then picks her fork back up and stabs it into a chunk of warm chicken. "Yes, she did say something about a fight between him and Mick."

I feel slightly triumphant on Joe's behalf, although I have no idea why. "He punched him in the nose," I say. She nods and looks uncomfortable.

"Yes, I know. And obviously I do not need to tell you that is no way for Joe to be treating his step-father."

"You called him a special boy this morning," I remind her. "Saving the day and all?"

"I know," she says tightly. "And I meant it. He is very good to you and always has been. But he cannot punch his step-dad in the nose! Poor Lorraine, she gets enough grief from the other two!"

"Well that's not Joe's fault, is it?" I try to point out to her. "He can't be punished his whole life because of what Leon and Travis are like. And also, why is it okay for Mick to punch him in the head then?" I look at her, waiting for an answer, a reaction. I wait for her to defend this man she thinks is so great, this man she is going out for drinks with on Friday. Her lips get tighter and she forks more chicken.

"I don't know anything about that," she says, not looking at me, and I feel the anger then like a great wave washing over me. I wanted so badly not to row with her, but I had no idea the anger was there like that, lurking and hiding, ready to unleash itself so readily. I bite down on my lips and try to think before I speak.

"*I* know about it Mum," I say through gritted teeth. "That's what I am telling you. I know because I have seen it a hundred times. Some people would call it child abuse, you know."

She looks at me in amazement. Her shoulders drop and she huffs and puffs and rolls her eyes and clicks her tongue all at once. "Lou!" she says this in her scolding voice and I want to laugh out loud at her. "Don't be so ridiculous! So melodramatic! It is *not* child abuse! It is nothing of the sort! Lorraine and Mick love those boys to death, I know they do, because I have to sit and listen to all her fears and worries about them!"

"Punching kids in the head is not child abuse?" I question, my tone rigid yet calm. She sucks in her breath. "And Mick loves *his* kids, mum. *His* kids can do no wrong. You just have no idea."

Mum shakes her head. She is really pissed off, I can tell, and this in turn pisses me off. How can she be so fucking blind? She puts her plate down on the floor and wipes her mouth again with the tea towel. "Lou, things are never as black and white as you think they are. Now, Lorraine is my best friend and has been for years. I will not sit here and listen to you accuse her of child abuse! For God's sake!"

"Not her, *him*."

"Lou, he tries to help her. He tries to back her up. Those boys would be the death of her otherwise! The older two have been running wild for years now. God only knows the truth of what *they* get up to! Now I know Joe is not like that, I know he is sweet and gentle. I know that Lou." She has turned herself towards me. She is leaning forward, trying to get me to look at her. I am glaring at my plate. "But if Mick and Lorraine left him to it and didn't try to guide him, he would probably end up like the other two, wouldn't he? They would lead him astray. They are probably extra strict on him for his own good love. They want to keep him nice!"

"You have no idea," I say softly. She blows her breath out this time.

"What does that mean, I have no idea?"

I look up then, right into her eyes. I am thinking about Travis kissing me, and Leon doing coke with Marianne, and Joe and me up on that bridge and the madman that almost threw him over. "You have no idea about anything," I tell her and put my plate on the coffee table.

"I don't want to argue with you Lou," she sighs, and presses her hands to her face for a moment. "God knows I don't know what I am doing with you either at the moment."

"Joe just stood up for himself for once, that's all." I push Gremlin gently from my lap and stand up. "He's been pushed around by all of them for years. The little ones wreck his stuff then tell tales to Mick if he tells them off, and the older two treat him like crap, and Mick and his mum just come down on him like a ton of bricks every time he does even the smallest thing wrong!" I have moved just in front of her. She remains sitting and I am staring angrily down at her.

"I am sure it is not quite that bad an upbringing for him," my mum says, attempting to remain calm, attempting to smooth things over. Expecting me to back down and agree with her. "I know for sure that it's a much nicer upbringing than either Mick or Lorraine had, I can tell you that young lady." I roll my eyes. I am not interested in that. I am sick of always hearing things like that. We don't know how good we've got it, in their day children were beaten with sticks, or whatever.

"Do you want to know what he said to me once?" I ask her. She looks irritated and glances over at my plate.

"Lou, you've hardly eaten a thing! Look at your plate!" Her voice is exasperated, panicked even.

"Mum, do you want to know what Joe said to me recently?"

"Lou, you cannot keep doing this! I made you a salad, a healthy salad, and you won't even finish that!" She is stubbornly ignoring my question, and won't look at me either. Instead her gaze is fixated on the bloody plate and the stupid salad. "You're going to kill yourself or end up very ill if you keep this up!"

"Mum!" I yell at her. "I want to tell you what he said! About Mick!"

"I'm calling the doctor in the morning, that's it young lady." She gets up, grabs my plate and hers and marches from the room. I follow her into the kitchen where she slams down the plates. "I've had enough. I'm calling her in the morning and that is final." She spins around to face me, her hands on her hips. "I'm not joking Lou. Maybe the doctor can talk some sense into you!"

"Mum, I am trying to tell you something!"

"You are fading away before my very eyes!" she wails then, and her face crumples with the tears that spring into her eyes. I guess I am meant to feel sorry for her or something, and beg for forgiveness or say the right thing to calm her down. She is trying to make me feel guilty and I won't let her.

"Joe said they're lucky he doesn't do what that kid in Redchurch did all those years ago!" I shout at her instead, because I just want to shock her out of her stupidity. I just want something meaningful and important to break through to her for once. She looks at me as if I am insane. "He said if they're not careful he'll just snap one day!"

"Lou stop it!" my mother points her finger at me and warns. "That is enough! How can either of you say such a thing?" Her eyes are confused, her brow furrowed, her mouth wide open. "That is…that is just…that is horrible Lou Carling! That is truly horrible!"

"I'm just telling you what he said," I say calmly and turn around. "Just so you know how much they get to him."

"That is meant to be some kind of sick threat?" she questions, her voice high and shrill. I go out of the kitchen and head for the front door. "That is disgusting! What happened over there was completely different and you know it! You bloody kids! You think you know all the answers don't you? Just you wait till you are parents! It's the hardest job in the bloody world!"

I slam the front door behind me.

I am staring down at the ground as I walk across the front garden, and then I bump right into Marianne. I look up and stare into her wide green eyes. Jesus Christ.

"Hi!" she says in amusement. I don't know what to say. I just stare at her. My brain has taken up its drumbeat again. My brain is killing me. "Are you okay?" she asks me, frowning slightly now. "Where are you going? You look like shit!"

"Thanks."

"Sorry, but you do! What's wrong?"

I start to walk down the pavement, no idea where I am going or why, and she falls in step beside me. "Had a bad few days," I shrug. "And my head is killing me."

"Oh. Well have you taken anything?"

"No. I keep forgetting to."

"You idiot!"

I look at her in annoyance. "Thanks again."

"Look, you've been avoiding my calls, so I decided to come and see you." Marianne has this kind of khaki satchel on her shoulder, and she shifts it to the other one and looks at me sideways. Her hair is down, and seems impossibly black and shiny, like ironed out oil, gleaming down her back. "I wanted to check you were okay. Why wouldn't you turn on your phone?"

"I told you, I've been ill. I've just been in bed."

"That's not what your mum said."

I shoot a look her way. "What did my mum say?"

"She said you were in bed, refusing to get out, refusing to eat. Just all depressed and stuff." She lifts and drops her tiny shoulders, and shakes her hair back over them. "I just worried about you, that's all."

"I'm fine. Totally fine."

"It wasn't anything to do with me then?" she asks carefully, as we walk along. I don't even know where we are going. "With the party, I mean? It was pretty wild in the end, wasn't it? A night to remember!"

"Yeah, I suppose."

"So you just ran off…"

"I was hammered Marianne," I tell her with a sigh. "I was probably the drunkest I have ever been in my stupid life. I didn't know what I was doing half the time. Forget about it."

"It's just that Joe called me. He was *really* angry with me. You know, because I tried to explain why I cut myself?" I look at her for a moment and all I see is this tiny, pretty girl, with jet-black hair and big green eyes. She is wearing black three quarter length trousers, a purple vest and a long black cardigan. I try to read her, to find her, to trace any sign of that wild girl with the glass.

"Don't worry about Joe," I tell her, and she smiles and looks visibly relieved.

"Okay, well good. I know how protective he is of you, and that's fair enough. But the thing is, boys will never understand something like that, will they? Boys have it so easy!" She looks at me with a broad smile. I just look back down at the pavement disappearing under my feet, while my head feels like someone is kicking it repeatedly. "They have nothing to worry about, compared to us girls, do they?" she goes on.

"I wouldn't say that."

"Anyway I tried to explain to him that I didn't exactly attack you or anything! I think that's what he has envisioned! Funny boy. I was drunk too, right?" She keeps looking my way. I have no idea what she wants me to say, so I just shrug. I can't actually concentrate on any of this while my head hurts so much. "I was trying to explain it to you, that's all, you know, the best way I could."

"Look forget about it," I tell her. We have ended up at the shops and I suddenly realise that I can go in and get some painkillers and a drink. What a fucking fantastic idea that is. "We were all pissed and stupid. We all did stupid things. Don't worry about it."

"But I just really needed to know," Marianne persists, and she reaches out and touches my arm softly. "I needed to know you were okay, and you weren't upset because of me or anything?"

"Course not. It's not you."

"Well what is it then? You don't seem yourself at all."

"I don't know," I say, and go inside the shop. I pass Lorraine on the till at the door. She is packing an old lady's bag for her, but watches me pass by with narrowed eyes, and a tight mouth. I get the feeling she is still coming to terms with Joe's new found courage. Maybe she blames me, who knows? Marianne traipses behind me as I locate the paracetamol, and then grab a bottle of water from the chilled drinks cabinet.

"Is that Joe's mum?" she whispers from behind me as we head for the till. I nod at her. "Yep."

"Sight for sore eyes," Lorraine announces when I drop my tablets and water on to the counter before her. Her eyes regard me with suspicion. "Your mum has been in a right state about you!"

"Can't help being ill," I shrug, not looking at her as she scans my things.

"Hmm," she says in reply to this. "Do you need a bag?"

"No thank you."

"You kids," she practically snarls at me as I pay her and leave. Outside I pause by the doors to chuck a pill down my throat and wash it down with water. Marianne is leaping about from one foot to the other, trying not to laugh. Finally, I shove the rest of the tablets into my back pocket and we head off again.

"She's *lovely*!" Marianne exclaims when we are around the corner. I nod at her.

"Oh yeah. She's priceless. Now you can see why Leon has such great social skills."

Marianne laughs, and swiftly slips her arm through mine. "Oh he has some very *interesting* social skills all right," she giggles. I am not sure I wish to know. "So where now?" she asks me. "What shall we do?"

"What time is it?"

"About half five, quarter to six?"

"I'm meeting Joe at seven."

"Oh right. Well I will duck out of that if you don't mind. I don't want him having another go at me. Maybe once you've explained it to him properly?" She looks at me pleadingly and I force a weak smile in response.

"Course."

"Want to get stoned somewhere?"

"What?"

"I've got weed," she says, and pats her bag. "Where shall we go?"

"I don't know if that's a good idea really," I say and stop walking for a moment. Marianne smiles good-naturedly and cocks her head to one side.

"Come on, why not? It'll be fun. I don't want to smoke it all by myself, do I? That's no fun."

A thousand questions pile up behind my lips. Who did she buy it from this time? Leon, or Ryan again? Has she slept with any of them again? How many times has she slept with them? Who else has she done it with that I don't know about? What did Leon think about her scars? I rub my head and let my shoulders drop. What does it matter, I ask myself, what does it matter?

"Okay," I give in. "What the hell. Come on then."

26

Dear World, we end up walking to the park. The fucking park. I look at it with a kind of hate and scorn I have never viewed it with before. How many hours of my life have I spent in this park? We sit up on the hill, just as I did with Joe earlier, and Marianne gets her stuff out of her bag and spreads it all out on the grass and proceeds to roll us a joint. I lie on my stomach, chew a stem of crispy grass, and stare out at the park, and the fields beyond. I think, look at this here, this is my entire life! This is it, right here. This park, and this field, and school, and the walk over the bridge to get there, and the town, and the bus ride in, and the quay and the tourists, and the ducks and the swans, and the Priory church, and a terraced house, and noisy neighbours, and the parade of shops, and everyone knowing who you are and where you live, and the men's club, and the car parks and the alley ways and the Provident loan lady and the Avon lady calling, and the Christmas hampers that take all year to pay for. This is it. This is all of it. I feel my shoulders shaking with strange laughter. Marianne looks and me and smiles as she rolls the joint.

"You okay?"

"I'm just looking at this fucking place, that's all."

"Looking, and thinking what?"

"I don't know. Thinking *what the hell*? Is this all there is to life? Do you ever think that?"

"I *always* think that," she grins, finishing the joint and packing her tin back into her bag. She sticks the smoke between her teeth, finds a lighter and flicks up the flame. "And I have a nice big house and rich parents."

"Oh yeah. And you still think that?"

"I think that even more. It's all pointless. It all means nothing really. I look at my parents, rushing around, full of stress, knocking back coffee and vodka and wine, on the phone all the time, fucking business suits and brief cases!" Marianne lifts her chin and grimaces at the sky. "Grrrrr!" she growls, and then looks at me and laughs. I smile. "Honestly! They kill me. On a daily basis. I swear, every single time they speak I want to puke."

"Oh Marianne, they can't be that bad," I laugh at her. "They seem lovely!"

"Lovely! Who wants to be lovely?"

"Not you obviously!"

"Hell no." She passes me the joint and lies down on her belly next to me, kicking her shoes off, and waving her feet back and forth. "No one should. Who would aspire to be *lovely*?"

"Did Leon think you were lovely?" I ask with a giggle. Marianne nudges me sharply with her spike of an elbow. "What?"

"Oh how did I know you were going to ask me that soon enough?"

"Well you wanted to come here and talk lady. I was quite happy minding my own business."

"How's your head now?"

I pass the joint back to her and grimace. "Not good. Come on then. Tell me what it was like with Leon. Now we are both sober. Tell me everything!"

Marianne giggles and looks down shyly, and plucks a stem of grass between her thumb and finger. "It was nice," she says, smiling. "It was very nice. He certainly knew what he was doing."

"I bet he did. I hope you were safe by the way. I hear he gets around!"

"Of course we were safe," she groans at me. "I'm not an idiot."

"Did you talk much?" I wonder. "He's never been much of a talker."

"*I* talked a lot!" she laughs, puffing smoke out in front of her. "You know me. I didn't shut up! He listened though. He seemed to really listen." She takes another long drag of the joint and hands it to me. She looks down for a moment, playing with the grass with her fingers, stroking the stems back and forth, and then she raises her glittering green eyes to me. "It might surprise you to hear, that he was actually incredibly gentle and loving." She nods and grins at my widening eyes. "It's true! He was really lovely Lou. Really gentle and considerate. He didn't even rush off after or anything. We laid in bed and talked for about an hour."

I am shaking my head slowly from side to side. "Un-fucking-believable." I think to myself, if there were two words I would never in a million years associate with Leon Lawrenson, it would be those two. Gentle and considerate. Unbelievable.

"Well it's true. I wouldn't lie. I would tell you if he was a complete shit, believe me."

"Have you heard from him since?"

"No," she answers too quickly, and that gives it away. I feel sorry for her then. I look away and smoke the joint, and feel my head getting fuzzier and fluffier, and the feeling spreads down through my body, lifting me up slightly, removing me from the reality of it all. I feel woozy and light-headed, and slightly sick, but my head is feeling better. "I don't expect to. You don't sleep with someone at a party like that and ever hear from them again, do you?" I don't answer her because how the hell would I know? "No," she answers for me. "I expect I'll bump into him again at some point, and that's fine. I am cool with it. Does it surprise you to know he's not the total arsehole you always thought he was?"

I laugh out loud and pass back the joint. "He's still an arsehole as far as I'm concerned! Well, actually, now that you mention it, he did kind of do one good thing for Joe for a change."

Marianne looks interested. "What was that?"

"Just stood up for him at home. Him and Travis. Joe and Mick got in a fight, and they came and backed him up. Don't think they've ever done that before."

"Wow," she says, looking both intrigued and surprised. "That's really nice! And speaking of Travis, that brings me to my question for you! Are you hoping to see *him* again?"

I just groan and moan and drop my face into my arms. My head is now too heavy and thick to lift back up again, so I stay like that for ages, just mumbling and moaning to myself, while she shakes and laughs beside me, and I am left wondering how I could have feared seeing her again so much, because I am actually enjoying myself, I am actually enjoying her company. She stubs out the joint and digs around in her bag again. She pulls out a bag of Haribo sweets, opens them, and places them between us. "Best thing ever for munchies," she remarks, plucking one out. I just roll my eyes and then close them again before I am tempted.

"It's all right for you," I tell her. "You can eat whatever crap you like and you never put on weight. It's so not fair."

"These are pretty low in calories," she assures me, taking another. I just shake my head and grab my water bottle instead. "So you're still at it then?"

"Dieting?"

"Yeah, and running. You're looking increasingly stick like Lou."

"Is that a compliment or what?"

"You look great," she grins. "But you should still allow yourself the odd treat. A couple of sweets won't do anything!"

I shake my bottle of water at her and unscrew the lid. I drink a few mouthfuls then screw the lid back on and chuck it in the grass before me. I drop my head back onto my arms and realise that I desperately want to sleep. "You're not passing out on me or anything, are you?" she prods me and asks. I moan.

"Nah."

"I thought we could talk for a while?"

"Talk then."

And so she does. Marianne talks about her night with Leon, and how she had instigated the whole thing, starting with the coy flirting I had witnessed before they vanished. She talks about him tracing his finger along her scars, without asking what they were or how she got them. She talks about how she spent the entire next day cleaning and tidying the house, and how her lovely parents never suspected a thing. She talks about having another party soon, and she talks about how she thinks Joe does not like her and never has.

Before I know it I am being prodded awake by urgent jabbing fingers, and I climb groggily out of pot-induced sleep. But thankfully my headache has subsided considerably. I look up at Marianne, who is kneeling down beside me and looking slightly anxious. "Sorry," I mutter at her. "Didn't mean to fall asleep. Don't know what's wrong with me lately."

"It's Joe," she whispers.

"Huh?"

"Joe. Coming across the field with his dog."

"Oh! Shit." I look across the field and sure enough, there he is, striding quickly towards us, with Rozzer running and darting around him, and a carrier bag swinging from one hand. He is walking fast and he does not look happy. "It can't be seven o'clock?" I ask in amazement.

"It's twenty past," Marianne replies. "Oh please don't let him kick off with me again." I am surprised that she cares. She can hold her own in an argument and we all know it.

"Oh Christ, I bet my mum is having a fit," I groan, rubbing at my eyes, and then at my head. "We had this massive row before I came out."

Marianne does not answer. Instead she packs up her things and slings her bag onto her shoulder. I cannot really believe that she is worried about what Joe will say to her. Since when has she ever cared what people think of her? "Are you off?" I ask her. She nods. Joe is upon us and does not smile at either of us.

"Hi," I call out weakly. He climbs the hill and stops in front of us and folds his arms across his t-shirt.

"Your mum is going mental," he informs me tightly. I grimace.

"Sorry Joe. Fell asleep here. Just woke up!" I smile at him uselessly. Marianne climbs to her feet and flicks back her hair.

"I'm off," she says brightly, looking down at me. "Better not be late home."

Joe looks at her darkly but does not say anything to her. He drops his carrier bag onto the grass and a bottle of cider rolls out. Marianne looks at it, and then at me, before shrugging her shoulders and starting to walk away. "See you later Lou. Joe."

"Bye Marianne. Thanks."

Joe says nothing. He waits until she has walked away, back across the field towards where you cut through to her house, and then he drops down beside me, still with his arms crossed tightly. "Joe," I start to say softly, as I can feel the resentment and anger coming from him in rolling waves.

"What the *fuck* are you doing here with *her*?" he snarls at me then. I blink in surprise. I think, the last time I saw him this angry was at Hogan's party, when he attacked Travis. I blow my breath out slowly.

"Joe," I say again, meaning to explain how I just bumped into her by accident, and everything is okay, and everything is smoothed out.

"You come here with *her!*" he says, sounding and looking like he would like to punch me in the face. I am finding it hard to look at him. "That mad bitch! What did you come here with *her* for? Come to sit here and carve yourselves up together or something?" I look up at his face in stunned silence. I cannot believe he has just said that!

"Joe!"

"Well, what then?" he yells. "What are you doing here with her?"

"I bumped into her by accident!" I yell back and I sit up. My head starts to pound a little again. I glare back at him, as he is glaring at me. "I had a row with Mum and stormed out of home, and just bumped into her! What are you so mad about?"

"I'm mad because she is a sneaky little bitch! I'm mad because you said if and when you spoke to her, you would do it fucking sober!" He runs his eyes over me and lifts his top lip in disgust. "And you obviously aren't! And I'm mad because you were meant to be meeting me! Instead I get your mother all crying and stuff, wanting to know where the hell you are!" He unfolds his arms and rakes one hand back through his hair. "Jesus Christ Carling! What the hell is your problem at the moment? You used to be normal!"

"No I didn't," I shake my head at him. Now I want to punch his face in. "What the hell is your problem? You knew I wanted to speak to her, and I have! We got stoned, not drunk, and if you want to know the truth, it's done me a lot of good!"

"Did she explain why she cut you then? Eh?"

"It's not like that," I press my hands against my face in exasperation. "I didn't want to really go into that. Look we were both hammered that night, Joe! People do stupid things when they are that drunk, you know that. She was really worried about me actually, about our friendship."

"Yeah, right, bollocks!"

"What do you think she is, dangerous or something? For God's sake Joe, you don't own me, I can be friends with who I like, and to be honest I don't exactly have that many options!"

He is shaking his head, his lips pressed tightly together. He tears his angry gaze away from me, and snatches the bottle of cider up from the ground. He lifts it, showing it to me. "Want some?" he sneers. "Because this morning you wanted to get drunk with me, remember? So you could talk and stuff."

"I still do."

"Can't believe you've been up here with her," he mutters this to himself, as he unscrews the lid from the cider, and the orange bubbles rise up and froths out over his hand. He swears and shakes it off, then lifts the bottle to his mouth and drinks. I watch him, not knowing what to say or do to calm him down. His face is flushed. His eyes are narrowed. He lowers the bottle, burps and drags his hand across his mouth. "I don't trust her," he says then. "I don't trust people like that! She knows what she's doing Lou. You just can't see it!"

"What is she doing then? You tell me." I take the bottle as he holds it out to me and I drink from it slowly.

"She's manipulating you all the time," he says. "You even said yourself you don't know if she's your friend or your enemy! Remember? She's sneaky and sly, and she should not have done that to you that night! For *God's* sake!" He snatches the cider back and drinks more.

"Just calm down," I try to tell him. "You don't need to worry about me so much, you know. I'm a big girl! And I'm not an idiot. I can figure Marianne out for myself. Maybe I'll always keep her at a safe distance, you know? Either way, it's nice to have female friends."

"Nice?" Joe practically explodes at me, cider dribbling down his chin. "Nice to have female friends who try to get you self-harming, or whatever the hell you call it? When you already have enough issues? Yeah, that's really nice Carling. Really, really nice of her. She's a fucking angel!"

I look down and say nothing. I think anything I try to say will just come out wrong and enrage him more. I wait for him to pass the bottle back and take a few more mouthfuls. I wonder vaguely what my mum will think now. Christ. I just seem to keep making things worse. I just seem to mess up every single day I exist in. We pass the cider back and forth between us silently for what seems like ages. During this time, Joe does not look at me once. He stares at the ground like he is in a trance, and just feels with his fingers for the cider bottle before raising it to his lips. Then he stares up at the sky, and at the field, and the hedgerows where we can see Rozzer having a shit. I wonder why he can't look at me. I wonder what the hell is going through his head. I start to feel really drunk and giddy and stoned. I remember uselessly that I didn't eat all my salad, and start to wish Marianne had left her sweets behind for us.

It seems a wise idea to lie down again, so I do, this time on my back with my arms folded behind my head. "I'm sorry Lou," I hear Joe say eventually, and I smile at him when he lies down beside me. He is still clutching the bottle of cider, but there is not much left.

"It's okay, you idiot," I tell him. "You had a right to be angry. I was meant to meet you."

"You fell asleep."

"And I'm sorry. I'm sorry you had to deal with my mum."

I watch him drop a hand over his face and leave it there. I look at him sideways and can just make out the creases of skin around his eyes, where he has screwed them up tightly. "What's wrong?" I ask him then. "You're not just angry about Marianne are you?"

He snorts in reply. "What are you, a mind-reader?"

"No, just your best friend who has known you since you were in the womb. I can tell when something is up. What is it?"

"Fucking…" he starts and then trails off, still with his hand over his eyes. I wait for him to find the words he needs. "Just…fucking Leon. That's it."

"What now?"

"You know."

"I think I know. You mean deliveries?"

Joe nods under his hand. "He won't take no for an answer."

"Well he has to. You want out. He can't make you."

"I kind of agreed to one more."

I roll onto my side and stare at him. "Joe!"

"I know, I know. Fucking idiot right?"

"Yes, you're an idiot! Why would you do that? Remember what you were saying this morning?"

"You have no idea how persuasive he can be," Joe mumbles, refusing to look at me. I watch his chest rising and falling under his t-shirt. It has ridden up where it is too small for him now, and I can see a slice of his bare stomach. I watch it go in and out as he breathes under his hands.

"Joe," I say to him. "Don't do it. You don't want to do it."

"I've said it now. Can't back out."

"Course you can! What's wrong with you? You don't have to do it. Why did you let him talk you into it?" I want to smack him I am so cross. I also want to hug him, I am so confused. What has happened to him since this morning for God's sake?

"Oh," Joe lets out a moan, drops his hands away and rolls onto his side to face me. He grimaces in anticipation for how disgusted I am going to be with him. "It's not the money," he says quickly, although this was not what I was thinking. "It's just hard to say no to him. You know how he is. Plus he reckons I owe him after he stuck up for me with Mick."

"You are joking?" I ask in disbelief. "He sticks up for you once, he does *one* nice thing for you and now you owe him? More like he owes you! Jesus Christ, he is one cheeky bastard."

"It won't hurt to do one last one," Joe says with a pathetic shrug.

"That's not the point Joe. You said this morning you were done with it all. You were different this morning!"

"I know, I know."

"And then you have the nerve to storm up here and have a go at me for trying to sort things out with Marianne!" I roll away from him then, shaking my head as I stare up at the sky. I am rather pissed, it has to be said. I am brimming with anger and disappointment. "I'm not coming with you," I tell him rather spitefully.

"I didn't ask you to."

"I don't know what is wrong with you. And you have a go at me!"

"Only because I care about you," he says quietly. I don't look at him. He sounds miserable and unsure. "I didn't mean to upset you. I probably felt like a shit for letting Leon talk me into it, and took it out on you and Marianne. Sorry."

"You can say sorry as much as you like," I snap, and suddenly force myself up from the ground. I am too angry to be around him. I think it is probably the alcohol and the state of my mind generally, but if he wants to let his bullyboy brother wreck his life and talk him into crime, then that is up to him. I can't be bothered anymore. I feel his eyes on me as I brush the dried grass from my clothes. "I'm going home."

"I thought we were gonna' talk?" he says, sitting up. "You know, you wanted to get drunk and talk? It was your idea!"

"Changed my mind," I say and start to walk away. "I'm going home to bed. I feel like shit."

"Lou!" he calls after me, but I don't answer him and I don't look back.

27

Dear World, well it would seem that you never really know anyone that well, do you? They don't know me, and I don't know them. He can fuck off. He has the nerve to shout at me and make me feel bad! *I* am not the one dealing drugs for my brother. I am just trying to be a decent human being, who does not run away from things the whole time. How easy would it have been to avoid Marianne and refuse to see or speak to her again? How easy it would be to vilify her and fear her, and bitch about her to the Stick Insects. Harder to listen to her, to try to understand her, to try to be a friend. Bloody Joe, I think, I rage, as I head home alone, wobbling all over the pavement at one point and shouting at myself inwardly, *for Christ's sake walk straight, you are not that drunk!*

It's not the drink, my nagging little friend in my brain tells me smugly. It's the lack of food. You used to be able to drink way more than that and still walk straight!

Yeah, so what? Who bloody cares? Not me.

Why am I so angry with him? Why am I so angry?

I realise how relieved I had been to hear him say the deliveries were over, that he had stood up for himself and said no for once. I had felt so proud of him. His courage, his nerve, had forced me out of my bed. That was it. I had done it for him. I had started to feel like a miserable self-pitying puke lying there like that, when he had bigger stuff to deal with. Oh Joe, I think desperately, why did you cave in again? Because it's not just one more time, and we both know that surely? One more time leads to one more time. One more time leads to a lifetime of being Leon's errand boy, Leon's scapegoat. One more time leads to other favours, other crimes, can't he see that? Is that what he wants? To be like them? I kick at the dead grass on our front lawn. Damn it!

Why do people let you down so much, I wonder? One minute you feel so proud of them, so *inspired* by them, and the next minute they reveal their true weakness in spectacular style. They just crumble. I am thinking of Mum and Les, and dad and his shitty sneaky little life, and me. Me.

Me. Christ, I am letting everyone down every day, and here I go again. I start to feel incredibly nauseous as I approach the front door. My headache has accelerated into a mind spin of pain. I gag, then swallow, gag then swallow. I watch my own hand reach out for the doorknob. I feel the metal in my grip, and then I am falling forward, I am tumbling in, I am sinking down. What a shock.

***

I come around to my mum panicking like a madwoman. She is practically slapping my face, trying to wake me up. When she sees my eyes open, she looks visibly relieved and starts to try to pull me in through the door, so that she can close it. I can manage a crawl to help her, but my head feels like play dough and every movement is a little kids fists pummelling and twisting it. I wonder where Les is. I hope he didn't see me go down.

"Jesus Christ! Jesus Christ that is it!" my mother is shrieking at me. She manages to get my feet past the door, shoves them up towards my arse, and then finally slams the door shut. I guess she didn't want to let the neighbours see me like that. Fair enough. "What the hell is wrong with you, as if I don't know?" she continues to squawk, as I heave myself into a sitting position in the hallway, with my back against the wall.

"Why are you asking if you already know?" I wonder out loud. She looks apoplectic now. She kneels next to me, hands splayed on her denim skirt, cheeks flushed with rage and eyes brimming with tears.

"Don't you dare start being cheeky!" she cries at me. "You've been out drinking haven't you? Look at the state of you. Right that is it, I warned you. I am not wasting another second of my breath trying to get through to you." She stands up abruptly and heads for the table in the hall where the phone is. I watch her angrily snatch it up and start to dial.

"Mum they won't be open now," I say quietly from the floor. She slams the phone back down and kicks the wall. "Mum calm down. I'm okay."

"I'm phoning the doctor first thing in the morning!" she turns on me, waving a finger my way. "I am not taking no for an answer! I will drag you there if I have to!"

"It's fine, it's fine," I tell her, and climb slowly to my feet. "I'll go. I've had enough of my head hurting anyway."

This seems to both surprise and placate her. She still looks like she would like to kill me, so I head for the stairs and she does not try to stop me. "I'll go to bed," I say meekly over my shoulder. I feel like such an idiot, if I am honest.

"First thing in the morning," she repeats to me. "I'll knock on your door. I mean it Lou. I cannot cope with this worry anymore."

"I said fine," I say, and go into my room and close the door. I hit the bed and don't get any time to think about any of it. I am asleep within seconds.

***

As promised mum wakes me up and hauls me to the doctors the next morning. We walk there in silence, and we occupy the waiting room in silence. I try to busy myself with a magazine, but they only seem to cater for the very young, (toddler bricks and baby books) or the very old (fishing and home makeover magazines.) I give up and just sit and wait with my hands in my lap, trying not to look at my mum. When my name is called, I go in alone, though I have a horrible feeling that my mother has already briefed the doctor. She has that sympathetic yet patronising sort of smile ready for me. The sort that says oh silly little you, what have you been doing to yourself eh? I find myself slumped in a blue plastic chair, waiting to be grilled.

Doctor Fielding is plump and grey-haired and has been my doctor since I was born. I almost expect her to say 'my haven't you grown?' when she opens her mouth, but instead she looks over her glasses at me with concern. "Now then Louise, your mum tells me she is very worried about you. She says you've been on a diet, is that right?"

"Yes," I nod at her politely. She has that elder lady quality about her. She also sounds rather posh, and I am tempted to call her madam or something.

"So how much weight do you think you have lost?"

"I think it's about two stone," I say with a guilty shrug. I can't help it. She is peering at me over her glasses; she is making me feel like I have done something wrong.

"Shall we get you on the scales and see what you weigh now then?" she asks brightly, speaking to me as if I am five.

"Okay."

She nods over to the big weighing scales parked next to the door. I slip off my shoes and climb on. I feel awful. I feel so small and stupid and childlike. Doctor Fielding has a look, writes a note and then motions for me to stand against the door where there is a chart to measure height. Again, she makes a note and then nods for me to return to my chair. "Okay," she says breezily, glancing down at her notes, before reaching for her keyboard and tapping out a few keys. "At five foot two, we would expect you to weigh somewhere in the region of seven stone, eleven pounds and nine stone, eleven pounds, and be healthy."

"I was about ten and a half stone once!" I say quickly, and she looks at me with a patient smile.

"Well, you weigh seven stone two today Louise. And that is too low." She gives me that smile again. The one she presented when she called me from the waiting room. She looks sympathetic and patronising at the same time.

"Oh," I say.

"Your mum is right to be concerned. That is not enough for your height, or your age. Don't forget you may still have more growing to do!"

"Oh."

"Yes, and losing weight by cutting calories and increasing exercise is all very fine, but you have to be sensible about it. Do you eat breakfast?"

"Yes." This is a half lie. I eat breakfast sometimes.

"What do you normally have?"

"Apples," I shrug, gazing around the room and wondering how much longer she is going to keep me here. "Yoghurts, that kind of thing."

She is looking at her computer screen. "And what about lunch?"

"Um, I don't know…just whatever. Toast or something." I shrug again.

"Your mum seems to think you are skipping meals a lot, is that true?"

Ah here we go, I think. Now she's getting to it. Now she's going to stop skirting around the issue. I think carefully for a moment as she looks back at me, one hand paused above the keyboard, and the other in her lap. I wonder whether I ought to lie, and see if she buys it. What can she do? Get out a lie detector or something? How does she know what I do or don't eat? How does anyone? I also wonder if I should tell her the truth, and see what she does with that. I am curious. So I nod at her hesitantly and she instantly frowns at me. "You seem like a smart young lady," she says. "You must know skipping meals is not a healthy thing to do." I just shrug at her. I don't know what else she expects me to say. She starts rifling through a bunch of leaflets she has already on her desk.

"Can I have something for my headaches?" I ask her then. I don't want anyone to forget about my headaches.

"You're getting headaches and passing out because you are not consuming enough calories, Louise," she tells me rather sharply, fixing me with a disapproving glare. "You don't need anything prescribed for your headaches. You just need to eat three sensible healthy meals a day."

"Oh," I say, and look at my hands.

"Are you worried about putting on weight?"

"Well, yeah."

"Louise, I want you to take these leaflets and these diet sheets with you. They document what a young girl your age should be consuming in terms of calories, and nutrition. You do realise that if you continue the way you are, your periods may stop? Your hair may fall out? You may have to stay in hospital?"

I just stare at her in confusion and feel tears threatening to come. Hospital? I know she is probably trying to scare me, but for God's sake! I swallow, and try to hold myself together in front of her. I feel angry with her then. How dare she try to freak me out and scare me?

"You need to put on at least nine pounds for me to be less worried," she goes on, and she is not even looking at me now, she is looking at the screen and typing again. "So I am going to leave those with you, and make an appointment for you to come back in two weeks, so we can see how you are getting on. How does that sound to you?"

I stare at her. I want to say that sounds horrible you mean old witch. That sounds like torture! That sounds like I have no choice and makes me want to kick you in the eye! I scrape back my chair and stand up nodding, so that she doesn't see the tears in my eyes. They are tears of rage, I swear to you World. She pokes the leaflets at me so I take them. She scribbles on an appointment card and gives me that as well. "You are not unlike a lot of other young girls I see in here," Doctor Fielding sees fit to tell me then. "We understand the pressures to lose weight, and look a certain way. But there is healthy, and there is dangerous, and I am afraid you are heading for the dangerous side Louise. I don't want to see you get thinner and thinner and end up in hospital. You don't really want that to happen either do you?" I shake my head. I cannot speak. "It's a slippery road, you see," she goes on. "You know I am talking about anorexia, don't you? This is how it starts. People try to lose weight, and when they do they get hooked on it. They can't stop. Eventually they are not even in control anymore. The disease is. I don't need to tell you it's a killer, do I?" I shake my head again, staring desperately at the door. "Can you send your mum in please?" she asks me. "I need to talk to her as well. I am going to suggest you arrange to see a counsellor as well."

"What?"

"A counsellor. Eating problems are not simply physical problems Louise. They are emotional, and psychological ones. A counsellor or therapist can help you understand *why* you feel the need to starve yourself."

I am staring at her open-mouthed. I am gawking at her. "Because I was fat!" I try to tell her, panicking. "That's why I started it! I won't do it anymore. I'll put nine pounds on, I will!"

"Louise, it is very worrying to see how quickly you have lost this much weight," she says this from her chair, her plump hands folded neatly on her lap. "I am concerned that you have already slipped quite far into a possible eating disorder."

I am outraged. I am gob smacked. "*Seriously?*"

"Yes," she nods twice. "I am very serious. Now send in your mother for me please."

I don't have any other choice. I have to go back into the waiting room and tell my mum it's her turn. She just barges past me with this tight look on her face. She makes me feel like I have done all of this on purpose just to wind her up, just to give her some more grey hairs or something. I sit back down and twist my hands together in my lap, and think about running out and running off, hiding somewhere, disappearing. There is a little kid on the floor, a little boy playing with the bricks. He is banging on brick on top of another, again and again and again. His mother is watching him with quiet adoration, and gives me a wet smile when I look up and glare at her. I feel like saying, you would have got a clip round the ear for that in your day. But I don't. I get up and walk outside and wait for my mum.

When she comes out, she is by no means impressed. I was right about feeling she is angry with me about all of this. It is as if she thinks I have led myself down this road deliberately to hurt her, to make her worry. "She thinks you have an eating disorder," she snaps this at me as we start to walk home. She is walking fast in her little black-heeled shoes. I am trying to keep up, clutching the stupid leaflets in one hand.

"She didn't say that," I attempt to correct her. "She said possible. Like borderline."

"That's not what she said to me!"

"Oh."

I think I don't want to have this conversation with you. I don't want you anywhere near me in fact. "She's going to arrange a counsellor," she goes on, and I feel my chest tighten involuntarily. I want to scream. "She thinks you need to talk to someone about your weight loss issues."

"I don't have weight loss issues!" I yell at her.

She wipes a tear from her eye. I don't care. "She says you are very underweight for your height."

"I know! I know all that! She wants nine pounds! She can have bloody nine pounds!" I am aware I am shouting and waving my hands about, but I can't seem to stop. "I'll give her bloody nine pounds!" I shout. "When we get in, just you wait, I'll show you! How much crap have you got in there? Crisps? Chocolate? Doughnuts? Give them to me; I'll eat them all! I'll get her bloody nine pounds in no time!"

"Lou, please…"

"I'll even round it up! I'll make it ten pounds!"

"Lou, listen to me, stop that shouting, you have to realise how serious this is, how worried we all are! We are just trying to do what is best for you!"

"Don't worry," I sneer at her. I hate her. "Don't you worry Mum, I don't want you to worry so I'll eat all that shit and put on bloody ten fat pounds all right? I'll do better than that if it makes you happy! I'll stop jogging and I'll sit in front of the TV all day and do nothing but eat! I'll get really fat again! Fat as a whale! How would you all like that then? You would all love that, wouldn't you? None of you cared when I was a big fat pig did you? None of you worried then!"

I run off. I run off before I can see her tears or hear her whimper of a voice, or listen to another word she can say. I run off because all of it is true. They are right, and I am right. I run off. I just keep running.

28

Dear World, I try to be left alone again, but it does not happen. Now that my mother has the doctor's words as ammunition, she is firing at me relentlessly, and she won't give up until I admit she is right, and I am wrong. She makes me read all the leaflets and the diet sheets. She sits with me and points out all the low calorie healthy meals I could be eating. She tells me no one expects me to eat chocolate or crisps or doughnuts if I don't want to. She tells me I can count calories and keep jogging if it makes me feel better, but that I simply have to eat three sensible meals a day, and that is final. She is being strict and motherly with me. Over protective and firm. Taking no shit. Taking no prisoners. She even has Sara phone me.

"Anorexic she says!" Sara is breathless with awe and disbelief on the other end of the phone. I am bored and cold.

"Borderline," I correct her. "Possibly."

"You don't believe it?"

"I don't get a choice. I have to put on nine pounds or else!"

"Or else what?"

"I don't know. I expect they will strap me down and force-feed me Mars bars."

"Christ Lou!"

"It's bullshit."

"You better do what they say. You know what Mum is like. She is right on one now!"

"Can't you get up the duff or something and get the attention back on you?"

Sara screams with laughter. "Glad you still got your wit little sister!"

"It's all I have," I sigh. "And a tiny scrap of sanity."

"Well we did try to warn you, you were taking it all too far. I can understand it though. Wasn't much fun for you being a chubster was it?"

"No fun at all," I snort in reply. "That's what she doesn't get. It's like she wants to keep me like that. Her chubby little girl who will eat anything. I mean, she never once told me to *lose* weight, did she? She never dragged me to the doctor about being too fat? Even though that's bad for you too?"

"You weren't that fat Lou," Sara giggles.

"I was an elephant Sara!"

"No, really you weren't. You have a somewhat distorted view of how fat you were. You were pretty normal really for a teenager."

"Easy for you to say," I remind her. "When you have always been a pretty little stick insect."

"Oh Lou," my sister sighs at me down the phone. "Just please do as they say and be sensible now, yeah? Passing out must have scared you, yeah?"

"It was quite funny," I lie.

"Lou!"

"Sorry. I've got to go Sara. I had a fight with Joe so I need to call him."

"Okay, okay. Pass me back to Mum then. I bet she wants a progress report."

"Okay. Bye."

I take my mobile out of my pocket and slip into the kitchen. My mum has made me lunch and left it on the table. Scrambled egg on wholemeal toast and an apple. Hmm. It doesn't look too bad, I reason with myself. I can probably manage it. I think about those nine stupid pounds, and sit at the table and force myself to eat it slowly. I wonder how much I can get away with not eating. I always feel like a total pig if I clean the plate, so I leave the crusts and about two teaspoonful's of egg. My mum hangs up on Sara and comes in to see me. She still has that disapproving and strict air about her. She folds her arms and frowns at my plate. I smile at her hopefully.

"Just about to call Joe,"

"What for?"

"Need to talk," I shrug.

"Okay then."

"When are you doing it?" is the first thing I ask Joe when he answers his phone. I hear him sigh heavily, because he knows what I am referring to.

"Friday night like normal," he says.

"I'm sorry I stormed off."

"My mum says you have anorexia."

"That's outrageous!" I hiss down the phone at him. I hear him snort, and I am relieved that he is not completely buying it like they all are.

"So you don't then?"

"What do you bloody think, idiot face? Do I look like I have?"

"Well," he says slowly. "Not quite."

"Jesus Christ, I can't believe she said that."

"You know what they're like. My mum was on the phone to your mum for bloody ages the other day. Then she comes and has a go at me. Apparently if I was a real friend, I would have noticed!"

"You're joking?" I squeal. "She said that? What a…" I want to say bitch, but my mum is in the kitchen, most likely listening in.

"Don't worry about it," Joe tells me. "We're okay though? You and me?"

"Well yeah. But I still don't want you to go. You know."

"Is your mum there?"

"Yeah, how can you tell?"

Joe laughs. "Look, it's all right," he tells me. "It's an old customer. Cool bloke. Then that is it. I have told Leon, I swear I have. I said last time. Last time! That's it and I mean it. I really mean it Lou."

I am leaning against the wall. In my mind I can see him disappearing into the darkness again, with that lump in his pocket. I wish there was something I could say to change his mind. "I just don't want to see you going that way," I say in a low voice. "You know, for all your life. Like they are. I don't want it to lead to other things. Other favours."

"Yeah, I know what you mean."

"Okay then."

"You're okay?"

"I'm okay."

"Okay. See you Saturday then? Do something fun?"

I sigh a misery-laden sigh at his hopeful suggestion. "Whatever fun there is to be had around here, we'll try to find it," I promise, and we say goodbye.

I spend the next few days trying to stay calm. I try to avoid looking in mirrors as much as possible, because it feels like every mouthful of food my mother watches me eat is already creating a nice layer of padding around my bones. I don't like it, and I tell my wall I don't. *Fat is wrapping around me, around and around, binding me up, tying me down, filling me out. They can't see it, but I can feel it.* I wonder if my mother ever looks at my wall? *Hi mum, thanks mum,* I write, just in case.

I have to admit that my headache goes though. But I tell myself this is because I deliberately avoid Joe and Marianne, and so do not smoke any pot or drink any cider. I am all clean and healthy, I think bitterly. I am getting filled up with nutritionally sound meals. My mother has read every leaflet with gusto. I go out for jogs, and long walks with Gremlin, and she just sighs. As long as I am eating the three meals, she seems calm.

"Counselling of some sort will be good for you," she tells me, and I can tell she has been thinking about this a lot. "Getting through the teenage years is tough enough for anyone you know. It will give you some tools to help you later in life."

"Is that what it says in the leaflets?" I ask her. She gives me a look. I feel like we are having a silent war with each other. I feel like doing it all the way she wants, then doing a Sara and moving out at eighteen so I can do what the hell I want, and eat what the hell I want.

On Friday night, I am thinking about Joe and sitting on the sofa nursing my swollen tummy, when the phone rings. My mum and Les are curled up together on the other sofa. I have Gremlin on my legs, snoring. My tummy feels too full, it feels gross, like it could split open if I move. Mum cooked salmon, new potatoes, green beans and carrots for dinner. "Very healthy, very low calorie," she nodded at me when I sat at the table.

"Not the usual greasy takeaways tonight," Les commented cheerfully, tucking into his. He has started talking to me lately, which is fair enough. Except that every single thing he says is cold and dull and I don't give a shit about it.

I got out of eating two potatoes, a chunk of fish and a few carrots. I felt my mother's eyes watching every single mouthful I ate. Now I am feeling too full, too heavy to move. I couldn't jog if I wanted to. Thanks Mum.

No one moves when the phone rings. There is no way I am getting it, even though I see my mum staring at me. I drop one arm over Gremlin, in case she has forgotten about him being asleep on me. She starts to sigh and untangle herself from Les, but then the phone stops. She rolls her eyes and leans back into Les. I yawn. I am thinking about going to bed. I don't know what time it is, but I reckon it must be nearly eleven.

The phone starts ringing again, making us all jump. Mum looks at Les and laughs out loud. "That gave me a fright!" she announces. "I better get it this time." She heaves herself free of him and the sofa and dashes into the hallway. Les just stares at the TV. He has nothing to say, and neither do I.

"Calm down, calm down," I can hear my mother saying in the hallway, so I sit up, looking towards the door. "Okay, just calm down Lorraine. I will come over!"

Lorraine? I get up from the sofa so quickly that Gremlin is hurled unceremoniously to the floor. I run out into the hallway and I can straight away see that something is badly wrong. Mum is clutching the phone with white knuckles, and her face is contorted with concern. She grimaces at me as I wait. I mouth 'what is it?' to her, but she just shakes her head.

"Okay, okay," she says, "keep calm, I'm coming over. I'll sit with the little ones for you. It'll be all right Lorraine, do you hear me honey? It will be a mistake, I am telling you! You just hold on. I'll be five minutes."

Mum drops the phone and starts turning around, looking for shoes. "What's wrong?" I ask her.

"It's Joe," she says, and my blood freezes. My heart stops. Every hair on my body stands on end.

"What?"

She is slipping on her shoes, pulling one over one heel, and then the other. She snatches her keys and her bag from the hall table and pokes her head into Les. "Got to go to Lorraine's," she tells him. "Emergency! You stay with Lou, and I'll call from there in a minute."

"Okay!" Les says, sounding alarmed. Mum heads for the door, seeming to have forgotten all about me.

"Mum! What about Joe? What is it?"

"Oh love I am sure it is all a mistake, a silly mix up," she turns to me as she unlocks the front door.

"But what? What? Is he okay?"

"He's at the police station," Mum says to me. "I've got to sit with the younger ones while Lorraine and Mick go down there."

"The police station?" I gasp, my hand fluttering to my throat. "What for?"

"Oh Lou," she sighs, going out of the door. "It really does sound so ridiculous, it must be a mistake, but he's been arrested! Arrested for drug dealing! Can you believe that? I've got to go, got to go."

She leaves me with that, and she is gone.

I feel cold, so cold. I feel sick. I cannot breathe so I lean against the wall. Jesus Christ, I think. "Are you all right?" I am dimly aware of Les stood next to me in the hallway, looking at me. I just stare in confusion at the floor. I think, maybe I should run after my mum, go with her? I look at the door, considering it. Les shifts nervously in the doorway. "Lou, are you all right?" I look back at the floor, trembling, on the verge of pathetic tears. Would she just turn me back though? Shit! Joe at the police station! I start to nibble at my fingernails. I know what I should do. I know what the adult thing to do would be. To tell them the truth. To tell them it's not his drugs. To tell on Leon and Travis. "Do you want to come and sit with me?" Les asks. I look at him and frown. Who the hell is he? What does he want?

"I should go with her," I tell him, looking back at the door.

"I think it's best to wait here."

"I'll phone her!" I take my mobile out of my pocket. No messages, no missed calls. I am trying to work out how long she has already been gone, and how much longer it will take her to get to Joe's house. Les sort of sighs behind me and goes back into the lounge. I chew my fingernails viciously and keep my eyes on my phone. I count inside my head. I count to sixty five times. That should be long enough. I snatch the phone up and punch in her number. It only rings twice before my mum answers it.

"Hello?"

"Mum, it's me!"

"Oh Lou, stop panicking, there's nothing to tell you! They've just left to go down the station."

"But quick, tell me what's happened!"

"I don't know any more Lou," my mum hisses back, as if she is trying to keep her voice down. "All I know is the police called the house because they picked him up and found drugs on him! I am seriously hoping this all turns out to be a big mistake, otherwise me and you are going to be having yet more words!"

Oh Christ, what does she mean by this? "I'll let you go," I say and end the call. I stand in the hallway with my hands over my face. This is a nightmare I think. This is the worst thing that could have ever happened! I want to punch the wall. Or myself. I tried to tell him not to do it again, didn't I? Oh why hadn't I tried harder? Why hadn't he listened?

I am standing in the darkened hallway, with my hands pressed tightly against my face. I try to calm down. I try to breathe, in and out, slowly and purposefully. I try to think. I think about Joe. My heart lurches and twists. My skin prickles. I drop my hands when I hear a noise at the front door, and I stare at it. I can see shadows moving there on the other side of the glass. I move towards it cautiously. I am shuddering from head to toe. There is a small, light tap on the door. It makes me imagine someone brushing their knuckles against it, trying not to make too much noise. I look back at the lounge, and there is no movement or sound from Les, so I presume he has not heard anything.

I open the door, and Leon and Travis are there in the darkness. Travis is just in front of his brother, wearing a white t-shirt that makes him look like a ghost floating in my front garden. He is rubbing at one bare arm, as he lifts himself from one foot to the other. The guilt and the shock are etched on his face. I don't get a choice about whether I want to speak to them or not. Leon reaches past Travis, grabs my arm and pulls me outside. He then pulls the door softly shut behind me. He is big and broad in his denim jacket, and he leans over me with one arm on the wall behind. "You know what's going on?" he asks in a low voice. I nod and look at Travis.

"You have to help him," I say. Travis drops his gaze to the ground and says nothing.

"It's not that simple," Leon tells me. "We've both got previous. We'll probably get sent down."

"But Joe…"

"He'll get a caution, a fine," Leon says this dismissively, shrugging his shoulders at me as if it is all very obvious. "He'll be home later. No worries." I can hardly believe what I am hearing.

"No worries?" I whisper, staring up at Leon in horror. "Are you serious?"

"He's not going to drop us in it," Leon tells me, and I can see by the look in his eyes that he truly believes this. "We just need to make sure you're not either."

"He's right," Travis finally speaks up, though he seems to find it excruciatingly difficult to look me in the eye. "Joe will be fine. He's not going to prison or anything."

"I can't believe you're prepared to even risk it!" I tell him. "He's your *brother*, doesn't that mean anything to you?" Leon rolls his eyes, looks at Travis, and spreads his feet as he straightens up. "He didn't want to go," I look at him then. "Did he? He said no. He didn't want to do it anymore, but you wouldn't take no for an answer would you?"

"It was the last one."

"You keep saying that! It's all lies! This is your new job isn't it? This is what you both do! This is it!"

Leon drops a hand urgently onto my shoulder. "Keep your voice down!" he snarls at me.

"You're going to ruin his life," I say, shaking my head in pure disbelief. "You don't care. You don't care what your mum and Mick will do to him!"

"We'll sort that," Travis says desperately. "Just let us sort it yeah? Say you'll stay out of it. It's between us and Joe anyway."

"Bastards," I say though clenched teeth. I point at Leon. "I won't say anything until I know what's happened to Joe. But if I think for a moment he's going to jail, I'll bloody run down the police station, right?"

"Don't forget you helped too," Leon reminds me then, and he sort of leans back a little, stretching out his spine and looking relaxed, arrogant even. "You and Joe. In it up to your necks. We didn't force you, did we?"

"I didn't take any money," I growl at him. "You fucking dick."

"Whatever. You went with him. You knew. That's just as bad. So keep your mouth shut and sit tight or you'll be getting arrested yourself." He moves away as I stare at him in silence. Travis moves with him, his arms hanging, and his shoulders slumped. I look his way.

"Scumbags," I hiss.

"We'll sort it out," he says to me, trailing after Leon.

"Liar!" I call after him. They don't look back. Neither of them do. I watch them go. I want to sink down to my knees and sob into the ground. I want to run after them, find a massive rock and bludgeon them around the head with it. I don't know what to do. So I go indoors. I go up to my room. I sit on my bed, and hug my knees and rock back and forth, trying to find the answers. But I am sixteen years old. I know nothing.

29

Dear World, I spend the rest of the evening sending frantic texts to Joe and to my mother, and neither of them get back to me. Later on, up in my room, I am dozing in and out of restless sleep, when I suddenly sit bolt upright in my bed, tangled in my duvet and sweating profusely. My door has opened a creak, and there is a shadow peering in. "Lou, are you asleep?" It is my mother. I throw back the duvet and leap out of bed, running to the door to tear it open. Joe is standing just behind her. He looks awful. He is trying not to cry. "Joe is going to stay with us for a few days," my mum informs me in hushed tones. "Until everything settles down again at home. Can you make him up a bed on the floor if I grab the blankets?"

"Course," I say. I grab his arm and pull him in. I have never been so glad to see anyone in my entire life. My mum gives us a sort of withering, concerned look before hurrying off to get blankets from the airing cupboard. Joe hovers in the middle of my room. I want to throw my arms around him, but I don't want my mum to catch me, so I don't. I just stare at him. He is wearing the same Arctic Monkeys t-shirt he had on days ago, with a checked shirt on top. There are mud and grass stains on the knees of his jeans, and a smear of dirt under his chin. He folds his arms around himself, shivers, and stares at the floor. He looks thoroughly beaten and disgusted with himself. I search for the anger and the pride he had that morning he got into my bed with me, but can see no trace of it. I look at his face as my mum goes back and forth dumping piles of blankets inside the door. His bottom lip is cut and swollen, and there is another thin trail of blood coming from his ear.

Finally my mother stops fussing, and stands in the doorway releasing a massive sigh. "I hope you two understand how much trust I am putting in you by letting you stay in here," she tells us sternly and we nod at her. "I am putting trust in you when neither of you has done anything lately to deserve it."

I want to tell her we are just bloody friends, and can everyone stop assuming that we want to get into each other's knickers constantly, but I bite my tongue and just look at her apologetically. "Things are too tense at home for Joe to stay there," she looks at me and says. I wonder if I can detect something in her eyes. Something she is trying to tell me. She does not take her eyes off of me. "So I intervened and brought him here. Putting my friendship with Lorraine at risk in the process," she adds angrily, as if this is somehow our fault. I just nod again.

"Okay Mum."

She finally turns to go. "Get some sleep," she sighs. "We'll all talk in the morning."

When the door is closed, I look at Joe. "Sit down," I tell him, nodding at my bed. "I'll make these up for you." He moves slowly, hesitantly and sits on the edge of my bed, while I wrestle with the blankets on the floor. "Are you okay?" I look up and ask him gently. "Why are you bleeding?"

"Had a fight," he croaks, staring at nothing. "Me and Mick."

"While my mum was there?"

"Yeah," he nods. "She stopped us."

"Jesus Christ Joe. What the hell happened tonight? I had a little visit from your brothers, once my mum had shot off to your house!"

"Oh. What did they say? I haven't seen them yet."

I stop making the bed up and frown at him. "You haven't seen them? So much for them sorting things out for you! That was what they said! They made me promise to keep my mouth shut while they sorted things. Those shitting scumbag liars."

Joe says nothing. He is sitting on the bed with his hands hanging limply between his knees. He looks like he is maybe in shock or something, but how would I know? I shuffle forward on my knees until I am right in front of him. He is just breathing very fast. He looks so pale. His eyes are full of tears, and as I pick up one of his hands and hold it gently between mine, the tears line up and fall one by one. I watch them skidding down his white cheeks, over his cheekbones, and down to his chin. "What happened?" I ask him. He sniffs loudly.

"Don't know. Police suddenly appeared when I was up on the bridge with the bloke. They must have followed me. They must have seen me before!"

My eyes grow huge. "What?"

"Was so scary," he whispers. I hold his hand tighter and rub it between mine.

"Oh, Joe. How much did you have on you?"

"Just one of them little bags Leon makes up. Twenty quid's worth."

"Shit. This is bad."

He lifts his other hand and wipes the tears away, but fresh ones line up to take their place almost instantly. He nods miserably. "Was so horrible Lou," he whispers croakily. "They put handcuffs on me and everything. I was so scared."

"Oh mate. What's going to happen?"

"Got to go to court," he shrugs and sniffs again. "They questioned me for ages. Wanted to know who I was running for."

"Let me guess, you didn't say?"

Joe just stares at me for a long, torturous moment. Then he drops his head into both of his hands and I watch his shoulders shake as he sobs into them. He shakes his head at me. I get up and sit next to him on the bed and slide my arm around his trembling shoulders. "Oh Joe," I murmur, resting my head against his other shoulder for a moment. "You idiot. You are such an idiot. Why didn't you say? You *have* to say. You can't take the rap for them, you just can't!"

"I need to talk to them first," he sobs.

"But *why*? I told you what they said already." I lift my head to stare at him. I keep rubbing his other shoulder with my hand, pressing his body into mine. "They said it was okay for you to take the rap, because they've both got previous and they'd get sent down, but you won't. That's what they think Joe. They're quite happy to let you take all the blame."

"I won't go to jail will I?" he asks suddenly, turning his tear stained face to mine. I swallow and fight the urge I have to wipe his tears away with my thumb.

"God knows Joe! How would we know? I have no idea! Did they get you a solicitor or something?"

He nods, frowning in confusion. "The duty one."

"And?"

"I don't know, I don't know, I can't remember..." Joe covers his face with his hands again. I hug him close.

"What happened with your mum and Mick?" I ask quietly. I feel his entire body shudder next to mine then. I feel the tremor of pain and shock and disgust twist right through him as he relives the memory.

"Just..." he shakes his head very slowly, staring through his fingers. "Just...really...fucking mental."

"Well my mum must have thought so, to bring you back here."

"They packed all my stuff," he says through his fingers. His voice sounds hollow, shocked to the core, devoid of emotion or belief. "They packed it all up and chucked it out the door."

"Oh my god! *Joe!*" I put both my arms around him now. I wrap them right around and hold him so tight while he shudders and sobs. I kiss the top of his head, and then the side of his face, and I taste his salty tears, as he must have tasted mine that night in his bed. "Joe, oh Joe. The bastards. All of them. Fuck them! They don't deserve you Joe. They never have. You can just live here with us then. Mum will adopt you. They don't deserve you!" I keep my arms around him and rock with him back and forth. "Don't you worry," I tell him, and plant another firm kiss on the side of his head. "Everything will be okay. We'll tell the truth Joe, that's what we have to do. We have to tell my mum the truth, about everything. Forget about Leon and Travis. Let them get arrested. It's their bloody mess."

"I don't know," he murmurs then, lowering his hands and sniffing loudly.

"In the morning," I tell him. "Sleep on it. You can't take the rap for them Joe, you just can't."

"Why not?" he asks, looking into my eyes and lifting his shoulders in a tired shrug. "I don't even care. I won't have anything to do with any of them after this. But I won't be a grass."

"Oh Joe, no."

He gets up then and rolls his head on his neck, then shakes out his arms and legs. His jeans are getting too small I notice. Creeping up his ankles. He drops down and gathers the blankets around him. He looks exhausted. He looks broken. I want to kill them all. I want to steal his perfect goodness away from them, and make it mine, keep it all for me. They never saw it, never nurtured it. They don't deserve him. That is all I keep thinking. They don't deserve him. He is a good apple among a rotting bunch of fetid cancerous ones. I watch him crawl in among the blankets, and I watch the sobs that still shake him as he tries to control himself. Finally he lays his head on the pillow and stares nakedly up at me. I want to cry.

"Thanks Lou," he says hoarsely.

"I hope you got a few good ones in with Mick," I reply with raised eyebrows. He does not even smile. He just closes his eyes. I get back under my covers and let him go. I seem to lie there for ages, just listening to him breathing.

At some point during what is left of the night, I hear him crying silently under his blankets, and I just cannot bear it. I get out of bed and slip in beside him. I pull his head into my chest and stroke his hair, and rub his back, while he just lets it all out. Neither of us speaks.

In the morning, I untangle myself from Joe and get to my feet. He just sleeps on. I look at my bedroom door, slightly panicked, while memories of the last time we were caught together in bed career through my mind. I lean down and cover him up and sneak quietly out of the room. I know that my mother is going to be in the kitchen, sat at the table with her hands wrapped around a steaming cup of tea, and a tea towel lying on her lap, or maybe on the table next to her cup. I know that she is going to look at me in that way, the way she always does lately. Like she does not recognise me anymore. I know that she is going to want to know what I know. I know that Joe will not grass his brothers up, but I have not yet decided if I will.

I creep in, feeling sheepish and young. She just looks at me, and I can't decide if it is disappointment or pity that I see the most etched on her face. Maybe a good deal of both? I slip into a chair at the table. "Joe's still asleep," I say, not looking at her. She drums her fingers gently against the teacup.

"Do you want some breakfast?"

"Yes please."

"Egg and soldiers? Used to be your favourite once. When you were a little girl." There is a note of terrible sadness in her voice that I can barely stand. I force myself to look at her long enough to smile and nod in recognition, but that is all I can manage. She slides out from the table and puts a small saucepan of water onto the hob to boil.

"How long can he stay?" I ask her back. I watch her sigh.

"As long as he needs to, I suppose," she replies. "I'm just going to have to be careful not to get involved, if you know what I mean. Not take sides."

I am not sure what she means. "Sides?"

"Yes. His side or theirs, I mean."

I still don't know what she means. I watch her turn the grill on, and slap a slice of wholemeal bread under it. "Mum, what happened at their house? I mean, why did you bring Joe back?"

She turns to face me and folds her arms across her breasts. "Look," she says slowly, and I can tell that she is thinking in her head, trying to work out the best way to say something. "I don't know what all this drug dealing business is about. I didn't ask Joe, and I don't plan to right now. I only know he has always been a lovely, decent boy, and I can only suppose the older two have roped him into something unsavoury?" There is an undeniable question mark at the end of her sentence, but I pretend not to pick up on it and just stare up at her expectantly. "Anyway," she goes on. "That's none of my business, because at the end of the day it's for the police and the courts to decide what's gone on. But I cannot justify, or make excuses for the way I saw…" She breaks off now, swallows, coughs, and then turns her back to check the toast and the boiling water.

"Saw?" I question, prompting her.

"The way I saw the adults in that house treat him last night," she finishes, and on the last word I hear her voice crack, and I see her lift one hand and drag it across her eyes. I watch her trying to compose herself.

"You mean, like the stuff I tried to tell you?"

"I suppose so yes. They just totally lost control. They were wild. Like animals. I kept telling them to calm down, calm down, leave it till the morning, let him go to bed, that sort of thing. They packed up all his stuff from his room and started throwing it out of the door."

"They've got vicious tempers," I say morosely. Mum shakes back her hair and stands over the hob, watching my egg as it bounces around in the pan.

"Well, I just didn't like what I saw," she says. "And I know Lorraine is my friend. My very old friend. And she has always been tough on her boys. Lord knows, the older two needed it, but Joe…" she trails off again, shaking her head slightly, as if she just can't fathom any of it. "He was just so pale, and frightened and so sorry, he was so sorry. He just kept saying sorry, sorry, over and over. They wouldn't even let him speak. I found myself stood in front of him Lou. I had to shield him. I had to get him out of there."

"You did the right thing Mum," I say then, and get up from the table. "They don't deserve him. I know he's in trouble, but it really isn't all his fault you know."

"Well if you know anything Lou…" She turns and looks me in the eye.

"I need to speak to Joe."

"Then I have to trust you'll do the right thing," she says, her eyes burning into mine. I feel such a wave of compassion and gratitude for her then, that it actually overwhelms me. I sort of stumble into her arms, and slide mine around her body, and end up with my face pushed up against her breasts.

"I'll do the right thing," I tell her. "Because you did. Thanks Mum."

I feel her playing with my hair like she used to do when I was small. She wraps it around her fingers and then unwinds it again. She presses her head down onto mine and breathes in. "You kids," I hear her mumble. "It still takes my breath away you know, when I see how quickly you've grown. You know what parenthood is Lou? It's not enough time. Not enough time to hold your children near." She kisses me twice on the head. "One minute it's all changing nappies, and rocking you to sleep, and holding your little hand, and then, in a blink of an eye…"

I squeeze her tight. In my head, I can just see her at Joe's house, scared and confused, standing in front of him, trying to tell Mick to calm down. I squeeze her again. "I love you Mum," I say. "I love you so much."

30

Dear World, we stay in all day. Joe sleeps for hours. When he finally emerges, he looks even worse, if that is possible. My mum sees him shuffle into the kitchen, and she can't help herself, the first thing she does is wrap her arms around him. I get up and make him tea and toast, which he barely touches. The whole time he can't stop shivering, even though it is a gorgeous summer day. I try to talk to him. I try to get him talking, but he just sits in silence all day with his head in his hand. My mum asks him when he has to go to court and he says he doesn't know. He sits there all day, with shiny eyes, but does not cry again. Eventually my mum gets up with a sigh and announces that she is going to speak to Lorraine. Joe barely looks at her.

When she is gone my phone rings so I answer it. "Hiya!" Marianne yells down the phone at me, hurting my ear. I roll my eyes at Joe, still sat in the kitchen. I am not in the right mood to talk to her or deal with her. She must be calling on her home phone, I think. If her mobile had come up, I would not have answered it.

"Hi Marianne, you okay?"

"Yes, more than okay, I am great! My parents have buggered off again, so got the place to myself! I was thinking about another party!"

I can't believe what I am hearing, so I sort of slump against the wall and groan inwardly. "Oh I don't know," I tell her. "I'm not sure about that."

"Well I mean a smaller one obviously," she goes on breathlessly. "I wouldn't have the time to contact everyone for a big one. I was thinking you and Joe, Josh and Ryan, Leon and Travis, maybe a few more? Anyone they want to bring!"

"It's probably not the best time, that's all," I try to tell her. I can tell by the look on Joe's face that he does not want me to tell her about his arrest.

"Why not? What else you doing? What you up to then?" She sounds sort of hyper, I think, like she is bouncing around the room while she speaks to me.

"Um," I say, while I try to think fast, try to think of excuses. "It's just I got family stuff on, you know. Stuff to do. I think I'm busy all weekend really."

There is silence from her end. I wait for her to fill it but she does not. I breathe out slowly and imagine her standing still, her eyes filling with rage towards me. "Marianne? You there?"

"Yes. Yes. I am here. Okay then fine. I could come over to you? Have a girly sleepover?"

Oh Christ, I think desperately. Why does she have to call now? Why does she have to be like this right now? "I'm really sorry Marianne," I say this firmly. "I really can't this weekend. I'll call you on Monday, okay?"

"Okay. Fine then."

"Don't be like that…"

"Like what? No, it's fine. Fine. Bye." That's it. She hangs up. I roll my eyes again look at Joe.

"Well that pissed her off," I shrug at him in exasperation. He nods very slightly. "Shall I make us some lunch then?" He looks down. I lean against the door frame and try to think of inspiring and encouraging things to say. But there are none. He has been arrested for suspected drug dealing. I have no idea what is going to happen to him, but in the long run it does not look good, does it?

So I fiddle around making us cups of coffee, and looking through the cupboards to see what we can eat for lunch. Not eating does not even enter my mind, though I am not sure why. It does not seem quite so important, that's all. Joe does. I am grilling some bacon for bacon sandwiches, when my mum hurries back in through the front door and slams her handbag down on the hall table. Joe and I both look up at her with wide, expectant eyes. "Well," she says, placing her hands on her hips and taking us both in. "I have good news and bad news."

"Good first," I say quickly. "I think we need it."

"Okay," she nods. "Well the police were unable to track down the other guy on the bridge, so they have no real evidence to charge Joe with intent to supply. Your mum spoke to them this morning," she looks at Joe and says. "They are charging you with possession. You'll still go to court, but at your age, with no previous convictions, you are more than likely to receive a fine, and maybe some community service."

I look at Joe in amazement. He looks confused. He pulls at his sore bottom lip with his thumb and finger and frowns at my mum. He has not brushed his hair and it is all over the place. "That's brilliant isn't it Joe?" I prompt him eagerly. "That's much less serious!" He nods, considering it.

"I guess so."

"What was the bad news?" I ask my mum. She sighs and folds her arms, and then I see her sniff and peer around me to take in the bacon under the grill. A confused look crosses her face and then she smiles ever so slightly.

"Oh," she says, "the bad news comes from Mick. He does not want you back. Well, not yet. Your mum is working on him."

"Well that's not bad news!" I laugh. "That's good news! You wouldn't go back there anyway, would you Joe?"

"Lou," my mum says softly. "It will be in Joe's best interests to make things right again with his family. But anyway, for now, he can stay here. I am sure Mick will calm down and change his mind soon enough."

I lean forward and punch Joe softly in the shoulder. "Not so bad then?" I ask him. He manages a small smile and nods at me.

"Are you making bacon sandwiches?" my mum enquires, trying to peer past me again.

"Yep. Joe's favourite."

"Any spare for me?"

"I think we can stretch to it," I say with a grin.

Five minutes later the three of us are gathered around the kitchen table, sinking our teeth into warm bacon sandwiches, smeared with tomato sauce. I think, this is crazy, but nothing in my life has ever tasted as good as this does. My mum tries not to look at me too much, and she certainly holds her tongue about me eating lunch, but I can feel it in the air around her, I can feel how happy she is, how relieved she is. I tell myself in a new calm voice I had no idea existed within me, that I can go for a nice run later. I've missed my runs. I can go for a nice run, and as long as I do that regularly, I'll never get as fat as I was, will I? As long as I am sensible. I wonder if I tell myself this enough, will I start to really believe it?

Joe and I return to my room after lunch. He seems a bit brighter, but is still not exactly talkative. He goes through the music on my iPod, his expression becoming increasingly disgusted. "You are stuck in the sixties!" he tells me irately. "You weren't even born then, but you're stuck in the sixties!"

"I like it. I like all that stuff."

"We could go back to mine and get my music."

"Oh. I don't know. Maybe not."

Joe runs his fingers back through his hair. "It's okay," he says, but his voice sounds unsure to me. "Mum and Mick will be at work."

"What about Leon and Travis?"

He shrugs at me. "What about them?"

"Have you decided what to do?"

"Nothing. I just want my music Lou. I want to get my music and my money. You know for the drums. I can't leave it there."

I had forgotten about his money. I had totally forgotten. I make a growling noise and cover my mouth with my hands for a moment, while I look at his pleading eyes and try to work out what to do. I don't want to go over there, no way. But I can see his point. "Okay," I say eventually. "I'll come with you. And we'll tell Mum what we're doing. I'm so impressed with her at the moment, I think she deserves my honesty."

Joe frowns and smiles at me at the same time. "How sweet."

"Fuck off."

"It is though. I'm glad. And you ate lunch! You ate bacon."

"I'll say it again. Fuck off."

Joe snorts and I see a small amount of light return to his eyes. "Wasn't really much fun collapsing all over the place then?" he goads me. I narrow my eyes and stand in front of him.

"I'm going to smack you in your sore lip in a minute if you don't shut up."

He slaps my shoulder. "Chill out Carling. I'm just joking." I push him towards the bedroom door.

"Come on, if we're doing this let's get it over with. I am all kinds of scared right now."

"Me too."

We find Mum in the back garden. She is on her knees, weeding her flowerbeds. Gremlin is lying next to her, panting in the sun. "Mum, is it okay if we go to Joe's house to get more of his stuff?" I ask her, holding up a hand to shield my eyes from the glaring sun. Mum sits back on her feet and looks at us worriedly.

"Oh I don't know guys."

"He needs his stuff," I point out. "His clothes and stuff. Toothbrush. His breath stinks you know."

Joe elbows me. "Oi!"

"Sorry. But it does. We'll be super quick mum. In and out. Mick and Lorraine will be at work, won't they?"

"I think so," she sighs. "But if their cars are there, I want you to turn around and come straight back, do you hear? I'll go over there later for Joe's stuff."

"Okay, we will," I promise. "See you in a bit."

We pile back into the house, and as we head down the hallway my phone rings again in my pocket. "Christ's sake," I curse under my breath and snatch it up. "Hello?"

"Lou, it's me again."

I mouth 'Marianne' at Joe and he rolls his eyes in sympathy and shoves his hands into his pockets while he waits. "Hi Marianne."

"I was just wondering if you wanted to come over?"

"Um, I can't, remember? I said I was busy all weekend."

"Busy with Joe?"

"No. Well yes actually, but look, it's a long story, loads has happened, and I can't tell you over the phone so…"

"I see."

"No, it's not like that, it's just actually he's sort of staying with us at the moment," I make apologetic faces at Joe as I see his expression darkening. "I can't go into it on the phone. He's got family problems."

"So you lied earlier?"

"No, I said family stuff didn't I?"

"You said your family."

"Oh Marianne, what does it matter?" I snap at her. "Look Joe needs me at the moment, and I'll explain it all when I see you, so…"

"Doesn't matter," she snaps back at me, and hangs up the phone.

"Oh Jesus Christ, what is her problem?" I cry at Joe, who just shrugs carelessly in return. "She's all pissed off with me!"

"She's a nutter, I told you. Forget about it."

"Why did she call back? For God's sake, I told her I was busy."

"Nutter," Joe says again. "Come on let's go. I'm getting all jumpy."

"Okay, okay."

The August sun pounds down on us when we step outside. It seems to bounce off the pavements, making them too bright to look straight at. Every car we pass seems to fire spiky rays of startling sunlight into our brains. We look down and walk on. Joe falls silent again, and I suppose I cannot blame him. His whole life has been turned upside down, one way or another. Even if he escapes jail and is allowed home, I know things will never be the same for him again. He looks increasingly sombre as we head towards his house. We go the long way around without even discussing it. Neither of us relishes the thought of passing the shop while Lorraine is at work.

We get to his road and look around. There are no cars in front of the house. It looks like no one is home. "Wonder where the brats are?" I ask quietly.

"Neighbours have had them lately," Joe shrugs.

"Have you got a key to get in?"

"No. Mick took it off me."

"So how do we get in then brainiac?"

"Around the back," he says, and walks off. I follow him around to the back alley and we walk down it, stepping over bags of rubbish and broken bikes and old TV sets. The back gate is open. He strides up to the back door and just walks in.

"Unlocked?" I ask, shaking my head.

"Broken," he corrects me, and shows me the floppy door handle. "It won't lock."

"Handy for us."

"Yep."

We stand in the kitchen for a few awkward moments, looking around us. I feel like it is a strange and hostile place all of a sudden, instead of one I have known since a baby. I am guessing Joe feels sort of the same. He certainly does not seem comfortable or at ease in the slightest. He rubs one arm up and down, shivers, and then heads for the lounge. "Come on then," he says. "We've got to be quick about it."

We pound up the stairs and into his room. It's a complete wreck. It looks like Mick has thrown a massive tantrum in here. Joe swallows as he looks around at it all. His posters have all been torn down and screwed up. His clothes are out of the wardrobe and scattered across the floor. It is creepy and shocking, and I want to get the hell out of there as fast as possible. I find his school rucksack on the floor and start to fill it quickly with clothes. Joe snaps himself out of his daze, grabs a holdall from the top of the wardrobe and kneels down on the floor, scooping up armfuls of his belongings and throwing them in. "Your money?" I say to him at one point, and he looks up and yanks open the top drawer of his bedside table. He grabs all the socks and boxers and hurls them into the holdall, and then holds up one bulging sock and smiles at me.

"It's okay. Look."

"Good. Come on, hurry up."

We crawl around the floor, grabbing everything we can salvage. His precious vinyl collection is half the size it used to be, as he hadn't managed to replace any of the ones Mick broke that day, but he packs them all in and zips up the holdall. He is breathless and his forehead gleams with sweat. I am still packing up, having found his schoolbooks under his bed, but he stand up suddenly and stares down at the floor, breathing quickly. "What are you doing?" I ask him.

"Just want to check something," he replies and walks out of the room.

"Joe!" I call after him impatiently, but I do not follow. I carry on packing his rucksack until I cannot squeeze any more in. I do the zip half the way up, and push my hair back out of my face. I feel my heart drumming quickly in a kind of panic, but I don't understand why. Just then Joe marches back into the room, his hair hanging over his eyes, and his hands full. I look at him in confusion. And then I yelp. "Joe! What the *hell*!" He is holding two bags of cocaine. Just like the bags we found that day in his brothers wardrobe. Christ how I wish we had never taken them. Christ, how I wish I had never opened that wardrobe door... He raises his head to stare at me, his mouth hanging open in awe.

"They've got more!" he practically screams at me. "They've got a load more!"

I climb to my feet. I grab both of the bags we have filled. I want to cry. "Joe," I say in desperation. "Just put it back, put it back now!"

"They've got more!" he says again, his eyes wide in wonder and disbelief. "It was all gone, and now they've got more!"

"Joe," I beg him, "it doesn't matter, leave them to it, let's just go! Just put it back and we can go!"

He shakes his head at me. I watch anger clouding his eyes. He keeps shaking his head and staring at the bags. "I can't believe they got more."

"Joe! Just put it back, I am begging you! It doesn't matter!"

"It does fucking matter!" he roars at me then, and his face is so dark, and his mouth twists in rage and grief. "They lied to me the whole time!"

"What do you mean?"

"That they nicked it, that they found it in a car they robbed. That the amount they had was it. Just one load. It was gone." He shakes his head, utterly confused, yet filling steadily with rage. "It was gone Lou! So what the hell is this? Where the hell did this come from? There's loads in there! They've got more!"

I walk forward and grip his arm with my hand. "Joe," I say to him. "Just put it back. Put it back right now. We have to get out of here. Just leave them to it."

"No," he says, pulling away from me and scraping back his hair. "No way. They lied to me!"

"They're always lying!"

"They lied to me about all of it!"

"Joe please, just put it back and lets go. I'm going!" I try to shock him by grabbing the bags and bundling past him. I head for the stairs. "Come on!" I call back at him. He storms past the stairs and into the bathroom. I am confused. "Joe what are you doing?"

"Flushing it!" he yells back, kicking the bathroom door open.

"*What*? Are you insane?" I drop the bags again and run after him. He is kneeling down in front of the toilet. He is tearing a hole in one of the bags. I am terrified and overwhelmed and desperate to be out of there. "You can't do that!" I hiss over his shoulder. "Are you crazy?"

"I'm putting an end to it," he says. He starts to pour out the first bag. I stare in horror as Leon's drugs pour in a neat white stream into the toilet bowl.

"Oh my God Joe, they will kill you," I say breathlessly. I try to stop him. I try to pull his arm back but he pulls away.

"I'm ending it," he says again. "I'm getting rid of it all."

"Joe they'll kill you. They will kill you! You can't do this!"

"You should be helping me!" he cries out, tossing back his hair long enough to glare angrily at me. "You've had enough of them too! Look what they've done to us! They've lied to us and lied to us. They've had us running all over the estate with this shit and I've had enough. So I'm ending it. I'm getting rid of all of it."

There is nothing I can do but stand and watch. He flushes the toilet and the first bag is gone. I have no idea how much money he has just flushed down the loo, but it is sort of horrifying and mesmerising at the same time. My stomach feels sick to the core. I can barely breathe. "Hurry up," I beg him, nearly in tears. "Don't do all of them Joe. Let's just go!" He ignores me and tears open the next bag. When that one is all gone, he gets up and stomps back into his brother's room. I stare down at the bubbling toilet. I chew my nails. He comes back and kneels down again and starts digging a hole into another bag.

"Drug dealers," he is snarling to himself. "They lied. They never found it. It was never a one off. They're drug dealers, and that's it. They lied, they lied, they lied to me. They've ruined my whole life. I can't even live here anymore, because of them!"

I don't know what to say, so I keep quiet. I only know I have never been so terrified in my entire life. But all that changes when I hear the front door opening. My eyes grow wider and wider. Joe does not hear. He keeps flushing the drugs. I listen again. Was I imagining it? Oh my shitting God. The front door. The front door. The front door!

"Joe," I put my hand on his shoulder. My hand is shaking so much it looks like a blur. Joe jerks to his feet when he hears the footsteps on the stairs. He has half a bag of cocaine in one hand, and as he stands next to the toilet and stares in terror at the landing, the rest of the bag empties slowly into the toilet bowl, and that is how Leon finds us, when he arrives at the top of the stairs.

31

Dear World, we are trapped in one of those moments that seems to stretch out forever. Leon, one foot on the landing, one foot on the last stair. Joe, frozen next to the toilet, so still, so silent, he looks like a dummy, like a waxwork image of himself. I watch the colour drain from his face. I watch his eyes widen into impossibly huge pools of horror. When I turn my head it feels like it is in slow motion. Leon is frozen too. His jaw juts out. His mouth disappears. It only takes him a second, a moment, to see Joe, to see me, and to see what is happening. And then he moves. He moves fast. He comes at us, he comes at us like a bear, like a bulldozer, like something impossibly fast and big and angry, and I find myself shrinking back against the wall. I feel him whoosh past me and I hear him snarling; *what the fuck are you doing?*

Joe does not get time to speak. Leon stares once, turning his head quickly, seeing the toilet, and seeing what is already lost. And then he roars again, but the words are not decipherable. He is on top of Joe. He is like a building falling down. I see Joe hurled across the room. I hear the dull thud as he hits the wall. I see his face screwed up in shock and pain as he doubles up on himself. I think he looks like a rag doll.

Leon snatches the broken, empty bags up from the floor. I am flattening myself against the landing wall. I watch him staring at them in utter horror. "What the fuck?" he is screaming. "What the fuck? What the fuck have you done?" It all seems to hit him then. The enormity of what he has lost, of what Joe has taken from him, of what it all means. I watch his face cave in on itself. It is like his forehead crashing into his eyes, and his eyes explode, and pure evil rage erupts from them, and his mouth spreads across his face, showing all of his teeth, as he spins around to see Joe. "You fucking idiot!" he is screaming. "You stupid fucking idiot what the fuck have you done!" These words, and others, collide into each other as he screams, spittle flying from his twisted mouth, they become one jumbled stream of obscenity and fury.

He steps over the toilet and reaches down to grab Joe by the front of his shirt and then he just starts punching him. It is horrible. I can see his fist, he pulls it back, then shoves it in, pulls it back, thrusts it in. I can hear the sound and the sound is almost wet. Before I know it I have moved, somehow I have got behind Leon, and I try to pull him away by his shirt, and when I can't move him an inch, I grab at his hand, the one he is punching with. I find it and hold it, but it gets away from me and goes in again, and the next few disgusting minutes become all about me trying to chase that fist. I grab for it, I miss it, I grab for it, I can't hold onto it. I do all I can to get that fist away from Joe.

At one point I nearly succeed, I hang onto the fist so tightly, that when he pulls it back to strike again, I am still on the end of it and I go with it. I end up toppling onto Joe, who is covering his face, trying to twist away, trying to protect himself. Then I feel Leon wrenching me away by my arm, and suddenly I am flying, I am being propelled, and I cannot stop myself, I cannot slow myself down. I land outside the bathroom, shaking and sobbing and screaming. I turn around and I see Leon is sitting on Joe. Joe has no chance of escape. Leon is holding onto him with one hand, and punishing him with the other. I see that awful fist flying in again and again. "Stop it!" I hear myself screaming this out, so loud it hurts my lungs. I scramble to my feet, desperate to beat that fist. I fling myself back at Leon. I am clinging to his back, scratching at him, pulling his hair, tearing at his shirt.

He ignores me for as long as he can. I am screaming and sobbing. I can see Joe's face is covered in blood. There is blood sprayed up the wall behind him. There is blood on Leon's fist, but still he does not stop. "You're killing him! You're killing him!" I am screeching into his ear.

I rake my nails into his head, plunging them in. I can see that Joe has gone all floppy. That Leon is holding him up to punch him.

Leon cries out in rage and frustration, and stops punching Joe. He grabs hold of my hands and pulls them violently out of his head. I feel something smack me in the side of the face, and I am flying again. When I hit the bathroom floor I am momentarily stunned into shock. I am just blinking. Blinking at the pale green lino. Blinking at the stained carpet on the landing. The little row of cars that Tommy has lined up right next to the wall. I try to lift my head and feel rockets taking off in my brain. I can hear myself grunting and groaning, as I try to get myself up. I plant my hands firmly on the floor and try to push myself up onto my knees. I hold onto my face. It is pulsing with sharp pain.

There is no more screaming now. No one is screaming. The only sound I can hear is the noise Leon makes as he beats Joe. It is like an 'oompff'. I sit back on my feet; I hold my face and turn around.

Leon is standing now. Standing over Joe and kicking him.

"*No!*" I am screaming again now. My throat stretches and yawns as the wails rip from me. "No, you're killing him! *You're fucking killing him*! Leon stop! Stop! *Stop!*"

I find myself back on my feet. I hold my head with both hands while I steady myself, and the room dips and rocks under my feet. A hand pressed to each side of my face I stumble forward bellowing; "Leon please stop! Stop! *Stop!*"

Jesus Christ, Joe is just lying there. He does not even flinch, or move, or cry when Leon kicks him. Leon's foot is flying in and out like his fist did. I think, he's killed him, he's killed him! I scream out, something feral and wordless and I land on his back, tearing at his hair, and digging into his face. I get him away from Joe, because he turns around and steps away, and in seconds I am slammed back into the floor. I feel my spine crack against the lino. I feel my bones jolted and jarred.

He is down and on top of me, and I see his face. His face is full of torment and rage and revenge and regret and violence, and I shrink away, I turn away, I try to roll away from him. He pins me down and his face is just above mine. "Little bitch," he pants down onto me, his big chest heaving up and dropping down upon mine. That is all he says, but I know what he means. I know what he thinks I am. His spit drops down onto my cheek. His chest is crushing mine.

I feel his hand down on the waistband of my shorts, and then I hear another voice, crying out. It is Travis. "What the hell? What the?" I feel Leon moving away from me, but he does not get very far before he is sent flying backwards. I hear him crash into the toilet and then he is up again, and I scramble out of his way. I press myself up against the door, and watch Leon shoving his way past Travis, who is staring at the huddled shape of Joe.

"He flushed it all!" Leon cries, as he gets past Travis. "He flushed it all!" He tears down the landing. We hear his feet pounding the stairs. Travis looks at me, eyes and mouth wide open.

"Joe," I say to him, crawling forward. "*Joe!*"

Travis snaps into action. He kneels down and pushes Joe's shoulder. Joe plops onto his back, one arm flung across his chest. Travis slides one hand under his head, and his eyes move rapidly over Joe's still body. "Joe? Joe?"

"Call an ambulance!" I scream, pushing him out my way. He scrabbles across the floor, uses the door to pull himself up, and dashes away with his phone in one hand. I am left alone with Joe. I put my hands on his chest. I try to feel him breathing.

"Joe? Joe? Joe wake up! *Wake up!*" I shake him gently. He looks dead. His face is awash with blood. His mouth is open and I can see his teeth and they are stained red, strung with stretchy trails of pink saliva. His nose is clogged with blood. And his head. His head.

"They're on the way!" Travis bundles back into the bathroom, skidding down onto his knees. I take Joe's hand and hold it tightly between mine. "Is he breathing!"

"I don't know!"

"Shit," Travis lays his head down upon Joe's chest, and his face tightens in concentration. I look at him in desperation, but his brow just furrows into lines of frustration. "I don't know!" he cries at me. "I don't know!"

"His pulse," I remember, and place his wrist between my finger and thumb. I hold my breath and pray for there to be something, anything in there, but I can't, I can't find anything. I wait and wait and listen and count, and there is nothing, nothing, no beat, no throb, no sign. "He's not breathing!" I hear my voice screaming at Travis. Travis stares at me. He does not know what to do. "He's not breathing!"

I don't really know what happens next. I feel like I am outside of my body and looking in. At some point I seem to be pressing my lips down upon Joe's, begging him to wake up. And then, out of nowhere, the room is suddenly full of people, of strangers. I am gently pulled away, and neon coats surround Joe, so that I cannot see him anymore. I am pulled out of the room. I am crying. I want my mum.

I find myself leaning against the landing wall, my knees too weak to hold me up. One of the paramedics is speaking to me softly, and touching my face and asking if it hurts. It does not hurt. It feels numb. I can hear Travis talking behind me to somebody else. I can't see Joe. They are lifting him up and carrying him out. I try to speak to him as he is bundled past me, but they are all in the way, and they are moving with a terrifying sense of urgency, and they are shouting and calling to each other, using the kind of terms I remember hearing on TV, on the soaps my mum watches. "I want to go with him," I say to the woman who is with me.

"They've got to go quick," she tells me, and I just stare at her, not understanding. I understand when I hear the ambulance screaming out of the street. I imagine the neighbours at their windows, wondering who is ill, what has happened.

I am led out of the house. I think Travis is coming too. But then he seems to change his mind, and he goes back, back up the stairs. When I step out of the house, the day is impossibly bright; it is almost white, the sun burns down on us all. There is a police car parked out there. They say they will drive Travis and me to the hospital. I am numb, in shock, unable to speak. All I can hear is my own voice, screaming at Leon to stop. It fills my head completely. All I can see is the blood. The blood that Leon has punched out of his brother's body. The blood that has erupted from Joe's face, from his head, and I shake my head, and I say to him, *please don't die, please don't die, please don't die......*

✳✳✳

The waiting room is full of bleeding people. Moaning people. Swearing, complaining people. Drunk people. Little kids whining and wailing. Old people swaying in and out of life. I sit in a hard plastic chair next to Travis, who is as white as a sheet. We do not look at each other or speak to each other. The police have asked me twice who attacked Joe, and I have not said. The doctors have told the police I am probably in shock and they need to give me time. "We don't have time," I hear the older policeman answer quietly, as he gives up and walks away. "The git could be anywhere by now..."

I am snapped back into imagining Leon. His fists smeared in Joe's blood. Where would he go? Who would he run to like that? I am sat on a plastic chair, the kind of chairs that are linked together by metal, so that people cannot pick them up and throw them at each other. This is a horrible place, I think, staring down at the floor, trying not to meet anyone's eye. This is a horrible place full of horrible people, and Joe should not be here. *Please don't die, please please please, don't you die.*

"I want my mum," I say to no one. Travis shifts next to me. He coughs, clearing his throat.

"Didn't anyone call her?"

"I don't know."

"Do you want me to call her?"

"Yes."

He gets up slowly, cautiously sliding his trainers out across the slippery floor, and gripping the handrails of the chair to push himself up. As he walks past me, I look up and I see the artwork of Joe's blood all over his t-shirt. I look down at mine and see that I have been daubed as well. I drop my hands into my lap, and I twist them into my stained clothes. Tears fall from my eyes as I stare down into the redness. My tears mix with his blood and I rub it into my fingers. His lifeblood, I think, and I feel the unbelievable swell of fear and grief trying to take me down. I am holding onto myself. Just. *Just don't die, don't you dare die, just please don't you dare die.*

***

Dear World, time does strange things when you are waiting like that. I try not to look at the clock on the wall. I try not to look up every time a name is called, and a broken person gets up and shuffles off to be fixed. I try not to stare when another emergency is rushed in on a stretcher. The sound of the paramedic's shoes slapping against the tiles echoes around the waiting room. Travis takes up his lonely post next to me. I can feel his questions but he does not speak. I can feel his misery, and most of all I can feel his guilt. Believe me, I can *smell* his guilt. I watch him twisting and wringing his hands together. Most of the time he just stares down at the floor, his head hanging low.

When my mum arrives, I am not aware of her until she is on top of me. Travis gets up quickly to give up his seat, and she plops into it, simultaneously enveloping me in her arms. I curl into them like a tiny child and I just sob and shake, and she strokes my hair, and kisses my head, and my face, and she says over and over again; "he'll be all right, he'll be all right, I promise you."

"He wasn't breathing," I whisper this into her hair. I feel her heart stop, and then start again.

"I'll try to find out what's happening," she tells me, and pats me firmly on the back, letting me know I can do this. "Has anyone spoken to you?"

"Nothing," says Travis. Mum looks up at him, standing there awkwardly, suddenly looking much younger than normal. She gives him a brave smile, but her eyes say something else. She pulls away from me, clutches my shoulder and squeezes it tight.

"I'll be right back," she says. "I'll see what I can find out. Don't move."

Don't die.

When she has gone, Travis sits back down, but he just perches on the edge this time, ready to spring back up on her return. He rests his elbows on his knees, and clasps his hands together in front of him. His hair is darker than Joe's and tumbles down over his forehead. I watch him. I say nothing. Eventually he coughs again and he says; "I got rid of it all."

"What?" My voice is a whisper. A croak. My throat raw from screaming.

"The stuff," he whispers back, not looking at me. "All of it. I finished off what Joe started. It's gone."

I stare at him. At the back of his head. At his neck. I can see the top of the tattoo he has curling up from under his t-shirt. He had it done when he turned eighteen. Barbed wire and roses. He looks back at me then. I see his eyes for the first time. He rubs at his chin with one hand. "Good," I tell him.

"Did Leon hurt you?" he asks me then, his eyes dipping once, and then rising to meet mine. I see him bite his lip with his teeth and then let go. "Before I got there?"

"I tried to stop him," I say, staring back at him. "I couldn't. I couldn't stop him."

We both look up as my mother returns. She slips in beside me as Travis rears up again. There is a lost, desolate look to her, that I just cannot bear. "Mum?"

She takes my hand and holds it between hers. "They're working on him," she tells me, her voice quivering.

"What does that mean?"

"It means that he has a lot of bleeding coming from his brain, and they are working on him, to stop the bleeding. He also has some internal bleeding they are trying to control."

I glance at Travis long enough to see him dropping his face into his hands. I look back at my mum. "That doesn't sound good."

"They deal with this every day love," she tells me, as if that somehow makes it less bad. "They know what they are doing. He is in good hands."

"That's what they say on TV."

"What?"

"On TV."

"Love," she says, squeezing my hand. "I've called his mum and Mick. They're on their way. The policeman wants to talk to you again. Are you up to it?"

"It was Leon," I say then, and I look at Travis as he reappears from his hands. He looks white. I expect to see him shake his head at me or something, but he does not. He just looks resigned, and his shoulders drop. I look back at mum and she is staring at me very intently.

"Darling," she says to me. "You have to tell that to the policeman. You have to tell him exactly what happened."

"Leon beat him up," I say to her. "I thought he was going to kill him." I collapse into her then. It all gets too much. Bleeding from his brain? His brain? Bleeding internally? From where? What does that mean? Something inside him must be broken for blood to come out, is that what it means? Like what? I bury my head in her shoulder. Like his heart? Can his heart bleed? His lungs? Was that why he stopped breathing? I cry so hard I cannot breathe. I feel her arms around me, so tightly, and her kisses and her voice, and I know what she is thinking, I know what she is feeling, like she has told me a thousand times before, 'if I could take the hurt away for you, I would.' I used to think that was stupid. I used to think it meant nothing. Like saying 'do one for me' when someone says they are going to do a wee. But now I get it. She would take all the hurt from me, and absorb it into her, soak it up and take it, and make it hers, because that is how much she loves me. And if I could, I would take all the hurt from Joe, all the leaking blood, all the damaged parts, everything they are trying to fix, I would take it from him, I would take it if I could.

"I don't want him to die," I moan into my mother's shoulder, and it feels like it is just us, and the hospital around us does not exist, and neither does Travis, because it is just us, entwined and holding on tight. Holding onto life. "I don't want him to die," I tell her over and over, "please, please, don't let him die, please don't let him die…I love him, I love him…"

32

Dear World, my mum wants to take me home. She says they will call us if anything changes, but I refuse. I just stay nestled into her like a small child, with my arms around her middle and my head in her lap. She drops one hand onto my head and keeps it there. I hear Travis offer to get her a cup of tea, and she sighs before she agrees to let him. At some point after this I might drift off for a bit, because I am suddenly jerking awake again, wiping my mouth, and hoping I have not dribbled all over my mum's lap. I wake up confused and unsettled, and I am reminded instantly of that strange night at Marianne's, how I woke up with my head on Joe.

"Joe?" I ask, sitting up, pulling away from my mum, who shushes me and smooth's my hair down with her hand.

"It's okay," she tells me quickly, "it's okay, he's okay."

"They say you saved his life," another voice, a cracked and broken voice tells me. I look beyond my mum. The waiting room has changed. New patients have replaced the old ones, but we are all still here. Lorraine is now next to my mum, and Travis is on her other side, with his head in his hands. I squint at Lorraine. She peers back at me through red ringed eyes. Her mascara has run with her tears. There are muddy grey tracks running down both of her cheeks. I look at her blankly, not understanding. She leans forward slightly, clutching her shiny red handbag onto her lap. "You gave him mouth to mouth, don't you remember?" she asks me. "Travis said you did. You kept him breathing."

"I tried to…" I frown back at her. The memory is not clear. The clearest memories I have are the ones I do not want to see. The image of Joe all floppy and bloodied. Of Leon pummelling his still body.

"You did, you did!" Lorraine says urgently. "You saved his life, that's what they are saying!"

"But he's okay now?" I ask slowly, looking carefully at all of their faces. I cannot see Mick anywhere.

"He's stable," my mum slips her arm around me and pats my shoulder reassuringly. "They managed to stop all the bleeding. He's stable. But he's in intensive care love. He hasn't woken up yet."

"They're going to let us see him any minute now," Lorraine adds, as fresh tears push yet more mascara down her cheeks. "Any minute. They said didn't they Shell? They said!"

"Yes love," my mum's voice soothes her. "Any minute now."

"Can I come too?" I ask them. Lorraine nods at me instantly.

"You and me darling," she sobs, breaking down again. "You and me go in first, all right?"

It is only another five minutes that we have to wait, but it feels like yet more impossible time that just does not move. I sit and stare at the floor. Lorraine falls silent, but I can hear her crying softly. Travis does not move or speak, not even when Mick comes in smelling of cigarette smoke. He looks at me briefly, taps Travis on the head, and slips into his seat when Travis vacates it. I can feel all their questions in the air. Who, why, how, how could he? How could he? I have my own questions for them, but I do not dare open my mouth. I bite down on my tongue, and keep my teeth pressed tightly together. Inside my mind I see Joe, slumped on the bathroom floor and it fills my heart with a raw and vile kind of pain that makes me want to be sick. I sit there in silence and I feel all their guilt because the atmosphere is thick with it.

Finally a male doctor with thick bushy ginger hair comes forward and motions for Lorraine to come with him. She leaps to her feet, passes my mum, and seizes my arm, practically yanking me out of my chair. I let her pull me into her side, where she captures me with her firm arm, and marches me along with her, her red heels click clacking on the floor as we follow the doctor. We go down long corridors, filled with swishing curtains, swearing patients, and bustling nurses. We follow the doctor into a lift and go up to the next floor. We are taken to a small room, and as we go in, two nurses finish their checks, smile at us in sympathy, and leave the room.

We shuffle hesitantly inside. In the movies, or on TV, I remember the loved ones always flinging themselves at the patient, wailing and falling onto the bed. But I realise it is not like that in real life. Lorraine is stiff and nervous, and I am terrified. The doctor has to gently persuade us to move further inside the room, so that he can close the door after us.

My best friend Joe is lying on the bed, but it is hard to make out where he begins, and the tubes and machines end. I do not know what any of them mean, or what they are doing for him. His head is heavily bandaged. His nose and mouth are covered with the tubes and a mask. All I can see of Joe is his eyes and his forehead. But even his eyes, which are closed, are so swollen that I wonder how it can really be him.

"Can he hear us?" I hear Lorraine ask in a squeak of a voice.

"We don't know, but we think so, on some level," the doctor tells her gently, holding his clipboard against his tummy. "We certainly believe it's worth talking to people who are unconscious."

"Is he in a coma?" I hear my own voice whisper.

"That's right," the doctor tells me. "But we think he will start to wake up once the swelling goes down."

Lorraine just stands there. She looks aghast. I inch forward. I am terrified of him, and yet I am drawn towards him. I slip into the chair that is next to his bed. I am staring at him, trying to find him. My eyes brim with useless, soundless tears. I swallow, and that is when I see his hand laying there. His palm is flat against the blanket. I lean forward and pick it up. I feel how cold it is, especially the palm. I rub his hand between mine, trying to warm it up, trying to reach him.

I feel Lorraine move behind me. She places her hands, awkwardly at first, on my shoulders. Then I feel her sigh massively, a juddery sob escaping at the same time. She massages my shoulders slightly. "That brings back a memory," she sniffles from behind me. "You holding his hand like that."

"Does it?"

"Yeah. I've even got a photo. Perhaps that's why the memory is so clear. You were both about one and a half. Not quite two. There's me and your mum, pushing you both home from the park in your buggies. You reached out from your buggy with your little hand, to Joe. And he took it."

I nod. I have seen the photo. It's at Lorraine's house, in one of her massive photo albums. All you can see is our hands linked, pulling the two pushchairs together as our mums push us home.

"I'll give you a few moments alone," the doctor, who we have both forgotten about tells us. We hear the door open and shut again.

"He held my hand on the first day of school," I say. "I remember that. We were both nervous. He picked up my hand."

"Always been stuck to each other like glue," Lorraine says softly. "Me and your mum Lou, we were always so thankful for you two, did you know that?"

"No."

"You were both so good. We used to say it all the time. Aren't they good? Aren't they so good together? We had our hands full with the others, but not you two. As long as you two had each other you were fine."

"He's gonna' be fine," I say then, and I look over my shoulder and up at her face. She nods bravely, but fresh tears are flowing from her eyes.

"He better be!" she smiles at me. "God knows, he better be. I've got to say I'm bloody sorry, haven't I eh?" She laughs, cries, and wipes tears and snot away from her face with a tissue she tugs out of her bag. I look back at Joe, holding his hand tightly between mine. I stare at his face, willing him to wake up. But he does not move. He just lies there. He is so still.

"Why don't you hold his other hand?" I ask Lorraine. I feel her hands leave my shoulders.

"I don't know," she says. "I'm scared. I don't want to…"

"You can't hurt him," I tell her. I nod at the chair on the other side of the bed. She sniffs, wipes her nose again and walks around the bed. I watch her slide awkwardly into the other chair, looking nervously at the machines that bleep and whirr all around the bed.

"I just can't believe this," she says then, resting her head in her hand just for a moment, before she looks up at me across the bed, across Joe. "My baby boy."

"He's going to be fine," I tell her again, and I mean it. I fucking mean it. I squeeze his hand to make sure he knows I mean it as well. "I'm not bloody going through my life without him," I say, and Lorraine laughs in surprise.

"What am I gonna' do?" she shakes her head at Joe. She lifts his other hand and holds it tenderly between her own. "He doesn't deserve a mother like me."

"You didn't do this," I tell her stiffly. The silence hangs between us then, and we meet eyes only briefly before it is too much, and we both look down at the hand we hold. The silence speaks his name. Leon. The silence speaks the truth. He has become the elephant in the room. The unspeakable thing. After that, we cannot talk. We sit, holding his hands, staring at him, listening to the machines. We sit in our own minds, reminded of how close we always are to death.

I remember my Nan's funeral. I remember how unreal it seemed that a person who was talking, moving, breathing, feeling and thinking just days before, was now inside a box. Going into the ground. While the leaves still shook on the trees that surrounded us, and the birds still screamed and glided over our heads. I remember that line they always read out; 'in the midst of life, we are in death.' I didn't understand it then. How can that be? How can we be in death, while we are still alive? It made no sense to me.

But it makes an awful kind of sense to me now. As I look at the boy on the bed, who is neither dead nor alive, I understand what it means now. He is with us, yet not with us. He is hovering somewhere in-between, like my Nan was in her final days. I remember going to see her in the hospital. I remember how tiny and ghostlike she seemed, shrunken under the blankets. I remember looking at her and knowing that she was close to death. I remember knowing that she could not and would not get back out of that bed. I knew it was only a matter of time.

I remember touching her hand, wondering what it would feel like, and discovering that it felt like cold paper. I was looking at her, I was watching her leave, and I was thinking about her soap collection. When she lived in her old house, before they made her move to the nursing home, my Nana had this collection of soaps. She kept them all on her dressing table. They took up nearly all of the space there. They were all different shapes and sizes and colours and scents. My favourite was shaped like a swan, a white swan. She never used them, she never got them wet, she just collected them, and her bedroom was heavenly with their smell. I never found out what happened to her soaps when she moved to the nursing home. She didn't even get a proper bar of soap there though. Just that antibacterial liquid soap that you pump out onto your hand.

I hang onto Joe's hand now. I press my lips down upon it. I smell his skin. I hold my cheek to his palm, letting him feel my warmth, my life. I beg him to come back. I beg him to wake up.

But nothing happens

Nothing happens. All that happens is, I have to go home.

33

Dear World, I find home is a strange, almost alien place when I get back there. Everything seems different now. I feel too far away from Joe, and I do not like it. I ask my mum when I can go back. I just want to sit with him, I tell her. She tells me that the police are on their way to speak to me, and I have to talk to them because they have already waited long enough. But I just want to sit with Joe, I tell her again and again. She insists that I sit in the lounge, and she brings me a blanket and a cup of tea and some Marmite toast. It all seems hollow and pointless while Joe is lying on a bed with machines keeping him alive.

The police do not stay long. The policeman I recognise from the hospital, but he does not say much. He leaves the talking to the policewoman, who looks like she is in her early forties, and wears her hair in a neat, tight bun. It does not take long. I tell them that Leon Lawrenson, Joe's older brother, attacked him. I tell them that I tried to stop him. I tell them that Travis eventually appeared and Leon ran off. They seem satisfied and they leave.

I see my mum hovering in the doorway, with her arms crossed over her middle, and a tea towel dangling. I look at her and she tips her head to one side, narrowing her eyes slightly at me. "What?" I ask her.

"The only thing you didn't tell them is why," she says to me.

"Huh?"

"*Why*," she repeats, before pulling away from the door frame and heading back to the kitchen. "Why he would do that."

My mind flicks back to the bags of white powder, pouring thickly into the toilet bowl. I wonder if Lorraine and Mick have been home yet, and if they have, what have they found there? I left out the bit about the drugs because I didn't want to get Joe into any more trouble.

We eat dinner in silence. Mum, Les and I. The phone does not stop ringing all evening. Twice it is Sara to get the latest news, and see if I am okay. Once it is my dad, who has heard about the attack. I don't speak to him, but my mum deals with him in careful, clipped tones, and I hear her advise him not to come rushing around as I am still in shock and not talking. I thank her inwardly for this. Lorraine calls twice as well. The first time I leap up to grab the phone but my mother beats me to it. Lorraine tells her that there has been no change, which is neither good news nor bad news apparently. She tells her that they have gone home to deal with the younger boys and left Travis at the hospital in case anything changes. The second time Lorraine calls it is to say she is back at the hospital, having sent Travis home to get some sleep, and that there is still no change.

I hover around my mother while she talks on the phone, trying to read her expressions, trying to hear Lorraine's voice on the other end. My mother keeps her eyes on me, listens intently, and then frowns and lifts her eyebrows at the same time. She makes a strange face at me. "Really?" she says to Lorraine. "How odd! Did you speak to her?" I mouth to my mum; 'who? What? Who?' She waves her hand at me and concentrates on what Lorraine is telling her. I watch her mouth opening and closing like a fish. "Oh my goodness!" she exclaims eventually, and I can barely stand it.

"What is it? What? What?" I beg, pulling at her arm and bouncing around her feet. She holds me away.

"Oh my goodness, that is terrible," she says again. "I can't believe it, how awful...Lorraine, hang on one tic, Lou is getting in a right state, hang on." She holds the phone against her chest and looks at me. "It's not Joe, nothing has changed, it's something else, I'll tell you in a minute," she blurts out to me, and then puts the phone back to her ear. "Really? Good God...Unbelievable. You wouldn't think it would you? I can't believe it Lorraine. Is she okay, the mother?...Oh right. I see...Good God, what a shock. What a day!...Okay, you've got to go...Oh yes, I will, I will, if she wants to. I'll have to talk to her...Okay then. Okay. Bye now."

Finally my mum hangs up the phone, exhales a huge breath and shakes her head at the floor, as if trying to clear her head. "What?" I practically scream at her in the hallway. "What else is it?"

My mother turns to look at me, and lifts one hand to scratch nervously at her neck. I can see that she is trying to work out the best way to tell me something and I am all over again filled with horrible fear. "Lou," she says, and reaches out to place her hands on my shoulders. "Lorraine is back at the hospital visiting Joe, and she called to say she ran into a lady there, a lady she recognised?" I stare at her, eyes wide, waiting, just waiting. "Anyway," she goes on, "she approached the lady, asking if she knew her from somewhere, and it turned out to be Marianne's mother, Mrs Sholing?"

"What? What was she doing there?"

"It appears Marianne is also in the hospital, darling," Mum says and tightens her hands on my shoulders, biting her lip, her eyes searching mine. I shake my head at her, not getting it.

"Why?"

"Um, I don't know the full story, but it seems she may have tried to end her life at some point today."

I pull back. I pull back from her hands. I stare at her as if she is insane. I think, no, don't be stupid, no way! "What?" I ask her. "What do you mean?"

"She tried to kill herself, Lou. *Apparently.*" My mother is blinking at me, staring at me as if she can't understand or believe it either. "Mrs Sholing is in a terrible state apparently. Lorraine had to calm her down. She wanted you to visit Marianne, but I said I would have to see...you've been through so much today already, I just don't know."

"I don't know either," I agree with her. "I don't know."

"Do you want me to take you back?"

I think quickly. I think of Marianne, and all I feel is wonder and confusion, but also anger. Anger. I can't somehow believe it to be true. Then I remember her strange phone calls to me earlier. God it seems like a lifetime ago.

"I think better leave it till tomorrow," my mum says then, making the decision for me, for which I am strangely grateful. I sigh, and let her lead me back to the sofa and my blanket. "Enough is enough for today," she says, as I sit back down and she covers me up. She sits next to me. "What a day," she says to herself. "I just can't believe any of it. Are you okay love?"

"I don't know. I suppose so."

"Why do you think Marianne would do that?"

"Attention probably," I reply, and the bitterness in my voice surprises both my mother and me.

"Well I suppose it could be a cry for help."

"She's okay though? She's not going to..."

"Oh no, no, no. It was her wrists apparently. They had to stitch them up. She was brought in by a boy. Did you know she had a boyfriend?"

"A boy?"

"Yes, that's what Lorraine told me. Mrs Sholing was told a boy found Marianne and brought her to the hospital, but then left. She doesn't know who it was." My mum pulls the blanket over her legs too, and snuggles closer to me. "Maybe Josh or Ryan?" she murmurs. I don't answer, because a strange little realisation is occurring in my head. I don't want to say a thing until I have spoken to Marianne.

"If you take me tomorrow to see her," I say to mum, "then can I sit with Joe as well?"

"Of course you can love. Definitely. But I want you to have a good night's sleep, and a decent breakfast. You've got to look after yourself you know."

I nod and look back at the TV. I am all out of words, and thoughts. I stare at the TV, taking nothing in, while my mind runs around on itself, hitting blank walls. I feel my mother watching me all evening. I see her wipe her eyes from time to time.

***

We leave the house at ten forty the next morning. Mum informs me that intensive care allows visitors at eleven. We are not sure where Marianne is, but my mum thinks we'll find her mother there somewhere. I feel conflicting emotions on the way over. I am both dreading seeing Joe, and desperate to at the same time. I cannot even fathom what I am going to say to Marianne, but the best way to deal with it so far is to just not think about it. Deal with it when it comes, I tell myself. Deal with it when it comes.

We go to intensive care first, and relieve Lorraine from her shift. She has been there all night, and barely slept by the look of her. My mum holds her for a while in the corridor outside Joe's room. I hover by the closed door, peering in, then looking back at Lorraine and Mum, not knowing whether to go in or not. I see Lorraine leaning into my mum, weak on her own legs, crying, and shaking her head. My mum nods at me over her shoulder. "Go on in love," she tells me, so I do.

Joe is there. Joe is still there. I look at him and feel a surge of impatience with him. "You lazy sod," I tell him, pulling up the nearest chair and finding his hand again. "Look at you laying there! Not gonna' get any riveting conversation out of you today, am I?" I shuffle the chair closer and lean towards him. I wonder if he can really hear me. He looks exactly the same as yesterday, except for the bruises on his face have increased in their vivid colour. "You won't believe what else happened yesterday," I whisper to him. "Get this. Marianne tried to top herself. Really. She did. She's in here somewhere too and wants to see me. I feel like telling her to fuck off. Remember those calls yesterday, when she was all snappy and pissy? God knows what's wrong with her." I sigh, and brush my hair away from my face. Joe does not move. I guess he can't move. I look at his face, at his swollen, closed eyes, and wonder where he is. If he is just stuck in an endless dream somewhere that he can't get back from.

The door opens from behind and Lorraine shuffles back in. "They say it's good to talk to him," she tells me. "Your mum is going to take me home to sort the boys out, then I'll be back. Can you stay with him till then?"

"Course I can."

"Thank you." She turns to go and then stops herself. "Lou, your mum said you told the police it was Leon."

I turn my head and look at her. I nod. "It was."

"Honey, I know. I know. Can you tell me something else?"

"What?"

"The drugs Joe was caught with. They were Leon's weren't they?"

I nod again. Lorraine steadies herself. I think, I have never seen her look so weak before. All the fight is gone. All the anger. She just looks exhausted and defeated. She does not say anything else. I don't think she has the strength. She just leaves and I hear her feet clacking slowly back down the corridor.

I stay with Joe all day. Nurses come and go, checking things, writing on charts. Some of them speak to me; ask me if I want anything, if I am okay. Some of them do their duties without even looking at me, as if I am a ghost they cannot see. I get a sore bum sat on the chair for hours, so I end up getting to my feet and going for a walk. One of the nurses tells me where I can get a drink and a snack, so I wander off, making sure the nurses know I will be back.

I find Mrs Sholing at the vending machine. She has her head resting on it, and is staring grimly into the void of chocolate and snacks, with her money in one hand. She is wearing a long black work skirt, and a long chocolate coloured cardigan. Her hair, so dark like Marianne's is twisted up neatly and pinned into place. I approach tentatively from behind, not knowing what to do or say. I hold the pound coin my mum gave me tightly in one hand. It burns a hot little circle in the centre of my sweaty palm. As I get closer, she must hear me, or become aware of someone behind her, because she straightens up, clears her throat and starts to feed her money into the machine. She only looks behind at me after she has punched in the code for the item she wants.

"Oh!" she says when she sees me.

"Hi Mrs Sholing."

"Lou," she says, and walks towards me, just as her item clunks to the bottom of the machine. I point towards it.

"Don't forget your food."

"Oh," she says again, sounding sort of vacant. She turns hurriedly, opens the flap and pulls it out. It is a Mars bar. "It's for Marianne," she admits. "I wasn't sure what her favourite was. Do you know?"

"I think she likes them all," I shrug, and take up my place at the machine. I get myself a can of lemonade and a packet of crisps. "Is she okay?" I ask, just to fill the silence that has consumed the corridor. "Mum told me last night."

"Oh." Mrs Sholing holds the chocolate bar in one hand, looks at me, and then looks away again, her brow furrowed in confusion. She reminds me of Lorraine. She looks utterly beaten and overwhelmed. "I don't understand it," she says suddenly, throwing up both of her hands. "I'm so confused Lou. Do you understand it? I hate to ask you, but do you have any idea why she would do something like this?"

I start to walk with her, back down the corridor. "Mrs Sholing," I say slowly, as we shuffle along together. "There is something. Something you might not know."

She is looking at me desperately. I am thinking of course, of lots of things. Of weed, and coke, and drink, and razors, and boys.

"What is it?"

"She cuts herself," I say. "I don't know if you know, but she cuts herself."

"Oh," Mrs Sholing exhales slowly. "Well, yes. We did know. I mean, it was a long time ago, before we moved here. We sent her for help and she stopped. It was because she was getting bullied so badly by these girls at her school. Which is why we moved her."

"She still does it though," I say in a small voice. I hate to be the one to tell her, I really do, but I find it hard to believe she thinks Marianne has stopped? The woman looks at me and her expression is one of someone who is totally lost and has no clue where they are going or why.

"Does she?"

"Yes. A lot. All over. I should have said before, I'm sorry." I bow my head, biting my lip and watching the pale green floor under my feet.

"No," Mrs Sholing replies quickly. "Don't say that. It's not your fault. It's mine. Of course it is. It's mine! A mother should know these things. A mother should know! I didn't know." She starts shaking her head. "I didn't know she was still doing it. I didn't know."

"People can be really good at keeping secrets," I try to tell her. "You shouldn't feel so bad. People can be really secretive. Kids especially." I grimace to myself, remembering all of the things my mother still has no clue about. Such as Joe and me going over the bridge to Somerley. Selling drugs to people. It makes my stomach turn over on itself and my cheeks burn with shame.

"It's our job to know these things though," Mrs Sholing says. "I didn't even know she was down, or depressed, or worried about anything!"

"Neither did I, really."

"Really?"

"Well she called me twice yesterday. She wanted to meet up but I was busy with Joe, you know, moving his stuff to our house, because he'd been chucked out." I look at her and see her big green eyes, identical to Marianne's staring at me in bewilderment. "You know, this was before, before he got...before he got in here."

"His mother," Mrs Sholing says, eyes still on me. "His mother is in bits. She told me all about it. How is he?"

"Still asleep, or whatever they call it."

"My God."

"I'm staying with him all day. I was helping him yesterday, before, and she called me, and I couldn't see her because of Joe. I think she was angry with me." I shoot a sideways glance at Marianne's mother, wondering if she will blame me now she knows this.

"Who knows what was going through her head?" she says to me softly.

"Do you want me to see her?" I ask.

"Oh yes. Oh yes please. Well, I mean, if you could. If you want to. I know Joe is, more, more pressing right now, but, if you could..." she trails off helplessly, wringing her hands and practically squeezing the life out of the Mars bar.

"Where is she?"

"Children's ward."

"Now?"

"Oh yes please. If you don't mind. She would love to see you."

I am not so sure about that, but I keep my thoughts to myself, and turn left instead of right. I feel guilty doing this, like I am being torn in two. I know I have to see Marianne. I have to. I have to speak to her. But I want to be with Joe. I want to be there with him, otherwise he is all alone. What if he wakes up and finds no one is there?

I can't allow myself to dwell on this, so I walk on. I follow Marianne's mother to the Children's ward, bracing myself for what I might find there. Initially, I am confused and surprised. I had been expecting a terrible place, rows of beds filled with deathly pale children on their last legs. But it is not like that at all. It is bright and warm and exuberant, with murals of cartoon characters all over the walls, and music playing, and a toy corner where lots of smaller children are gathered in front of a man who is putting on a puppet show.

Mrs Sholing traipses past the children, staring right ahead, almost as if she cannot bear to look at them. She leads me down to the far end, where I can already see Marianne, sat cross-legged on a bed, fiddling with her mobile phone. Her hair is loose and hanging down over her face. She is wearing purple jeans and a black top, with a scruffy green cardigan hanging over her tiny shoulders. I see her, and I am surprised by the anger and resentment that flood me. I go ahead of Mrs Sholing, who hangs back nervously. I get the feeling she is afraid of her own daughter, afraid of what she will say, or do. I don't blame her for that.

I approach the bed bravely. I think of Joe. He can't sit cross-legged in his bed yet. He's not even there. When she looks up and sees me, she does not even look surprised, or pleased, or worried, or anything. She gives me the same look she always does. Her eyes, as always, almost totally unreadable. "Hi," she says flippantly, throwing her phone onto the bed. She shakes her hair away from her face, and her little pointed chin juts out at me defiantly.

"Hi," I say, because I don't know what else to say. She motions for me to sit next to her, so I do, taking care not to actually touch her. I think I am afraid that her insanity will rub off on me. She gets up abruptly and yanks the curtains around her bed.

"No privacy in this place," she complains, hopping back onto the bed. I stare at her, amazed. "Can't believe they put me in the kiddies ward."

"When can you go home?" I ask her.

"Dunno," she shrugs. "Some time later. When they've done all their checks I suppose. It's so boring in here!"

"Well what did you expect?"

"I didn't expect anything did I?" she stares at me and asks. "I expected to be *dead*." I stare back at her. She holds my gaze, but then breaks away and giggles.

"I don't believe you," I tell her coldly. "I don't believe you meant to die."

"Don't you? Oh well. Think what you like."

"So why did you do it?"

"Lots of reasons," she cocks her head at me. "Some of which you know. Some of which you don't know."

"Is that why you wanted to see me yesterday? Because you were feeling so bad you wanted to kill yourself?"

"Well sort of," she shrugs again, and she leans back on the bed with her hands behind her, and her legs kicking out at the curtain. "I suppose if I am truthful, I wanted to give you a chance to be a good friend."

I stare at her, open mouthed. I am utterly stunned. I feel like I have been slapped in the face. "You what?"

"You know," she goes on casually, kicking her legs. "I wanted to see if you'd come. I wanted to see if you'd choose me for once. Instead of Joe."

"Joe needed me," I say this through gritted teeth.

"He always needs you. And you always need him. It's so predictable and boring, and yet you wonder why you have no other friends!" She rolls her eyes at me sulkily, and looks away for a moment. "Wonder why you two don't just sleep with each other and get it over with," she mutters.

"You bitch," I mutter back. She whips her head back to stare at me.

"Why am I?"

"Joe was thrown out of home, that was why I was helping him yesterday," I tell her, trying to keep my voice down. "He was busted carrying you know what for you know who, did you know that?"

She narrows her eyes. Shakes her head at me. "When?"

"Friday. He got arrested. Thrown out of home. Leon and Travis even came to me to make sure I kept my mouth shut."

"So why is he in here?"

"You don't know?"

"My mum won't tell me anything," Marianne wails, sounding like a spoilt little child. "She thinks anything will send me over the edge! How did he get in here? What's wrong with him?"

I stare down at the bedspread under us. I pick at it with my finger and thumb. I take deep breaths, in and out, calming myself down, telling myself it is not her fault she does not know. "Leon attacked him," I hear myself say, my eyes on the bedspread. It's awful really, because every time I think of it, it rushes through my head like an unwanted movie. All of it. The dull sound of a curled fist beating flesh that cannot escape. The gurgling choking noise Joe made in his throat. I fight the tears that threaten to swell in my eyes.

"Badly?" Marianne whispers this. I look at her.

"He's in a coma."

I watch her green eyes grow larger. "You're fucking joking."

"I'm not joking Marianne. He's in intensive care. I've got to go back in a minute, because I'm the only one there."

"Well what's wrong with him? When will he wake up?"

"They think when the swelling goes down. He had bleeding in his brain and his internal organs. They had to operate. He nearly died Marianne." I find my eyes meeting hers, and the tears come too fast for me to stop them. "He still might die," I tell her. I feel her hand land on mine, and I pull away quickly, dragging the hand across my wet eyes.

"Why are you mad with me?" she asks.

"Because you did this to yourself!" I hiss at her. I reach for her arm and snatch back the cuff of her over-sized cardigan. Her wrist is bound in thick white bandages. I raise my lip and drop her arm again. "You're always doing things to yourself. Joe didn't. He didn't ask to have a family full of maniacs, and he didn't ask to be thrown out of home for something his brothers did, and he didn't put himself in hospital, unlike you!"

Marianne is silent for a moment, and I can see her considering what I have said, what I have accused her of, as she folds her arms across her middle and crosses one leg over the other. She looks petulant, watching my face, waiting for me to add anything else. I sniff and wipe my nose on the side of my hand. "And you did this for attention," I say, not looking at her. "You called me twice. You couldn't accept I was busy with Joe, so you did this! Are you happy now? Are you happy you got my attention?"

"Don't flatter yourself you stupid bitch," she says to me in a low, cold voice which is so startlingly different to her normal voice, that I move back slightly, unwilling to be too close to her. "You think I'd slit my wrists over you?"

"Why then? Why?"

"Just like you to expect it to be so black and white," she says scathingly. "Do you not think there might be millions of reasons why someone tries to end it?"

"But did you really want to end it, Marianne? Did you really?"

"At the time, yes. I was angry. I was pissed off at you and Joe. Always together, always shutting me out, unless it's convenient for you. I was pissed off with my parents." She leans forward, over her folded arms, and her hair drops over one shoulder, gleaming black. "Off they go again on another little trip. Business, they say. *Business.* Yeah, right. Do they ever think to invite me along? Do they ever think I might get bored and lonely on my own? It's like they can't wait to get away from me."

"You should tell them then," I say. "You should tell them how you feel. They don't know how you feel."

"Then how do I know exactly how *they* feel?" she shoots back viciously. I frown at her, not understanding. "How is it I can empathise with them, but they can't with me?"

"What do you mean?"

"The baby. My twin. Melissa. I know how they feel because I feel it too. I've felt it my entire fucking life. It drags me down. I wake up in the morning, and it is there Lou. *She* is there. Because she isn't there!" She is getting worked up now. She stops and tries to compose herself by rubbing a hand across her mouth. Then she pulls at her top lip with her finger and thumb and glares at the curtain that shields us from her mother. "I live with it every day," she goes on, one leg twitching angrily on top of the other. "I wake up and she's there, the misery of it, the why's and the what if's. I have to put on a brave face, try to cheer them up. I've been doing it since I was a little kid. Trying to make it okay for them. Trying to be enough for them, to make up for losing her. But it's never enough, because they are still sad. They are still grieving for her, every day Lou. Can't you see it when you look at them?" She turns to look at me questioningly. "Their faces. They're so good at pretending to be fine, but it's not real, it's never real. It's fake. It's pretend. It's not there. Do you know what that means Lou? That means my entire life is fake and pretend, and not there. Maybe I decided I just didn't want to do it anymore."

I exhale the breath I have been holding in. I scratch my cheek, and then rest my forehead in my hand. I don't know what to say to her, I don't know what to say for the best, so I just say what I am thinking. "You should tell them all of this," I sigh. "They don't know Marianne. You may be right about all of that, and it's not fair and it's not nice, but they're not doing it to you on purpose."

She does not answer me. She brings her feet up onto the bed, and wraps her arms around her knees. I watch as she presses her face against her legs, closing her eyes tightly. "Marianne," I say to her. "Our parents aren't mind readers. They don't know what's going on in our lives if we don't tell them."

"So when did you get so wise?" she says into her knees.

"Me?" I snort. "I feel like a hundred years old today. I am a little old lady, you know. Sixteen is like, gone."

"I'm sorry," I hear her say. She mumbles it into her knees, and her hair falls all around her face, blocking her out. "I'm such a bitch."

"It's what I like about you," I joke. "It's what makes you so intriguing remember?"

"I don't think I deserve any friends, really."

"Maybe none of us do. The way we've been acting lately."

She pulls away from her knees finally and pushes her hair back behind her ears, and there are real tears in her eyes. "I'm sorry about Joe," she whispers and I nod at her. I know she is.

"He'll be all right. I know he will."

"I just never, I never thought Leon could do something like that."

I look down at my lap. "Neither did I. Maybe he was high."

"Why did he do it? Why did he attack him?"

"The drugs," I say softly. "Joe was flushing the drugs." Marianne opens her mouth slowly, disbelievingly. I nod at her. "When we went to get Joe's stuff from the house, he found loads more of it. They'd told him it was all over, all done. He could just about cope with being arrested if it was all over. But they lied, Marianne. It was never a one off. It was never a once in a lifetime thing. It was a career choice."

Marianne shakes her head at me. "I can't believe he flushed them!"

"He lost the plot a bit. He was so angry. He just wanted it gone. And then Leon appeared and he just..." I stop, biting at my lip. "Fucking hell," I tell her. "It was awful Marianne. I never want to see anything like that again in my entire life. I tried to stop him. I kept trying. I just wasn't strong enough. He kept shoving me away."

Her eyes move up to the bruises on my face. "Is that what they are?"

"Yeah, I guess so."

"And then what happened?"

"Travis appeared," I remembered. "He shoved Leon off me. Leon ran out. Then we tried to help Joe. I can't really remember it all after that."

"You were probably in shock."

"The police know Leon did it," I tell her then. Her face is sombre as she nods at me in reply. "I had to tell them. He might die, Marianne. What if he dies?" I can't help it then, I start to cry. Really cry. Marianne puts her arm around my shoulder and pulls me into hers. I cover my face with both hands.

"He'll be all right," she tells me, rubbing my arm. "He will be. Lou? There is something else I have to tell you."

"What is it?"

"It was Leon that found me."

"What?" I pull back, staring at her.

"He found me," she nods, biting at her lip again. "He found me at home. He stopped the bleeding. He wrapped his t-shirt around my wrists and took me here. He carried me out to his car and drove me here."

I am just staring at her, blinking, shaking my head, trying to believe it, trying to understand. "You mean, he saved you?"

"Yeah. He saved my life Lou."

I don't know what to say, or think. I suddenly remember Joe, and how he is all alone, and I am meant to be sitting with him. I slip slowly from the bed. "Marianne I have to go back to Joe," I tell her, wiping my eyes. She nods in understanding.

"It's all right. I'll be all right."

"I've got to go." I turn and stumble through the curtains. I see Mrs Sholing hovering nearby, and she falls into step beside me and follows me all the way back out of the ward.

"What did she say?" she asks me, wide-eyed and frantic as she hurries along beside me.

"It's a lot of stuff," I tell her. "But some of it is to do with her twin. You probably need to talk to her about that."

"Oh!" Mrs Sholing stops walking and I go on. "Thank you for seeing her," she calls after me in a small, timid voice. "I hope your friend will be okay."

34

Dear World, how much more can I take? I ask you. I walk back to Joe's room with my head spinning. He is still lying there, doing nothing. I sit down next to him and open my crisps and my lemonade. I watch his face as I eat. It seems weird to think he is in there somewhere. "Can you hear me?" I ask him. The machines beep and whirr in reply. I watch his chest rising and falling slowly, gently. "You're gonna' have one hell of a headache when you wake up," I tell him. "I won't envy you." I finish the crisps and chuck the empty packet into the bin in the corner. I take a long sip of lemonade, and then wedge the can between my thighs, so that I can lean forward and hold his hand again. I press my forehead down onto it. "Oh why won't you just wake up? It's been long enough. This is getting boring now, Joe." I look back up, willing him to move, or try to speak, or to open his eyes. But he seems so totally shut down. He is like a window with the curtains closed. He is locked down, buried within.

"I'll tell you something really interesting," I say to him then. "I'll tell you what I just found out. It's a pretty good story actually. You won't believe it Joe. This will make you sit up and listen! Listen to this. I went to see Marianne. Just now. She tried to slit her wrists probably around the same time you were flushing Leon's stash. It was Leon that found her! I *know*. Crazy right? Totally fucking crazy. He practically kills you, runs from the house covered in your blood, and drives to her house. To *her* house. It's so ironic it's unbelievable." I pick up my drink and take a few more sips. I have this insane image of a blood soaked Leon zooming in his car to Marianne's house. He must have known her parents were out. He must have run up to her room. "Then he saves her," I tell Joe. "He uses his t-shirt to stop the bleeding, can you actually believe that? He takes off his t-shirt, and wraps it around her wrists. Jesus Christ, she better hope you don't have any nasty diseases, because your blood's probably in hers right now!" I laugh a little, but the sound is awful and hollow in the empty room, so I stop quickly. His hand is lying on top of mine, and I am stroking each of his long fingers with my other hand. I wonder if I can drive him mad with soft tickling. If that will work? "So your brother who nearly killed you, is actually also a hero," I murmur, feeling suddenly very sleepy. "Who would have thought it possible? Not me. Maybe Marianne sees something else in him. Maybe he sees more to her than we do. Who knows?" I shrug my shoulders.

My head feels heavy on my neck. I rest it in one hand, and keep my other hand entwined with Joe's. "I think they all feel guilty as hell," I tell him. "Mick couldn't even make eye contact with me yesterday. And your mum, your mum, well, I've never seen her like this. It's weird. I've never seen her upset about anything before. Not *upset* upset, I mean. I've seen her angry upset plenty of times. She feels bad you know. She knows the drugs were Leon's. She knows she was unfair on you. So now you've got to wake up see? Wake up so you can see them all worried about you, all feeling guilty, even Travis. They're all ashamed. They all want you to wake up so badly, so that they can say they are sorry. So that everything can be okay. So you've just got to wake up yeah, so you can enjoy it! Imagine Joe, having them all at your feet! We'll have fun with it won't we?"

I yawn widely and fold my arms on the bed, taking his hand with me, holding it to my face. I close my eyes. "If people like you die," I whisper to his hand. "Then I don't want to be part of this world again. I'll go back to my bed, won't I?" I kiss his hand and fall asleep.

When I wake up, it is because I feel a cold hand on my shoulder. I shudder into consciousness and look up. Lorraine is standing there with Mick hovering behind her. I look at them, blank and sleepy, but part of me already starts to think of unkind words I can fling at Mick.

"I'll take over," Lorraine says in hushed tones, her eyes moving from me to her son. "The doctor says still no change."

"I can stay longer," I say, stretching out my limbs.

"No love," she shakes her head at me. She has not bothered piling up her hair, so she looks very odd. She has her brass blonde waves all sat around her shoulders, framing her face. It at once makes her look younger as well as older. "You look done in, and your mum wants you back. Did you visit your friend Marianne?"

"Yeah."

"How was she?"

"She's fine," I say, scraping back the chair and standing up. "Did you know it was Leon that found her and brought her here?" I don't know why I say this. It is not like I wish to help him, or make him look good, but I suppose I want her to know the whole story, the whole bizarre circle of it. I watch her forehead creasing in confusion. She sort of pulls her face back into her neck, as if she does not believe me, as if this version of what Leon is capable of, does not tally up with hers. She looks over her shoulder to frown at Mick, who stands hunched and silent near the door.

"He found her? Well how did he find her? What was he doing at her house?"

"They kind of hooked up recently," I shrug, not sure how to put it politely. Lorraine nods now, understanding better.

"He *saved* her?"

"He stopped the bleeding and drove her here."

"Right after he nearly killed his brother?"

I shrug again under the glare of her outraged eyes. "I guess so."

"Well you think you know your kids," Lorraine says with a sigh as she drops her handbag to the floor. "But then you realise you don't know them at all. Not one little bit. I had no idea he was capable of either of those things Lou Carling, did you?"

What a question! I think I have been watching Leon from afar since I was a little kid, and I have never been able to figure him out. When Joe and I were little we looked up to him and Travis, only because they were older and cooler, and we wanted to be like them. We wanted them to let us join in. Eventually we realised they were mostly just mean to us, and there was no point. Since then we had kept a certain polite distance from them. Until recently. Until they needed us. "I don't know," I tell her uselessly. "Has anyone found him yet?"

"Police are looking for him," Mick speaks up then, his tone as gruff and snappy as ever. I only give him the briefest of looks.

"When can I come back?" I ask Lorraine.

"This evening?" She reaches out and ruffles my hair. It is an odd, clumsy gesture, as I am taller than her, and not a child, but she does it just like I am a little kid at knee height. Her eyes remain on Joe. I have an awful flashback of her slapping in him in his bedroom that morning, after catching us in his bed. She sort of jolts, and bites her lip, and I wonder if she is having the same thoughts as me. "Go on," she says to me, taking my chair next to Joe. "Go on home and get some rest. We'll call you if anything changes. Mick will give you a lift."

I look at him in distaste. "It's okay I can walk."

"Don't be fucking stupid," he says, and holds the door open for me.

***

We ride back to the estate in Mick's car. He drives like Leon, I notice. Impatiently and aggressively, swerving around corners that he should take slower, and taking a long time to brake at traffic lights and junctions. I feel close to shutting my eyes, so convinced I become that he will crash. I sit nervously on the passenger seat, arms crossed, wondering whether to talk or not. Mick smokes a cigarette as he drives, and swears loudly at people who annoy him, and people who drive too slowly.

"Have you looked for Leon?" I ask him tentatively, thinking at least one of us should try to be well mannered. His eyes swing towards me briefly as he sucks on his cigarette and steers the car one handed.

"Nah," he says. "Wouldn't know where to start. Travis has tried."

"Oh. Is Travis at home now by any chance?"

"Dunno," Mick shrugs.

"I can get out there," I say to him. "Easier for me to cut through past the shops than you drive around."

"All right."

That is as far as the conversation goes, and once more I am left with the burning question, what does Lorraine see in him? What kind of conversations do they have, for God's sake? What is it about him? I sit in silence until the car swings round the corner into their road. Right away I can see Travis, sat on the front door step, smoking. As Mick pulls up, Travis stubs out his smoke and flicks his hair out of his eyes. Tommy is crawling around in the front garden, pushing plastic trucks through the long grass. As Mick climbs out of the car, Tommy sees him, leaps up and runs to him. Mick drops his cigarette, stamps on it and holds out his arms for Tommy.

I look behind at Travis and catch his eye, as Mick makes a big show of swinging Tommy around in a circle. They go inside together, Mick planting one rough hand on Tommy's small shoulder as he steers him through the door. He passes Travis, not saying a word to him, not even acknowledging him. He is staring at me, and gets to his feet, settling his hands in his pockets as he approaches. "How's Joe?" he asks me, squinting in the sunlight, and shaking his hair out of his eyes again.

I stand in front of him on the path. I feel sleepy and disorientated; as if I have been curled up inside a dark cave somewhere. "The same," I nod at him.

He nods at the ground. "And your friend? How's she?"

"She's fine. She'll probably be allowed home later."

He lifts his eyes to meet mine. "She really tried to top herself?"

"Looks like it yeah. You know who saved her?"

"No, who?"

"Leon."

I watch the confusion and disbelief flood his face just as it did his mothers. He lifts his top lip and screws up his eyes. "You what?"

"That's where he went when he left here, you know when you…" He nods at me, remembering. "He went there and found her. She says he stopped the bleeding and drove her to hospital. Saved her life."

We stand in the sunlight, while the information bounces around Travis's mind. I drop my shoulders and sit down on the step and he does the same. I watch the way his long legs stretch out before him, as he crosses them at the ankles, leans back on the door frame, and keeps his hands in his pockets. I am reminded of Joe, every time I look at Travis, and it is hurting more than I knew was possible.

"Can't believe it," he shakes his head and says.

"I know."

Travis pulls his legs back in then, and leans forward, crossing his arms over his knees. He looks sideways at me. I can feel his bare elbow brushing my arm. "I flushed the whole lot you know," he whispers to me.

"I know, you said. All of it?"

"Yeah. All of it. Before we went to the hospital. I went back in."

"Why did you?"

"Same reason Joe did," he shrugs at me. "Wanted rid. Wanted it over."

"But why?"

"Just a nightmare," he muses. "From start to finish. Leon got us into it, you know. He told Joe we found it in a car we were trying to rob. That's bollocks. He's been getting into dealing for a while now. He thought we would get rich quick."

"You stupid idiots," I say, staring down at the ground. Travis sighs and rakes one hand back through his hair.

"I know. Look at the fucking mess we're all in."

"You know you don't have to spend your whole life following Leon, don't you? You know that, don't you?"

Travis nods at me, his top teeth pulling at his bottom lip. He leaves his hand in his hair, and props his head up over his knee. "We'll probably never see him again."

"That would probably be a good thing."

"I'm sorry, you know."

"For what?"

"Everything. Being a dick. Following Leon. Letting him involve you and Joe. I should have said no, at some point." He sounds angry with himself, and I see him curl his other hand into a fist. "At some point along the way I should have said no."

"Leon is not easy to say no to," I remind him. "Joe found that out."

"I think Leon was high when he, you know." His eyes, darker than Joe's but more human than Leon's, jerk back to my face. "Otherwise, I don't think he would have…I mean, I don't think he could do that, the way he did. You know."

"He was like an animal."

"I know."

"He was like possessed or something. He wanted to kill Joe, I know he did. He really wasn't going to stop." I bite down on my tongue, fight to control myself, force the tears back. "If you hadn't come up the stairs like that, I think Joe would be dead now. Maybe me too."

Travis is silent. I feel him watching me, but when I look at him, his eyes drop down to the ground. I sit next to him and I have so many questions I could just burst with them. Questions I have held for years, about Leon and him, and what they do and where they go, and who they are. Questions about now, and what next, and what is he thinking and feeling? But I do not have the energy to ask any of them. It seems to be zapping all of my strength just to sit there next to him.

"What will you do?" I ask him. "If he doesn't come back."

"How will I cope on my own you mean?" he looks at me with a wry grin.

"You know what I mean."

"I was thinking it was about time I moved out actually."

"Yeah?"

"Yeah. Not exactly welcome here, am I?" His grin spreads a little further, touching his eyes slightly. "I was thinking, maybe if I moved out, got a proper job or whatever, then maybe me and Mum would get on better, you know."

"Proper job?"

"Yeah. Never wanted one before."

"So why now? And why do you suddenly want to get on with your mum?"

"I don't know. It would just be nice, wouldn't it?" He shrugs his shoulders, drops his hand down from his hair, and lets it hang over his knees. "Maybe if me and Leon had moved out ages ago, given them all some more space, there wouldn't be so much tension and shit in the house."

"So why didn't you then? Move out before I mean."

"Don't know," Travis shrugs. "Leon always said why should we? We were here first, I mean, before Mick. Think he felt like Mick was always trying to push us out, so we shouldn't make it easy for him. Stupid really."

"Mick's strange," I sigh. "I think I understand you and Leon more than I do him, these days."

"He just wants his kids to be safe."

"His kids?"

"Yeah. He feels like the rest of us are a bad influence on them. He's probably right to be fair."

"Joe is a good influence," I hear myself say fiercely. We look at each other and then look away almost instantly. It feels like Joe has become the unspeakable thing now, the elephant in the room, whatever the hell that means. To speak his name brings him back, reminds us of the horrible limbo he exists in. I feel a cold shiver wring right through me, and all of my hairs stand on end. My stomach lurches and churns whenever I think of him. It is horrible to be apart from him, I realise, like anything could happen while I am not there.

Travis is nodding at me. "Joe," he says. "Joe was always this good kid. But annoying because he was so good and quiet. Used to wind Leon up. I think he wanted him to be up to no good like us. But then it was like he was too good and quiet, because no one noticed him, they just put on him."

"Well I hope you all feel pretty shit about it, that's all," I say, getting to my feet quickly, and rubbing my wet eyes dry again. Travis looks up at me in alarm.

"Where you going?"

"Home."

"I do feel shit about it!" He gets to his feet and grabs my arm. "I feel shit about everything Lou, I want you to know that. I didn't mean to be such a complete prick. I didn't know how *not* to be one, if that makes sense."

I stare down at the ground. I am thinking how close we all are to death, to the end of us, every single day. How a car could swing around the corner, mount the pavement and wipe you out, at *any* fucking time. How you could bite into an apple, and be alive, then choke on a chunk of it, and then be dead. How easily you could trip on the stairs, and plummet down onto your head, breaking your neck as you land. How these things happen every day, to millions of people. How human life is so extinguishable, so disposable, like snuffing out a candle flame, poof and you are gone, you are over. You are dust in the ground. Disease, I think. They could be creeping around your body like a silent killer at any time of your life. Death is not just for old people like my Nan, whose life is as paper thin as their skin. Death is for young people too. People who have not even started to live yet. I stare at the ground as Travis holds onto my limp arm, and I think about Joe and Marianne. How different it could have been. How close Joe was to dying at any given second. How one more punch or kick to the head could have been the end of him. And

Marianne, I see her soaking into her bed, the expensive quilted bedspread absorbing her lifeblood like a tampon. Soaking her up. Sucking her dry.

Why did Leon go there, over anywhere else? What did he hope to find there? Did he think she would help him or hide him, or soothe his guilt? Did he hope he would find an answer there? To what he is and what he has done? And what must he have looked like when he ran in and discovered her? Was she unconscious by then, or could she speak to him, tell him why she did it, why now? Did he speak to her as he wrapped his t-shirt around her wrists? Did he tell her it would all be okay? If he had not gone there, if he had never been involved with her, then she would be dead. Right now. She would be dead and stiff and over.

I am crying as I try to pull my arm out of Travis's grip. He places his other hand on my shoulder. "What's wrong? Why are you crying?"

I shake my head, because I am unable to tell him how fragile and thin life really is, how we walk through life never realising that we are balancing on a tightrope, with life and death on different sides. One wrong move, and that is it. One piece of bad luck, or bad judgement, and it's all over. I picture Joe, my best friend; lying in that hospital bed, more object than person, because he is not there. Where is he? Wherever he is, I want to be there too.

"He'll be okay," I can hear Travis telling me. "I know he will. He'll wake up. He'll wake up soon."

I nod, because that is all I can allow myself to believe. He will wake up. He will wake up and be just fine. It will all be over. We will keep our heads down for the rest of the summer, and then we will go back to school. School. Christ, I nearly laugh remembering how much I had loathed and scorned the place just days ago, and yet now the word itself tastes delicious in my mouth. *School.* Where we will be safe, and people will tell us what to do and how to do it, and when we walk home, it's all over and you forget all you have learnt until tomorrow, because it is home time and you just switch off. I can't believe I am looking forward to going back to school, but I really am. Kids go to school. We will still be kids.

I keep nodding, as the warm tears flow down and over my cheeks. I taste them between my lips, drawing them in. Travis keeps his hands on me, one on my shoulder and one on my arm. I can feel his sadness, rolling from him in waves as he stares into my eyes. "You really love Joe," he tells me then.

"Yeah."

"I mean, *really.* I mean really love. I mean, you two are going to end up together, aren't you?"

"What?" I snort with laughter, wrench my arm away and put my hands on my hips. "What the hell are you talking about?"

Travis straightens up. "I just think you will," he says quietly.

"Don't be bloody stupid. We're just friends. How many times a day to I have to tell you people, *we're just friends*?" My voice has climbed loudly, and Travis glances uncomfortably into the hallway. I glare at him.

"All right, all right," he says. "I'm sorry, I just think you will. Everyone thinks you will."

"Who the hell is everyone?"

"Everyone, they all do, they all think it. Me and Leon joke about it all the time."

"Oh do you now?"

"Yes, but it pissed me off," Travis shoves his hands back into his pockets and looks at me sulkily. "Leon was always saying it. Making a joke of it. But it pissed me off. It pissed me off that Joe could have you, but he didn't even notice."

"*Have me?*" I practically bellow at him. I am half laughing, half crying, just staring at him in amazement, shaking my head and standing my ground. It feels like familiar territory at least, battling with one of them, defending myself, thinking up good comebacks. "What the hell are you talking about Travis? What a load of shit! I'm going home. Me and Joe are not like that. It's not like that."

"Keep telling yourself that then," he replies. I shake my head at him.

"Fuck off."

"All right let me tell you something then," Travis says this suddenly, urgently, stepping closer and peering into my face. "In case he dies."

My jaw hits the floor. I nearly strike him. "Don't you fucking say that!" My voice comes out as a scratchy, croaky hiss.

"Let me tell you what he said," Travis insists. I turn away in disgust and start to walk back down the path. He follows me, talking into my ear. "After Mum and Mick found you two in his bed, after that party? When it was all kicking off here. When he was standing up for himself for once. He told me to back off! He told me never to kiss you again. He warned me to leave you alone! He said he was going to kiss you, he said he was the only one who was going to kiss you." Travis pulls desperately at my arm, trying to stop me. "Do you hear me?"

"I'm going home," I tell him, pulling free. I keep walking. I don't look back. I walk on. I think, I don't understand anything anymore. I really don't. I walk home with my arms folded across my chest. The day is warm but I feel chilled to the bone. I am thinking of my bed and my duvet, and just hiding for a while. When I get home, I have the place to myself. I gather Gremlin up in my arms, and carry him upstairs with me. He wriggles and slops his oversized tongue across my face. We curl up in bed together. I close my eyes and hope that sleep is not too far away, because otherwise I am going to lie here and think about everything that Travis just told me. I am going to think about it until I go mad.

35

Dear World, I sleep and sleep, and for once they all just let me. They all just leave me alone. I sleep the rest of the day away, wake up mid-evening and stagger to the toilet, and then find myself back in bed, and sinking quickly back into yet more sleep. I can sense my mother hovering anxiously on the side-lines, pausing in the doorway, sighing and catching her breath. I know she must be worrying about meals, and what I have and have not eaten. But she leaves me be.

When I finally wake up properly it is half way through the next day, and I arise from bed with a sense of panic drumming in my veins. I get washed and dressed, and whip back the curtains to reveal the day outside. Joe. I am panicked about Joe. What if something has happened? What if something has changed, and I wasn't there? What if he is gone? What if he left me and I missed it? I hurry down the stairs, hoping my mum can give me a lift to the hospital, and wondering why the hell they didn't wake me up sooner.

"It's all right!" she tells me at once, as I fly into view. She is drinking coffee at the table. "There's no change. Joe is still the same. I would have woken you if I needed to. Don't panic."

I breathe out. I wonder how scared I must have looked. My mother smiles warmly at me. "I'll take you as soon as you've had something to eat," she reassures me. I sit down, nodding okay. She gets up and starts to make me a sandwich. I try to remember the last time I went for a run, and I can't. I start to feel a little creeping guilt crawling up from my belly. I wonder if my waistband feels a little tighter. A bizarre and twisted part of my mind tells me that when Joe wakes up, *if* he had wanted to kiss me before, he certainly wouldn't now. Travis must be wrong, I think. Why would someone like Joe want to bother with someone as messed up as me? He knows all about me, I remind myself rather viciously. He knows what a mess I really am. I tell myself to shut the hell up but I do not listen. I play strange scenarios out in my mind. Such as Joe opening his eyes dramatically, and finding me the only one there, me looking fresh faced and beautiful. Ha! What the hell is wrong with me? "Marianne is back home," Mum tells me, as she slides a plate with a ham sandwich on it under my nose. I pick it up and take a bite. She watches with her hands on her hips. "Funny girl that one. And I still can't believe Leon was the one that saved her." She smiles at my widening eyes. "Lorraine told me, of course. News travels fast round here! I think, to be honest it's made her feel better that he did that. She's coming to terms with her son being some kind of monster, but now she can have some hope for him too. I mean, if he did something like that? Oh I don't know. I still can't understand any of it."

"Me neither."

"The other thing is, he's in custody now."

I stare at her. "What? When?"

"Last night. Apparently he just walked into the police station and handed himself in."

I am speechless. "*What?*"

"I know," my mum nods in amazement. "I can't fathom it. Just walked in. Just gave himself up." She walks past me to get her shoes and bag. "I don't know what to make of any of it," she adds brightly.

"Neither do I," I tell her.

***

I walk with my mother into the hospital, which is now starting to feel like an old friend. We know the way; we don't have to ask for directions. I walk along, listening to my mother complain about the smell of hospitals, but it is not the smell that I notice. It is the heat. You walk in and feel like peeling off a layer almost immediately, which I do, slipping off my cardigan and tying it around my waist. My mum herds me along, one hand on my back. "You know you were all born in here," she tells me distractedly. I do know. She has told me this a hundred million times. That is how she met Lorraine. On the labour ward, with Sara and Leon. Through fretting and chatting about new motherhood, they discovered they lived around from the corner from each other, and the rest, as they say, is history.

When we get to Intensive care, we have to buzz the button and wait to be let in. "You're quiet," my mum says to me as I yawn.

"Am I?"

"Yes."

It is Mick that lets us in. He grabs my mum by the arm and pulls her through, and I immediately sense his urgency, and my heart hammers into action, and I break out into a horrible cold sweat. "What is it?" my mum calls to him, as he starts to pull her down the corridor.

"Joe?" I cry out.

"Come on!" he yells at the two of us. "Quickly!"

"Mum?" I look at her for help. I find her sleeve and cling onto it. Mick rushes towards Joe's door, just as Lorraine appears through it, blinking and shaking her head, and her face a picture of trailing tears and disbelief.

"Lorraine?" my mum seizes her. Lorraine grips her arms.

"Go and see!" she says to me, before collapsing on my mum. I am so confused. I cannot understand what is going on. I am too afraid to move. I look to Mick, and he nods at the door as he holds it open for me, and I force my feet to move, but they feel like concrete. He gives me a gentle push, and I am in. I am in the room.

Joe is still lying on the bed. Joe is staring at me.

My body reacts violently to the shock and the relief. I feel a massive shudder wringing through me, and my knees go weak. I put out one hand and find the end of the bed and hold onto it. He is staring back at me. His hazel eyes are like slits through all the bruising and swelling, but I can still see them. He does not have the mask or the tubes anymore. He looks confused, and so pale, but he smiles at me really slowly. "You motherfucking bastard!" I tell him, and burst into tears.

I hear them laughing outside the room. I wonder if they have their faces pressed up to the glass. I don't care. I fall into the plastic chair, I shove it forward and I snatch up his hand. This time his fingers tighten on mine. They feel weak and fragile, but they move, *he* moves them. I squeeze them back and he winces.

"Ahh that hurts," he says, and his voice is a hoarse whisper.

"You bastard," I tell him again, shaking my head from side to side.

"Bitch," he grins at me.

"How's your head?"

"Numb."

"Are you gonna' be okay? Are you brain damaged or anything?"

He snorts at me. "You wish."

"You were brain damaged to start with," I say to him, as the relief floods through me, warm and tingling, making my limbs fizz with excitement and energy. I want to grab that feeling in my hand, snatch it up and shove it in a bottle somewhere to keep, because to me right then, that feeling is life. *Life*. I hold his hand in mine, rubbing my thumb back and forth against his skin. I just stare at him for a few moments. I am smiling, and shaking, and I can't take my eyes off his face, his eyes and his mouth. "Where were you?" I say eventually. "Do you remember anything?"

"Not really," he croaks, moving his head a tiny bit. "It's all a blur."

"I've been sat here talking to you for days. Feels like years!"

"I'm sorry."

"What are you sorry about retard? Tosspot. Dick brain!"

"Witch," he grins at me, curling his fingers into mine. "Fuckwit. Reject."

"You arsehole," I tell him, laughing, wiping my eyes with the sleeve of my cardigan. "I've never been so scared in my entire life. Or so bored!"

"Sorry," he says again, still smiling. "So do I get a kiss or what?"

I frown at him. I think I want to hit him. I want to wrap my arms around him and check he is real. Put my head against his heart and listen to it thumping. "Kiss? Are you insane? Why would I want to kiss you?"

"Because you missed me, because I scared you, because it's the last fucking chance I'm gonna get!" I laugh out loud. I stand up and lean over him, as if threatening him. Christ, I think, I have missed him. "You don't deserve a kiss," I tease him, coming closer. His smile is huge in his swollen face. "You look like the Quasimodo or something," I tell him. "You look like you're wearing a Halloween mask."

"You can't insult a man on his death bed, whore."

"One kiss," I tell him. "And if your breath stinks, you're for it!"

"Okay," he grins, wriggling slightly under his blankets. I laugh out loud again. I feel like an idiot. I feel so, so happy. I wish again that I could grasp hold of this feeling that I have. I want to capture it and keep it, and be able to speak of it and explain it, because it is better and stronger than any other high there is. It does not even have a name, I think. Happy to be alive. Happy to embrace life. What the hell? I don't know! I am sixteen remember, I don't know anything! I stop thinking and I lean down and press my lips upon his. I close my eyes. My hair slips down and covers his face. He kisses me back. It feels like coming home. It feels like a breath I have been waiting to take. I pull back and stare at him in triumph.

"About fucking time Carling," he winks at me. I sit back down. I feel kind of giddy and sick, but I can't stop smiling.

"You didn't have to go to all this trouble just to get me to kiss you," I tell him, jokingly.

"But it helps though."

I look over my shoulder. I see Mum and Lorraine and Mick all at the window, eyes on us, all of them smiling sickly. I sigh and look back at Joe. "We're so gonna' regret this," I tell him.

And I laugh.

***

About the Author

Chantelle Atkins was born and raised in Dorset, England and still resides there now with her husband, four children and multiple pets. She is addicted to both reading and music and is on a mission to become as self-sufficient as possible. She writes for both the young adult and adult genres. Her fiction is described as gritty, edgy and compelling. Her debut Young Adult novel The Mess Of Me deals with eating disorders, self-harm, fractured families and first love. Her second novel, The Boy With The Thorn In His Side has been developed into a five book series, and follows the musical journey of a young boy attempting to escape his brutal home life. She is also the author of This Is Nowhere, This Is The Day and a collection of short stories related to her novels called Bird People and Other Stories and the award-winning YA dystopian adventure, The Tree Of Rebels. Her latest release is Elliot Pie's Guide To Human Nature.

Books by Chantelle Atkins
- The Mess Of Me
- This Is Nowhere
- The Boy With The Thorn In His Side – Part 1
- The Boy With The Thorn In His Side – Part 2
- The Boy With The Thorn In His Side – Part 3
- The Boy With The Thorn In His Side- Part 4
- The Boy With The Thorn In His Side – Part 5 – coming soon
- Bird People and Other Stories
- The Tree Of Rebels
- Elliot Pie's Guide To Human Nature

Find out more by following Chantelle Atkins;

Facebook: https://www.facebook.com/chantelleatkinswriter/
Website/blog: http://chantelleatkins.com/
Twitter: https://twitter.com/Chanatkins
Wattpad: https://www.wattpad.com/user/ChantelleAtkins
Pinterest: https://uk.pinterest.com/chantelleatkins/
Instagram: https://www.instagram.com/chantelleatkinswriter/

Sign up here for Chantelle's fan-club newsletter and receive freebies, the latest news, sneak peeks and more! http://eepurl.com/bVVbGD

Finally, if you enjoyed this collection of short stories, please consider leaving a review on your favorite ebook retailer and/or Goodreads. Reviews really do help authors by encouraging readers to purchase the books.

Printed in Great Britain
by Amazon